YESTERDAY IS TOMORROW

Books by
MALVINA HOFFMAN

YESTERDAY IS TOMORROW
HEADS AND TALES
SCULPTURE INSIDE AND OUT

MALVINA HOFFMAN, SELF-PORTRAIT, CARVED IN STONE IN PARIS

YESTERDAY
IS TOMORROW

A Personal History

By

MALVINA HOFFMAN

CROWN PUBLISHERS, INC.   NEW YORK

ACKNOWLEDGMENTS

IT IS DOUBTFUL if this book would ever have been completed without the
guidance and helpful criticism of certain friends who were kind and altruistic
enough to give me of their time and patience to study the manuscript in its
varied stages of development.

Guiding the often discouraged and weary mind of the author to coordinate
and bring to some definite conclusion such a mass of memories was no easy task.

My sincere thanks go to the poet Marianne Moore, to the writer Marchette
Chute, to my indefatigable editor Millen Brand, and to my secretary Gullborg
Groneng.

CONTENTS

YESTERDAY IS TOMORROW

Wax miniatures of Ann Cooper Hoffman, wife of Andrew, and of Andrew Hoffman (*Frick Art Reference Library*)

PART I

CHAPTER ONE

THE FAMILY TREE:

Father's Branch

THE PAST is indeed a curious creature that for years may reside in silence and apparent oblivion, and then may stir and come to life for some descendant.

During my childhood and the hurricane years of maturity, I took little thought for my forebears and what influence they might have had on my character. They seemed something mythological that my parents occasionally mentioned, beings remote from the sphere of my daily discoveries. However, I was always fascinated by the old photographs and daguerreotypes in the house, and above all by the earliest record of my ancestors on my father's side, a pair of wax miniature portraits of exquisite workmanship. They were mounted on black glass and framed in oval gilded shadow boxes, and portrayed my great-great-grandfather Andrew Hoffman I (1737–1799) and his wife Ann Cooper Hoffman (1751–1841). They appear aristocratic and self-assured in their well-modeled profiles. Ann was evidently a plump, self-satisfied lady, her nose turned up pugnaciously. She wore a high coiffure of curls and a lace shawl draped over her shoulders. Andrew sported a high-collared cloth dress coat with the typical lace-trimmed stock of the time about his throat. The only statement I could find as to his business was that he was a "draper and mercer."

It would be easy to surmise that these parents of my great-grandfather considered themselves very genteel and certainly had no high regard either for actors or for musicians who appeared on the stage. However, children dart off in unexpected directions. Their son Andrew II, born in 1772, was at an early age determined to follow the art of the actor, and to circumvent his parents' objection to his tarnishing the family name by associating it with the stage, he decided at the beginning of his career to add the name of Andrews after his family name of Hoffman. From then on, he was known as Andrew Hoffman Andrews, and he called his children by that name.

When I came upon his diary—a simple day-by-day listing of incidents recorded in 1804, without italics or other emphasis, they seemed, after some 150 years, to assume almost heroic proportions, and startled me into a sudden state of awareness. The pages of this compact little red-leather volume were neatly and closely written in perfect penmanship. On the first page I read the following surprising statement about this great-grandfather of mine: ". . . Commission of Bankruptcy, when residing in Charles St. Covent Garden, London. Feb. 7. 1804. Certificate allowed and dated . . ."

Andrew II was thirty-one at that time, and it seems evident that he resolved to start anew and follow his chosen profession as actor and singer in spite of obstacles that must have tormented him during the early years of his life. Two years later, he wrote that he left London and went to Welshpool in Peyton's Theatrical Company. Then he joined Mr. Crisp's company at Worcester, and acted every night for twenty-one shillings a week. After he had set up his wife in business at Worcester, his company moved to Stourbridge and each night he played different parts.

Now, the entry that made the past begin to stir:

> . . . June 5th, after the play I walked to Worcester 11 P.M. to five in the morn —23 miles. Returned at 6 A.M. and arrived at half past noon. Played that night in the "Village Lawyer." . . .

When I realized that this ancestor of mine had walked forty-six miles that he might spend an hour with his wife, the sap in my family tree began to rise; as my friend Marianne Moore writes:

> What is there like fortitude? What sap
> Went through that little thread
> To make the cherry red?

I read on, with new interest:

> . . . During this month of June, I played in 16 benefits. Total receipts 123 pounds and 5 shillings. . . . Once in July I walked to Ludlow, and in August after the play I walked to the Hereford races and returned in time to play in "Secrets Worth Knowing." August 27 walked again 23 miles to Worcester and next day to Birmingham to join my wife. . . .
>
> Jan 26. "Mountaineers." Mr. Crisp fined me 1 pound 10 for refusing to sit on a broken chair on the stage (I considered it dangerous), therefore got my discharge sooner than submit to his imposition. . . .

My great-grandfather certainly had a mind of his own.

In June, 1815 he noted: ". . . Rejoicings for Victories this week (no salary). Napoleon defeated at Waterloo, Belgium." To come upon this sudden historic statement with its personal meaning for my ancestor gave me a start, and made Waterloo immediately alive.

Ten days later, he stated that his own benefit brought in £126.19. Perhaps he felt that the victories were worth the temporary cessation of salary.

In 1829 Mr. Andrews became an auxiliary manager.

. . . In the company were fourteen gentlemen and eight ladies. This number gradually increased, a corps de ballet and a band added.

[1830] . . . June 26. His Majesty George IV died. Theatre closed by order of the Lord Chamberlain, which order was revoked the same day by his Majesty King William IV who ordered the theatres to be closed only the night of death, two nights lying in state, and night of funeral. —The King is dead, long live the King—

Play'd 15 parts in 4 nights. Went to Margate where we play'd 246 nights. Company play'd 542 parts [!] Open at *Drury Lane*. October, 1830. 111 members in company.

[1833]. Liverpool. Lease of theatre to Mr. Lewis began March 25. Entirely beautified and repaired. All very elegant. 157 performances.

I was intrigued to read that his "dear son Richard" (my grandfather, born in London in 1803) "appeared for the first time, at the age of six, in a play called 'Tom Thumb.'" Reading between the lines, we can sense the affectionate pride Great-Grandfather felt for his talented son—and shared by me, I confess, 150 years later. But that talent was to turn to music.

Two years after his debut, my grandfather was articled as apprentice to his "kind and affectionate master," Mr. Andrew Ward, then leader of the band at the Royal. When he was ten, he led the band in a benefit performance for his father. In the four succeeding years he came frequently before the public of Manchester and Liverpool, and, for something like half a century, he was a leading music teacher in Manchester, but it was as composer and adapter of music that he was best known. In this field he was so prolific (and how hard a worker may be inferred from the fact) that he either composed, adapted, or arranged something like nine hundred pieces of music! And he kept his performing skill. I recall my mother telling me that when Grandpa was seventy-five years old she had seen him play all the scales on the piano with velocity, while balancing a wineglass full of water on the back of his hand without spilling a drop.

The atmosphere of Grandpa's house was certainly steeped in music, and it was not surprising that his children came under the spell. My father was born in Manchester on May 24, 1831. Following the family tradition, it was quite natural that his musical training was intense at an early age. His genuine love of music was evident, and we find that he, too, made his debut in public life at the age of six, playing three musical instruments—piano, violin, and concertina. This tour de force struck me as almost unbelievable, but Father never thought of it as anything unusual.

As a youngster in Manchester he was often taken to the "Gentlemen's Concerts" performed by an orchestra of seventy carefully selected musicians in which my grandfather was First Violin. Father was permitted to sit in Grandpa's chair

PORTRAIT OF ANDREW HOFFMAN ANDREWS,
MY GREAT-GRANDFATHER

PHOTOGRAPH OF RICHARD ANDREWS, MY GRANDFATHER

while the orchestra was playing, for in those days all the men, except the cellists, stood while playing. He confessed that during some of the concerts he fell asleep and that Grandpa, during a pause, would prod him with his bow to wake him up.

Father also studied the organ, but was hampered because his feet could hardly reach the pedals. At the age of twelve he was asked to play before an assembly of guests at the country estate of Lord Wilton, an excellent musical amateur who was considering applicants for the position of organist at Prestwich Parish Church. On the eve appointed, after a long and solitary drive, Pa was faced with the ordeal of reading at sight and playing some old chorals with figured base on an organ he had never before seen. The result was satisfactory, and he was offered the position.

The following week, during the afternoon service, while reaching for the swell pedal to emphasize a climax, his little foot slipped and he fell on the keyboard, all stops out, and then tumbled to the foot pedals. The congregation was scandalized. His brothers, knowing that he had not really wanted the position as organist, never referred to the incident as an "accident." Be that as it may, Lord Wilton wrote to Grandpa, praising his son Richard's talent, but stating that the boy seemed a little young to play the church organ and direct the choir!

When Father was sixteen, he was offered the chance to go to Birmingham and write an account of the Festival performance of *Elijah* conducted by its composer Felix Mendelssohn. By good fortune he had a pass to the rehearsal, and Dr. Henry John Gauntlett, the organist for the performance, asked Father to pull out the organ stops for him. It was one of the supreme moments of Father's life when he had the privilege, in this way, of participating in the premiere of Mendelssohn's oratorio. Mendelssohn entered, a small, lithe figure with rather a large head and lustrous eyes shining with the light of genius. Once or twice during the rehearsal, he came up to Dr. Gauntlett to tell him not to be so loud and to push in such and such a stop. But as soon as his back was turned, Gauntlett would say quickly to young Hoffman, "Pull them out again, pull them out again."

The next day Father waited for four hours to get into the festival hall, and then described the Mendelssohn part of the concert as "music that begins where language leaves off," and parts of it as "beyond human conception." After the oratorio, Giovanni Mario and Madame Giulia Grisi sang other works, but my father felt that "when Mendelssohn left the stage, all the lights seemed to go out."

Father had hoped to be sent to Germany to study under the direction of Mendelssohn, but the latter was so overtaxed with engagements that this plan was dropped, and Pa had lessons from Leopold de Meyer, the "lion pianist," as he was called. He was one of Father's youthful infatuations; in spite of the fact that he behaved like a mountebank when playing in public, Father admired the superb power and controlled delicacy of his touch.

Father's devoted friend in London, with whom he stayed, was Giulio Regondi, an outstanding virtuoso on the guitar and concertina. His trills and shakes brought thunderous applause from audiences who marveled how the little concertina could produce such brilliant and rhapsodic music. Regondi made Father a skilled concertina player, but although Pa actually gave concerts on this instrument, the piano was his first and last love. I still have the concertina in its velvet-lined case. The leather bellows decorated in gold has no cracks or blemishes.

Pa told us how Regondi became an idol of London society, not only for his musical talents but also for his aristocratic and mysterious personality. The nobility studied with him and became his close friends. My father dearly loved this gifted musician, with whom he went to Paris when he was still in his teens. I became fascinated by the mystery of Regondi's origin, and asked endless questions, but they were always brushed aside by Father, who merely told me Regondi was probably descended from royalty. He described how two old ladies of the Bourbon aristocracy in London always rose when Regondi entered their salon. He was treated *en prince* at these gatherings, which he constantly attended. Pa considered him a true and noble artist filled with an exalted love of music.

Another outstanding performer remembered by Father was Franz Liszt, who in 1824, as a boy of thirteen, was sent by his father to England to give a concert in Manchester. There he was confided to the care of Mr. Ward, who was my grandfather's partner. Fifteen years later, when Liszt was twenty-eight, Father heard him play a concert of bravura piano compositions. Pa recalled Liszt's tall, lanky figure, his long light hair hanging down to his shoulders, and his tightly buttoned frock coat heavily trimmed with braid. His technical velocity was indescribable and the audience was wildly enthusiastic. The press extolled his electrifying effect when he played a sequence of thirds in scales, and the dramatic volume of tone he produced in the execution of a double shake or a trill.

Grandpa's ardent desire that his nine children be trained as musicians must have necessitated strict discipline in a household overcrowded and noisy with youngsters practicing both voice and various instruments. For this reason I suspect that Father's thoughts were turning toward greater freedom, and when his Uncle George, then living in New York in 1847, invited him to come to America, Pa accepted willingly.

On arrival in Boston he was met by a friend who presented him to old Mr. Jonas Chickering at his workshop. Pa was asked to sit down at a grand piano and play for the old gentleman, who soon gathered an admiring audience of friends to hear the "lad from England," who was dressed in an Eton jacket and broad white collar. Pa was so pleased by the tone and action of the Chickering piano that he was faithful to that make during his entire life.

After a day or two in Boston, Father went to New York by the Sound boat—alone and very homesick. He drove to his Uncle George's house on Spring Street and rang the bell, but no one answered. Having reached the house very early, before anyone was awake, the poor youngster was obliged to sit on his little leather trunk and reflect on the wisdom, or perhaps folly, of his daring voyage to a strange land.

ENGRAVING FROM A DAGUERREOTYPE
OF MY FATHER AT THE AGE OF SIXTEEN

An old lithograph shows him at this time—he was sixteen—with a thick shock of curly hair, eyes wide apart, and an expression of innocence and wisdom, a certain dignity and grave charm. (Father used his lithograph, which was made before he left England, for his American publicity.) Soon after his arrival in this country, he dropped the name of Andrews and reverted to the simpler name of Hoffman, to which he was entitled.

While staying with his uncle, who was an actor, Pa met many members of the dramatic circle, and musicians as well. One of these was Joseph Burke, an Irish violinist, who became Pa's first real friend in New York. Burke, who was also a youthful prodigy, had gone on the stage at the age of eight and was known as "Master Burke," but he soon forsook the theatre for the violin and a musical career. When Father and Burke met, they were immediately drawn to each other, and they decided to try their luck in a joint concert at the Tabernacle, a huge circular hall seating two thousand people. Though the auditorium was dismally lighted, and had but one entrance, reached by a long narrow alley from Broadway, the two young musicians were quite successful. In fact, Pa was so encouraged, he took the risk of giving a concert on his own in the same hall. He felt very grand that night because, as stated on his program, he was playing on "a superb Chickering piano, specially made for a gentleman in this city." But, alas, the hall was only half filled. This overambitious effort might have been disastrous had it not been for the prompt generosity of a group of friends who insisted upon paying the cost of the hall and other expenses. Pa wrote: "Possibly I was suffering from a swelled head caused by over-praise. This experience of over-confident youth taught me a lesson in humility and had a good effect upon my character." It was also comforting that Mr. Charles A. Dana, who was associated with Horace Greeley on the *Tribune,* wrote a kindly as well as a favorable notice of the concert.

Good fortune came to Father's aid soon after this financially disastrous debut, when he was asked to play with the Philharmonic Society on November 27, 1847. This was his first appearance as a classical pianist. He chose the Mendelssohn G Minor Concerto, and press criticisms were excellent:

J. Otis, music critic of the New York *Express,* wrote:

> Mr. Richard Hoffman deserved richly the compliment paid him by the management in inviting him to take part in the first concert of the Philharmonic for the season. His admirable performance of Mendelssohn's Grand Concerto in G Minor gave him an opportunity of stamping upon the minds of some of our most distinguished judges an idea of his genius and talent. . . .

The *Evening Mirror* said:

> Mr. Hoffman, a youth scarcely sixteen years of age, made his debut on Tuesday evening. He is a pianist of extraordinary merit, and may be marked among the executive wonders of the present day. His hand possesses an immense grasp, his wrist is strong and flexible, his touch is exquisitely delicate, yet firm and crisp. His taste is exceptional and his feeling and expression perfectly genuine. . . .

Father used to say that the fine music critics of his day, in giving him such good notices and wise counsel, stimulated him to far more intense cultivation of his art.

With renewed enthusiasm Pa and Joseph Burke went on a tour in 1849 under difficult and exhausting conditions. Beginning with Albany, they performed in Boston, Worcester, Springfield, and Portland, Maine. At Newburyport they were warned not to ask more than twelve and a half cents for a ticket! They reduced the usual price of fifty cents to twenty-five upon that memorable occasion. Pa's share of the profits was under one dollar. They discovered that by reaching a place two days in advance, they were able to advertise their arrival and concert, and gradually the tour became more successful.

Their next trip included Philadelphia, Baltimore, and Washington, bringing them back to New York in the spring.

After touring as far west as Chicago, something of a feat in those difficult days of slow travel, they tried Milwaukee, Buffalo, Rochester, and Montreal, with tickets invariably fifty cents (except for the occasion in Newburyport). After these concerts, their earnings during their first summer were $401.50. Expenses were about $164.

In some of the towns they visited, the problem of procuring a piano became acute. Sometimes the owner of an instrument would lend it only if it was returned the same night. Thus, after an exhausting concert, they would have the additional burden of pushing the piano over the pavement back to the owner's front gate! Father and Burke must have been relieved and thankful to return to New York after a tour that required such endurance.

FATHER AND JENNY LIND

Then something wonderful happened to Father: his first real chance of a long engagement. He had been aware of the great reputation of the Swedish soprano Jenny Lind, and before coming to America had stood in a queue for four hours to hear her recital in London, but he had not dreamed that he would ever be engaged to play in her company. However, in 1850, he received the following letter:

> RICHARD HOFFMAN, ESQ.:
>   Dear Sir: By advice of Mr. Julius Benedict I write to inform you that I will engage you to play for Jenny Lind's concerts, Etc. . . . I expect the 1st concert will be given about the middle of Sept.
>   Very truly yours,
>   P. T. BARNUM

Everyone knows of Barnum's connection with the circus, but it is less generally known that he began his career as an impresario for touring musicians. Perhaps the greatest gamble of his career was undertaking to bring Jenny Lind to America. Her contract was for 150 concerts during the first year at $1,000 a concert. After her first appearance she broke the contract, and demanded $1,000 a night *plus* one half of the receipts above $3,000 with all expenses paid. The

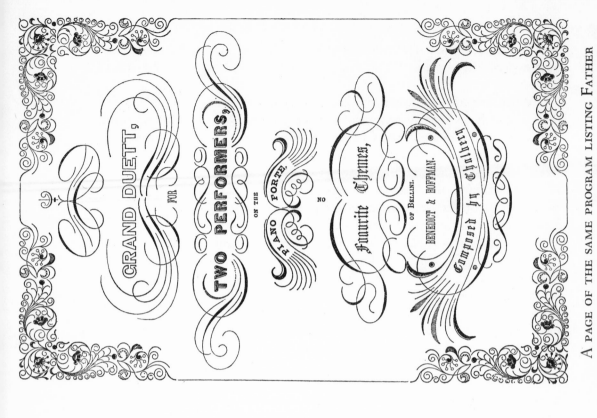

A PAGE OF THE SAME PROGRAM LISTING FATHER
AND JULES BENEDICT IN "GRAND DUETT"

CASTLE GARDEN

First appearance of Mademoiselle Jenny Lind on Wednesday Evening, 11th September, 1850

COVER OF THE PROGRAM FOR THE FIRST
AMERICAN APPEARANCE OF JENNY LIND

musical public in New York was not very enlightened, and Barnum could not be sure how he would fare elsewhere, but, feeling he had discovered a gold mine, he accepted the singer's terms.

When Jenny Lind arrived in New York, thousands of people had gathered along the piers to get a glimpse of the much-heralded "Swedish Nightingale." From docks, roofs, and the decks of steamers the public shouted an enthusiastic welcome. Great arches of garlands and branches had been built over the gates to the pier, and it was with difficulty that Miss Lind and her escorted party were able to force a way out and drive in the captain's carriage to the Irving House, where she had to appear on the upper balcony of her rooms to quiet the tumultuous throng in the streets below. I remember hearing Father describe how at midnight many members of the Musical Fund Society arrived to offer a serenade to Jenny Lind, and how they were accompanied by torchbearers and several companies of New York firemen and a well-behaved crowd of many thousands of people. After cheers and speeches the multitude retired, and Miss Lind was at last permitted to do the same.

Arrangements were made for a first concert in Castle Garden (originally known as Fort Clinton), on the west side of Battery Park, and the seats were put up at public auction in the same place. Pa said about four thousand people attended the sale. Gemin, a hatter, procured the first ticket for $225, and the total receipts for the first concert amounted to about $28,000. One of Pa's favorite stories told of the little boats crowded around Castle Garden, then connected with the Battery by a short causeway, and how ladders were leaned from the boats to the wall of the building, people buying places on the rungs of these precarious perches. He said the boatmen, pocketing their earnings, could row away after the concert under cover of darkness. Though Mr. Barnum had tried to arrange for sufficient police protection at Castle Garden to enable the concert audience to enter without undue confusion at the gates, it was only by determined effort that ticketholders elbowed their way forward.

Because Father was performing at this concert, he secured a good place in the wings where he could watch and hear the singer at close range. Facing her first American audience was obviously so formidable an ordeal to Miss Lind that for the first few phrases her voice faltered. Father was apprehensive, but she regained control immediately, and he said that by the end of the cavatina the applause and cheering were vehement. Flowers were heaped on the stage, and when Father and Mr. Benedict came out to play a duet on two pianos it was with difficulty that the audience was persuaded to quiet sufficiently to listen. Had they attempted an encore, Pa felt, they would propably have been lynched.

Joseph Burke was engaged as concertmaster, and played at all of Miss Lind's performances in this country. Where an orchestra could not be produced, Father and Burke generally started the concerts off with a duet, and solos by each would follow. Father, who listened offstage to all the numbers on Miss Lind's program, remembered her voice as a deliciously rounded tone with fine musical phrasing and possibilities of great volume. Inexhaustible reserve force enabled her to sustain a clear tone for an unbelievable length of time. Her appearance, though she was not precisely beautiful, had great attraction, for her manner on the stage was perfect, and she seemed always in an ecstasy of delight, giving her audience a sense of sharing her pleasure in singing for them. At one of her concerts she sang the aria "I Know That My Redeemer Liveth." The rapt expression of her face and the prolonged volume of her voice were spellbinding. Daniel Webster, who was seated in the center of the balcony, rose at the close of the aria and made her a profound bow.

For a concert in Boston, the Fitchburg railroad station was engaged by Barnum, who, by miscalculating the floor space, sold tickets for many more persons than the station could accommodate. The result was a mob that could not be controlled. Police had to take charge, and when Father reached the entrance they helped to pass him along on their shoulders until he got to the stage—more dead than alive, as he used to say, and so disordered in appearance that he had to be put together with safety pins before going onstage. He felt as if he had been tossed in a blanket. He and the other participating artists were indignant with the manager for having arranged this railroad-station concert, for the wild confusion it caused distracted the audience as well as the performers.

My father thought that a contributing factor that helped keep Miss Lind's highly temperamental character on an even keel, despite such upsetting experiences, was that she became enamored of Otto Goldschmidt, a pianist who was a member of her company and who was her accompanist as well. She would sit at the side of the stage whenever he played a solo, paying rapt attention to his performance. It was not long before they were married in Boston.

Miss Lind was beloved by thousands, not merely for her accomplishments but also for her humane and magnanimous heart. Her gifts to charity were tremendous, a large percentage of her receipts always being shared with those less fortunate than herself. Father recalled her invariably gracious bearing to him and the other members of the company. But as a contrasting instance of her complex character the following story always struck me as revealing:

Father's sister Helen, one of the most promising singers in England at the time, had also been engaged by P. T. Barnum to sing with Miss Lind's company in America. During a London tryout, however, when she and Miss Lind appeared on the same program, Aunt Helen's contralto singing in an oratorio just preceding Miss Lind's part caused such sustained applause that Miss Lind was forced to sit down while Aunt Helen repeated her aria. This angered the Swedish Nightingale, and after the concert she notified Mr. Barnum that Aunt Helen's contract must be canceled. Father used to try to explain this unfortunate event by saying, "Perhaps Miss Lind felt she was embarking on a perilous venture, and out of sheer self-preservation she could not add to her anxieties by sharing honors with a rival singer." As it happened, Helen soon married, and her husband was thankful to have her abandon a public career.

On his return to New York after the tour with Miss Lind, Father had many opportunities to play both with chamber-music groups and in recitals. His own standards were high, and enabled him to resist the natural temptation to

JOSEPH BURKE, VIOLINIST

JENNY LIND

Jenny Lind

play bravura style, which always brought forth enthusiastic applause from audiences.

Father was only twenty-two when he played the Chopin Concerto with the New York Philharmonic and was unanimously elected to honorary membership in the Society. He played with them as soloist for thirty years and decided at the beginning never to accept any remuneration, because he felt that by turning his fee over to the members of the orchestra he helped them and also set an example of practical idealism. After one of his orchestral appearances H. C. Watson wrote in *Frank Leslie's Illustrated Newspaper:*

> . . . Richard Hoffman played Mozart's Piano Concerto with fine poetic feeling and freshness of sentiment, that conscientious art principle which is the attribute of the truly classic artist. . . . He arrested the attention of the audience from the first note to the last. We have rarely heard anything more exquisite. . . . Hoffman's technique is superb and its perfect quality could not have been exhibited to greater advantage. He achieved a triumph. . . .

The fact that Father might be called upon at short notice to play a concerto, or fill in for some emergency, such as a pianist being taken suddenly ill, drove him to practice a varied repertoire, with an impassioned determination to commit the compositions to memory and feel confident of his ability to perform them in public. The result was that when the moment came he could play without nervousness and feel serenely secure.

One of the personalities of that era was Sigismond Thalberg, a virtuoso pianist who was one of Father's idols. During Thalberg's season in America, in 1856, Pa attended all his concerts, on a free pass, and learned by heart all his operatic arrangements and compositions, which he played at intervals throughout his life, never having to refer to notes to refresh his memory. He said that the audience would rise during Thalberg's astonishing feats of virtuosity to see how such marvelous tours de force could be accomplished. So great was his popularity that he often gave three concerts a day, two in New York and one in Brooklyn.

Father went to England for a summer during the early sixties, and one of his happiest associations there was being welcomed by the family of John Leech, the great illustrator for *Punch.* Leech's brilliant pen-and-ink drawings had few rivals, except perhaps George du Maurier's illustrations for *Trilby,* a novel that seemed to infect the public with an enthusiasm Father described as almost a malady. He fell a victim to it himself when he compiled an album of Trilby melodies.

During the Civil War, Father helped organize a series of concerts to raise money for wounded soldiers, and took part in the concerts himself. Some of his best pupils joined him, and together they played duets for two pianos and quartets for eight hands.

Father remembered the musical season of 1870 as a brilliant one, with the coming to America of Christine Nilsson, who had just triumphed at the Paris

Grand Opéra. In the seventies there were also concerts by Anton Rubinstein, whose playing style Father admired for its nobility, and by Hans von Bülow.

My father in those years used to visit the home of the Sedgwick family in Lenox, Massachusetts. Miss Elizabeth Sedgwick married Mr. Frederick Racke-mann, who became Father's particular friend and was himself a fine musician. At the Sedgwick home, the great actress Fanny Kemble mingled informally with the guests and often recited poems. Father and Mr. Rackemann furnished musical interludes. I heard from many of Pa's friends later that his natural dignity and quiet friendliness were enhanced by a native talent for telling amusing incidents and stories. Another good friend of Papa's in those years was Dr. R. Ogden Doremus, president of the Philharmonic Society, who insisted on addressing Father as "The Beloved."

Between his recitals and other activities, Father gradually built up a clientele of diligent and talented pupils. His teaching stimulated their imagination; he impressed upon them the importance of supplementing their technical skill with profound understanding. He warned them that no matter how brilliantly they could maneuver their fingers, their playing would never be able to move the hearts of their listeners without a complete knowledge of the composer's original conception. Pa would advise his pupils to hear as many great opera singers as possible, both to train the ear and for musical impressions of conflicting emotions—love, honor, despair—as interpreted, for instance, by Nilsson and Italo Campanini in the duet of the Fourth Act of *Les Huguenots*. He recommended hearing Jean de Reszke phrase and enunciate the "Salut" cavatina of the garden scene in Gounod's *Faust*. He wanted his students to attend fine orchestral concerts whenever they could to develop their appreciation of music and to try to grasp its inner meaning. He emphasized that his pupils should never shirk using their minds and critical faculties. He urged them to note the variety of tone and the infinite shading of harmony that charm and uplift us. These are not the result of technical study, he insisted—the player must have gone deeper than this. Where the piece was difficult, for reach or fingering, he felt that the passion for playing would stimulate the technique of the pupil and overcome all difficulties.

He asked the pupils if they had noticed that Hungarian airs commence on the downbeat, or first of the bar. In the concluding movement of the Chopin Sonata that contains the funeral march, there is much to be thought out and studied, my father said, adding that only one player, and by that he meant Vladimir de Pachmann, succeeded in giving a perfect rendering of the whistling wind sweeping the hurrying clouds before the face of the moon and lashing the trees in relentless fury, then moaning itself away like a restless spirit.

One teaching method of Father's was to explain variant scales (Scotch and Chinese) and from that he would branch into a description of Gregorian chant. Everything that could stimulate the curiosity of the pupil or enlarge the scope of his musical ideas Father found useful.

Another intricate study he recommended was following the different modulations of a composition, for example, Chopin's Nocturne in G Major, Opus 37, Number 2, or the first movement of Beethoven's Sonata, Opus 53.

He wrote in his article on *How to Stimulate Thought and Imagination in a Pupil*: "All . . . head knowledge will be sure to come out at the finger-ends. Those great pianists who can charm their hearers by their interpretations can be quickly counted, while those who excel in digital dexterity alone are as innumerable as the stars of the firmament." This article of Father's is filled with wise guidance drawn from his own experience, and I was always impressed in later years by how thoroughly informed his best pupils were, knowing the history and individual accomplishments of a host of musicians. The wisdom of a real master may rub off on his sensitive pupils, and certainly this is a consoling thought for every generation unless they are blinded by their own egotism.

Father's reputation as a teacher came to the notice of Charles and Elizabeth Lamson, who at that time lived on West Twenty-first Street with their family of nine children. They decided to engage Richard Hoffman to give piano lessons to their eldest girl, Fidelia, who had shown a rather marked musical talent.

I like to think of Fidelia swaying along in her tight bodice and full skirts, poke bonnet and tiny parasol, past the Union Club, down Fifth Avenue under the ailanthus trees to her teacher's studio in the Chickering Building on Eighteenth Street. Her thoughts were busy with sonatas and her heart was singing with happiness, for she and her professor were deeply in love. Her mother, however, was firmly opposed to any such romance. Mrs. Lamson was an imperious lady who felt that family traditions must be observed and that her children should continue to live within a strict social code. The idea that her daughter wanted to marry a music teacher and "public performer" on the stage was anathema to her. So the romance flourished in secret, and I remember Ma often telling me that one of the most difficult problems she had to face was her mother's disapproval of her interest in Pa, and having to suppress her emotions, avoiding any mention of her pleasure in studying with him.

Fidelia waited until she was twenty-one; then, when there was no hope of winning her mother's consent, she took her future into her own hands, agreeing with Father to elope. On the day set, it rained so hard that she could think of no convincing excuse for going out into the deluge. When it appeared that there was no other way, she slipped down the back stairs. The lovers had confided their plan to a few close friends, among them Ma's great friend Adele Smith (later Mrs. Edgar Bass), who waited in a four-wheeler at the corner of the street. Destiny held the reins, and Fidelia and Richard were married in 1869 at St. John's Chapel in Varick Street, the church in which he was organist. After the ceremony the small group drove up Fifth Avenue in the still-pouring rain to the home of their friends, the James M. Farrs, who gave them a heart-warming welcome and a wedding breakfast.

Though their wedding day was inclement, the young couple embarked on their daring new adventure undaunted and happy, determined to go forward despite possible ostracism by Mother's family and despite having many problems to solve, very much on their own. They rented a little red brick house at

116 West Forty-third Street, halfway between the Hippodrome and Henry Savage's Theatrical Agency. At that time a respectable-looking street, it was later known as the "Red-Light District." The Lamsons showed no signs of forgiveness until a daughter, Helen, was born two years later. Then they relented and decided to have a party of reconciliation. I am told that a large heart-shaped floral shield was set above the mantelpiece in the Twenty-first Street house, with the letter "L" in red carnations at one side and the letter "H" in white at the other. Refreshments were served, and the *pièce de résistance* was a huge three-tiered cake covered with nougat and ornamental frosting. Truly, it was a happy reunion for all; everything was forgiven, and the families were united forever after. When the Lamsons knew my father better, they succumbed, as did everyone else, to his quiet charm. Acquainted with his real character, they were gradually convinced that what they had feared might be a Bohemian and wild existence for their carefully brought-up daughter was actually the sharing of the romantic and dedicated life of a serious artist. Father, a devoted and faithful husband, was beloved by them all.

CHAPTER TWO

THE FAMILY TREE:

Mother's Forebears

MOTHER'S FAMILY TREE also had its roots in England. The three Lamson brothers, whose origin has been traced back to the Earl of Durham, sailed from their British homeland to the coast of Massachussetts in 1630, and formed part of the group who founded the settlement of Agawam, later known as Ipswich.*

In 1635 the Massachusetts Colony granted William Lamson 350 acres of land near "Labour in Wayne" Creek, which have remained in the possession of the family ever since. Industrious, William was held in high esteem and was made a freeman of the town in which he held a position of high authority. He married Sarah Ayers (although no marriage certificate has ever been found), and they had eight children.

One of his sons, John, was also a freeman of the town, and served on the grand jury of "Tryalls" of Salem, at the time of the famous witch-hunts. The court tried to calm the hysterical townsfolk who accused and insisted upon punishments for so-called witches, and under pressure of judicial wisdom the wild excitement gradually abated.

The story of another son, Joseph, has often fascinated me, for he seems to have been the only artistically inclined ancestor on Mother's side. He was a cordwainer, cabinetmaker, and stonecutter, but it is said that when he carved the coffins or tombstones he often added little winged figures as decorations. The times were not propitious to his artistic leanings, but I like to think that at heart he was a sculptor. When not occupied with stone carving, he looked after the "yoking and runing of swine," was also a tithing man and a sealer of leather. When he died he left his wife only "what she had brought with her when she married"; to his four sons he left an estate valued at £203.

The settlers at Ipswich must have been a rugged lot. They built their own

* *The information about the Lamson family in Ipswich was given to me by Colonel Daniel Sanderson Lamson of Weston, Massachusetts, one of the "Sons of the Revolution," who sent me his family records about 1910.*

houses of hand-hewn timber with hand-forged nails, raised large families, and cut through the wilderness to make their roads and gardens. Firearms and swords hung over the large open fireplaces or stood near the doorway for defense of the household against Indian attacks. Bedrooms were upstairs, and sparsely furnished. The only central heating was the human blood circulating in these hardy Puritans, reinforced by a warming pan and feather bed, their only protection from the cold on wintry nights.

Life was austere, a Spartan survival-of-the-fittest existence. Everyone worked hard throughout the week until 3:00 P.M. on Saturday, when all were expected to study the catechism and prepare for nine o'clock service on the Sabbath at the Town Hall Meetinghouse. Baptisms followed the afternoon service, which began at two o'clock. Apart from cessation of farm labor, there was little reason for the early Puritans to call Sunday a "day of rest." To survive under such conditions was a challenge. They must have had iron constitutions and endless patience and faith.

The Bible was the source of the names for the Lamson children—Obadiah, Amos, Jonathan, and Caleb; Elijah, Zachariah, Gideon, and Lucinda; Lucretia, Amaritta, Ebenezer, Isaac, Abigail, Naomi, Mehitabel, Reuben, and Asa. Though we may smile as we read these names, we infer from the early chronicles the fearless tenacity of purpose and deep-rooted reverence for the Bible and its teachings that underlay these pioneers' sense of duty.

A goodly number of the Lamson clan became soldiers, and served in the Revolutionary War. One of these, Jonathan, received after five years an honorable discharge signed by Washington's own hand. He then migrated to western New York, driving an ox team and one horse as far as Rome.

Dr. John Lamson served as an army surgeon and was captured by the Cohnewagoe Indians and held prisoner for many months; when he was freed he was transferred to Europe. After a siege of smallpox and nervous fever, he sent a petition to the Governor of Massachussetts and was allowed damages of £160 in new tenor bills.

Three (though not successive) generations of the Lamson family commanded regiments from Weston, Massachusetts, in three wars, the only such instance on record in the Massachusetts State House.

Samuel Lamson fought in the Indian War of King Philip in 1675. His great-grandson Colonel Samuel Lamson fought at Concord and served with Washington's army on the Hudson. This Colonel Lamson's grandson was Colonel Daniel Sanderson Lamson of Weston, Massachusetts, who fought in the Civil War. I well remember as a little girl going with my mother to visit his old homestead, which was built in 1765. I was prewarned to be sure to notice and inquire about his war medals. A typical old soldier, he proudly displayed his medals and mementos, including one of the first rebel flags, the white stars of which were cut from the petticoat of President Tyler's daughter.

My own interest in mechanical gadgets and how they worked made me all the more keen to read of the many Lamson forebears who seemed to have made their mark through their own inventions. These included a "snath," or crooked scythe handle, which was a great boon to farmers. In 1847 another Lamson built several types of kites and airplanes that were used in meteorological observations. Still another inventor was Dr. Daniel Lamson, an excellent surgeon, who wrote a paper on aphasia from brain surgery that was considered a great contribution to medicine. He perfected an automatic vaccinator that is still in use. As early as 1855 this same man built a steam engine that actually worked, as well as an improved mowing machine.

I felt sincerely sorry that I never knew this ancestor of mine, for I feel sure we would have had a wonderful time together.

Around the turn of the century, Alexander Otis Lamson, a specialist in wireless telegraphy, invented a phonograph record that did away with jarring and unsteady tone. This greatly widened the range for recording the human voice. The array of talents revealed to me just in reading the long list of Lamson inventions in New England made me proud to belong to their clan.

Other branches of Mother's family tree followed widely different roads. Some were ministers of the church and missionaries to far-off countries, while others were intrepid explorers who brought back valuable collections of prehistoric pottery and jewelry which they presented to the Smithsonian Institution, and to the Yale and Peabody museums.

Perhaps the most often referred-to ancestor on Mother's side was my great-grandfather Captain Charles H. Marshall, who was born in New York State in 1792. Both his parents were of Nantucket descent, and he was born with a love for the sea. At the age of fifteen he begged his parents to let him try his luck on a whaling ship commanded by a friend of the family. His mother packed his sea chest and added a quantity of "prog" (ham, bread, and pies); this, with thirteen dollars in coin, comprised his entire baggage.

I have always had a leaning toward this spunky and determined young lad who was told by the captain to whom he presented himself that he was too light for his purpose and was a mere boy. This remark shocked the boy visibly. The captain, noting his embarrassment, said: "I will take you, my lad; I dare say you will make up in smartness what you lack in size!"

So it was that Charles Marshall began his life on the sea, and made good in such a variety of adventures that it was only about ten years later that he was offered the command of a 350-ton ship, the *Julius Caesar*, and was enrolled as a shipmaster. He sailed it to Charleston, South Carolina, where he took on a cargo for Liverpool, England.

A fast ship named *Martha*, commanded by a well-known shipmaster, was due to sail from Charleston ahead of the *Julius Caesar*. The owner of Charles's ship heard of this, and promised to reward him with a new suit of clothes if he could beat his formidable rival and so make his own reputation, as well as that of his new ship, by establishing a record from Charleston to Liverpool. Charles accepted the challenge.

The *Martha* sailed one day ahead of Charles's ship. It was well known to all hands on both vessels that they were entered for a race across the Atlantic, and on each ship every nerve was strained. The *Julius Caesar*, handicapped a day at the start, was kept under all the canvas she could carry. It was boisterous March weather, with high winds and rough seas. Charles drove the ship night and day, the seas breaking over her so that there was hardly a dry man on board throughout the voyage. She reached the Channel in eighteen days from the day she left Charleston. Here the weather was very thick and rainy, and they could make out neither land nor lights. But all risks must be taken, and Charles crowded on sail, running through the fog at full speed, keeping the course in accordance with his best judgment.

On the twenty-second day the *Julius Caesar* reached the mouth of the Mersey, where they learned that the *Martha* had not yet been sighted. Young Charles's excitement was unbounded, and on landing he rushed to report his victory. His story was hardly credited; but when the *Martha* arrived, the consignees agreed that he had beaten her by eighteen hours, exclusive of her day's start. The new suit was fairly won and promptly worn.

About this time the Black Ball Line of Liverpool packets was established, and Captain Marshall was soon called into the corps of shipmasters who by their skill and fidelity gave the line its high reputation.

In 1822, at the age of thirty, he married Fidelia Wellman, a woman of rare beauty.

Aside from his whaling trips and an East Indian voyage, he crossed the Atlantic ninety-four times. He identified himself with the leading movements of commerce in New York City. In 1861 he rallied the Union League Club to work more actively for the imperiled liberties of his country. He was elected third president of the club, and served as such until he died in 1865.

His daughter Elizabeth married Charles Lamson who was a member of the business firm Lane, Lamson & Co., Importers of French Silks. They had nine children, and the eldest daughter was my mother, who was named for my great-grandmother Fidelia.

She was born in 1848 in Paris, in a little house at 13 rue de la Victoire. It was at the time of the Commune, when the city was in a state of siege. Grandpa Charles Lamson, the anxious father of the newly arrived Fidelia, had gone away to Lyons on a business trip, and when he tried to return to Paris he found the gates of the city closed. He at once initiated proceedings to obtain a special permit; and as the French always seem to have great sympathy and love for children, he prevailed upon the high officials to permit him to return to his home, and rejoin the family.

When I was in Paris in 1948, I had the good fortune to visit a Centennial Exhibit that showed the life of Paris in 1848, from old prints, maps, and documents. Many of the shops familiar to us today were well established then, though on a smaller scale. The ladies in pursuit of fashion wore voluminous hoopskirts and endless flounces, ruffles, lace jabots, capes, and lace-trimmeed negligees. All of these accessories were worn by my grandmother. Her elegant appearance and carefully coiffed white hair made a lasting and rather awesome impression upon her grandchildren.

My grandmother, Elizabeth Lamson (*Frick Art Reference Library*)

My grandfather, Charles Lamson

Children in Paris have always enjoyed an open-air life in the city's beautiful gardens and parks. In the middle of the nineteenth century, as today, Punch and Judy shows delighted young and old, shallow pools provided seas for sailing boats, and multicolored booths selling candy and *gaufrettes*, pinwheels and balloons, did a thriving business. My mother must surely have been happy in her first years, and she did, in fact, always like the thought that she began her life in the "city of light and romance."

On their return to New York from Paris in the early fifties, Grandpa and Grandma Lamson bought Number 11 West Twenty-first Street. During the subsequent years their family grew until there were nine children, seven girls and two boys.

Twenty-first Street was considered quite fashionable in those days. The Union Club was on the Fifth Avenue corner, with the Presbyterian Church across from it. One of the diversions enjoyed by the Union Club members was watching the comings and goings of the seven Lamson sisters, who generally went walking in a group.

The Jeromes, whose daughter Jenny became the mother of Winston Churchill, lived on the south side of Twenty-sixth Street, opposite the old Madison Square Garden, which was topped by the gilded figure of Diana, by the sculptor St. Gaudens. It is hard to believe that the residents of that quarter were scandalized by the nude figure of this goddess, but they were.

At Number 28 lived the Hermann Oelrichs, and at Number 6 the De Lancey Nicolls whose Aunt Glory came for a week's visit and stayed for forty years! It was a custom for the maids of those families to hang gray corduroy covers over the iron railing of the front balconies to protect hands and elbows, since watching one's neighbors was a constant diversion.

Fifth Avenue was the formal avenue for handsomely attired walkers. The Forty-second Street Reservoir, in the Egyptian style, was massive and gray; extending from Fortieth Street to Forty-second Street, it was surrounded by walls with a coping wide enough to walk on. Its height forced water to the top of three-story houses, and obviated the necessity of carrying water upstairs in brass cans.

Central Park in the 1860's was surrounded by squatter farms and was reached by horse-drawn cars. Stages were used on Broadway, starting from Bowling Green, and passing Barnum's Museum, the Olympic Theatre, and Tiffany's on their way uptown. Children rolled hoops and played hopscotch on the sidewalks and enjoyed trips with their mothers to Jefferson Market where customers knew the salesmen by name.

The Lamsons' holidays were spent at the Surf Hotel on Fire Island. Their little tribe with many others of the neighborhood attended Easter Sunday services at the Union Church; and on one occasion after the sermon Dr. Osgood announced from the chancel steps: "Let all the little lambs and all the little Lamsons, too, come up here!" and the congregation smiled as the children filed in good order up the steps and shook hands with the friendly minister.

THE SEVEN LAMSON SISTERS

Fidelia and her sister Lily were sent to Miss Green's School on Washington Square for their education and finishing "frostin'." The girls all went to the Dodsworth dancing school in the Delmonico building at Fourteenth Street and Fifth Avenue. Coming-out parties were numerous, and much time was spent on the "debutante wardrobe" of the seven sisters. It must have been a costly household to maintain!

One of the highlights of my grandmother's life was described to me as a child. It was her attendance at a magnificent ball given in 1860 in honor of Albert Edward, Prince of Wales (afterward King Edward VII). At this brilliant affair Grandma wore a gown of rose-colored brocade, the skirt a series of stiff flounces topped by a close-fitting bodice. She carried a tight little "Valentine" bouquet of rosebuds with knotted streamers. This ball (for which the Academy of Music had been rented) was the greatest that had ever been held in New York.

EUROPEAN HOLIDAY

A year after my parents were married in 1869, they decided to take a holiday together in Europe. Father's previous hard work and savings made them feel they could afford the trip. They went to England, where Pa proudly presented his young bride to his parents, who were living in Manchester. Father had assumed the responsibility of supporting his parents in their old age, and he never allowed anything to prevent the sending of the regular stipend.

While in London, Pa and Ma had the good fortune to hear the singer Adelina Patti in her prime. In both *Rigoletto* and *La Somnambula* Pa remembered her as a surpassingly fine artist with the throat of a bird and a trill that left her listeners speechless with wonder.

From London Father and Mother crossed to France and while in Paris they went to the Cemetery of Père-Lachaise on "le jour des Musiciens" when it was the custom to decorate the graves of musicians. They carried a wreath past many tombs piled high with flowers and came to the grave of Chopin. It stood bare, and they laid their wreath on it as they had intended, though not expecting that theirs, a tribute from so far away, would be the only one.

They stayed at Dinard for a short seaside holiday, and then returned to New York, happy and eager to establish their home life in West Forty-third Street.

Their first child, a girl, died in infancy. The year after this, my eldest sister Helen was born, and my parents decided upon a simple solution of a summer holiday in America. They went to a small country boardinghouse on the New Hampshire coast overlooking a long curving stretch of sandy beach, a paradise for children. The place was called Little Boar's Head and the boardinghouse grew into a hotel, always run in an informal and efficient manner by Pa and Ma Batchelder as they were fondly called by generations of growing families. As the resort grew, a number of residences and cottages were built along the ocean-shore road, and many of them have been lived in by four and five generations of the same families, coming from as far away as Chicago, St. Louis, and Washington.

Mr. George M. Robeson, Secretary of the Navy under Grant, had a cottage near the Inn for many years, and one year an influx of Washington diplomats added zest to the summer colony. Many foreign secretaries of Legations also joined the group. James G. Blaine, Secretary of State during President Garfield's administration, was a frequent visitor, and one evening he gave a vivid account of President James A. Garfield's assassination at the railroad station in Washington, D.C., when he had been with him. So dramatic was his story that the assembled guests felt as if they had personally participated in this tragic event.

The following year President Chester A. Arthur on a trip of inspection at the Portsmouth Navy Yard drove down for luncheon and talked to friends and other guests at the Inn.

It was about 1860 that President Franklin Pierce built a house there. He and his wife enjoyed many summers by the sea. He was considered attractive in appearance and an eloquent speaker.

The first summer that my parents spent at Little Boar's Head was enlivened by the arrival of Harriet Beecher Stowe, who took a nearby cottage for herself and two daughters. The fame of *Uncle Tom's Cabin* had spread over the continent, and the book had been translated into many languages. She was a simple and unassuming person who spent the greater part of every fair day on the beach attired in her bathing suit, chatting most amicably with other summer residents. Although her book has been criticized as having no great literary distinction, it certainly touched off the spark that fired public opinion and showed how contradictory the existence of slavery was in a country proclaiming itself to be free. My mother used to say that the power of *Uncle Tom's Cabin* reminded her of Mercutio after he received the fatal thrust in the duel with Tybalt: "No, 'tis not so deep as a well, nor so wide as a church; but 'tis enough, 'twill serve . . ."

About this time plans were afoot to build a stone chapel for the summer residents by the sea at Rye Beach, a mile north of L.B.H. Mrs. Stowe was prevailed upon to give a reading of her recently published *Oldtown Folks*, and this helped to launch a series of concerts, tableaux and fairs. My father was also a participant in these benefits. After a few years the necessary funds were raised, and St. Andrew-by-the-Sea was built and a small bellows organ installed. Father became the organist, and played there every summer for thirty years.

He also rehearsed the voluntary choir every Saturday morning in the large parlor of Professor Bennett Nash's cottage across from the Hotel. And every Sunday evening from six to seven o'clock a large group of children gathered in the hotel "playroom" to sing hymns selected and played by Father, who by some magic was able to control this noisy and chattering crowd of youngsters so that they promptly took their places and sang fervently to his piano accompaniment and behaved like "li'l" angels. After supper, on this "day of rest," Father would give an informal recital on his own piano in the hotel parlor. Many of the selections were in response to requests from his listeners who came from far and near, driving sometimes from Portsmouth nine miles north, or from nearer points along the coast. Every variety of horse and buggy and "surreys with the fringe on top" drove up as near as they could, their passengers eager to listen to Father's music, the sound of distant breakers and the open-air setting under the stars adding charm to these unforgettable evenings.

As the years went by, our family grew, and Helen, Richard, Elizabeth (Elsie), and Charles were brought up in the Forty-third Street home. Father was never happier than when surrounded by his family. He would join no club, saying his children were the only diversion he desired. My sister Elsie had a marked musical talent, which was a source of great pleasure to the family and to her many friends, but Father never had an ambition to see any of his children follow the profession of music. I suppose he recalled too many hard knocks suffered in his own childhood. When he was musically tied up in the front parlor, the children gathered around the dining-room table to do their homework, under a double kerosene lamp, their murmur kept from the front room by sliding doors and heavy portieres.

The only moment of visible anxiety or tenseness in the family was when the agent was due to collect the house rent. The children never were told of the economies needed to meet this obligation, but they sensed the strain twenty-four hours before the "ogre," as they called him, arrived. After his visit the atmosphere cleared and they all felt relieved.

Pa had a stiffly bound notebook that was really an old grocer's day-by-day listing of the family's purchases. On these pages he glued all his concert clippings with furniture glue that has now turned the papers yellow. Between these clippings occasional items appeared, such as "1 lb. butter 26 cts—1 doz. eggs 22 cts.—1 lb coffee 34 cts." Pa never bought any unnecessary items for himself, one of the ways in which he practiced economy.

Helen and Elsie were in their teens when a surprising event occurred. Mother was to have a new baby, and felt frightened and none too happy about this unexpected addition to the family. She had a photograph taken, which she felt might be her last, and the picture has a wistful and sad expression. In her apprehension, she asked Helen to stand ready to help care for the newcomer. All went well, however, and I was born on June 15, 1885, and was named Malvina after my godmother Aunt Malvina (Cornell), Mother's youngest sister.

There was later some question about the year I was born, and it may be of interest to discuss it here since it may explain discrepancies that exist in the record of that date. My birth certificate once was lost along with my baptismal certificate, in fact all evidence that I existed at all. When Mother then mentioned the year I was born, I said, "Mother, you're two years wrong," and she said, "How do you mean, I'm two years wrong? After all, you're my child." I said, "Yes, I wasn't registering the date of my birth at the time, but I *have* come across odd notes of yours and Father's and I think I have to look them over." She was holding out for 1887 and I for 1885. I found a note in the family history that established unquestionably that I was born in 1885.

Not that I much cared, for I never took any interest in anybody's age, and especially in my family, I never knew whether anyone was older or younger.

It never occurred to me to calculate, probably because I was the baby of the family. And yet nobody seemed to feel that I was particularly young any more than I felt they were particularly old. When I heard my father referred to as "old," I was shocked. To me he was always the same age and he was consistently and (so it seemed to me) unchangingly active with his music up to the day of his death.

This lack of a sense of time will probably make itself felt in this account of my life. Of course, war and other recorded events are hardly subject to misdating; but, on the other hand, I myself have always been highly unaware of dates, even to never having had an interest in my own age.

Perhaps I was born partly grown up and with a congenital conviction that my parents were young.

Be that as it may, I never felt left out. Either the natural affection of my parents and brothers and sisters or their good management made me feel always a part of the family doings.

MY MOTHER   MYSELF (MH) AT THE AGE OF TWELVE

CHAPTER THREE

CHILDHOOD WITH MUSIC

I HAD BEEN but two weeks in this world when the time came for our family to go to Little Boar's Head. Securely attached to a pillow with safety pins, I was deposited in the corner of a red plush seat of a railroad coach. The train carried us from New York to Boston in six hours. With no pullmans or dust screens in the windows, cinders blew in, and many found their way into my eyes. It may be considered artistic license for me to say that I remember (but I certainly do) this annual ordeal of being carried to the ladies' room in the North Station in Boston where the attendant in charge put an "eye stone" under my lids, as well as a soothing eyewash, with the miraculous result that the cinders disappeared. I was then transplanted to the Boston and Maine Railroad car for North Hampton. As the sea breezes blew in from the ocean, we became elated in anticipation of our seashore holiday.

Truth is so often stranger than fiction that I shall again risk the raising of eyebrows and tell how clearly I recall being taken out in my baby carriage for pleasant rides. My nurse was a good-natured German woman named Bertha who seemed to enjoy caring for me long after I was a baby and who taught me little German verses as soon as I could talk. The remembrance of my daily homecoming to our house in Forty-third Street in my carriage includes the fright I felt every time we reached the basement gate, as I was bounced down two high steps and heard "Berrta" warning me to hold fast, saying, "Sei ruhig, mein Kind!" then two formidable bumps—and she would sing " 'Oh, Tannenbaum, wie grün sind deiner Blätter,' " and all would be forgiven.

There was great excitement one day when fire broke out in my nursery. I was bundled into a heavy knitted shawl, carried across the street to the house of Mrs. Charles Foote, taken into her arms, and allowed to watch the fire engines as hose pipes were hauled up the steps of our house. The fire was quickly extinguished. They found that the maid had put hot ashes from the coal fire into a straw wastepaper basket!

I was a very little girl when a serious accident frightened us all. My brother Charles was rehearsing a play at Callison's School on our street when a heavy

31

curtain pole fell on him and cut a deep gash in his head. Hearing a commotion on the front stairs I ran out, peered between the bars of the balustrade, and saw our beloved friend Evart Wendell carrying Charles, whose face was gory with blood dripping from his forehead. He was laid on the sofa in Ma's and Pa's big front bedroom, and I was dispatched for a basin of water and clean towels.

The doctor came soon and put in a few stitches, and in a few days all was well. Mr. Wendell stayed a long time and insisted upon playing nurse, telling us funny stories to dissipate our apprehension.

Thanksgiving Day was a time of elaborate preparations in the front basement. Mother gathered together those who came to do extra laundry work and cooking for parties, and we packed baskets of turkeys, cranberries, vegetables, and fruit for them and a number of needy families. These baskets were ranged on a long table, and we children were on hand for the happiness of distributing them.

Our neighbors were our friends and playmates. They often came in to see the rabbits and guinea pigs penned in our back yard and forever burrowing under wire fences and nibbling our flower beds. There was an obliging tree growing in the next-door yard that hung its shady branches over the fence and added to the green leaves of the lonely catalpa tree that grew in our own back yard.

PAUL AND RUTH DRAPER

Two of my best companions in the neighborhood were Paul and Ruth Draper, who lived at 19 East Forty-seventh Street, just a few blocks away. Ruth was a year older than I, and Paul a year younger, and they already showed signs of their future artistic talent. They were the youngest of eight children. Ruth had a smooth olive complexion, almost a kind of pallor, that set off her black hair and big dark eyes, and she had well-marked and well-modeled features. She was a very good-looking child. On certain afternoons, especially when it was raining, we would meet in her third-floor playroom, which was upstairs in the front of the house—her father had his doctor's office on the ground floor— and Paul, who was fond of pranks, would make us fold little boxes of newspaper smaller than a shoebox. We would fill them with water, and when people came along with umbrellas we would drop a box of water into the areaway, quickly shutting the window. We would hear an explosion, and shiver with excitement. Then we would peek out from behind the curtains and see the consternation among the passersby. We enjoyed that very much until we were discovered. (One always does get discovered.)

Another favorite prank was to tie a threadlike wire to a purse; after dusk I darted out and placed it on the sidewalk, and then we hid behind the basement curtains with bated breath until someone noticed it. He would hesitate for a moment, look around to make sure no one was watching, and then, just as he bent over and reached for the purse, we would pull the invisible thread and draw it between the iron grilles into the areaway and observe our victim's embarrassed stupefaction.

We used to visit the firehouse between Fifth and Sixth avenues in our street, hoping always to be on hand when an alarm came in and the three black horses would dash from their stalls and stand under the suspended harness at the front of the station. Excitement had no limits when the engine pulled out of the building and smoke began billowing from its funnel. The firemen were all very friendly, but strict about our keeping out of the way. Once they let Paul Draper and me try sliding down the brass pole. The firemen warned us not to grab the pole with our hands but to hold on by elbows and legs. We were so scared that we forgot and scorched our hands. We never tried it again.

All in our family were fond of roller-skating and ice-skating, the former in Bryant Park, the latter in Central Park. One good dipping in the thinly frozen pond, luckily where the water was shallow, rather chilled my enthusiasm. My brothers were always on the alert for a chance to go skating. They would run around the corner to see if the white flag with a red circle was flying on the top of the horse-drawn crosstown cars on Forty-second Street. This meant that the ice on the lake was safe for skating.

Those of us who played and roller-skated in Bryant Park, the little oasis of trees and benches between Fortieth and Forty-second streets on Sixth Avenue, will never forget the dripping old stone fountain basin and, beside it, hanging on a chain, the rusty, dented tin cup from which we were forbidden to drink, and wisely so, since every homeless drunk or vagrant of the neighborhood slaked his thirst from it. One can no longer see the old fountain and the ever-wet paving around it, on a slight decline to the avenue level. When skating madly across this slanting area in our races to see who could circle the park most swiftly, we would frequently skid upon this hazard and pick ourselves up with ignominious filthy wet spots on our clothes, entailing a tirade from the nurses who grouped themselves, their baby carriages, and very young charges under a big tree near the Forty-second Street entrance and west wall of the reservoir—where the New York Public Library now stands.

When I was given permission to visit Mrs. Hyde's toy shop on Sixth Avenue above Thirty-ninth Street, it was usually to buy some trifling bag of marbles or a skate strap or a new leash for my dog. My little friends often accompanied me and, of course, our nurses Bertha, Rosa, and Mademoiselle would walk behind us like prison guards. All the more expensive and fancy toys were merely a display of "forbidden fruit," and my playmates and I seemed quite content with our few simple toys, which demanded ingenuity to keep mended and in service.

Probably I differed from most other little girls because dolls were no diversion, whereas electric batteries, mechanical toys, and toy horses were of real interest to me. I was always taking the toys apart to see how they worked and how the wheels went round. I would make harness for the horses from leather straps, and bandage their legs like those of racehorses. I would patiently study pictures and try to copy the patterns of blankets and harness and bind the flannel headpieces with bright red braid around the openings for their eyes and ears. Dexter was my favorite horse; he was about fifteen inches high. On snowy days I would blanket him from nose to tail and set him outside in the areaway that led into our basement. He was left there until covered with a thick layer of snow. One day the old postman coming to deliver our mail noticed Dexter almost buried under the snow; he rang the bell and asked for the little girl who owned the horse. He lectured me severely for leaving a poor little beast out in the cold. "Cruelty to animals 'tis," he said, "and them that has horses should know how to take care of 'em. Take him in and give him a good rubdown with horse liniment and he'll forgive you." Abashed and unhappy, I bundled Dexter into the kitchen, where I dutifully dusted off the snow and almost rubbed his hide off.

Finally, his sawdust began to leak out from the seams, and he disintegrated.

While leading Nellie, my smart little fox terrier, on a leash along our street one day I noticed that something had startled a pair of horses hitched to an open truck; their driver was not to be seen and the horses had started slowly toward Broadway. I gave my dog's leash to my nurse and, before she could stop me, ran across the street, climbed up the back of the cart and, as I ran to the driver's seat, the horses broke into a trot; luckily I caught the reins, which were hung over the seat, and bracing my feet against the front of the cart and pulling with all my might, just before reaching Broadway I managed to pull the horses against the curb. This slowed them up and enabled a streetcleaner to catch the bridles and stop them.

The driver had come out and discovered his missing team. Starting after them on the run, he jumped into the cart just as we stopped, and shouted accusations against me, believing that I had willfully climbed in and started the horses as a mischievous prank. When he lifted me to the ground, the surprised onlookers took him soundly to task, explaining how I had really saved his horses and truck from a crash. He was slow to believe it, but just about this time my terrified nurse and Nellie arrived on the scene. I was furious and, snatching Nellie's leash, ran home crying, frightened, and thoroughly indignant, refused to talk, and was a general annoyance to everyone.

At one time when Nellie lost her appetite and seemed to be in need of medical care, my brothers took her in a cab to a veterinary in East Fifty-fourth Street to be under observation. I was desolate and sulking about the basement when suddenly I heard a violent series of barks at the front gate. Nellie, without collar or leash, was pawing at the grille and panting as if she had run a marathon, which in fact she had, for she had sensed trouble and imprisonment on the threshold of the dog clinic, slipped her collar, and made a dash for freedom and home a mile and a half away, over streets and avenues she had never explored.

Nellie was my constant companion, permitting me to harness her as a horse, to drag an express wagon loaded and strapped down with every kind of bale, bundle, barrel, or box. One day while we were crossing Forty-second

Street, the cord on Nellie's wagon came loose, and the barrels and bales rolled over the tracks in front of an approaching crosstown trolley. Far more concerned in gathering up the bales and barrels than by the fact that I was blocking traffic, I began to reload the cargo. The motorman was calling to my nurse to pull me and my dog out of his way, and started clanging his foot bell. Terrified, I gathered everything into my skirt and pulled Nellie and the cart over to the curbstone.

After many years of devotion to us, Nellie grew blind and infirm, and it was considered by my elders only humane to put her out of her misery by a whiff of chloroform. I was sent off to the country to be safely out of the way. On my return I was told that Nellie had gone to sleep and would never awake. This experience made me aware that even one's own family can carry out secret projects that exclude you and that one can never detect what is really going on in someone else's mind. Suspicion of motives began to appear.

I well remember how sympathetic three old ladies were the summer after I had lost Nellie. Miss Martha and Miss Caroline Palmer and Miss Light had rooms at the same hotel as ours at Little Boar's Head, on the same top floor. They would ask me in to play with them. Using gaily colored worsted reins they had knitted, they hitched up two big rocking chairs, first side by side and then as a tandem, and would rock away violently while I drove and snapped the whip to speed them along. I wondered how these three spinsters could understand and comfort a child so spontaneously when they had no children of their own. In fact, I once dared to ask Miss Martha about this, and I recall her reply: "Why, Mallie dear, you will find out someday that people who don't have certain things understand more than people who do have them, for they often grow indifferent to their blessings."

Just outside the entrance to the Misses Palmer's rooms was a steep narrow staircase leading up to the cupola on the roof of the hotel. Four little square windows facing north, south, east, and west overlooked the whole countryside and the coastline of the ocean. This hideout, covered with dust and cobwebs, was a delight to a child. I felt atop the world, and sometimes in a storm I would muster all my courage and hide up there, watching the lightning and the northeast wind furiously lashing the sea into breakers. The windows rattled and the gales whistled and seemed to hold me hypnotized by their ferocity. As time went on, other children discovered the cupola, and then the spell was broken, the elemental contact destroyed.

I was drawn to the companionship of elder friends of the family, and seemed to feel more at ease with them than with children. One of them was Joseph Burke, the violinist, Father's lifelong friend. He used to come to Forty-third Street for lunch on Sundays, and I recall sitting on his knee and watching him do card tricks, entranced by his sleight of hand. He could shuffle two packs of cards from one hand to the other. He would imitate the motion of Pa's hands while playing the concertina, pulling his hands apart and approaching them, all the while keeping a stream of cards flowing between them.

Father and Mr. Burke were chess enthusiasts, and patiently taught me the rules and maneuvers. I suspect that I was pretty good at this subtle game, for otherwise I do not think Pa would have taken me to the Eden Museum of Wax Works where an automaton chess player would challenge all comers. The mysterious setting, with heavy curtains behind the chessboard through which only the hands of the automaton projected, excited me to a point approaching terror, but I never dared flinch while Father was watching, and bravely started the games, over and over, always vanquished by the Mystery Man who swept the pieces off the board into a basket and withdrew his hands behind the curtains as soon as checkmate was evident. After three or four visits, my invisible opponent, apparently enjoying my frequent efforts, lured me on, permitting me *almost* to win a game, but just at the apparently crucial moment made a brilliantly decisive move, countering my strategy and opening the way to the inevitable checkmate.

FATHER'S PIANO AND FATHER

The focal point of our life in Forty-third Street was Father's piano in the front parlor. There he practiced, gave endless lessons, and rehearsed chamber music for trios and quartets, usually until five o'clock. I always looked forward to spending an hour in the parlor at teatime, generally curled up on the old red sofa, beside Father, who might be studying some orchestral score or reading the piano parts of some composition or chamber music. He would explain to me how he could *hear* the written notes and interpret their phrases on paper without having to play them. This seemed to me a sort of magic faculty that I could never fathom.

After a while he would close the scores, put his arm around my shoulder, and ask me to tell him everything I had noticed during my walk: with whom had I played—were there any new games—what children had roller skates—how many horses had I noticed—how many dogs—what had tempted me in the shop windows? He insisted on my memorizing these things. When he went with me on my walk, we would play the game of making lists to see who could remember the most. This ingenious idea served to sharpen my power of observation and increase my memory. As we chatted, I was not aware of any great difference in our ages. He was like a big brother who seemed to understand my spoken and unspoken thoughts. I felt protected and blissfully happy with him. I would watch his face and confide my secrets, telling how a certain horse had tried to push off his nose bag and could not get it on again; how I had tried to push it back over his nose; and how my hands were so small and the rope so stiff that I had a severe struggle, during which the big horse had suddenly tossed up his head, almost knocking me down, scattering a cloud of wet oats over me. At this point I recall my father's laughter as I jumped up, shaking myself violently and scattering oats out of every crevice of my clothing and over the parlor carpet.

In our more serious moments Pa would explain how the same principles that guide music are those needed in the practice of any of the arts—construction, rhythm, balance, and harmony, and everlasting hard work. We often had sessions on how to set poems to music. I would work out the melody that seemed suited to the words; if Pa approved the effort, he would add the accompaniment. It was great fun to sing these to the family after supper. His patient efforts to have me read and play printed music were in vain, however. I simply could not read and watch the keyboard far below the desk at the same time. I even invented an adjustable desk that could be moved down almost to the keyboard level, but, alas, this did not do the trick, although it proved very helpful to Father in teaching other children.

In 1897, when I was about twelve years old, an event that seemed of enormous interest and excitement to our family was planned by a group of Father's most devoted pupils. One of them, Mrs. Charles Foote, a fine pianist, undertook the management of a testimonial concert to commemorate Father's fiftieth year of playing in public. It was to take place in Chickering Hall, and some of Pa's most talented pupils were to perform certain solo pieces. Mrs. Foote was to play the second piano in Bach's C Major Concerto. The Dannreuther Quartet volunteered their services to complete the group of players who, with Father, played the Hummel Septette, which was one of Father's favorite compositions. As the news of this concert became known to friends, our house was flooded with congratulatory letters and telegrams. Endless good wishes and messages of affection arrived from far and near. When the great day came, we all drove down to Chickering Hall, which was crowded with admiring friends, many of whom had studied with Father at one time or another. The atmosphere seemed charged with emotion. I had never before experienced such a thrill of excitement. I felt as if I were personally responsible for the whole affair, especially for Father's solo numbers, of which I knew every note.

After the final applause I went backstage and burst into tears as I threw my arms around Pa's neck; then I helped collect the flowers and pack them into a cab that drove Father and Mother and me home to Forty-third Street where the other children had preceded us. In the cab, I told Pa that he had not made a single mistake while playing but that I felt exhausted from the strain. Patting me fondly, he smiled and said: "Well, Malvina, you won't have to worry again about my making any mistakes, for this is my exit from playing in public. I've decided to play for friends only from now on!" Then, looking sadly at the beautiful flowers all around us, he said, "Rather like attending one's own funeral, isn't it?" Ma was very quiet, and hardly spoke, but I noticed that she held Father's hand tightly all the way home.

The press was unanimous in its praise of Father, both as an artist and as a teacher—a man who had made an enviable place for himself by having contributed so much to the musical life of New York during the fifty years of his professional life. We all felt that this testimonial concert had been a historic event, and its impact was never forgotten by any of us. By his art and his idealism Pa had built himself a fortress of loving admiration, and in a new way we realized our privilege in being his children.

1847 **1897**

TESTIMONIAL CONCERT
TO
Mr. RICHARD HOFFMAN
ON THE OCCASION OF THE
FIFTIETH ANNIVERSARY
OF HIS FIRST PUBLIC APPEARANCE IN NEW YORK
AT
CHICKERING HALL
WEDNESDAY AFTERNOON, DECEMBER FIRST
AT THREE O'CLOCK

PROGRAMME

1. QUARTETTE, G minor, . . . *Mozart*
   MR. RICHARD HOFFMAN, . Pianoforte
   MR. GUSTAV DANNREUTHER, . Violin
   MR. OTTO K. SCHILL, . . . Viola
   MR. EMIL SCHENCK, . . . Violoncello

2. CONCERTO, C major, ... *Bach*
   Two Pianofortes with String Quintette.
   MRS. CHARLES B. FOOTE and
   MR. RICHARD HOFFMAN

3. PIANO SOLOS,
   Nocturne, Op. 27, No. 2,
   Ballade, Op. 23, . . . *Chopin*
   MR. RICHARD HOFFMAN

4. SEPTETTE, ... *Hummel*
   MR. RICHARD HOFFMAN, . Pianoforte
   MR. WM. SCHADE, ... Flute
   MR. JOSEPH ELLER, ... Oboe
   MR. OTTO K. SCHILL, ... Viola
   MR. EMIL SCHENCK, . . Violoncello
   MR. FELIX LEIFELS, . . Contra Bàsso

PROGRAM OF FATHER'S TESTIMONIAL CONCERT

CHAPTER FOUR

SUMMERS BY THE SEA

EVERY SUMMER I looked forward with excitement and joy to the two months of holiday at Little Boar's Head. We would go to the edge of the ocean; we would bathe and build sand castles and moats on the beach between the rising of the tides. I knew the hiding places of little speckled crabs, and year after year I turned over the same stones in the rocky pools and found the same crabs or their descendants in their perennial hide-outs. At Little Boar's Head the sea line never seemed to change; it represented permanence. Winter storms tore out stretches of beach, but the rocks and their pools remained. The gulls were forever soaring about in groups, scavenging the seaweed and diving for fish. The seaweed was of every kind, strange long, wavy-edged strips of brown kelp, spongy golden tufts, and greens of every shape and shade. A walk on the beach was an adventure in discovery: stones rubbed to an incredible smoothness, spars from ships that might have been lost at sea inciting the imagination to hunt for more signs of wreckage.

Clambake parties on the rocks were great fun. We all pitched in to gather driftwood for the fires, and bedded the clams between layers of seaweed that steamed and sizzled on the hot rocks; loud pops from the pods of rockweed added to the excitement. Many ears of corn were baked in their husks and eaten on the cob. When sweet potatoes came into season about the end of July, these were added to the clambake. Clouds of aromatic smoke enveloped us as we crowded about the fire and added driftwood to the glowing embers.

One of my early trips along the beach was with Father when he was out shooting snipe and yellowlegs. I once begged to be allowed a shot. The gun was a heavy double-barreled affair, and as I pulled the trigger the backkick knocked me over into a shallow pool. I never asked again.

Father and I would go out in Harvey Brown's rowboat, a dory, over the breakers to the deep water to fish for perch, cod, haddock, and mackerel, and we would watch other fishermen gather lobster pots and pile them high in the stern of their boats. Dr. Bennett Nash, Professor of Classic Languages at Harvard, who spent his summers at Little Boar's Head, would take me for walks along the shore, and we would explore every cranny in the reefs, collecting all kinds of seaweed, shells, or bits of sea-weathered wood washed up on the beach.

It was from seasoned wood of this kind that he taught me to carve, an occupation to which I felt immediately responsive, for I had already been drawing and was already under a powerful impulse to copy the world around me. This impulse had no name. I certainly did not think of it as art.

Dr. Nash showed me how to carve small models of canoes, boat hulls, and racing shells. I used a penknife and the simpler tools that were available. Meticulously he made me fit the shell with seats, oars, oarlocks, rudders, and keel. In his kindness and thoroughness, he hunted with me as far as Big Boar's Head for the right kinds of wood, naming the different varieties for me and showing me their grain.

I made a little chest with partitions and trays, which I lined with suede kid cut from old gloves, to become a present for Mother, a "jewel case" we called it to make her smile.

So important was this that I told about it in *Sculpture Inside and Out*:

Professor Nash took infinite pains to show me just how to miter the corners, countersink the hinges, and sandpaper every edge, even though these were to be covered by the leather lining. "Remember, Mallie, that the Japanese craftsmen stand out above others because of the perfection of their workmanship. They even carve the underside of bases and boxes, where only a few eyes ever discover their hidden, delicate designs. We Americans forget that the angels can see through and around and under just as well as from the front."

Concurrently with Professor Nash, my father, too, was unknowingly preparing me for my later work. Every morning he and I took a drive in a runabout pulled by "Topsy," a small patient horse with good manners. Often Pa would deliberately go to the fish houses or little bathhouse cabins that were being built that were primitive in design, and he would explain the basic process of construction—how they put up the roofbeam and then the beams that slanted down, how they made frames and poured in concrete, how they held a level to line up the courses of a brick wall. Once he made me get out and see if I could break a brick with a trowel the way the mason did, break it cleanly, not on the slant, and not hitting my finger. It was to give me some idea of the work of this world, of manual work. He said: "Watch the best one, the one who does it the fastest and most accurately. There will always be something you can learn, even how to hit a nail straight." All this was long before sculpture, that emphasis on my hands, on the manual thing—I never forgot those lessons; I never forgot my father saying, "You can pretty much tell a carpenter by the way he picks up a tool." When I have to nail two boards together for an armature, and one is hard wood and the other soft and I have to watch that the nail won't bend part way through, I salute again my lessons of those days.

My mind was like a film ready for the impression. It took everything and "fixed" it. It was long before my formal art teaching, but it was all-important.

BATCHELDER'S HOTEL AT LITTLE BOAR'S HEAD

From ten to fifteen, in many departments of life, I was first cousin to a sponge.

Little Boar's Head was also where I got thoroughly acquainted with horses. Here I was able to drive them myself, a great pleasure. I started with pencil and paper to catch fleeting impressions. The urge to do so was constant, and my many sketchbooks with notes on equine anatomy would suggest insatiable curiosity. While still so small that I had to stand on a soapbox to reach over a horse's head to put on a bridle, I had no fear of entering the stall of any horse in the livery stable, despite warnings from the men that one might kick or another bite; after a word of greeting I merely pushed a horse aside and went to the manger with a lump of sugar or a handful of oats.

I can remember the smell of the great feed bins as I strained to lift up the heavy wooden covers . . . the warm, soft pungence of bran, a sharper smell from oats, and the aroma of freshly stacked hay . . . odors that even now arouse nostalgic memories.

As I went into the stalls I would observe the different shapes of horses' heads, the way their nostrils quivered as they sniffed the oats in my tiny fist. Gradually I became so familiar a presence that they would let me open their mouths, examine their jaws, count their teeth, or push their ears about to discover what muscles made them look excited or angry.

After watching the village smith at work, for I always went to the blacksmith shop whenever I could, I would, on my return to the stable, lead the horse into his stall, pull off his bridle, slip on the halter and, lifting each foot in turn, examine his shoes. My back was hardly strong enough to lift the heavy legs, but I soon discovered a little trick for myself. Since certain tendons lifted the hoof, I would tap them with the side of my hand, which seemed to release an inner spring of the Achilles' tendon, and it was then easy to raise the hoof between my knees, like a real blacksmith. There were times when I thought the old horse "Spot" was actually laughing at me over my shoulder!

These were some of the lures of L.B.H. And then the dark mysteries of the pine woods where we could roam in the afternoon to our hearts' content and discover the miracle of Indian pipes pushing up through the damp pine needles, and many other forest treasures such as wintergreen with its vermilion berries and the sharp tang of its leaves.

One summer four playmates formed a little group, and our plan was to build a secret house in the woods. We spent weeks collecting boards, nails, tools, shingles—and by begging, borrowing, or sawing down trees, we managed to get together all we needed. Well do I remember having to carry great loads of supplies through an apple orchard behind the stables, so as not to be seen by anyone. Before reaching the place we had selected for our cabin in the woods, we had to cross a forbidden spongy swamp over which we laid planks, making it possible to carry our supplies. If we slipped off, we sank into black ooze up to our knees. As the last one crossed, he picked up plank after plank and passed them ahead, and so obliterated all traces of our trail.

The first thing to be done now was to clear away the underbrush. Then we dug holes and set up the framing poles, put the roof beams in place, and

Family at Little Boar's Head, Sunday after church. Left to right: Charles, Mother, Father, Helen, Elsie. Seated: MH and Richard

fitted wallboards and nailed them up. A small area outside the cabin was fenced about with pine boughs higher than our heads. We collected flat rocks and built an open-air oven. My special assignment was to assist in shingling the roof and weaving the pine boughs into a garden wall. We were only four youngsters, and the building took us six weeks. It included a rustic table and chairs made of small trees. A locked corner closet, in which we kept our tools and supplies, we made from weathered boards picked up on the beach. A small supply of cocoa, crackers, and sweets was secreted on the premises and, at the end of three or four hours' labor we would refresh ourselves regally, light a discreet little alcohol lamp so there should be no smoke to disclose our where-abouts, heat the milk for the cocoa, and sit around our table, triumphant and happy. We had built a lookout up in the tree about twenty feet above the ground. For this we had a rope ladder made with wooden rungs, which we pulled up after us when suspecting an intruder, and, hidden by the boughs at the top of an ancient pine, we listened for approaching footsteps, but were never discovered.

Our one mischievous prank was rolling dried cornsilk into cigarettes and smoking them after our cocoa and biscuits.

The boys lifted and carried the heaviest burdens, but we girls were never supposed to complain or be afraid of anything, and I cannot remember that we ever gave cause for a reprimand.

One day I mustered courage to ask the other three if I might invite my old friend Professor Nash to our hideout. I promised to take him there by false trails and, at the end, blindfold and lead him in zigzag paths to our jungle fortress. Permission was given, and the dear soul was as intrigued and excited as we were by our secret. He came to the edge of the wood with me, and there I started him off in the wrong direction. When we came to the swamp, he was blindfolded and told to lift his bandage just enought to see his feet and place them on the boards until safely across. One of us led him by the hand, with another following, holding his other hand to give him balance and confidence. His first sight of our retreat was the high green barricade; the strong gateway was then unlocked with due formality, disclosing the little clearing where ferns and Indian pipes were growing between the rocks and tufts of velvety moss, all transplanted from distant corners of the woods; even cardinal flowers and blue-berry bushes were included. When he had entered the cabin, our delighted guest threw his arms around me and his eyes filled with tears. "Oh, the wonder-land of youth," he sighed. "How good you all are to let me share this with you!"

He began pulling little packages out of his pocket, candies, a fine pocket-knife, a collection of various tools, brushes and paints; odd bits of fishing line, scissors, a foot rule and pencils—anything he could think of that might be useful. His astonishment reached a climax when we had him sit down in our enclosed garden and watch us all mount the rope ladder to our hideout in the trees, pull it up after us, and disappear in the dizzy concealment of the grand old pine.

After a little feast, topped off with ginger ale that we had carried in a pail of ice, we all went home very happy, and as proud as we would ever be again in our lives.

The next day we were all invited to Professor Nash's workroom. There he presented us with a pair of fine field glasses, an electric flashlight, and a brass padlock, which he said was stronger and more difficult to break than ours. It is hard to imagine what a fortress of confidential affection this old gentleman had created for himself in our young hearts! He never divulged our secret, and realized quite soberly what a matter of life or death it was to us that no suspicion of our activities be aroused.

About three years later a tragedy befell us. We heard that a trolley track was to be laid through the woods from Little Boar's Head to Rye Beach. . . . Our hearts tightened with dread. . . . Finally, we found the construction men approaching our hidden abode. In desperation we decided that we must pull down our precious cabin and treetop lookout. Imagine it! After deciding, we could hardly bring ourselves to speak of the impending destruction. With heavy hearts we began to pull down the wall, harrowed by the sound of ripping boards. When the roof had fallen in, we pulled up the little thatched fence, and it did not then take long to wipe out all trace of our efforts, but long enough to brand each of us with a sense of irrevocable loss. We could not share our sorrow with outsiders; indeed, we could hardly mention it among ourselves. It was as if our land of dreams had been plundered and spirited away. We seemed suddenly and painfully to "grow up"; uncertainty had entered our lives.

We did not attempt concerted action again. I don't know what the others did in their own secret worlds, but I went off by myself whenever possible in the woods, finding another distant spot where no one ever seemed to pass. There I collected stones and as much rich earth as I could find, and between the stones I planted little curling ferns, Indian pipes, wintergreen, and what wild flowers I could find. On this rocky mound I built an altar of stones, and on it I would light a little fire, the pungent smoke of which would rise in arabesques and delicate spirals up into the treetops, a sort of pagan holocaust that seemed to soothe my spirit. For years afterward, I would escape at frequent intervals and spend hours with my ferns and rocks and smoldering fires, at peace with the sounds and spirits of the forest. I could hear Panpipes, and—free in heart and body—would dance to the music of ages past, a living part of the tall dark forest, feeling the pulse of the warm, fragrant earth, and, oh, it was hard to come home and change back into myself as others knew me!

On the back porch at 116 West Forty-third Street. Left to right: Pa, Ma, Elsie, Aunt Georgie Andrews, Charles. Seated: Nellie

CHAPTER FIVE

HOUSEHOLD IN FORTY-THIRD STREET

THE CHARACTER of the street in which I lived during childhood had great color and interest. Not only the appearance of the houses: but the endless stream of people, horses, dogs, postmen, milkmen, ice deliverers, and the black coal carts backing into the curbstone with their heaped-up cargoes—all these constituted a great slice of the world for a child to observe and learn from, and never to forget.

It was such fun living in West Forty-third Street. Our house was on the south side, three stories high, made of brick with a stone stoop leading up from the sidewalk to the front door. The more affluent neighbors had brownstone-front houses, and all of us had spacious back yards, giving us room to play out of doors and in winter to pile up the snow, which seemed far more plentiful in those years than now.

My brothers and I were able to make a seven-foot-high snowbank in the far corner of the yard, where we pulled our sleds and then pushed each other down for a rapid descent, ending sometimes with a good bump against the wooden "cooling closet" next to the kitchen door. We stuffed a few burlap bags with straw and old newspapers and hung them on this wall to make the finish a bit less dangerous. When Pa realized the risks of this sport, he insisted on throwing ashes on the last ten feet of the slide to slow us down.

On the street there was always a hopeful chance that some of the members of the circus at the Hippodrome would be taking their animals for an airing; some days it was the elephants, then the zebras and ponies; occasionally even a giraffe would be led up and down as far west as Broadway and back again. I made friends with some of the clowns, giants, and sword swallowers by going to the circus early, before the performances. The spell of excitement was thus

47

prolonged as much as possible, and I could wave at them and get smiles of recognition.

While exercising my dog Nellie, I would walk ever so slowly in front of the Savage Theatrical Agency, nearer Broadway than we were. I watched the constant stream of actors and actresses of all ages going in with hopeful and happy faces, but often coming out with grim, worried expressions, while I invented all kinds of disappointments to account for the transformations. Many of them would stop and give my dog a friendly pat, and I decided that actors must be rather special in their love of animals. Some of them carried their little pets with them. Deep down in their hearts perhaps they were lonely, I thought, in their make-believe world of entertainment—always pretending to be some-one else.

Diagonally across the street from our house lived the flamboyant Lillian Russell, and the never-ending line of colorful visitors to her home always lured me to our front windows to watch the ladies in their finery and furs.

Early one snowy morning I went into my parents' room and looked out. In the house next to Lillian's a second-floor window was suddenly thrown open by a woman clad only in her nightgown. She climbed quickly onto the window-sill, prepared to jump. A trained nurse rushed to her and took hold of the nightgown to pull her back, but the lady deftly slipped out of the gown and plunged down to the areaway just as our friendly old postman was about to deliver the morning mail. She missed him by about a foot. I watched fascinated as he threw off his pack, took off his heavy overcoat, and with instinctive chivalry and gentleness spread it over her. My heart was pounding so that I could not find my voice to call my parents to the scene. As it turned out, the woman was not seriously hurt by the fall, for the pavings were padded with a heavy cover-ing of snow, but her act of desperation haunted me. That ivory-colored body that swayed and fell! It was my first sight of lovely nakedness, and the shock of wonderment has never left me.

My father often took me to the opera matinees on Saturdays. He would give me a libretto and tell me to read it carefully beforehand so that I would know the plot. When there was some superlative singing of one or two of the important arias, he would nudge my arm and at the close of the act would insist on our leaving. This was a great disappointment to me, but he wanted me to remember the high moments of perfection, and on our return home he would play over the arias and make me follow the wording in the score, so that they would be locked in my memory, promising to take me again later in the season to stay through the whole performance. Perhaps this heroic treatment was the reason why Emma Calvé's singing of "L'Amour est un oiseau sauvage, il n'a jamais connu de loi. . . ." and Emma Eames's singing of Micaëla's prayer remain as clear today as the day I heard them for the first time.

Hero worship formed a major part of my emotional life, and Mme. Eames became one of my earliest musical gods. I was transported when she sang "Le

Roi de Thulé" at the spinning wheel in *Faust* or when she did her dramatic aria, "Visi d'arte, visi d'amore," in *Tosca*. I was so inspired that I read vast amounts of poetry until I found just the right selections to describe her in her greatest operatic roles. These I copied out carefully and made watercolor illustrations for each one, showing her in costume. This precious little album I bound in stiff parchment, and after Father had looked it over and added a few bars of music for the different high spots in the singing parts, he offered to escort me to the Plaza Hotel where Mme. Eames was living at the time, and there I left my passionate little offering to be sent up to her room. My knees were shaking. I had never met her, but she was evidently moved by such a genuine expression of admiration, for the following day she sent me an autographed photograph of herself as Marguerite.

Somehow it was arranged that I could meet her later in the season, and from that day we became fast friends until the close of her life. The little album was burned in the San Francisco fire when she was forced to flee from her hotel and lost all her belongings.

Another intense impression was made upon me when I attended the performance of *Parsifal*. This magnificent spectacle filled me with religious fervor, and the massive Wagnerian music's overwhelming climaxes remained in my mind for days.

Language is a clumsy medium to express the pounding surge of intense feelings. Our senses build up a world of their own—beyond words. Music could drive my blood and suffuse my entire being with its mysterious magic. Of course, my musical treats were carefully geared so that they did not interfere with my schooling, which my mother and sister Helen directed for about a year.

During these regular study hours, on the second floor of our house, the distant strains of Father's practicing floated through the air and were like a constant accompaniment. Mother supervised English and history and urged me to learn many French songs and other poetry by heart. As she was an excellent French scholar, this part of the home lessons was sheer delight. I became familiar with the poems of Victor Hugo, Verlaine, and Alfred de Musset.

On Saturdays Paul and Ruth Draper joined us, and we were drilled in reciting and diction. Paul would frequently act out the parts, and I shall never forget how he took the stance, pulled a lock of his flaxen hair down over his right eye, and started off in stentorian tones:

> "You know, we French stormed Ratisbon;
>   A mile or so away,
>   On a little mound, Napoleon
>   Stood on our storming-day;
>   With neck out-thrust, you fancy how,
>   Legs wide, arms locked behind,
>   As if to balance the prone brow
>   Oppressive with its mind."

Said Paul: "I want a key to lock my arms behind!"

Ruth liked to recite, and did it well and rapidly, and whenever we were told to do it for anyone else, which Mother thought was good practice for us, Ruth always—her bent this way so much stronger than ours—gave so potent a demonstration of her talent, and with so much ease and accomplishment, that even as children we knew she was something beyond us. She excelled in monologues and charades, and very soon gave her own family entertainments, which started off her brilliant career as a solitary performer, impersonating a host of characters on an empty stage, an artist of unique and transcendent authority.

A happy rhythm of affection blessed our family life. We never seemed to have violent arguments or feel jealous of one another. Though my sisters and brothers were quite a bit older than I, this never caused any worry or unhappiness. Helen was fourteen years my senior, and treated me more like her own child than like a sister.

Neither my brothers nor my sisters tried to go to college. In those days there were no such things as scholarships or foundation grants, so they knew that the cost was beyond our parents' budget, and all looked upon the idea of getting an early start earning a living as a privilege rather than a hardship. It certainly added discipline and a healthy sense of responsibility to their lives.

During the winter months, after graduation from the Brearley School, Elsie and Helen were engaged as social secretaries, sending off long lists of wedding announcements which they addressed in their strong and controlled handwriting. My part in this activity was to seal and stamp the hundreds of envelopes, and Charles cheerfully would lend a hand when he returned from his office work downtown. He would carry the boxes of envelopes to the corner of Sixth Avenue and post them. We enjoyed this teamwork, and my sisters made quite a neat little sum from these secretarial labors.

Charles was the plump and cheery member of the family, and as he grew older he developed a most thoughtful nature with a deep sense of responsibility about supervising his family's affairs. He had a host of friends and kept in a constant good humor, which added greatly to his popularity.

An attack of appendicitis stopped my activities for a time, and I remember that ten days after the operation, which was performed in our house, Charles took me on a gentle outing—a drive in Central Park in a hansom cab. Halfway around the reservoir, a piece of paper flew out of a baby carriage crossing our path; the horse reared, kicked a hole in the dashboard, and ran away. A mounted policeman caught up with us while Charles held me in his strong arms, terrified lest the swaying hansom would topple us over on a curve. When the runaway had been caught we were helped out, transferred to a four-wheeler, and driven home, with no more excitement and, fortunately, with no ill effects whatever.

Being the youngest of the family, I suppose I was often spoiled by the affectionate attentions of my elders. My sisters were apparently amused by my unpredictable antics and my inquisitive questions about their grown-up activities. When they prepared to go to some social function, I would act as lady's maid and take great delight in their appearance in party dress. I loved to watch them brush their long wavy hair and then deftly twist it into a firm figure eight at the back of their heads. Elsie had golden-brown hair, and her handsome head was well set on strong, beautifully sloping shoulders, a physique seemingly made for outdoor sports. She was a joy to behold as she stood on the golf course and swung her driver for a long shot which never seemed to swerve or go astray. She won many cups, and sisterly pride filled my heart when she brought back these silver trophies that I kept shining on her mantel and showed off to our friends.

In spite of my interest in this sport, I never seemed to find the time to go in for it seriously. I did my best to learn the essential rules of the game, and managed by considerable effort to keep within the bounds of civilized behavior on the links and out of the way of the better players, but after a few seasons I gave up not only golf but all temptations of outdoor sports. I left the honors to Elsie.

Helen, who was smaller in build, like Mother, had dainty little hands and feet and an inexhaustible store of nervous energy. Her bronze-colored hair had a glint of gold in it, and it was a matter of great pride to her, all her life, that it never lost its brilliant color.

Strangely enough, though neither Father nor Mother had even a hint of red hair, Richard also had curly bronze-colored hair like Helen's.

I always eagerly watched the clock for Richie's return from his office. When I heard his key in the lock, I would slide down the banister and greet him with a hug as he entered the hall. Constitutionally rather frail, he began suffering from an inflammation of the spine, and it was found necessary for him to wear a brace. He even had to stay in bed for a number of weeks, and I concocted a means of joining my room at the rear of the house with his at the front. Having watched the subway being excavated in Forty-second Street, I made a sort of traveling crane strung on a strong wire along the hall between the rooms. Electric batteries gave me enough current to throw a switch and start the drum turning that would roll up the pull cord and drag the improvised bucket along the wire to Richard's bed. We would unload silly objects and reload others, and keep ringing the bells and blowing whistles to start and stop the load en route. Ma and Pa would often join us; sitting at some halfway point, they would whistle for the bucket to stop and fill it with unexpected cookies or a bit of chocolate, and Pa would sometimes add funny pictures or jokes cut out of *Punch*. All went well until one night the jar of one of my sulfuric acid batteries broke and everything spilled over my carpet, burning ugly holes. I had pretended that the batteries were dry to forestall possible parental objections. (The little table under which they hung has served me in my studio ever since as a tea table.) The game was stopped and a general order issued that I should cease my experiments with dangerous acids and confine myself to more girlish diversions, such as paper dolls or learning to bake cookies.

At another time Richard was home for three weeks with pain in his head and back, and then was taken with pleurisy and pneumonia. After a long con-valescence he accepted an offer to work in a Pittsburgh steel business.

My sisters were fortunate to have generous friends who at various times took them along on trips to Europe. On their return home they shared their wonder-ful experiences with the family, and these tales of travel and a constant stream of picture postcards whetted my desire to fly off myself to the Old World.

Our talented cousin Herbert Haseltine was a great pal of Richie's, and while a freshman at Harvard he often spent weekends with us. He was always gay, and joked about his work in college where he made many humorous illustrations for the *Lampoon,* but he neglected some of his courses and after his junior year he did not return. He was a wizard with a pencil and would amuse me for hours on end by drawing horses standing and galloping and in long lines of diminishing perspective. Later on, he became a celebrated sculptor of horses and other ani-mals.

We were often taken by our parents to the old Sherwood Studios in West Fifty-seventh Street to meet the artist friends of Edgar Kinsley, a painter, and his daughter Georgie, who was the great-niece of my father. These friends included the well-known easel and mural painters Edwin Blashfield, Siddons Mowbray, John Sargent, Kenyon Cox, Winslow Homer, and Elihu Vedder. An exciting event was when the incandescent Spanish Carmencita danced in Carol Beck-with's studio, before Sargent painted her great portrait, now in Mrs. Gardner's Palace in Boston. These studio parties initiated me into a new world of art. Mr. Blashfield, the mural painter, had a gentle voice and a kindly, understanding manner. I was happy that later in my life I was able to know this sensitive artist better. He radiated a spiritual consciousness reflected in his paintings.

Toward the end of Mr. Kinsley's life, a long illness affected his mind, and it was necessary for him to live in a sanatorium. His daughter gave up every activity to care for him, and, being a gifted pianist, offered to play the piano at the in-stitution for any of the patients who cared to listen. She continued this generous playing until the last year of her life.

During her final illness I went to see her in the hospital. She was in a pri-vate room, and the nurse told me: "Yes, you may go in; she was speaking of you before she went into a coma." The icy unconcern with which she said it seemed to chill the air. I walked in, and as I took Georgie's hand, she opened her eyes, and smiled from far away, but still with recognition and the strange kindliness that had served her as a shield against the years of torment.

She was too weak and too far along the shadowy journey for words. We had to be content with looking into each other's hearts—one can if the silence is deep enough. Then we both heard the nurses talking in the hall, for the door had a rubber pad to keep it from closing. . . . "Now, be a good girl, dearie, and order the things we'll need. They've attended to the coffin business, and my feet hurt so. . . . I'll just sit down here and wait. 'T'wont be too long, I'm thinking, for Number Nine!"

Georgie opened her eyes a bit wider. "That's my number," she whispered. "They think the dying are always deaf!"

Our house seemed to be a gathering place for all ages, especially on late Sunday afternoons when many friends would stay on for supper and musical diversions in the evening.

Elsie could read music at sight and was a good pianist. I of course had given up, and I think it was a great disappointment to Father. I could learn songs by ear, and had no trouble memorizing melodies and words, but perhaps it was just as well that I had abandoned the piano, for Father's in the parlor was in constant use, and upstairs the upright piano was used by Elsie, and occasionally by Mother, who, alas, had little time to keep up her music. So it was evident that if I insisted upon being an artist I had better take up a *silent* art.

I was about twelve years old when we began to notice that a young man, Dr. William K. Draper, Ruth and Paul Draper's half brother, was a pretty constant visitor to our house. He kept a bicycle-built-for-two in our basement, and in the spring evenings he and Helen would go off on this tandem and ride up along Riverside Drive. Because there were no motorcars in those days, they could really enjoy this outdoor recreation. It was quite evident to us that Will's attentions were serious.

Their wedding took place the following year. Will was recovering from an attack of pneumonia, and it was thought unwise to have a church wedding, so the ceremony was performed at his home. Ruth and I were flower girls. We were both rather high-strung and nervous, and to add to our anxieties the flowers we were to carry arrived only five minutes before the ceremony was to begin. Our tension relieved, we clutched them firmly and walked through the rooms to each side of the improvised altar, which was banked with flowers. The wedding, a simple, quiet one, was performed without further obstacles.

Will had recovered from his pneumonia successfully, but a year or two later, my beloved brother Richard was stricken with a second attack of that illness, so terrifying in those years, while on a business trip to Chicago. He died there.

This first tragedy to smite my family shattered my childlike confidence in the sacrosanct safety and happiness of my home life. My brother Richie, whose devotion and companionship added such zest to life, had suddenly left us and become a part of memory, a totally new extension of consciousness, yet the miracle of his living spirit bound us to him more closely than ever. He seemed a very part of the air about us, vividly alive in our hearts. This experience was a devastating upheaval of values. A child doesn't find it easy to give up the belief that no final catastrophe can happen to her or her family. In surrendering that belief, the whole strength of my child's mind and soul was involved.

The awarensss that other members of my family were suffering with me comforted me and gave a new dimension to my sense of their mutual loyalty and love.

Four or five years after Helen's marriage, Elsie married Arthur W. Butler. How frightened I was to be the only attendant and to have to walk up the long aisle of the Church of the Heavenly Rest, trying to keep my flowers from shaking too visibly!

Life at home seemed so much quieter now that there were no more constant visits of my sisters' numerous suitors and admirers. The question that obsessed me was: How can a girl be absolutely sure that a certain man is really the one she can marry and remain faithful to for a lifetime? I was torn between all the attractive beaux, as if it was I rather than my sisters who had to make this fateful decision.

I finally asked Mother how one could be completely convinced one was making the right choice. She smiled and said: "Oh, you will find that out for yourself someday. When love really takes hold of you, there are no questions, no doubts, no fears, no shame!"

CHAPTER SIX

I EMERGE AS AN ARTIST

AFTER MY FIRST stint of being tutored by Mother, when I was nine or ten, the time came for me to be entered in the Chapin School for Girls, which was only a short distance from home, just east of Fifth Avenue. It wasn't easy to give up the relative freedom I had been enjoying and undergo the discipline of regular classes, and I was "broken to harness" by a group of worthy but rather heavy-handed trainers.

After a few seasons there, I progressed to the Brearley School at 19 West Forty-fourth Street and found the atmosphere friendly. There were many children in the classes and, although at first we were a bit formal in our manners, we soon settled into the daily routine and enjoyed the lessons and the friendship of some splendid and stimulating teachers. Some frightened us, but some aroused our young hunger for knowledge.

Another passion kept persistently driving me. I've mentioned observing horses and harness down to the last detail and recording them with pencil or ink, even studying the anatomy of horses. Cousin Herbert Hazeltine may have conveyed to me how he started. He once told it all to me outright years later when I said I just drew without any teaching when I was young "except maybe yours." "Well," he said, "it begins like that. That's what I began with, drawing so many horses I couldn't unlearn it, didn't want to, but I wouldn't have learned it from anybody. Nobody's going to *make* you work like that. It has to be instinctive desire."

But there was another influence: my father's practicing. It was a daily lesson that woke me in the morning and put me to sleep at night. It was my earliest recollection as a child and it lasted the rest of his lifetime. In all that time I never heard Father slur over anything or bang down the piano lid or say, "That's enough for the day."

I soon realized I couldn't be a pianist myself because of the difficulty I've mentioned, that I couldn't read the printed page and play it at the same time.

55

But, sketching in a notebook, there was no hurdle. I don't know why I turned to it. Nobody told me to. Perhaps it was handy, and perhaps I found that I could make a pencil work where I couldn't coerce a piano.

Father was aware that I was drawing. He didn't compliment me, for he was a man of few words, but he took note of it.

A time came when I made that transition from my own persistent drawing to a first awareness of art—not that I necessarily connected the two. I read a life of Michelangelo, and that was enough to put a light in my mind. I studied at every opportunity, collected photographs and books on Egyptian and Greek arts, and became familiar with some of the masters of painting and sculpture. I didn't go to the museum, for I was too young to go alone and I was shy about asking others to chaperon me: they might not want to go. But I found my own ways to study, and, although it was extracurricular work, my parents never objected; they seemed to sense the sincerity of my effort to learn.

It was after my second year at Brearley—I must have been about fourteen—that I decided to attend two evening classes at the Woman's School of Applied Design on West Twenty-third Street. There, through hard work and countless efforts to control washes of ink and accuracy of line, I managed to learn the fundamentals of composition and the use of watercolors. I also had some training in pen-and-ink drawings and illustrations, so that after a few months I took some of my designs to music publishers for their song covers, and to some of the less important magazines for their color covers. Their remuneration for this was meager, but the experience was rewarding in many ways, and encouraging. Some of the editors were sympathetic and gave me helpful suggestions. They sensed my embarrassment and seemed to find time to give me honest advice and real guidance.

I always carried a tiny sketchbook in my pocket during the frequent trips I made on the subway and trolley cars to my classes. Whenever I noticed a passenger settle into position while reading his newspaper, I stealthily started drawing him, noting the folds of his clothing, the creases in his sleeves and at the knees of his trousers, the tilt of a felt hat, or the position of hands holding a magazine or newspaper. By working faster and faster, and consciously forcing my memory to retain impressions, I could often carry in my mind an entire composition. Sometimes it was a mother carrying her sleeping baby with its head hanging limply over her shoulder. The subways were not nearly so crowded then, and if by good luck I saw a derelict asleep or huddled in a corner I could draw him from various angles without his noticing me. On reaching home I would try to draw my sketches in larger scale on stray sheets of wrapping paper that I collected. To remove the creases I dampened the paper and ironed the folds carefully.

LIFE CLASS

I felt the need of knowing what went on beneath the clothes and draperies, the reason why creases and folds fell as they did. The urgency for studying the nude became so strong that I persuaded my parents to let me enroll as a student in a "life class" at the Fifty-seventh Street Art Students League of New York. Noisy, chattering students swarmed about the hallways, and I felt pretty isolated in this mass of strangers. The first night when the bell rang and we were settled in our places in the studio, the model climbed up on the stand, threw her wrapper off her shoulders, and assumed a series of poses from which one was selected by the class monitor. Everyone started to work, holding the pencil or charcoal out at arm's length, trying to determine proportions of the figure. The serious, almost desperate expressions all about me made me realize how keenly interested the students were, and how uninitiated I was.

I was so bewildered by the sight of a beautiful woman, apparently immobilized for my special observation, that everything else was obliterated. Here was the miracle of life itself, the curving forms reflecting lights and strong shadows, the pose and balance of the ivory-colored body. I, too, was immobilized, unaware of time until the monitor's bell called for a five-minute rest period. I had not drawn a line. I went out into the hall in a sort of daze. I knew I must face reality and discipline myself. The monitor's instruction rang in my ears: "Draw the entire figure on your 24-inch paper."

I went back and started to draw, but my figure seemed to grow too long and I had no room for the feet, so I drew them on the side of my paper, trying to keep them in correct scale with the figure. When the time was up again and the model rested, she instinctively fell into a relaxed pose, and I began trying wildly to catch these variations in my sketchbook, forced to use a simple line to suggest the curve of her back or the sweep of an outstretched leg, no time for details or shadows. As I continued doing this, it gave me important lessons in leaving out unessentials.

Sometimes we had the good luck to have a strong young man as model, and the thrill of seeing the light flowing over the shoulders and following the curves of his pale flanks was like seeing the first Adam. I found that I understood the construction of his anatomy more easily than that of a woman. His muscles showed clearly which ones were used in each movement, and the strong overhead light brought everything dramatically into relief. The Greek statues that I had studied in photographs now came vividly to life, bathed in a golden glow.

Those first weeks at the League were full of excitement. There were so many students in each class that the instructor could scarcely find time to give a word of individual criticism or guidance. But I was learning much from studying the models. I no longer felt isolated, and I enjoyed the stiff competition.

When the classes were over, I went out into the city streets, thoroughly exhausted. Would I, even in a lifetime, learn all there was to know about the human body! It seemed doubtful indeed. A force far beyond my ken was driving me on, and I felt completely in its power. My imagination was sparked into such a state of awareness that it was difficult for me to go to sleep, and still more difficult for me to get up and reach school the next morning at a quarter to nine. To concentrate on the lessons in history, mathematics, English, French, botany, and geography was a perpetual struggle. There was little time for rest. I wonder where all the energy came from that drove me from morning to night six days a week!

One day, in the sixth form at Brearley, I was listening to the English teacher analyzing the pupils' compositions, when an unfortunate girl was accused of cribbing her story. "Very good, for a change," the teacher said, "written with a silver pen—but was it yours?" There was a heavy silence; my feelings got the better of me and I said, "This is unfair!" Another silence. I was promptly sent to Mr. James G. Croswell, the headmaster, with a note from the teacher. It was my first real meeting with him. As I entered his office, I handed him the note, saying in an embarrassed voice: "I have wanted so often to come and talk to you, but apparently one cannot come here except as punishment."

His eyes opened with surprise, and he beckoned me to sit down. After reading the note, he said, "All right, Malvina, if I must punish you I shall read you verses of Sappho in Greek." I listened, fascinated, wondering why he did this. Then he translated the lines "Sapphic Fragments":

> "Songs that move the heart of shaken heaven,
> Songs that break the heart of the earth with pity,
> Which still like sparkles of Greek fire
> Burn on through time, never to expire. . . ."

After a long pause I said: "I'm sorry I was naughty in class, but I couldn't help myself. I'm sorry, too, that my marks are bad." I said it solemnly.

He looked again at the note. "I read here the word 'insubordination.' We must get to the bottom of this. Are you overtired or dreaming of other things?"

The kindly words startled me, for they hit close to the mark, and I did not answer. He asked again: "What do you do after school hours?"

"I go to night school," I said, "at the Art Students League twice a week, and to the Women's School of Applied Design on West Twenty-third Street once a week." (A little jaunt that caused my mother much worry and anxiety, since it meant coming home alone pretty late at night.)

"Well," said the headmaster, "from now on I want you to bring me your drawings. You need not speak of this to anyone else in school, but I intend to keep track of what you're doing outside school hours. You must learn to save energy for each task you undertake."

This, thought I, is a real headmaster. From then on, we were the greatest of friends. I never had to be sent to his office again.

The following summer I was taken ill and had a continual fever and bad cough; the doctors decided I would have to give up school and live in the country for a while. When Mr. Croswell heard of this, he invited me to Deer Island, in Penobscot Bay, Maine, where he and his wife had a country home. They took care of me with thoughtful affection, and I gradually regained strength, although for the first few weeks I was unable to walk even a few feet from the house. He would support me on his arm and help me to the big hammock under the pine trees, where I rested and read while he cut firewood and busied himself about the place as only a woodsman can do. I often asked him to read and translate the Greek poets for me.

In the afternoons of the following year, I painted his portrait in oils, in his school office, leaning over his desk, reading aloud as I had so often seen him. I heard the school wanted a portrait of Mr. Croswell; but unfortunately the school authorities considered my portrait too faunlike in expression, and declined it. He told me, however, not to change it, that he had always known that his eyebrows and ears went up in points, and that I must paint the way I felt was right.

After our summer vacations Mr. Croswell and I would meet and compare our discoveries. I had made a number of watercolors of all the wild flowers I had gathered and cut into sections, with enlarged studies of stamens and pistils and a little album of botany studies. The designs and variety of colors fascinated both of us, and he encouraged me to new efforts. Endless curiosity spurred me to explore the secret ways of nature; any leaf or fern I could find was drawn and colored. Not satisfied with merely outward forms, I managed to borrow a microscope, and by its aid I found enchantment in the hidden seeds and cross sections of flowers and ferns, impressions so revealing and unexpected that they pierced my consciousness with their sting of beauty; such discoveries overwhelmed me and often left a kind of pain behind. I felt a driving need to record these impressions; they acted as a sort of anodyne; I was aware even then that beauty is akin to sorrow but that by consecrating our whole being to its service we are somehow healed and given new strength.

Mr. Croswell collected every kind of seaweed and waving sea grass, and taught me how to float and mount them on the leaves of an album, which I still treasure, and the happiness of those days revives as I turn the leaves, amazed by the variety and delicacy of lacy patterns preserved on these pages of fairylike seaweeds that most of us might not even notice. "Always keep your eyes alert, Malvina. Try not to miss too much! We do, you know—so many just look *at* things. You must look *into* them and *through* them to make them a part of yourself and learn their secrets!"

I kept constantly drawing and recording my discoveries. Sometimes it was action poses, sometimes profiles of people; often it was incidents about my favorites or "crushes." I filled many notebooks. One especially crowded one was illustrated in pen and ink, interspersed with newspaper clippings, all referring in some way to the activities of a certain handsome young clergyman who served as chaplain to the New York Fire Department. He was a frequent visitor to our house and seemed very devoted to my mother and sister Elsie. As I was only fourteen years old at the time, I was not taken much notice of, but I had secretly started compiling an illustrated record, which I kept up for over two years. I kept it hidden in a drawer and told no one about it. I suppose many girls in their teens feel impelled to express their rather overscale enthusiasms in some such secret manner. It was exciting for me to write up a fairy-tale saga of this man, but I did not wish to share it with anyone lest it be ridiculed.

The chaplain came to dinner quite often. Sometimes he was called away to a fire, and the next morning I would scan the newspaper for the story. This would immediately be cut out and pasted in my notebook, and illustrated. I always watched for him on the evening he was to dine with us, and when his smart little runabout and glossy black horse pulled up at our door, I would run out and give a lump of sugar to his horse, and note the details of harness and style of the cut-under carriage, especially the brass gong that was set under the rear end.

One day Mother found me drawing one of the illustrations. I knew I was caught. "But these are really amusing," she said. "You should show the book to the chaplain. I feel sure he would be delighted." I begged her not to tell any of the family, and she never did. However, on my sixteenth birthday the chaplain came to our dinner party, and later in the evening Mother came over to where he and I were sitting and whispered to me, "Come into the dining room for a few minutes; no one will notice, and, Malvina, please go and get your notebook and bring it down to show the chaplain." I knew if I argued or refused, the other guests would hear us and surely be curious, so I ran upstairs and brought the bulging notebook. Embarrassed beyond words, I showed it to him in private. He became very serious, and as he handed it back to me he drew a little silver cross from his pocket and laid it on the cover and said: "Attach this and keep it as a memento. I'm very moved by your interest. I don't quite know how to express myself, but I do thank you with all my heart." I took the book and fled upstairs while Mother and the chaplain rejoined the other guests, and kept my secret inviolate.

Then came a time when we didn't see or hear from the chaplain for quite a while. We had known he was married and that his home life was not too happy, but we were all shocked to read in the paper one day that he had been very ill at a hospital and that on his recovery he had eloped with his nurse and they had sailed for Europe. He must have suffered a total blackout to have done something so destructive. As his wife was socially prominent, the papers proceeded to play up this startling news that naturally caused quite a scandal; and a few weeks later, when the chaplain and his nurse returned to New York, they met nothing but icy and unyielding ostracism. He was defrocked by his church, dismissed as fire chaplain, and all his former friends and associates closed their doors to him, refusing to forgive any such breach of the social code.

All this gave me a shock of bewilderment and disillusion. My father spoke to me very seriously after the notice appeared in the papers, saying that he would never permit this man to enter our house and that we should not make any appointment to meet him elsewhere. My heart sank, but I promised I would obey his order, feeling that Pa's judgment was always fair, and based on real wisdom. A few weeks later, as I boarded a Sixth Avenue open trolley car at Twenty-third Street, going uptown, I found myself sitting in the front seat directly opposite my forbidden friend. There was no other place for me to move, as the car was crowded. When we reached the Forty-third Street stop, I jumped off the running board and to my dismay found myself standing face to face with him. We walked toward my house very slowly. My head was swimming, my heart pounding in irregular thumps. My distress must have been evident, for my friend placed his hand on my arm and asked if I wished him to leave me at once. I shall never be able to erase the memory of the look in his face as he held out his hands in a sort of mute supplication. I found enough voice at last to tell him of my promise to Father and how much it cost me to keep my word. I had to close my eyes to keep the tears back. When I opened them, he was gone. After I collected myself and was able to walk home, I found my father at the dining-room table, writing a musical manuscript. I sat down in silence, and waited. I knew that Pa never had approved of this man, although he had never said so in so many words. When he looked up and saw the expression on my face, he came over to me, put his hand on my shoulder, and asked what had happened.

MY PAINTING OF JAMES G. CROSWELL

"DESPAIR," MY FIRST ATTEMPT AT SCULPTURE

I told him of our accidental meeting and how it had ended, and that I had felt a terrible pity for the wretched man, but, remembering my promise, had felt it impossible to give the former chaplain a single word of sympathy. "And now," I said, "I feel as if I had been a coward, and I'm ashamed and miserable." My father was moved, and tried to comfort me, realizing, however, that his love and sympathy were of little avail. When the storm had quieted down, he said: "My poor child, you can rest assured that I shall never again ask you to promise anything that goes against your conscience. Your own judgment will be your guide."

During the weeks that followed, I felt a sense of impending disaster. Then the newspaper again ran a headline: our unfortunate friend had committed suicide by jumping from a window in a high building.

I was put to bed with a fever and in a state of nervous collapse. I had never known anyone who had committed suicide, and this act of desperation shook me to the roots of my being. It took me quite a while to recover. I felt withdrawn and restless. While I was in this groping state, something instinctive made me buy some modeling clay and try to work my way out of the mental impasse. There would seem no other reason why I should have turned to sculpture at that time. There was a consolation in this new struggle in three-dimensional silence that claimed my whole mind and attention.

I modeled a small standing figure of a woman. The pose, the bowed head held in both hands, even the folds of the drapery suggested desolation. I had trouble making an armature to hold this figure up. I began with a large spool into which I set a pencil, to which, with wire hairpins, I attached a metal shoe-horn. When the figure was completed, I remember feeling a sense of relief that helped me to go about my daily tasks with more assurance. This experiment in sculpture was an effort in self-preservation, and it worked.

My father, taking notice of it, said in his gentle way: "You might knock it over. Put it in plaster, for someday you might be interested in looking at it again." I did have a plaster cast made of it as he advised. Father said: "I'm sorry you felt so strongly that you were that unhappy, but it's an awfully good idea, when you can, to get what's troubling you out of your system. Music is the same sort of consolation to a musician."

ILLUSTRATIONS FOR "POOR CHILDREN OF NEW YORK"

CHAPTER SEVEN

MY OWN ROOM:
FIRST STUDIO

WHEN IT became evident that I wished to devote every moment of time after school to my artwork, my parents decided that rather than strew my drawings and papers all over the house I should have a room of my own where I might confine my work. My excitement was unbounded. The room was on the third floor of our house, where I felt safely isolated with my Daemon. The door from the hall was opposite a ladder that led to an attic in which, as children, we used to hide our agate or tamarind-striped marbles, or prowl under the cobwebs and low beams that roofed a place of secrets and shadows, a place where anything might happen—a hideout for gremlins and piles of "lucky stones," encircled with white lines, picked up on the beach. I loved the spiral twisted shells that we held to our ears to hear the murmur of the sea.

Because the two windows in my upper room faced to the north, the light was steady and clear. The furnishings were a couch, a kitchen table for my paints, a chair on a model stand for my sitters, and an easel—that was all, except for two long poles fastened to the stand to support whatever drapery I used as a background. A few carefully chosen books on the anatomy of human beings and horses, as well as my favorite poets, were in constant use. On the mantelpiece, over a coal-burning grate, stood my little plaster figure, "Despair."

It was a lucky coincidence that while I was trying to find some purpose and direction for my enthusiasm about drawing, a friend, Frederick C. Walcott, interested in poor children of the lower East Side, persuaded me to try my hand at illustrating a short book on the subject by Kate Douglas Wiggin. On Saturdays I wandered about the Bowery, sketching the children and the background of pushcarts and fruit vendors. The need for intense observation and rapid recording of gestures and expressions was good training. I began to understand why musicians must constantly practice, and I began to sense the unending

65

daily sacrifice and attention art demanded. If you're not one who is instantaneously and constantly recording what's going on, I thought (much influenced by
Father), you're not an artist. Art isn't just doing one picture; it's a state of being.
In this spirit, I made far too many pictures for the needs of Walcott's little book,
but I learned a great deal about the poor in that area of my own city.

As I progressed in the use of colors, I ventured to ask a friend or two to
pose for me. The results in both oils and pastels encouraged me. With considerable trepidation, I undertook to make a life-size portrait of Ruth Lambert Cheney,
a close friend of my sister Helen. When it was framed and under glass, I was
excited and proud because it was the first thing I made that was thought worthy
of a frame.

Then came my uncle Judge Robert Cornell. He was infinitely patient, and
I can remember the difficulty of painting his bald head, which seemed to shine
like a beacon above his face. He would divert me by recounting anecdotes of
the Court of Domestic Relations where he had presided for many years. The
idea of taking one's domestic troubles to a court seemed to me strange and
impossible.

A good friend, Henry C. Fairbanks, asked me to make a pencil drawing of
his head, one half life size. This was rewarded by a camera and a green carpet
for my room.

One summer at Little Boar's Head, Emeline Kellogg, aged about six, posed
for a pastel portrait. Because she was a willing sitter, I embarked on a full-length
picture of her sitting on an old Shaker chair, her foot resting on one of its rungs.

Always searching for willing victims to pose for me, I asked Jim McLane,
a beguiling youngster with a strong southern accent, to let me try my luck on
a picture of him. He and I would play together on the rocks, hunting crabs
and collecting seaweed. I caught him in various action poses and made a number of pastels of him during that happy era, long before he became a bishop.

When some of my young married friends asked me to make pastels of their
babies, I found it a challenging opportunity and, as the commissions continued,
I decided to start a little fund toward buying steamer tickets that I hoped someday would enable Mother and me to go to Europe. Though only a distant hope,
the idea of studying in Paris possessed me.

I began to live like an artist and know that I was one. Art became a labyrinth in which each lesson led into a new maze of enchantment. Many were
the dreams born in my little room, and how often did they return throughout
the years! We may live a thousand lives and die a thousand deaths, but the
magic of our dreams never lessens, nor are their patterns dimmed by what we
call reality, or by the passing of time. Any moment that could be snatched from
school I spent in my top-floor room.

It wasn't that I made uninterrupted progress. You make mistakes over and
over. I was never sure I could do it better, but I hoped. That was what kept
me going: the innate feeling that I hadn't done it yet, but I would try again.

Even more discouraging were the contradictions of art. As I learned more,

I would think, Well, I know that and I can go on from there. But to my surprise, there were relapses when everything had to be learned again. I did it well and then, unbelievably, I did it worse again. While I was going through this period, I sought reassurance from my cousin Herbert Hazeltine. It was a great privilege to see him draw, doing so easily the things I wondered if I'd ever live long enough to do. And he knew about the phase I was going through. He'd say: "The other horse I did is better than this one. This one we'll throw away." He'd say, "A lot has to go down the drain; a lot you don't keep."

Father also encouraged me in his laconic way, saying those things happened in music, too. And with his steady interest, he trained my memory. I've mentioned our exercises of taking mental memoranda of the store windows. It is a patient ear that will listen to a child tell lists of objects. Father also always made me learn the songs I sang by heart. He said: "I don't want you peeking over my shoulder. When I'm your accompanist, you stand down there in the bend of the piano. You don't need to look at the song, or if you do, then you haven't got it ready." That was to make me memorize. I've mentioned also that Mother made me read and memorize French songs and poems. It all seemed like an extension of the one thing: music, poetry, art.

TEACHERS

So I studied and dreamed, in that new room of my own. Everything was finally subordinated to art. Harper Pennington, a great friend of my parents and a gifted painter, with endless patience taught me some of the mysteries of the palette and of oils, keeping up a steady stream of comment on the old masters and their individual methods of mixing their pigments, and how they prepared their canvases or wooden panels. Harper's intense admiration for Whistler led him to perfect himself in etching to such a point that Whistler insisted that one of them would have to choose another road and leave the etching field to the other. So Harper, almost sacrificing his livelihood, in his quixotic manner concentrated on oils and pastels. Besides his other paintings, he made fine copies of Gilbert Stuart's portraits of George and Martha Washington, which luckily were in demand at that time and brought in good returns. Harper had a sharply waxed moustache, wore smartly tailored clothes, white silk socks and black patent-leather pumps, and a monocle on a long black ribbon as the final aristocratic touch. While spending the day at our house, he always rose to his feet when Father began playing, and he remained standing until the music ceased. It was in no way a pose, but a natural way of expressing his admiration and esteem.

I knew that I wanted, and needed, instruction in modeling, and when the opportunity came to join some night classes twice a week with a group of girls at the Veltin School, I enthusiastically enrolled.

Herbert Adams and George Gray Barnard alternated as our instructors in sculpture. The two were the antithesis of each other—Adams, a quiet, dependable Vermonter of impeccable taste, arriving promptly and regularly. With his head tipped slightly to one side, at an angle that gave him a quizzical look, he taught us gently and earnestly, trying to help us without laying down rules. "Be thankful if you like to work," he used to say, "for art is a hard taskmaster, and there are no shortcuts worth taking." Then the lines about his eyes would crinkle into a smile. He was a sympathetic friend, and the relationship in my case lasted far beyond the student years—in fact, until the end of his life.

Barnard, on the other hand, would appear late at classes, or not at all. His was the manner of the "grand master"; his massive head and shoulders, his powerful forearms, and his deep resonant voice dominated the studio as he declaimed his opinions about art. We were slightly awed by his manner, though we were seldom able to extort practical advice applicable to our elementary efforts in modeling from the nude.

On Saturday mornings I attended John W. Alexander's class in painting. He was always smart; he had a carefully trimmed Van Dyke beard, and his eyes sparkled with a glint of mischief at times. Seemingly discouraged by most of our efforts, he would admonish us to put more paint on the canvas and less on aprons and fingers. However, we enjoyed his classes and occasional visits to his studio where he was painting a series of murals for the Carnegie Institute of Technology in Pittsburgh: floating figures enveloped in clouds of gray and pink smoke, with faint silhouettes of furnace and foundries in the background.

PORTRAIT OF FATHER

At home I finally gathered enough courage to attempt a three-quarter-length, life-size portrait in pastels of Father seated before the old Chickering grand piano. The light was inadequate—in fact, he sat with his face in shadow and his back to the window, so I placed a tall lamp on the piano and was delighted by the soft illumination that fell on his shock of white hair and his sensitive face. Hours of intensive effort followed. It was a difficult problem to find space and support for the large board, four feet long and three feet high, to which my pastel canvas was attached. I wanted to show both of Father's hands on the piano keyboard; but if I sat down to draw, the heavy black frame of the instrument blocked my view, so I tilted the board backward, setting the lower edge on a bench and leaning it against the back of a heavy high-backed chair, laden with many books to keep it from shifting on the carpet. I drew the upper portion of the picture standing up, leaning over the canvas; for the lower portion I crouched on a low stool. In this way enough light fell on the canvas from the lamp on the piano to enable me to see what I was doing.

The sense of progress, however, soon rewarded me for my aching back, and the excitement of feeling the composition come into being, with enough areas to include the seated figure, both hands, a little of the piano, and a shadowy background—this was enough to drive me on for two more days until suddenly I realized it was finished. Both Pa and I were happy in the result, but I was completely exhausted and felt as if I had fought a long battle. Father quietly remarked: "Nothing good ever comes without a struggle."

Being limited to two dimensions in painting made me feel the need of a third. There are so many other sides of a character that I could not seem to feel satisfied with a profile portrait. I begged Father to pose for a bust I wanted to model in clay. I was sure it would not take me long, for doing this pastel portrait had taught me much, and I knew just what I was searching for. Father reminded me that we were soon to give up our old home and move to a little house in Thirty-sixth Street, near my sister Helen's, but he agreed to pose for the bust if I would wait until we were settled in our new quarters. He even added, "We'll give you the room with north light, and I'll pose there so you will have really favorable conditions for work."

This new encouragement took a good deal of the sting out of parting from my old habitat. We moved into 125 East Thirty-sixth Street without too much difficulty, and I was immediately installed and started to work in clay, in the room with high north windows, that was now to be my studio. Every day when I stopped work I wrapped the clay in damp cloths and covered it with a square of oilcloth and cleaned up the floor and washed the tools so that all would be ready for the next sitting.

I did not foresee the many pitfalls that lay ahead.

At first the clay seemed like a slippery and unreliable medium. If it was too wet, it slipped down and refused to hold its form. When it was too dry, it caked on my tools and hands and became crumbly. By trial and error I finally managed to work it into soft, malleable lumps that adhered to one another as I applied them to the makeshift armature. I bought a collection of tools, most of which proved unnecessary. The fingers were the most reliable tools, and one or two strong wooden spatulas with which I could shape the large planes and yet keep the work simplified. Otherwise, the masses were broken up uselessly and lacked scale and solidity. The head seemed to be solid, and I had become so familiar with Pa's features while doing the pastel portrait that I was able to get a resemblance. But a likeness is not half the battle; I was interested in what went on behind the facial mask. What lines could show the inner character, the submerged struggle and patience of a man as dedicated as my father? Revealing this truth demanded an intensity of observation beyond just making the shape of his features. This probing for what lies beneath the surface has been the search of my whole life, and I confronted this high barrier on this first portrait, as well as on every one I have made since. I discovered that not one profile from the side, but countless profiles all around the head had to be modeled in the clay, and every one of these had to fit into the next one from front and back and sides, from above and below; every viewpoint was essential before the head would have living authority in its forms and entirety.

The clay began to respond to the pressure of fingers or the palm of the hand; the surface was important, too, for to give life to sculpture I found it must have a pulse, a breathing quality that could change in a flash, and it must never appear static, hard, or unrevealing. All these demands formed themselves in my thoughts, and became like an endless obsession.

However, after a few days I noticed that the shoulders were lower than when I started. Their weight was too heavy for the wooden framework I had put under them, and the neck seemed insecure and had begun to crack. I was still floundering in this new world of forms and planes when fortunately, one day, a friend of Mother's asked if she might bring the Danish sculptor Gutzon Borglum to see the portrait and possibly give me some guidance. When he came and I uncovered the clay, to my dismay the shoulders had sagged down quite out of place, and I was too embarrassed even to attempt any explanation. Borglum gave a piercing look and asked what I had put inside as an armature. "Three sticks of kindling wood fastened to the base, a tin can upside down over the top ends, and a short board tied across those to hold the shoulders!" He gave me a thunderous look and almost shouted: "Stop this nonsense and come with me to my studio. I'll show you how to build a decent armature. You must begin all over again. The study of the face is not too bad, but you'll have to do that over, too; it's insecure. When you have finished the new portrait, I'll come again and have another look at it. Now, come along to my studio!"

Despite his gruff manner, his smile was reassuring, and I was thrilled to go to his studio, only two blocks away, on Thirty-eighth Street, near Third Avenue. Although I had been there before, this was the first time I had gone alone with Borglum, and it was all very different. He unlocked a door in a wooden fence fronting the sidewalk, led me through a narrow alleyway to the studio vestibule, and then directly into a vast high space that had once been a stable. The hayloft had been removed, leaving a room two stories high, and covered over in part by a skylight. All about stood great masses of clay, groups and single figures, one covered with dripping rags, others of marble glistening in the white light. My eyes were drawn to the life-size figure of a woman standing over a man whose recumbent figure was turned away from her, the face of the woman bent slightly forward, and the closed eyelids swollen from weeping. One had inescapably the sense of tears held back. On the stone base I read: "I have piped unto ye, and ye have not danced."

The vast space in the studio made me wave my arms about. I heard a voice from the clay bins: "Better learn to use your hands before you sprout wings." I stopped short, and felt the blood rush to my cheeks, but Borglum paid no heed to my embarrassment as he returned from the far end of the room with several lumps of clay and lengths of lead pipe. Deftly he bent a piece of pipe in his large square hands, set it into a larger iron pipe screwed to a wooden base, then opened a penknife and whittled several short bits of wood that he wired together to make "butterflies" (little crosses), handling his tools without a waste motion. When he had constructed a firm, professional-looking support, he tossed me the lumps of wet clay and told me to start pushing them tightly against the iron base pipe. He hung the butterflies on the curved arch of the lead pipe above. "These will keep your clay from slipping down," he said, "and don't ever let me see you build up an amateurish, nonsensical armature again."

I set up the new and sturdy armature and proceeded to model another portrait of Father, this time with the feeling of a secure support. The work went

FATHER POSING FOR HEAD

MARBLE OF FATHER

well, and the character of Father's personality gradually took form and gave both sitter and sculptor a feeling of satisfaction.

When Borglum came to see the finished bust, he was pleased, and he even encouraged me to attempt to carve it in marble.

Phimister Proctor, who also approved of this idea, very kindly offered me the use of his studio in Macdougal Alley while he was staying in his country home at Bedford, New York. He helped me to select the marble block at an Italian carver's studio opposite his own and gave instructions to rough off the surplus material, following my plaster model, and leave a quarter-inch all over the surface for me to carve myself. Months of hard work and careful study were demanded of me, for I knew nothing about carving or how to keep my chisels sharp. When faced with some especially difficult problem, I would run across the alley and beg the Italian carver to give me a word of advice. I became terrified that, when I was finishing the eyes and details of the face, I might chip off too much, realizing that such a slip could spoil the whole thing and that it would be irreparable.

When I began this portrait I was in a state of anxiety about my father's health; his strength seemed to be ebbing away.

The work had so engrossed me that I was unable to think of any outside problems. Carving became a harbor of safety into which I could steer my thoughts and sense a sort of salvation by self-obliteration. It became the deciding factor in my decision to be a sculptor.

When the marble was finished, I sent it to the Annual Exhibition of the National Academy of Design in New York. While waiting for the jury's decision, I felt as if my fate were hanging in the balance, the destiny of my whole life. The portrait was accepted and put in a good place. So, for better or worse, the die was cast.

Mr. Alexander was president of the Academy at that time, and when he saw my name on the marble base he sent for me. "Well, Malvina," he said, "so you have forsaken painting for sculpture. If this is your first attempt at carving a portrait, I think you had better give all your attention to sculpture. It is far better work than you've been able to show me in painting."

CHAPTER EIGHT

SAM AND FATHER

WHILE I WORKED in Proctor's studio in Macdougal Alley, I prowled in and out of the transformed stable studios that lined each side of the little dead-end streets running west, just south of Eighth Street. On the north side, James Earle Fraser had his studio, with much work going on, portraits and figures in plasteline in every stage of construction. At that time he was teaching at the Art Students League, and Laura Gardin was one of his gifted pupils; later she became his wife and had a career in sculpture nearly as successful as his. Fraser was of strong, stocky build, with the squarest jawbone I ever saw. It was always surprising to hear him speak, for his voice was low and gentle in contrast with his aggressive appearance.

Near him, Edward Deming was ever painting his scenes of American Indian life and modeling wild animals. This quiet, industrious man worked among a confusion of dusty relics, and a swarm of little Demings took delight in the Indian war bonnets, bows, arrows, and other trophies of western trips that filled corners and hung on every wall.

In sharp contrast was the perfect order of Gertrude Whitney's splendid place on the north side of the alley, with high, well-lighted studios and fully equipped workrooms. The array of modeling tools and glistening saws and chisels that hung over the workbenches, turntables that really turned, stands that did not wobble—the whole atmosphere of the place excited me and filled me with awe. Mrs. Whitney herself, tall, thin, and fragile in appearance, worked tirelessly but was never too busy to help young sculptors; her generosity was well known to the profession. In Paris, where I knew her later, she was working as diligently under the inspiring tutelage of Rodin, in a studio near the Bois de Boulogne. Her interest in art led her to found the Whitney Museum on West Eighth Street.

Herbert Adams's studio on West Eleventh Street I had known for a long time. He had enclosed his back yard in a spacious brick-walled workshop that was always tidy and well ordered. When I remarked upon the advantage of having everything in its place, he told me he owed the inestimable comfort of this order and cleanliness to his studio man Bill. "Without such a man, Malvina, I cannot guess how anyone can keep his studio in any sort of order." So I added a "Bill" to the list of my objectives, not guessing that later on, this very Bill was to keep my studio clean for twenty years!

Between Fifth and Sixth avenues, on the south side of Eighth Street, Daniel Chester French had built a studio and casting room on the ground floor and in the back yard of a wide house. Here was a true New Englander, indefatigable and efficient, of the academic school so characteristic of his period. In his gentle, kindly way he took time to show me whatever he was doing, and to explain the contrivances he had designed to aid his work, especially a platform that could be raised and lowered above and below the floor level. By placing an equestrian statue or any heroic figure on this, he could study it from the correct angle of its prospective setting. When it was lowered, he could work on the upper portion of a statue without climbing uncomfortable ladders. There was a splendidly equipped casting room in which iron pipes, rolls of wire, burlap, and brushes were assigned to their special places, and Vincent Russo was kept busy casting Mr. French's many commissions. I adopted Russo as my caster whenever he had free time, and he has done all my plaster work ever since.

My thirst to learn was unquenchable, and I was grateful to these eminent artists who went out of their way to help a beginner who seriously wanted to study and work.

One day I was invited, with other pupils in his class at the Veltin School, to George Gray Barnard's studio uptown, overlooking the Hudson, on land known as "God's finger." The gigantic proportions of the high rooms made his many heroic figures and models for triumphal arches and war memorials seem shadowy dream fantasies. The effect was heightened by endless blocks of stone that lay about the courtyard, casters busily covering finished clay models with plaster, and stone carvers pounding on colossal figures. As Barnard escorted his class through these studios, he described in his grand manner great projects that seemed, even to our youthfully daring minds, beyond any probable realization.

The illustrator Charles Dana Gibson occasionally took me to lunch near his studio in the Carnegie Building; oysters, pigs' feet, and apple pie would be his favorite order for us both. He would tell me how important it was to learn to draw, to observe light and shade and every plane, which is the basis on which one must build forms. "Remember, Malvina, when you're out in front, you can't afford to make a slip or a stumble. It takes years to build a reputation, but only one failure to lose your place. We're just like racehorses in some ways!"

Vista of Rodin

I was studying in books and pictures the work of Rodin when a chance meeting with Mrs. John Simpson enabled me to see many of the actual marbles and bronzes by this French master in her collection. Her house on upper Fifth Avenue was crowded with his figures and groups; among them was a marble portrait of herself in which the sculptor had caught her stately dignity and subtle smile. Mrs. Simpson's ardent admiration and understanding of Rodin's work seemed to take fire each time she laid her hand caressingly on the marbles and bronzes. On the first floor were two or three glass cases filled with tiny studies in clay, terra cotta, and plaster. The infinitude of observation and knowledge embodied in these studies made the finished groups more eloquent; indeed, they opened for me new vistas in the field of sculpture.

When I was allowed to open the cases and examine these fragile objects in my own hands, the power and scope of Rodin's art took possession of me. To this day I can close my eyes and feel the spirits of Good and Evil hovering with their heavy wings over the seated figure of Youth attracted and bewildered by both; or the bronze figure of St. John striding with the defiant inevitability of Faith. The Age of Bronze was there, the standing youth lifting one arm and sensing the flow of life through his awakening body; and the brother and sister, and "She who had been a helmet maker"—a wreck of a woman who still remembered the days when she was beautiful; Sorrow, the tear-stained face of a woman; "The Thinker," in bronze, muscular force brooding and dumb before the wonder of life!

For hours I sat studying and drawing. Sometimes Mrs. Simpson would come in and talk to me and give me tea, telling me stories of her many sittings with Rodin, and the fascination of his unpredictable mind. Later I told Chester Beach, the sculptor, of this treasure house, and he was as excited as I when we went together, for Mrs. Simpson enjoyed having artists study her collection.

Of course, the stimulation resulting from this close-up examination of Rodin's sculpture made it clearer than ever that the road I had chosen was a long and challenging one. But I was young and had boundless energy, and youth dares the apparently impossible with high hope and an accepting, come-what-may philosophy. The goal was a distant one, and there was no desperate need to exclude everything social along the way. Life was exciting, and many friends added pleasure and diversion to our family activities. In fact, I felt the need of knowing all kinds of people, for each presented a mystery to be studied and understood; no two were ever alike, and many hid their true characters under masklike appearances. For the artist, all this was a vital education—a journey of discovery.

> Experiment to me
>   Is every one I meet
> If it contain a kernel?
>   The figure of a nut
>
> Presents upon a tree
>   Equally plausibly
> But meat within is requisite
>   To squirrels and to me.
>
> —EMILY DICKINSON

I reached the "coming-out" age. I find in my scrapbook a little engraved card stating that "Mrs. William K. Draper and Miss Malvina Cornell Hoffman will be at home Wednesday, December 14th, four until seven o'clock, at 121 East Thirty-sixth Street." (She and Dr. Draper lived in that same house for forty years.)

I felt afraid that the social life this would surely entail would take far too much of my time. I soon found myself in a whirl of engagements. The best were the evening parties before a cotillion, or some less formal dancing. The preparations were complicated. One could not wear the same dress too often, and a seamstress was kept busy changing the appearance of party gowns, for our limited exchequer did not permit buying many new ones. The formal balls were often given at Sherry's, then on Fifth Avenue at Forty-fourth Street. The excitement of filling a dance card with partners was intense. Every boy seemed to present a new problem in human relations; some were precocious flirts who enjoyed sitting out their dance in the conservatory, and others seemed timid and introspective, but the variety kept the evenings lively, and the music was a constant delight. As I was reputed to be a good dancer, it was generally very late when I finally went home, exhilarated by the thought that life could be so filled with joy and anticipation.

Many were the hours spent with our dear friend Ethel Sterling, of Washington, D.C., who taught me French and German songs and corrected my accent.

The following spring the peak of my social activities was Princeton Commencement—not only the exercises, but dinners, dances, and moonlight walks with the seniors, and being escorted home in the early dawn. I felt thoroughly spoiled, and enjoyed it.

A day I shall never forget was when Father took me to a Carnegie Hall matinee to hear Paderewski for the first time. Father had known him and had spoken with ardent admiration of his playing. So I went well prepared. To my joy he played the Schumann "Fantasia," the Beethoven C Sharp Minor Sonata, and Variations on a Theme by Paganini by Brahms. After the intermission, during which Father had all he could do to calm my excitement, Paderewski played a group of Chopin pieces, starting off with the Ballade in G Minor.

The early years of the twentieth century were the golden age of opera, and my sisters and I happily had many invitations from friends to hear the really great singers.

Under the direction of Mr. Maurice Grau, in 1902, Mme. Emma Calvé appeared in *Carmen*, with Emma Eames as Micaëla and Antonio Scotti as Escamillo, but best of all was *Faust* with Emma Eames as Marguerite, Jean de Reszke as Faust, and Edouard de Reszke as Mephistopheles!

One of my favorites for years was *Tosca* with stately Emma Eames, Scotti as Scarpia, Caruso as Cavaradossi, her lover, and Gilibert as Il Sagrestino. These artists could cast a spell over the audience with the force and conviction of their interpretations. As Elsa in *Lohengrin*, Emma Eames's beauty was radiant, and her voice "so smooth, so sweet, so silvery, as could they hear, the Damned would make no noise."

Otello was another favorite, with Desdemona sung by Emma Eames, Emilia by Louise Homer, Iago by David Bispham, and Otello by Albert Alvarez. I was taken to hear Madame Adelina Patti at Carnegie Hall, and I can still remember with delight the purity of her voice. To hear Caruso in *Pagliacci* was a revelation; I thought his voice, so natural and effortless, was like a torrent of tone.

Besides opera, Father often took me to song recitals. On our return home he would play the German or French songs over and over until I had learned them by heart, adding them to my repertoire.

At that time I had a friend who met my mood perfectly—Frank Walter Taylor, a gifted artist in Philadelphia whose work often brought him to New York. A few imaginative friends composed a pantomime in which Walter was the perfect Pierrot and I was Columbine. When our two or three informal performances were over, Walter and I decided to continue our make-believe characters whenever circumstances permitted us to meet, either in New York or in his studio in Philadelphia. By the mere fact of getting into our costumes and preparing our makeup, our personalities shed all vestiges of realism, and we spent many delightful afternoons and evenings together, preparing supper, reading from favorite poets, and sipping red wine from tall slender glasses that we had seen in the Parisian drawings by Willette.

When parting time came, we would drink a standing toast to fantasy, and separate without another word.

In 1904 Wassily I. Safonoff, of Moscow, became the conductor of the Philharmonic, and since he was a great friend of Father's, he was a constant guest at our house. I loved making studies of his gestures while conducting, and with my father I attended any performance under his leadership. It was a real education to be permitted to share the long evenings at home when he and Father would discuss the great composers, one or the other going at intervals to the piano, playing the themes of symphonies or concertos and expressing his opinions.

TROUBLE BUREAU

Surrounded by artists and musicians who were forever getting into financial difficulties, pleading dire need of assistance to be able to keep afloat and continue their professions, some friends and I started a fund known as the "Trouble Bureau"—a plan to aid artists needing money or medical care. Donations were sent to the Fifth Avenue Bank by friends wishing to share their good fortune with others less fortunate on the understanding that an artist was never to know from whom assistance came so there need be no letters of thanks or sense of indebtedness. As there was plenty of "trouble" to keep the bureau active for many years, "Happiness is a change of trouble" became our slogan.

We had a small group of representatives in New York and in a number of other cities. The cases that came to our attention were looked into and, if they seemed honest and worthy of assistance, were helped. When the account was first opened at the bank, I remember how puzzled the elderly directors were, first by my description of the idea, then by the title under which the funds

STUDIES OF WASSILY SAFONOFF IN 1907 CONDUCTING THE
THIRD MOVEMENT OF TSCHAIKOVSKY'S SYMPHONIE PATHÉTIQUE

were to be deposited. Because the "Trouble Bureau" was initiated with two generous checks bearing the signatures of two well-known wealthy men, the bank did not wish to lose the account; but it required a bit of argument to get them to inscribe in their important-looking records the somewhat informal title insisted upon by me, not to mention my subtitle: "Brotherhood of Brave Poor Things." One of the old gentlemen finally cracked a smile, and we parted cheerily, hopeful that the idea would flourish and find supporters as time went on. Alas, the funds were finally exhausted, and after the First World War the books of the Trouble Bureau were closed.

I initiated my own private version of the Bureau when I read a newspaper account of an accident on the corner of our street. A youngster selling papers had tried to jump aboard an open trolley car, missed his footing, and fell under the rear wheels, which cut off his right leg and crushed the left one below the knee. The boy was taken in an ambulance to Hudson Hospital; the article stated that he never lost consciousness and that he told the intern in the ambulance that he might as well take off the rest of his left leg to make a neater job of it!

The words seized my imagination; I cut out the article, called up the hospital, and asked if the lad had survived. "He's alive," was the laconic answer, "but we don't expect him to live."

I told Mother that I was going to see the boy if I could. My sister Helen knew Dr. Lewis A. Stimson, the surgeon attached to the hospital, so when I arrived I went straight to him. He told me the boy was very weak but was emerging from shock and had a good chance of recovery. Without considering the difficulties involved, I said I would supply the boy with artificial legs and that I would talk to him. Dr. Stimson took me up to the ward and led me to the bedside. There a pale gaunt face turned toward us with a look of surprise. Beside the bed sat a tear-stained woman holding a child in her lap, and another small boy stood beside her.

"John," said Dr. Stimson kindly, "this is a friend who read about the accident in the newspaper. I shall leave her with you, for she has some good news, and it will help you to get well."

We had a long talk, John, his sister, and I. They told me how he had worked hard to make extra money after school hours so that he might help support his widowed sister and her two children. This accident would make him a cripple and a burdening expense. It was grim and heartbreaking.

In leaving I assured him that somehow I would find a place where he could recuperate and that I would find him a job.

When I reached the hospital desk, I was faint and frightened under the responsibility I had assumed. My voice shook as I asked the cost of artificial legs. "Oh, anywhere from $125 to $300." A body blow—I had guessed $50 or $75 at the most. I sank upon the nearest bench.

In due time the boy went to a home for cripples, where his education was continued. He became interested in electrical work and prepared for a career in it. All during his two years' convalescence I had been constantly going to parties and "coming-out" balls, and I became known as "Wooden Legs" because

I warned my partners for cotillion or square dances that it would cost them $5 as donation to John's leg fund. Finally we had enough for his shorter leg, but the other had to wait nearly a year. Then, one day, out of the blue, the telephone rang and a man's voice asked to speak to the young lady who was collecting money for John's leg. I said I was the culprit. He laughed, and said: "Well, I'm down at Cantrell's leg shop now. He's a good pal of mine, so he told me your story, and I want to know how much more you need to get that second leg. I lost my own in an accident twenty years ago, and I'll give you the balance —whatever it is. Just tell me."

I was so astonished I could hardly find words to answer. "I think it's about $150," I managed to say, "but Mr. Cantrell knows!"

"O.K.," came the gruff answer. "I'll tell him to finish it up, and I'll pay him off, but neither you nor John will know my name. Tell the boy this is my way of being grateful I'm still alive and can help along another guy. And tell John to remember that he can help others too, later on when he gets back his strength."

When John was finally ready to walk with the aid of two artificial legs and a cane, my sister obtained a position for him with the New York Telephone Company. During the First World War, he came to the Red Cross and offered his services in the evenings to show the amputees how to use their new false legs and arms, and teach them to repair them and keep them in good order. He no longer needed his cane, and his courage and cheerful disposition made him the best possible morale builder.

Toward the end of Father's life, I became acquainted with the maze of troubles, usually financial, which Father's pupils and other music students seemed always to be bringing to him. He would spend time and effort getting clothing or instruments for them, or legal help; he would try to free them from unscrupulous agents or a "phony" contract demanding large advance sums before dates were determined.

The condition of artists struck me as unfair and even disheartening, and I decided to call together a group of influential people I knew who were genuinely interested in the cause of music. Some of them had known of the existence of our Trouble Bureau.

When I look back now at the list of sponsors and the talk I gave—they insisted upon having it printed—I marvel at my foolhardiness in attempting such a project. However, "Fools rush in . . ."

Mrs. John Hammond offered her drawing room for the meeting, and Mrs. E. H. Harriman, Mrs. W. Havemeyer, Mrs. Otto Kahn, and Mrs. Edward S. Harkness, and others assured me of their support. So, with one foot on the head of a lion before the great stone fireplace, I began trembling, but determined, " 'That's a valiant flea that dare eat his breakfast on the lip of a lion.' "

Within an hour The Music League of America was founded, the first of its kind. The sum of $25,000 was pledged to its support, and officers were elected, as well as managers and office staff.

Those were the days when patrons would get together and back an artist's dream. For many years the League obtained engagements at low commission fees, and ran a *vestiaire* where singers could get lovely evening clothes to make their debut. Donations to this service and to the general account came in generously. The idea took root and became a living part of New York's musical life.

During a visit to Southampton, Long Island, at the home of one of my classmates, I had the fun of meeting some of the well-known theatrical stars of that era; among them were John Drew and his niece Ethel and nephew Jack Barrymore. They were visiting in his home near the dunes.

All the young people would disport themselves on the beach at bathing time, and many parties were planned. I was quite shy, but really very excited when, at a Saturday club dance, the highly popular "Jack" took me for a stroll in the moonlight. It was evident that he was in high spirits and full of mischief. So was I. I urged him to keep on walking and talking, for he could tell some wild and lurid stories. Suddenly he stopped short, pointing to the moon.

"Do you see those black spots on the moon, Malvina?"

"No," I said. "It's all clear and dazzling. Maybe we'd better go back before you see too many black spots; they're not good omens." He looked deflated, and I bade him good night, smiling.

The next day was Sunday, and the beach was crowded. I was basking in the sun when Jack appeared. He leaned over and nervously asked if I could see the black spots that were far out on the ocean. To my surprise, I could see them quite clearly. "Why, yes, this time I see your black spots, and I wish I could know what they really are."

"Your wish will be granted, my lady!" and he made a deep bow and kissed my hand, much to the surprise of those who were watching us.

He ran down and plunged through the breakers and swam out toward the spots. He went far beyond the limits set by the lifeguards, and John Drew, who was nearby, became very nervous and ordered out the lifeboat and climbed into it himself.

They shouted at Jack to turn back, but he kept on swimming until he had become just one more black spot in the sea. I was terribly worried and embarrassed, for many of my friends accused me of daring him to swim too far out, just to show off. Suddenly, as we watched, Jack's arms waved in the air, and, lo and behold, the original mysterious black spots rose and flew away toward the horizon.

Jack turned and swam back to the lifeboat and his distracted uncle. Just as he reached the bow, he dived down and came up at the stern. This last stunt was indeed a show-off, but it frightened the guards and his uncle, who pleaded in vain with him to get into the boat. He came up the beach to where I was sitting, and bowed. "Black ducks, milady, and maybe the same ones that were on the moon last night!" Then he fell flat on the sand, completely exhausted, and his friends gathered around him excitedly so I decided to escape as quickly as possible, for Mr. Drew was shaking his finger at me. That same afternoon Jack, on his bicycle, came to call at the house where I was staying. He told us the story in dramatic style, saying that his uncle had "cooled off" and that all was forgiven.

MH BY HERSELF

SAM BY MH

SAM

In November, 1905, Samuel B. Grimson, a young English violinist, was introduced to Father by Mrs. Draper. Late one afternoon I was reading upstairs with Mother when I heard the doorbell and ran to the head of the stairs to see who it was. A pale young stranger went into the parlor where Father was practicing. The music stopped, and my curiosity increased. I crept downstairs, peeked furtively through the crack in the heavy portieres, and saw the young man's finely chiseled profile. He was standing by the fireplace, listening to my father, whose voice sounded unusually interested and sympathetic.

Something strange and overpowering happened to me; suddenly the pounding of my heart frightened me. I closed the curtain and tiptoed upstairs. Mother asked me where I had been. I was trembling and could scarcely find my voice to answer. "Something wonderful has happened to me," I said, "not like anything else in the world." My whole life had changed. I knew I must bury the tumult in my heart and try to live on as if life was the same as it had been. My feeling was far too deep to express in words.

One might wonder why I hadn't simply opened the portieres and walked in and said, "Here I am." But it was impossible. We were brought up with the knowledge that the portieres were inviolable when Father was busy. There were things you just didn't do.

But I had the premonition that I would see the young man again, and in fact Father invited him to lunch the following Sunday. Already they were planning to play together, and Father wanted to discuss repertoire, what composers and pieces they admired in common. It was one of our usual family Sunday lunches, but I can't remember with certainty who was at table with us; I suppose it was Mother and my sister Elsie and perhaps Helen, who came often, and Aunt Georgie Andrews, a cousin of Father's, who was nearly always there. Before I gave up piano, with two pianos in the house always in use, I used to go to Aunt Georgie's on Thirty-eighth Street to practice.

Now I sat at the table with Sam Grimson. But not in comfort. You get awfully scared at that age in the presence of "that person." You hardly dare look to see what's going on. Fortunately—and again this was our family training, like the portieres—we were expected to maintain complete silence when Father talked. That gave me some protection.

But I was aware that a new person was there, a young man with a thin straight nose and lips that had an English hint of superiority, but were actually humorous and tender. I knew that all my family had fallen immediately under his spell. Mother loved him from the moment she knew him, and included him in the household. Father too. The "Sunday waitress" served food that the cook sent upstairs by a little dumbwaiter. As we ate, I was conscious that it wasn't so long since I myself as a child had helped serve just such dinners as this. It had been my job to heat the dishes on the hall radiator and have them ready for the table. Nobody, of course, knew about my activity, and later, if it was evening, I could come in for ten minutes and meet the company before I had to go to bed.

Now I was part of the company and found myself at the table with this altogether special person, Samuel Bonarios Grimson, and glad of it, but disturbed, too, because he had an overwhelming effect on me. Only as I recovered did I learn that the name Bonarios came from his mother, who was Greek. Perhaps that accounted for his Greek nose, I thought.

I also learned that he was working up a repertoire with the hope of being able to play as soloist with the New York Philharmonic Society. This was apart from what he was going to do with my father, which now began to resolve itself into a choice of Beethoven sonatas. After lunch, they went to the music room to continue their discussion, and shortly afterward, for the first time, I heard Sam play the violin. His technique, I recognized at once, was entirely comparable to my father's on the piano, and I could see how inevitable it was that they should (as Mrs. Draper had suspected) take to each other. His playing was part of himself.

What I next remember—and it was on another day—is that Father made me sing for Sam. By then I was less scared; still, it was nerve-racking to be placed in the bend of the piano and told to perform. I wore the modest dress of those days, and as to my appearance, Papa said I was "wide-eyed like a spaniel." The piano sounded, and, comforted by it, I managed to find my voice. I can't remember now what I sang, but it was very likely something in French, perhaps Verlaine's "Chanson d'automne":

> Les sanglots longs
> Des violons
>   De l'automne
> Blessent mon cœur
> D'une langueur
>   Monotone.*

I sang two or three songs, and Sam listened, sitting in a big chair, his head to one side. There was a kind of fatality to it. Even as early as this, though not a word about our feelings was spoken, we knew we were fated for each other.

Sam wasn't long over here from England, and our country hadn't yet restored him from his native fogs. Though he was pale and frail-seeming, he was strong. I discovered, when he went to Little Boar's Head, that he was an excellent swimmer.

He and his brothers and sisters had been brought up and educated by his father. His mother had died when he was very young. Mrs. Grimson was a beautiful-looking woman, the kind—so often sought by strong-minded Englishmen—who unfortunately blow away after having produced a few obligatory children. Sam's father, a violinist, was a strict disciplinarian, and the children were trained like a little orchestra. The sisters played the piano. One brother

* *The long sobs of the violins of autumn wound my heart with monotonous languor.*

played the cello, another the violin. Sam became a child prodigy, and before he was ten he had such command of the violin that he was asked to play for Queen Victoria at Windsor Castle. When we were in England together in 1925, we visited the royal residence, and he paced off those rooms and remembered how nervous he had been when he was invited there as a child, to play for the Queen.

He studied at the Royal College of Music. When he was older, he wanted to go to Germany to study, but his father forbade him. His sisters, however, were on his side and wanted him to go. He ran away. He left without even an overcoat. And he completed his studies in Berlin.

Of course, such stories as this, told in growing intimacy, sealed my love for him. He worked hard at his repertoire, preparing confidently to play with the New York Philharmonic Society. Before long, he was engaged as a soloist for the Bruch Concerto. When the time came, we were at Carnegie Hall to hear him. At the close of the composition, he was recalled five times. I was so proud of him and excited by the whole experience that my nerves were tingling and my knees shook, and it was quite a battle to be able to walk down the long flights of stairs from the dress circle. I felt as if I were living a double life, in being part of Sam.

We realized that we both were dedicated to art with all we had of spirit and determination. Sam had studied much on his own; he had an encyclopedic mind and a phenomenal knowledge of classical music and musical instruments. He brought much to Father. All of us noticed that whenever they played together, their interpretations of sonatas and other compositions seemed to be spontaneously suited to each other; one would have thought they had worked together for years.

Now I have to tell my part in this. At the series of Sunday-afternoon musicales of Beethoven, which were held at Mrs. Draper's, at 18 West Eighth Street, I was permitted to turn the pages. I turned them also at rehearsals. Father demanded absolute precision in this. He would say: "Learn the parts. Know when to get up. Don't just stand there," and that really trained me in the classical repertoire. He would say: "You have to do it on the snap, just at the right moment. You have to be fast, but don't knock the music off the stand." Sometimes Paul Morgan, the cellist, joined Father and Sam to play trios, but even with three I turned all the pages and kept up with the score.

What Sam knew of my own work was mostly drawings and pastels and not too good oils and watercolors. But, after one Sunday luncheon at our house, I remember that I took him upstairs to see my studio, and he noticed on the mantelpiece the plaster reproduction of my figure "Despair." It was the only piece of sculpture I had at that time. I thought he looked somewhat curiously at that girl who hid her face in her hands and who was obviously weeping. I don't remember that he said anything, but that was the premonitory first sign of my sculpture on his horizon.

After that, on Sundays after lunch during the times he came, I would ask him to pose, and I made a number of life-size charcoal portraits, always thinking of the possibility of modeling his head. As I drew him, I felt more definitely the patrician quality of his delicate bone structure and fine profile that came

BUST OF SAM

from his mother, who was born on the island of Cos. I knew that his father, too, was fine-looking.

The day Gutzon Borglum came to see the finished clay portrait I had made of Father and gave me his approval to cast it into plaster, Sam happened to be present.

"Why don't you model a clay head of this young man, Malvina?" Borglum said, reinforcing my own unexpressed idea. "He'd be an excellent subject for you, and such a different type from your father. You can come to my studio in Thirty-eighth Street and have it to yourself, for I'm going out of town for a few weeks. You'll find all you need for the work there, but don't forget to lock the door when you leave!"

In ten days or so I had completed a head of Sam—my third piece of modeling, counting "Despair"—when Borglum came to give me a most helpful criticism. He noted every detail. "These lines are a bit sharp," he said, "but here you've accented the chin and jaw forms with free strong strokes of your thumb—leave them—they give freshness to the surface. Try to work spontaneously. Don't use *little* tools; they tend to make it look fussy. Use only your fingers to get the feel of life into the clay—emphasize the forms of character but don't carry it too far. Above all, keep it fresh and alive. It takes courage to know when to stop. Don't forget that! I'll come in again tomorrow."

The next day he came as he had promised, and seemed pleased. "Now call the plaster caster, and try to remember what I've told you. You're on your way. So long, and good luck!"

So it was the heads of Papa and Sam that confirmed me in sculpture.

During one of the summers of this period, Sam was seriously ill. He never thought it necessary to get out of New York in the summer, for he was absorbed by practicing, and hardly noticed the weather. During this particular summer he was boarding at 47 Fifth Avenue when he developed a perforated ulcer and had to be hospitalized. The long jarring trip by ambulance up to St. Luke's broke the ulcer, and blood poisoning set in and he became desperately ill. He had no mother or sister—no one to be with him—so I left Little Boar's Head and took a train to New York. In those days people didn't understand how my mother could approve of my going alone to see Sam. But to her it seemed natural for me to do what I could to comfort him and to look after him. He was operated on and moved as soon as possible from the ward to a semiprivate room. After many weeks of convalescence, he recovered and was able to resume his playing.

The Beethoven sonatas continued at Mrs. Draper's for about two years, and then Father wasn't strong enough for them, but he and Sam continued playing together privately with the same unchanging absorption. Sam had begun to get engagements as a soloist and so we would see him only when he was back in New York or, during the summers, when he would visit us at Little Boar's Head or Mount Kisco, where my brother-in-law had a cottage. But the sonatas would resume at once, and I would watch and listen, filled with love for both of them.

Sam and I had begun to learn some songs together, I singing and he accompanying me on the piano as Father would. We'd do that if we were asked to when we went out to dinner together. If Sam was coaxed to play the violin, he would say, "The violin doesn't eat at night so we didn't bring it," but there would almost always be a piano, and I would go, as I did with Father, into the bend of it, and sing, "Si vous croyez que je vais dire qui j'ose aimer . . ."* That was very pleasant, and Sam and I could hide behind it. And I would sing further: "Et je puis, si'l lui faut ma vie, la lui donner." But it was to be many years before I could give Sam my life, as the song said, though the willingness was always there.

We had many private messages to each other in songs. One was in a poem of Robert Louis Stevenson that Sam had put to music. He and Father both wrote songs; sometimes they would even do different songs from the same poem. Sam had a great rush of them for a while, and I later bound his and Father's songs together into a book that I still have.

This song from Stevenson was one of them:

> Dark brown is the river,
> Golden is the sand.
> It flows along forever
> With trees on either hand.

And then the poem said "boats of mine" are set afloat and go drifting away and, "Where will all come home?"

> Away down the river,
> A hundred miles or more,
> Other little children
> Shall bring my boats ashore.

This became a private message. If things just refused to go right, we'd say, "Well, 'other little children shall bring my boats ashore.' "

In that book I bound, there is manuscript with Father's writing on one side and Sam's on the other, so close we were. As I look at these sheets of paper, I seem to hear again Sam's nickname, "Sambo," from the first syllables of Samuel Bonarios. I seem to hear the affectionate name echoing through the house.

I even wrote one song myself to a poem by Oscar Wilde, "Under the Balcony":

> O beautiful star with the crimson mouth,
> O moon with the brows of gold,
> Rise up, rise up from the odorous south
> And light for my love her way.

What I wrote must have satisfied my father, for he smiled and wrote the bass accompaniment, saying I was too young to be alone with Oscar Wilde. It reminded me of how we used to write songs together years ago. Father took this one—Oscar Wilde, moon, and all—to G. Schirmer, and all of us were pleased and excited when they decided to publish it as "Song for a Medium Voice."

* *If you believe that I am going to say whom I dare love . . .*

If Sam now should seem at times to disappear from my narrative, it is only because he had become so much a part of me that in my recollection it seems as if he was always present. There were, of course, those gaps during his seasons of engagements when he was not back with us for any great length of time, and yet he always seemed there. When he was away, we wrote, and our letters, young and filled with endless details of what we were doing, were like being with each other. So we seemed always together.

During the summer of 1908, I was glad to go to Mount Kisco to stay with Father and Mother in the cottage on Chestnut Ridge. The inn we used to go to at Little Boar's Head had closed, and just about that time my brother-in-law Arthur Butler offered us the use of a small farmhouse he had (we called it "the cottage") so that we could be near him and Elsie during our vacations. This summer he had begun making over an old barn into a studio, and he asked me to direct the workmen and see about setting a skylight in the roof. We built a fieldstone fireplace, planted moon vines to climb over a trellis on a covered porch, and laid out a little garden with a pool in one corner. There I could work in clay and make drawings of the farm animals, dogs, and horses.

My excellent tutoring by Harper Pennington continued there, for he used to come up and stay with us. He and Sam were devoted friends, and Harper was much a part of our lives then. He showed me how to use charcoal, and continued his other instruction. He taught me very seriously and very well. He gave me a pen-and-ink sketch of Whistler that he had done. There was a depth and sadness to Harper. On some of his old drawings I'd see "R de l'A," and I asked him what it meant. He said, "Risen from the Abyss."

At this time Charles Scribner's Sons were to publish a book by Richard Harding Davis, and an encouraging surprise came when they asked me to make a frontispiece drawing of the author at his desk. As he was our near neighbor in Mount Kisco, he very kindly offered to pose for me—he may well have been the one who suggested me for the work—and to my delight the drawing was published.

During the summer, Arthur gave me a saddle horse so I could ride over the countryside to my heart's content. I often rode over to visit the sculptor Phimister Proctor and his family on Indian Hill, near Bedford. I watched his young children playing about, quite unconcernedly, near a large cage made of chicken wire in which was a mountain lion Proctor was using as a model for a group of wild animals. He felt no anxiety about the children, saying in a cowboy drawl, "I don't reckon they'll be so foolish as to put their fingers through that there wire or try to tease a real wild animal." Then we would go to his studio and see his latest group of cowboys and buffaloes.

Riding home through the woods, I was enthralled by the leafy silence and the thrushes singing their evensong to the setting sun.

At our cottage in the evening Pa often asked me to sing some of our favorite songs together. We would perhaps do the ones I've mentioned, but at that time I remember one that we both particularly loved: "Come to me in my dreams, and then by day I shall be well again. . . ."

Father and Mother at Mount Kisco

In answer to my wishes, I often had wonderful dreams, but the daylight brought me back to my senses with stabbing reality. There was heavy sadness in the air during our last two summers in Mount Kisco. My sister Elsie, who had been married to Arthur Butler only a few years, was stricken with a fatal illness known as Hodgkin's disease. Her courage never wavered. After months of pain, she was released from torment and died at the age of thirty-one, radiant and smiling as she passed from us, her spiritual strength a revelation to us all. At the end of that final summer, before she died, she had been moved back to her New York home, and during her last hours Father played her favorite compositions on a piano in an adjacent room.

My father never really recovered from the loss of his beloved daughter. His life was very quiet, for he could not enjoy seeing many friends.

The year after Elsie's death, on his seventy-eighth birthday, on May 24, 1909, he unfurled the little British flag as always—it was Queen Victoria's birthday too—and, with cake and candles we tried to drive away the apprehension we all felt because of his failing strength.

We moved up to Mount Kisco for Decoration Day. During the following weeks, Charles came up weekends to be with us, and generally stayed over Sunday night and went back on Monday morning, wanting to be with Father as long as he could without seeming to make too much point of it. On July Fourth we went to see the fireworks over the lake at Dick Davis's. Arthur Butler arranged a reunion later in the summer with Ethel and Jack Barrymore, the Stephen Bonsals, and Cissie Loftus. This was the only outing we planned. A week later Father asked me to go to Little Boar's Head for the dedication of a bronze memorial tablet to my sister Elsie at the Chapel of St. Andrew's-by-the-Sea. At Rye Beach, Dr. Floyd Tompkins of Philadelphia, who had known Elsie and Father for many years, made a beautiful address on the text: "The world was not worthy of such." That same evening I wrote a detailed account to Father and posted it to him, heavy of heart and full of foreboding.

> Presentiment is that long shadow on the lawn,
> Indicative that suns go down;
> The notice to the startled grass
> That darkness is about to pass. . . .

At five o'clock the next morning, August 17th, I was awakened from a nightmare by a knock on the door. I saw my friend Mary Southworth holding a telegram in her hand. My heart contracted violently as I read: "Father died in Mother's arms tonight."

In a daze I packed, and Mary kindly accompanied me to New York and then to Mount Kisco. Such loyalty in friendship is never forgotten.

When I thought of life without Father and without music, I could not find the courage to face it. I felt the silent gallantry of my mother, and prayed for strength to help her. She told me that Pa had been composing a trio all the afternoon of the day of his death.

A few nights later I had a vivid dream. Father was playing a Chopin ballade for me; the notes fell like crystals on the air, and at the end he turned to me and smiled. . . . The next night I had another dream and Father played the "Polonaise. . . ." Could my dreams be the answer to the song I had so often sung with him: "Come to me in my dreams, and then by day I shall be well again"? But the days continued just as dark, and the dreams that so consoled me stopped. I felt broken and full of pain.

Sam did all in his power to comfort us, and so did Harper Pennington and other good friends, but Mother and I were far away in our sorrow. "J'ai pris l'habitude du chagrin. . . ."*

We made a dreary move; we packed our belongings and decided to try living at the Schuyler Hotel in West Forty-fourth Street. Later, I had a few days of respite by my beloved ocean to gather strength and renewal.

Sam completed the trio Father had been working on the day he died.
He did it for me.

* *I have fallen into the habit of grief.*

FATHER AT THE PIANO

MYSELF ON MY FIRST TRIP TO EUROPE, 1910

PART II

CHAPTER NINE

FIRST TRIP TO EUROPE: 1910

In 1909 my godmother, Mrs. Van Nest, died. With farseeing thoughtfulness, she left the sum of $1,000 to my mother to help out in my art education and enable us to live for a while in Europe. I had been able to earn and set aside enough to buy our two steamer tickets, so, after disposing of most of our furniture and other belongings, Mother and I joined a group of friends who were sailing on March 5 on the S.S. *Carmania* with Italy as our point of debarkation.

I was armed with a photograph of my portrait bust of Father and another of Samuel Grimson, and a letter of introduction to Rodin from Gutzon Borglum.

Those were hard days for both Mother and me. It meant cutting familiar ties and saying a long good-bye to all our friends. But for me it was especially hard, since I had to leave Sam, not sure when or how we could meet again. We accepted our fate, feeling sure and safe in our love for each other and directing our hopes and strength to making good in our chosen paths—he as a violinist, I as a sculptor.

Fortunately, to occupy him Sam had a full season of engagements, necessitating a great deal of traveling, while I was embarking on a voyage of discovery, determined and hopeful that my dream of becoming a pupil of Rodin in Paris would come true.

Except for the separation from Sam, my mind was settled and my spirits lifted as I set out at last on my long-delayed first trip to Europe. I had been patient. Now a new world of art opened before me. On the steamer *Carmania*, in spite of the difficulties involved, I tried to paint a series of small panels of

95

the changing sky colors and clouds, from dawn to dark, and in moonlight. This effort helped to train my observation and discipline my will. The studies were of use to me in America later when I developed them for a mural decoration in the house of my classmate Julia (Dodge) Rea in Pittsburgh, as a wedding gift from her father, Cleveland H. Dodge.

The Dodge family and Mr. and Mrs. Edward S. Harkness were our companions and joined in all our excursions to the towns and hills of the Azores, Madeira, and Gibraltar. On the hillside of Madeira, Mr. Harkness and I somehow became separated from the others and almost missed the steamer. The long strident blasts of the whistle alerted us and saved us from what might have been a serious predicament.

ITALY

We landed at Naples, where the fragrance of spring filled the air, and sunlight glittered on the bay. Not knowing a word of Italian, we were left stranded with our luggage for hours in the customhouse on the wharf. It grew windy and chilly, and I was worried about Mother, for she had an attack of rheumatism and was quite lame. Since there seemed to be no way of hurrying matters, I wandered about and came on a flower vendor and bought the most enormous bunch of fresh violets I had ever dreamed of, and carried them back to Mother as a consolation. Customs finally let us go, and we installed ourselves comfortably in a hotel. I bought an Italian dictionary and conversation book, and we studied it diligently, fearing that otherwise we would die of starvation or neglect, our Italian vocabulary being limited to such musical terms as "Pianissimo, presto, fortissimo"!

Mother's rheumatism grew steadily worse, and she was unable to accompany me on any of the trips to the museums or the aquarium, but after a week of rest and care she felt well enough to go with me to Pompeii and Herculaneum. The fragmented ruins were haunted with pathos. When I heard the story of the eruption of Vesuvius and the rivers of lava that poured down over the hills, destroying humanity and the villages, the incident that stood out was that of the sentinel at the gate who, ordered to keep guard, obeyed to his last breath, though a stream of lava rose over his body, burying him alive with his spear held at attention. He was found years later, in the exact attitude in which death had overtaken him. The deserted houses seemed to echo with the footsteps of an ill-fated people.

In Pompeii I was continually aware of the grace and proportion of the temples and houses, and was fascinated by the color values and tone of the paintings, the figures full of life and motion, harmonious, pale, like evocations of a dream.

I had been warned in America that when visiting museums abroad I must beware of their death-dealing chill; they were never heated, and so, whenever I ventured forth, I wore a thick tweed coat, a muffler, two pairs of wool socks, and heavy woolen underwear!

I remember the wonderful walks in the late afternoons up to the hilltop above the harbor of Naples. Winding downward through the woodland paths and mossy gardens, I would come back in a state of reverie. Across the valley from our hotel, one of the paths allowed me to wave to Mother, who watched at the window, and she would know that in about half an hour I would be home to tell her my adventures.

We moved on to Rome, where we lived for six weeks with Mother's aunt, Mrs. William Haseltine, the widow of the gifted landscape and marine painter from Philadelphia. Her apartment occupied a whole floor of the Palazzo Altieri on the Piazza del Gesù. Every room opened on a balcony filled with flowering shrubs and plants, and overlooked the wide paved courtyard.

One day a letter from Sam arrived, and the sight of his handsome writing moved me so intensely that I nearly fainted, and was forced to lie down for a while before I could read it. The emotions that I had tried to keep under control since leaving New York suddenly overwhelmed me.

When I did read the letter, I found that Sam wished us well on the journey and was very glad that we had arrived safely—I had cabled him that. He wrote about his own activities, practicing and preparing his concerts, and he casually described the places he had visited. He said that we had done right in making our decision. Nothing must interfere, nothing must shake my faith in myself and my determination to study and develop my art. Surely in Rome I would be overcome by the opportunities surrounding me. He told me not to worry about anything and that everything would be all right.

Comforted by his letter, I plunged straight into life. As a dramatic introduction, Mother and I went to the Easter service at St. Peter's. The "Pieta" marble by Michelangelo held me spellbound as we crowded into the cathedral with thousands of worshipers. All the bells of Rome were ringing, and the air shook with their vibrations; everyone seemed in a state of religious fervor.

In visiting the Forum and churches, we found Aunt Ellie Haseltine a good guide, for she had lived in Rome many years and spoke the language fluently. We spent hours studying collections. We explored the Capitol Museum, the Villa d'Este, the Appian Way, the Catacombs, the Colosseum, and the Baths of Caracalla. Hadrian's Tomb (Castel Sant' Angelo) was familiar to me from the last act of the opera *Tosca*. My mind nearly burst with the multitude of Old World discoveries.

A short way from Rome we visited the Protestant Cemetery and found the graves of Keats and Shelley in the shade of the sentinel cypresses. Shelley once wrote, "It makes one in love with death to think of being buried in such a place as this."

KEATS'S HEAD

The house in which Keats had lived in his last days was at the side of the steps leading up from the Piazza di Spagna. When I found myself in the room where the poet had died, something inexplicable happened—I had a startling vision of Keats. I saw him steadily and clearly, reclining on a couch and propped up with pillows. I did what seemed natural—I told the guide I was an artist, and asked him if he could give me a piece of paper as I had not brought my sketchbook, and I persuaded him to leave me alone in the room for a while and not admit anyone else. I began to draw the profile of the poet. I did the entire head on the grayish square of paper and then thought it would be well to check the absolute accuracy of this profile by getting a front view. When I walked in front of what I imagined was there, the vision disappeared.

I showed the drawing to the guide, and he seemed surprised and impressed. There was actually no couch in the room, and neither he nor anyone else later was able to tell me where the couch had been in Keats's time. When I was in London later, I went to the Keats Memorial House, and there the curator showed me the portraits that were available. I examined them and the death mask and the life mask. The death mask had nothing of my drawing, but I knew a death mask can be taken so that the person becomes unrecognizable. The weight of plaster pressing down on the features distorts the expression totally. But a life mask is different. There were perhaps twenty different versions of Keats's appearance, and as I examined them carefully, in some I could see a decided resemblance to my drawing but in some I could not. But I had a growing conviction that some power had directed me and that my drawing was an exact likeness. I never changed it. Those who had made a careful study of Keats portraiture and best knew what he may really have looked like were impressed by the resemblance.

No head of Keats had been made in sculpture during his lifetime, and I had the impulse to do one. After returning to New York, I made a life-size model. I referred to the existing portraits to make them fit my profile, but my main confidence was in myself, in what I had myself seen and recorded. Even if it might have been some illusion or dream, this was what Keats was to me; this was my sense of his presence and poetry.

After I had done the plaster model, I wanted to do it in marble, but it took me many years, perhaps seven. I couldn't seem to find out how to make it in marble the way I had made it as a drawing, with the same feeling of sureness. I kept it available in my studio and would work on it from time to time, in different lights and at different times of day. After I finished it, I thought it would be with me all my life; that's why I had made it, for myself.

It did stay with me for a while, but then came the big traveling exhibit of my work in 1928, some fifty or sixty pieces, among them the head of Keats. The exhibit was shown at the Carnegie Institute in Pittsburgh. Before the opening, I went up on the balcony of the gallery where part of my work was on display, and there I saw a man standing and speaking in a low voice to this marble head of Keats. When he finished, he still stood there meditatively, and finally I approached him and said that I would appreciate knowing who was talking to Keats in such a familiar way and reciting his poetry. He said his name was John G. Bowman. "I'm the Chancellor of the University here, and I've been so taken with this I'd like to find out who did it." He asked me if I knew, and when I said I had done it, he was startled and then took my arm and walked with me down the gallery, talking with me. Finally he said the marble was going to stay

STUDY OF KEATS

MARBLE HEAD OF KEATS (*Peter A. Juley & Son*)

there. And that was what happened. The exhibit as a whole continued to many other cities and museums, but the head of Keats did not accompany it and never returned home.

Years afterward, when I had a hiatus between commissions, I took down the plaster original from which I'd made the first marble head and made a second one for myself. In some ways I like it better. It's a little older looking and a little sadder around the eyes, as if the poet had been sleepless for some time and the lids were swollen from lack of sleep. This later one I still have.

So there was the long result of my visit to the house near the Piazza di Spagna in my first days in Rome. To go back to them—those days had a mounting intensity. The Michelangelo paintings in the Sistine Chapel were almost more than I could bear. I was overcome by the magnificent figures and their immortal power. In "The Last Judgment" the titanic scope of imagination left me exhausted; I could not go out or attempt more sightseeing. The line from Michelangelo's sonnet kept repeating itself in my mind: ". . . No one knoweth how much blood it cost. . . ."

One day in Rome I went to the Capitol Museum and was absorbing the beauty of certain masters with whom I was unfamiliar when I noticed some striking portraits, one of Michelangelo, another of Benvenuto Cellini, and another of Velázquez—all attributed to "Lui Stesso." Astonished by the differences in style, and curious to know why my teacher in New York, Mr. Alexander, had never told us about this great painter Lui Stesso, I came back to the Palazzo Altieri and wrote Mr. Alexander a letter. Fortunately, I happened to read it to Aunt Ellie before posting it. She burst into laughter, explaining that Lui Stesso meant a "self-portrait"! This story went the rounds for a long time afterward.

My friend Stéphanie de Neuville and I would go on painting trips, carrying our folding camp stools, our easels, and boxes containing palettes and tubes and little wooden panels. By some good chance Stéphanie had obtained a permit for us to paint in the Vatican Gardens. We started early in the morning and selected our view. We had just finished our sketches and were leaning back to admire our efforts when we heard footsteps. Looking around, we saw His Holiness Pope Pius X in a white robe, approaching with two attendants for his morning walk in his garden. Just as he was within a few steps, my camp stool collapsed and I fell backward with my masterpiece butter-side down in the gravel! I quickly picked myself up as His Holiness with a broad and very human smile continued on his walk, while my friend and I, much embarrassed, gathered our goods and chattels and hurried home.

It so happened that our friends had arranged for Mother and me to have an audience with the Pope on the following day. We wore the traditional black lace mantilla over our heads, and, bowing in silent reverence as His Holiness walked past us, evidently I was not recognized.

Occasionally Aunt Ellie drove us beyond the campagna outside Rome to visit Mr. and Mrs. Samuel Abbott at their beautiful Villa Lontana. From their garden, framed between the marble columns of a circular terrace, we could see the golden dome of St. Peter's in the distance. The gently rolling hills surrounding the Eternal City spread out before us in their fine green light and the air was filled with fragrance and vibrations of church bells tolling the hours of vespers.

My visits to the American Academy introduced me to several young compatriots who were there on their Prix de Rome scholarships. One of them was Paul Manship, then struggling with the group that later on won him fame, "The Centaur and the Maiden." When he heard I was a student of sculpture, he told me he was having trouble with his centaur: "Where do I put his navel?" he growled. "How can we know where the man ends and the animal begins?" "How can we indeed?" was my guarded answer.

Being a woman, I was admitted merely as a visitor, but in 1926, when I was again in Rome, for a longer period, I was permitted to study in the library and dine in the big room with the other students. During this visit my friend Phimister Proctor was at work on his huge group of an American pioneer family and was living at the Academy as resident sculptor. This made me feel very much at ease, and he welcomed me to his studio at any hour.

On my first visit to Rome, I had the incomparable privilege of hearing Ossip Gabrilówitsch play in the privacy of his hotel. Mother and I were friends of his wife, Clara Clemens, who was Mark Twain's daughter. I had known Mark Twain in New York, and we had enjoyed several delightful sails on Cleveland Dodge's yacht up and down the Hudson River. Now Clara and her husband showed us the kindest hospitality while we were in Italy.

The glorious sunsets in Rome have never grown dim to me. I can close my eyes now and see the sky diffusing its iridescence, edging pink clouds with gold, irradiating the horizon with lavender and poets' green, while the echoing bells answer each other, calling in wistful minor notes, calling the listener to the benediction of evening prayer and peace. I celebrated the last day of my stay in Rome by climbing the 642 steps to the dome of St. Peter's to lock my precious memories in my heart.

At our next destination, Lake Como, we found a modest pension overlooking the lake, drenched in azaleas, wisteria, and moonlight, the air filled with serenades of invisible nightingales.

We would hire a boat, taking in a basket our lunch of ripe figs and wine, sketchbooks, and Ma's knitting. So enchanted was I by the miracle of spring all about us that I frequently forgot in what direction I was rowing, and Mother would patiently remind me that we were going in circles or had drifted too near the shore. We presently reached the stone steps that descended down under the water of the lake from the garden gateway of the Villa Barbianello—deserted, tangled, and locked in its wilderness of roses, like a castle of dreams. My heart pounding, I tied the boat line to the iron gate—and a sudden thought of suicide swept over me. I managed by a desperate struggle to dominate it and, creeping back to where Mother was sitting in the boat, put my head in her hands and wept. My tears blotted out all else save the sense of our being together. This saved me. I can never forget her look of infinite compassion. She realized that my decision to leave America and Sam had not been an easy one and that there would be many difficult moments for me. This was a poignant one that swept over me without warning. No word was spoken, but the boundless tenderness and understanding that was in my mother's face drove away my sense of desperation.

In Florence we lived in a little pension on the Arno; Mother was lame with rheumatism again and was cared for by a kindly nun. After a week or so we went to see Paul and Muriel Draper, who were living in a suburb with their baby Paul, then a year old. We lunched at the villa of Mabel Dodge, and there met Janet Scudder, the American sculptor. She told us the mirror in her room had fallen down and broken, that a ghost was haunting her, and that she had decided to leave for Paris. She seemed spellbound by a sense of impending danger. I was intrigued to the point of wanting to see her again, and planned to visit her studio when I reached Paris.

Each morning I made a different trip: to the Uffizi Gallery, the Palazzo Pitti, Michelangelo's "David," the Medici Tombs, or by an endless rough walk over cobblestones to the Casa Buonarotti. There I would draw and study. My fatigue was increased by pain in my left foot, which I had caught under the edge of an elevator and sprained badly. I had to use a cane to limp over the rough streets; our budget never permitted me to indulge in a cab unless Mother was along and the distance too great for walking.

The Bargello and Cellini's "Perseus" lured me forth time and again after a long excursion, before the evening church bells warned me of my pension's early supper and exacting regulations.

Owing to financial limitations and Mother's continuing lameness (my youthful one had mended), we decided to go to Paris where my two aunts were anxiously awaiting our arrival. We took a train by way of Switzerland, and I slept a dreamless sleep and awoke in the morning to see from the train windows little pink-roofed houses and feathery poplars. "Oh, Ma, darlin'," I cried, "let me hold your hand. C'est la France!"

PARIS

Now, after the long overture, the hope of years, the curtain rose on the new scenes in the City of Light—Paris. We moved into a small pension called Villa des Dames at 77 rue Notre-Dame-des-Champs. It had a garden with winding paths and a heavily laden chestnut tree, in full bloom, that seemed the essence of Paris. Just at that time a comet had been predicted to be "the end of the earth," and I looked up to the moon and seemed to see a little bird on it with all its feathers standing on end with excitement and its beak wide open—perhaps like me. At any rate I could hardly bear the rush of new experience. My brain was strained beyond its capacity, and ached continually.

I thought of "Astiquette," a name my friends had given me back in New York when I used to do the pantomime and plays with Walter Taylor and later Sam and the whole group who turned to the imagination for release. We'd play Schumann's "Carnival" and act out the parts—Walter was particularly good at changing his personality. So they called me Astiquette, diminutive for an Italian

JANET SCUDDER AND MYSELF AT GIVERNY

wine, Asti Spumonte, and the nickname persisted. Now, when life seemed to take on an unreality compounded of new scene and overwhelming sensation, I thought of myself as Astiquette, as on a stage or in a dream.

I had been trying to see Rodin (as yet unsuccessfully), and on our fourth day in Paris Mother and I went to the Musée du Luxembourg. I felt so young, so inadequate. For no reason my throat ached and tears filled my eyes, and in the center of a room "La Main de Dieu" of Rodin suddenly appeared to me. I took Mother's hand, asked her to be patient with me as I felt a sort of wildness. If she would only be patient, I said, I would study forever, but just now my thoughts were in a tumult. I was abjectly humble and yet believed inexplicably that some unknown power would come to my rescue. The suffocated state I was in must have come from the great things I saw, but I knew that before I could interpret them or other subjects from life "I must live long and deeply and probably tragically."

After a few days, both of us were so exhausted by our emotions and new experiences that we were forced to stop everything and try to regain our strength.

I had called at Janet Scudder's studio at 1 rue de la Grande-Chaumière. The woman at the door said Mlle. Scudder was busy, and I received this identical greeting the next several times I came. Not discouraged, after my period of rest and recuperation, I persisted. At last Miss Scudder let me in, and I thought she looked at me in rather a strained way, but this passed and I somehow felt I ought not to refer to the strange episode in Florence that had so aroused my curiosity. She offered to take me to a "soirée" at Gertrude Stein's, and there I met some of the many painters and writers who flocked about that curious personality. Miss Stein received them genially, seated like a great Buddha surrounded by worshipers. Paintings by Picasso covered the walls of the salon, and there were also many pencil and pen-and-ink drawings by Matisse so meticulously executed it made me think an etcher might have made them. I was told that Matisse had given up this type of work and was doing free and bold line painting.

Janet took me for apéritifs at l'Avenue's and other Montparnasse cafés where we met more of the artistic coterie then working in Paris.

Everyone was talking about the coming Quatre-Arts Ball. I went under protest—by no means in the gay mood of the others. They dressed me up as a court page and, so disguised, I spent a wild night dancing and drinking absinthe, singing my way home with the crowd of artists, arm in arm, winding along the Boulevard St.-Michel.

In all these new experiences, much seemed familiar to me from descriptions in books, but the sounds and colors, the immediacy of Paris defied the written word; the air was charged with beauty and newness. Here was something I could never have known from writing or tales of travelers, but only from the blessed good fortune of being able to live it.

CHAPTER TEN

LONDON

AFTER STAYING in Paris two weeks, Mother and I went to London where we had lodgings—"Bed and Breakfast"—at 88 Oakley Street, Chelsea. Visiting friends in Cheyne Walk and the Mews permitted me to learn the ways and haunts of London artists. We particularly enjoyed being with Wilfred de Glehn, a gifted painter, and his wife. They took me to John Sargent's studio, adding that moment to my other flooding discoveries in art. His watercolors seemed to glitter before the eye, and I was to learn more of his virtuosity later in Mrs. Jack Gardner's Museum in Boston.

In his studio outside the city, Frank Brangwyn showed me a series of his large murals, nearly completed. Eventually these were placed in the entrance hall in Rockefeller Center, New York.

Emanuele de Rosales, the Italian sculptor, had an interesting studio where he was working on his inlaid, highly finished bronzes. He was planning to go to Paris, and promised to give me lessons there. An ardent admirer of the Russian dancer Anna Pavlova, he had made portrait statuettes of her and Nijinsky and Fokine. One of these, of Pavlova in "The Swan," which he made in silver inlaid with gold, was acquired by the Luxembourg Museum in Paris. The miracle of the Russian Ballet had only just been revealed to the Western world, and I had not yet seen it myself, but Rosales's report was like a first luminous intimation.

Mother and I saw London from bus tops, but walking was our usual form of transportation. One day we went to St. Leonard-by-the-Sea to visit Father's older sister, Helen Lewis, who had many traits that reminded us of him. Her lonely old age saddened us. How can one find the needed patience and courage to grow old slowly, be alone, and radiate serenity? We then visited Father's other sister, Mrs. Loew, who was tragically incapacitated.

105

CHARCOAL SELF-PORTRAIT

Gathering our courage for our only social effort, Mother and I put on our best and went to a reception given by Mr. and Mrs. Whitelaw Reid at the American Embassy. Pablo Casals and eight members of his orchestra played Reynaldo Hahn's songs arranged for strings, songs I knew by heart, having sung them so often with Pa and Sam in New York.

One day I happened to come on a most wonderful collection, Art in Medicine, in the Wellcome Medical Museum; I realized at once that with my interest in anatomy and all the mysteries of the embryo, I had in this extraordinary place a vast opportunity for research and study. Sir Henry Wellcome had spent the greater part of his life collecting art symbols relating to medicine in sculpture, paintings, and etchings—every kind of black magic, white magic, and medicine-man and witch-doctor mystery from archaic times to his own day, a huge assortment. The rooms were interconnected in a series of five or six little houses on Wimpole Street. There seemed to be no end to the collection. I went day after day and filled my sketchbooks with drawings of models, ivory carvings, wax bas-reliefs, skeletons, pygmies, babies, freaks, and giants. The guard lost patience with me after the third day as I never would leave at closing time, but sneaked back into the anatomy rooms, turning on the light and continuing my work. He would then have to come back and start arguing all over again before I would consent to leave. The third day he said he was going to register a complaint, and he insisted that I follow him to the director's office.

I found myself facing a kindly person by the name of Dr. Malcolm. After the guard had made his case, I noticed the suspicion of a smile on the director's face, but was not quite sure. He dismissed the guard and asked me to state my side of the case. I handed him my sketchbooks, telling him I had very little time left in London and that I had discovered in the Wellcome Museum a mine of information, that I was quite ready to plead guilty, and awaited his judgment.

He asked why I was doing this, and I said I was just starting my studies as an artist and that—though I had not thought of learning medical draftsmanship when Dr. Cushing had asked me to last year—now I found myself terribly interested in it. I looked up and saw that Dr. Malcolm's face had completely changed its expression. "Do you mean to tell me," he said, "that you know Dr. Harvey Cushing?"

"Why, yes," I answered. "We often walk on the beach in Little Boar's Head in New Hampshire. I have known him since I was a very young girl."

Dr. Malcolm closed my books, handed them back to me, and said: "What time will you be here tomorrow? We open at nine."

"I guess I will be here at nine, too!"

He rose and escorted me to the door, put his hand on my shoulder, and said: "If you will promise to come to this museum every time you come to London, I guess I will have to give the guards special instructions! Dr. Wellcome is very interested in art, and I think he will be delighted that you value his collection and want to work so hard at your studies."

From that moment Dr. Malcolm and I became fast friends, and on subsequent journeys to London I have seldom missed paying a visit to the Wellcome Museum.

PAVLOVA

Toward the end of this first visit to London, I was able to see Anna Pavlova dance. From a top gallery in a theatre I saw her and Mikhail Mordkin in Glazunov's "Autumn Bacchanale." Fireworks were set off in my mind, and I understood what Rosales had told me. Here were impressions of motion of a new kind, of dazzling vivacity and spontaneity and yet with a control that could come only from long discipline and dedication. The incomparable Anna cast her spell over me, and it was inevitable that I should wish to portray her in my own work, in sculpture. I went to further performances, standing up when necessary, and made sketches. These precious sketches and impressions I took back to Paris.

After exploratory trips to Oxford and Cambridge, Mother and I went to Antwerp, where I could study the Dutch school of painting. Our little hotel was near the cathedral, and for the early part of our first evening we thought the church bells had charm and quaint European atmosphere as they tolled each quarter-hour. But about 4:00 A.M. of the second night we agreed we could stand them no longer, for in spite of shutting the windows and wrapping cotton over our ears we had hardly slept since our arrival. We decided to pack and find another hotel. When we found that none was available, we took the first train to Paris.

There we took up our modest abode in *chambres meublées* at rue de la Grande-Chaumière, known as the "rabbit hutch." Our two tiny furnished rooms, only five or six doors from Janet Scudder's, looked out on a picturesque old street in which there were two well-known schools, Colarossi's and the Grande-Chaumière. On Monday mornings a long line of models of all colors and nationalities filled the sidewalks leading to these two academies—colorful characters looking for all the world like the drawings of Toulouse-Lautrec, Daumier, Willette, and all the French artists one had ever seen or heard of!

The calls of the knife sharpeners and mattress makers, the Pan pipes of vendors of goats' milk leading their bleating flocks filled the air, and the stage was set for the opera *Louise*!

Mother and I enjoyed walking about our *quartier* in Paris, hunting for little sidewalk cafés where with our limited budget we could get our meals at low cost. All week long we had no desserts, but on Sundays we would celebrate with old favorites like *gateau de riz* (rice cake) and *fraises des bois* (strawberries) with crème d'Isigny, which would be a real treat. Gradually we grew familiar to shopkeepers and academy students, and Mother's charm was not long in working its customary magic, attracting friends to us. Musical evenings in Janet Scudder's studio were soon supplemented by romantic gatherings of poets, musicians, and artists.

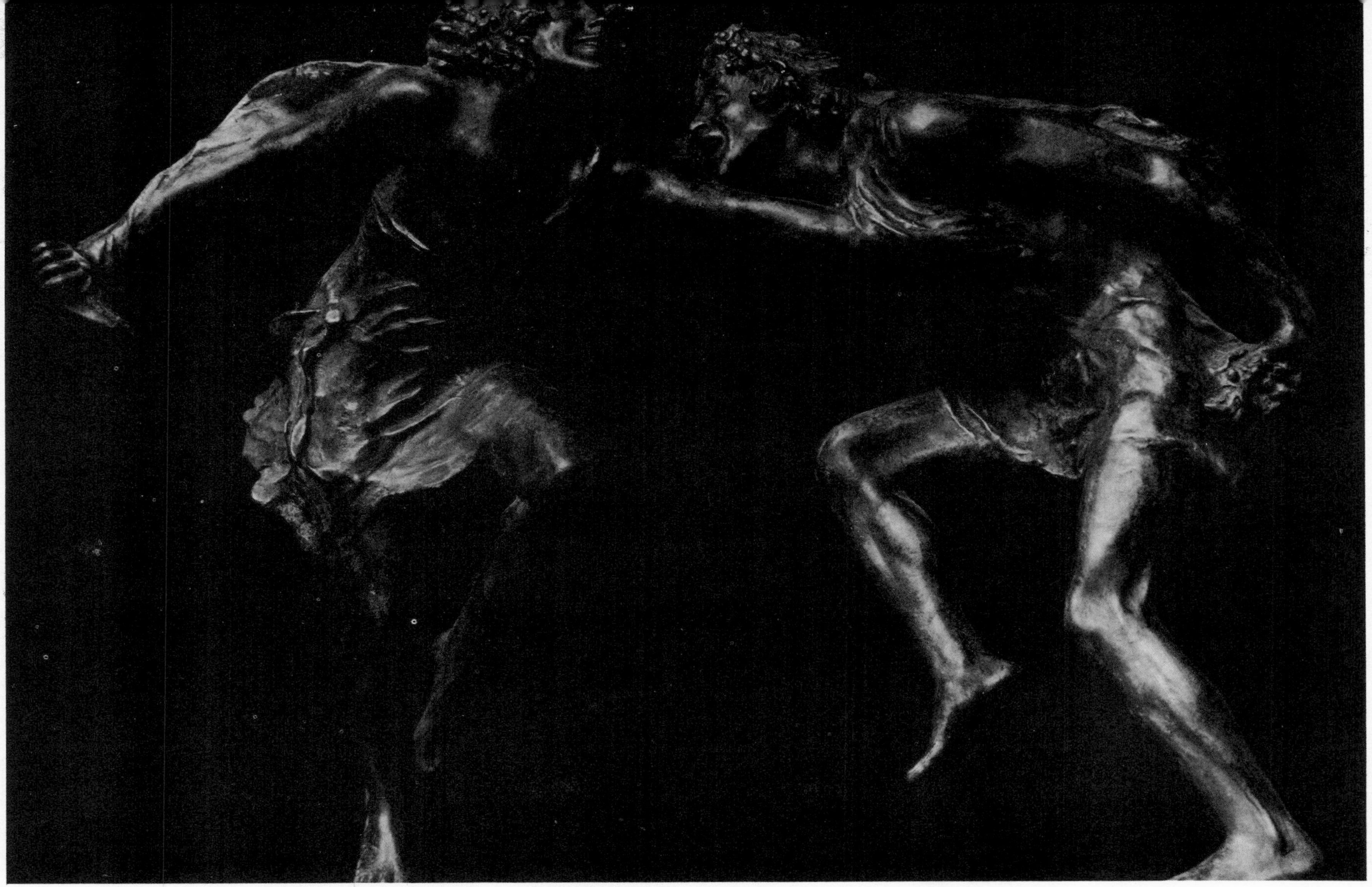

"Russian Dancers" (© *MH*)

We enjoyed visiting my cousin Herbert Haseltine in his splendid studio in Passy, luxuriously equipped to model equestrian statues. In large cages around the garden he kept a leopard, parakeets, monkeys, snakes, and all sorts of animals and birds, a place of enchantment for those who loved animals!

Knowing my constant need for models to paint, my patient little mother willingly submitted to posing. I made a number of studies in oil that were later to help me do a marble portrait of her, but it took years of thought before I felt capable of undertaking such a task. I felt if she were to pose forever I could never achieve a worthy interpretation of her spiritual qualities. I used to call her my "mother of sorrows"; suffering had left unmistakable lines on her delicate, sensitive face, and there was nothing in the books about how to reveal such inner serenity.

About this time Janet Scudder engaged me as a studio helper, knowing I needed work. She said if I would do the work, she could use me for half a day, preparing clay out of barrels, getting it in good condition for modeling, and then building up, from six- or eight-inch sketches, fountain-size figures such as babies playing with dolphins. I was able to do this work satisfactorily, and she let me use her front studio in the afternoons. She was from the Midwest, had a slow drawl, and took life at a relaxed pace, but sometimes smoldering embers ignited. I had lunch with her every day, and we got to know each other well. Then, on her own, she broached the subject of Florence. She had felt something ominous in my connection with her terrifying experience there—and it *had* been terrifying. In the room she had been occupying at Mabel Dodge's, a ghost not only had broken the mirror but had also spoken to her about murder. "The result was, when I got back to Paris, I told the maid not to let anybody of your name in. That's why you couldn't get in at first." I had the feeling that she was still upset.

Through Janet I met Frederick MacMonnies, who was living and working at Giverny. Janet had been a pupil of his, and she rented a peasant's stone house there in which the owner, Mère Porchet, cooked the meals. She washed the heavy linen sheets on the banks of the river, a tributary of the Seine that wound through the valley toward Les Andelys under the shoulder of the high hill on which stood the ruins of Richard Cœur de Lion's fortress, the Château-Gaillard. Often we went over to see MacMonnies in his studio, which adjoined the house. This thin, elderly faun with the mischievous bright eyes worked with nervous movements while his remarks fell like a shower of sparks, often singeing some of his listeners.

Not far away Claude Monet was painting his famous water-lily garden, remote from the outside world. I loved to watch this gentle old man in the long linen blouse and wide-brimmed straw hat as he wandered about the garden, crossed the little footbridge, chose the exact spot to set up his easel, opened his camp stool, and began painting his beloved lilies.

In Janet's front studio I made the portrait of William Astor Chanler who had recently returned from a safari across Africa. He posed in his linen burnoose and regaled me with endless tales of travel and adventures, puffing a cigarette the entire time. So lurid were some of his tales that we decided to inscribe on the pedestal of his portrait "A brother of lions and a companion of owls." This bust was exhibited with the one of my father at the Salon des Beaux-Arts in 1911.

Mr. Chanler took me on many delightful trips to show me the neighboring countryside and environs of Paris, not omitting horse races at Longchamps and luscious tea parties at Rumpelmayer's. As a souvenir of a drive to Pierrefonds, he gave me a set of dinner plates depicting the life of a young man of the fourteenth century. "Someday you will have a home of your own, Malvina, and then they will be useful and remind you of today." And as I write this today, I still use these plates and I still have the complete dozen!

Then came my first north-light studio in Paris, at 72 rue Notre Dame-des-Champs. This great new installation was up two flights of squeaking wooden stairs, and had a tap of water down the hall, and a concierge with the inevitable black cat. It was a stage setting worthy of a scene in *La Bohème*. My first commission in this little studio, the portrait of Robert Bacon, then our ambassador to France, nearly paralyzed me with fright. His big limousine, with two men in livery, would drive up, causing a flurry of curiosity in the quarter. He would often come in polo togs on his way to Bagatelle, and his good humor and hearty laughter would soon set me at ease; but modeling his portrait was a major test, and caused me many a week of struggle. Each sitting I made drastic changes, and I often felt a fierce desperation: What if I failed in such an important task? But with patience we brought the portrait to a satisfactory completion.

In June, Mother and I left our furnished rooms to install ourselves in a studio and alcove at the well-known artists' abode—17 rue Campagne-Première. We piled our belongings on a rickety *voiture à bras* (hand truck) and followed it on foot to our new address. There we could keep house, sleep, and work to our hearts' content. We even rented an upright piano, and dear Ma, though so many years past her girlhood talent for music, found to her delight and mine that she could quickly refresh her memory and soon had quite a repertoire. Many of the pieces were old favorites of Father's or songs I had sung to Sam, and it was a kind of balm to hear them again. We had suffered from the absence of music in our daily life, and our sorrow found comfort in these hours of singing and playing, in our first Parisian home.

We took a trip down the Seine; the silvery fronds of the willows trailed their tips in the water, and the clouds were massed in splendid chaotic sky mountains as we went in a little river boat to Bas-Meudon where for the first time I saw the romantic country shores of the Seine. Corot's trees smiled familiarly, and the forests beyond drew me toward their deep shadows.

After luncheon at a little riverside café, Pêche Miraculeuse, we strolled along the shore and witnessed a water tournament then in full swing. From the woods came a haunting flourish of huntsmen's horns, that even now resounds in my memory. The *Joute Ancienne* on the river held our attention for over an hour, and we joined the cheering crowd as the fighter on the raised platform in the prow of one of the boats was catapulted into the water by a long pole held by his opponent. Gondola-shaped boats competed twice yearly in this affair, an echo of medieval times.

Wonderful days of study were relieved by such diversions. Emanuele de Rosales had come to Paris as he planned, and gave me lessons. He was like a medieval craftsman. He worked meticulously; he was a perfectionist and was slow to complete anything. I tended to be more fluent, but I learned from him and was helped by him. He took a particular interest in my Pavlova and Mordkin "Bacchanale" and several other small studies of Pavlova and her company that I was doing. Pavlova had danced in Paris and I had seen her again, but I had to work mainly from memory. I knew that what I would do wouldn't be finished work; it would be an *esquisse,* or sketch. But I believed I could catch something and I was burning to try. I wanted to show Pavlova and Mordkin running together; I wanted to show that new kind of freedom in the dance. Since of course I didn't have her or members of her company to pose for me, I used models to reinforce my memory. This is standard procedure; it's something you learn. You don't make a literal copy in any of your work.

Rosales guided me with great sympathy and understanding. He showed me how a model would move around in such a way that you could catch the pose or construction you needed. He once sent me his own model Loulou with a note saying that, as he was leaving the city, he would be unable to use her, but for the balance of her engagement she would pose for me free of cost. From her I got necessary anatomical detail. For Mordkin I used Ventry, another model. Though not a dancer himself, he had the same kind of strong, limber legs as dancers. Rosales found other models for me, and so I managed to make my likenesses.

All this was along with my regular studies. I spent intense hours at the Louvre, analyzing, trying to identify the techniques of the great masters of painting and fathom the secrets of Egyptian and Greek sculpture.

After my day's study or work, Ma and I often sat in the Luxembourg Gardens late in the afternoons, watching the children sail their little boats in the pool or listening to the music under the trees beside the Medici Fountain. When the drums announced closing time, we could wander past Jean-Baptiste Carpeaux's fountain above the rearing bronze horses by Emmanuel Fremiet, and watch the crisp new moon cut its crescent light across the dark water. We would salute the aristocratic and spirited statue of Maréchal Ney by Rude, near the Closerie des Lilas, and slowly wend our way homeward along the Boulevard Montparnasse.

At that time many American sculptors were working in and near Paris. The first time I met Paul Bartlett in his studio he was just then covering a huge clay figure with wet rags. I liked the way he tossed one of these over to me and told me to climb up and cover the head; this heroic equestrian statue of Lafayette, which now stands before the Louvre, dominated the place. Later I enjoyed watching him make his own bronzes by the lost-wax method; patining them with a blowtorch and various acids, then dousing them with cold water to anneal their surfaces. Like Rosales, he believed in fine craftsmanship.

Andrew O'Connor was another American sculptor who lived in 17 rue Campagne-Première. This was, and still is, a familiar address to many Americans; Mahonri Young; Paul Dougherty, the painter; William Stanley Hayter, the surrealist etcher; and many others have had their studios there.

Many evenings we walked along the banks of the Seine or went to the Concerts Touche on the Boulevard de Strasbourg; twenty excellent musicians played together, and we could buy a fauteuil for 1 franc 25 centimes and sit at a little table where a refreshing "bock blond" was served, or other gentle beverages. The Concerts Rouges also provided good musical programs.

I recall meeting the gifted young French painter Emanuel Gondouin, whose work was well in advance of his time; his fine Greek profile and the musical voice in which he read aloud the poems of Victor Hugo in the late afternoons in the gardens of Versailles, where we had spent the day lunching on bread and cheese and red wine, seemed to me the epitome of an art student's life. So intense was his admiration of Hugo's works that he finally saved enough money to buy a complete edition at a secondhand bookstore, whereupon he took a tiny room at Versailles and lived there for months until he had completed all the volumes, existing the while on bread, potatoes, and milk.

On rare occasions there were gatherings of the artistic and literary élite on the roof of Mrs. Georgie Duval's luxurious apartment on the Quai d'Orsay. The windows opened on a terrace overlooking the Seine and the Place de la Concorde, and on moonlit nights we enjoyed hearing renditions of eighteenth century music by the best musicians from the Conservatoire. Then followed readings by poets or solos by singers and pianists. Jean Cocteau was often one of the guests, a young man already invested with an aura of the intense and the avant-garde.

On Sundays Mother and I would take the omnibus over to the Place Victor Hugo and lunch with my aunt, Lady Drummond. Her apartment in Avenue de Malakoff was a labyrinth of Dresden ornaments, paintings, and rare furniture. Like all others in Aunt Lily's presence, we were on our best behavior. When she entered a room, she moved like a princess. She was tall with lovely features— de race in every gesture, a perfect wife for the distinguished diplomat, Sir Victor Arthur Wellington Drummond, godson of the Duke of Wellington. Though safely removed from the world of art, they took a lively interest in what I was doing. I told them of my first group of "Russian Dancers" that I was exhibiting in Paris and about which one critic wrote: "This bronze is imbued with joy and motion transformed into sculpture. . . ." This and other notices had given me a good send-off, and the show did well, for any fresh approach was considered "news." It was in the sense of motion and immediacy that I differed from Rosales. I wasn't medieval. I was, in intent at least, as modern as Pavlova herself. It was a beginning, and much was to come of it, in my own work and in the impetus it seemed to give other sculptors to interpret the dance.

SIR VICTOR DRUMMOND

LADY DRUMMOND

CHAPTER ELEVEN

AUGUSTE RODIN:
1910—1917

My FRIENDSHIP with Rodin began in 1910, and at the start was beset with obstacles. I had presented a letter of introduction at his studio five successive times; each day some excuse was given by the concierge and the letter returned to me—the fifth trip found me in rather a desperate mood, so I added to the letter from Gutzon Borglum a verbal message from Mrs. Simpson, Rodin's great friend in New York, and to my relief and astonishment Rodin sent for me to come to his studio at once. It was about the noon hour, and as I entered the big door of the studio in the rue de l'Université (*dépôt des marbres*), I faced a group of six or seven *députés* in black coats, each with a red rosette in his lapel—*La Tomate,* as the French call it.

Rodin, wearing his velvet tam-o'-shanter, stepped forward and shook my hand. I noticed the letter still unopened in his other hand and I ventured to ask him to read it as I knew it contained some comforting remarks about my desire to work, and certain recommendations that I felt might ease my first cold plunge. He smiled and replied that letters never interested him very much, but he was happy to hear I knew Mrs. Simpson. He asked what I wanted to study and what I intended to do in Paris. He gave me the impression of dynamic force; an elemental giant was facing me, short and stocky, with a keen hooded look as he peered out from under a massive brow.

I carried with me two photographs of my own sculpture, which at that time consisted of but two portrait busts, my father and Sam. Rodin looked at them with a critic's eye, seemed to approve, and said, "Good character study—not bad, not bad!" and then, without further ado, joined the group of formidable-looking deputies. When, shortly afterward, he faltered in trying to quote them a poem that described a great marble angel with broken wings, I realized that the verses

115

were familiar to me so I touched his arm and recited the next lines of the poem, picking it up where his memory had failed him: *". . . J'ai perdu presque la fierté qui faisait croire à mon génie."** This was luck, and good luck for me, for Rodin's expression seemed suddenly to soften into gentle astonishment. He motioned me to continue the Musset poem to its end . . . and by the grace of my guardian angel I did so!

Rodin took down a large key from the wall and led me into another studio filled with marbles and plaster groups. "Now, my child, you are at home. I will leave you here to look at whatever you please and I will return later. I am off now to a formal *déjeuner* with these gentlemen, so *au revoir!*" He closed the door, which he locked from the outside, and I was left alone with this new white world of marble.

After exploring and uncovering everything for an hour or more, I selected a small, carefully modeled hand in plaster and began to make drawings. After a while I realized that I was both cold and hungry; it was long after two o'clock when the Maître returned, knocking at his own door before entering. I called, "Come in, if you can," and the key turned and in he came, smiling most genially. Immediately aware of the cold dampness inside, he threw fuel on the stove fire, inquired if I had felt cold, and if I had lunched before coming. On finding that I had not, he became very concerned, took off his long cape, and wrapped it around my shoulders, seriously advising me to care for my health above all things. He looked at the little plaster hand on the model stand and raised his eyebrows questioningly. I told him I had covered up the marbles because their number bewildered me, and that I had tried to concentrate on one hand and one drawing. "Can you draw, Mademoiselle?" "I *think* I can," was my naïve reply, but after his first criticism I had no such illusion. "You have the *sacré* American facility for making sketches. Michelangelo never made a sketch, he made only drawings." Slowly tearing up my first attempts, he said very solemnly: "You must also never make anything but careful drawings; take this plaster hand home with you, and make a series of studies from all sides. Now quickly go to your *déjeuner* and come back here next week to continue your studies." He lifted a rag hanging on a nail on the wall. "Here you see where my keys are for the other studios; you may use them, but always put them back before leaving, and cover them with this cloth."

This visit set things moving for me, and I plunged into work of my own all day long, except when I spent half the day as a studio apprentice with Janet Scudder. In the evening I had classes at Colarossi's School, and each week I carried my studies to Rodin for criticism. When I was lucky, I would spend Sunday with him at Meudon, his country place, seven miles outside Paris, overlooking the Seine. We gradually became good friends, lunching together, going through the sculpture galleries of the Louvre, and walking in his wild and beautiful garden near the Invalides, back of the Hôtel Biron on the rue de Varenne, the one-time convent of the Sacré-Cœur. My construction of French

* *I have almost lost the pride that made me believe in my genius.*

A STUDY OF RODIN BY MH

sentences amused him highly, and as my conjugation of the verbs was very limited, he used to call me *"l'enfant des infinitifs."*

During that period, Rodin made many studies of Cambodian dancers, their
lithe arms waving in sinuous motion; then a mask in wax of a Japanese dancer,
Hanako, and a series of drawings of Loie Fuller, the American dancer who used
voluminous soft draperies in lines of rhythmic motion.

I remember how excited we both were after seeing Nijinsky dance his
"L'Après-midi d'un faune." The next day I urged Rodin to tell me his impressions of the Ballet Russe. He said thoughtfully: "It was Youth in all its glory,
like the days of ancient Greece, when they knew the power and beauty of a
human body, and revered it. Such grace, such *souplesse!* An evening to be remembered forever. Go often, Malvina—it is a revelation to inspire us all. They
have recovered the soul of tradition founded on respect and love of Nature.
That's why they are able to express all the emotions of the human soul. . . ."
After seeing Nijinsky, Rodin wrote, in May, 1912:

> A faun dozes
> Nymphs dupe him
> A forgotten scarf fulfills his dream
> The curtain falls so that the poem
> May begin in everybody's memory. . . .

When I showed Rodin the first study I made of the Russian dancers, the
"Bacchanale" danced by Pavlova and Mordkin, he asked me what emotion I had
tried to express. *"La joie, l'ivresse!"* joy, intoxication! I answered. He studied the
group for a long time in silence, and then said: "The difference between ecstasy
and tragedy is no greater than the thickness of a sheet of tissue paper. When
you carry joy to its full intensity like this, you are already on the borderline of
exquisite pain. Don't forget that these dancers could be drunk with joy or mad
with despair. It is all so closely interwoven in human life! Socrates once said that
Joy and Pain should have been a fabled creature with one head and two bodies,
so inevitably do they go together and follow each other!"

Perhaps the most surprising and significant lesson I ever had was in Rodin's
studio soon after I had begun my studies under his direction. One day he led me
into a room adjoining his salon and showed me five or six portraits in marble and
bronze. "Choose one of these," he said, "and examine it carefully while I look
over some letters. I will return in twenty minutes." He left and closed the door.
I suspected I was in for some sort of examination or acid test.

In half an hour he returned and told me to follow him into the next studio,
where he pointed to the clay bin and said: "Now show me how accurate your
observations were. Model for me the head you selected in the other room, from
memory, about half the size of the original. French clay is strong, and you will
not need any support or armature." So saying he closed the door and locked it
from the other side—*à double tour* ("double-locked") as they say in French.

As a test of memory this was *it*. My heart was pounding, and I knew I had
to burn through my fog of panic. Memory is both illusive and piercingly bright.

Rodin's studio

Once started, I was carried along by some inner sight that re-created the forms that had impressed their planes upon my mind. Gradually the face took on the look of the gaunt and severe personality I had selected without knowing who it was. The expression of the eyes and general outline of the head were so unusual that my memory had caught them, but when it came to other details I found that they had not registered.

Rodin returned, asking me if I had completed my task. I said Yes, as far as my memory would guide me! He took the clay head and examined it from all sides. *"Pas mal, mon enfant!"* (Not bad, my child!) He led me back to the original bronze in the little gallery. "Now," he said, "in five minutes check your mistakes and bring it to me. Then I will take you to lunch at l'Avenue's!" Before we left, he placed the clay on a high shelf in a closet so that it might dry and harden. "You will come back in a few days, and it will be like stone. I want you to keep it for a reminder. You will never forget this lesson, for most people *look* at things without *seeing* them, and very few know the value of cultivating memory. But you will need to do this *all your life!* Don't forget it."

A trip to Rodin's Villa des Diamants and museum in Meudon on Sunday was my reward for a week of hard work. There we would chat and experiment with pieces of plaster casts that he would fit together, recomposing them into imaginary groups, pushing lumps of wax between the fragments to hold them in position. We would walk in the garden and explore the vast collection in the museum, and sometimes go down the road for luncheon at the wayside café.

He urged me to take up the study of dissection during the coming winter in New York. Knowledge of anatomy, he felt, was of major importance; he said he had always regretted not having had a chance to do any dissecting. The study he recommended for me was made possible through the kindness of Dr. George Huntington at the College of Physicians and Surgeons in New York, where I worked for three winters under his direction. These sessions at the college took all the nerve and willpower I could muster, but they gave me a fundamental understanding of the construction of the human body.

In my old diary I find the words of Nietzsche: "Tu t'es toujours approchée familièrement de toutes les choses terribles. . . ."*

The spring came after the first winter of these studies, and Ma and I returned to Paris. Living and working in the building next to my studio was a very talented young woman, Mademoiselle O'Donnell, who sometimes carved for Rodin. Her admiration and devotion to the Master possessed her to such a point that if he failed to keep an appointment to see how her work was progressing, she would come to me and burst into tears, imagining all sorts of exaggerated reasons for his absence. Had she cut too deeply? Was he displeased with her execution? I tried to calm her, for she was high-strung and lonely, living on the edge of an emotional precipice. Once I went to see Rodin and asked him to try to go to her studio soon, for I feared she would have a nervous breakdown.

A few months later another *crise* was enacted in my studio; she begged me to return with her to see what she was carving. When I had admired her tech-

* *Thou hast always approached all terrible things familiarly.*

nical skill, she thanked me for my sympathetic understanding and gave me three or four good marble tools. "Keep these," she said. "They were given me by Rodin, but I feel he is no longer interested in my work. He has grown very indifferent, and I feel ill and discouraged."

As I left, I felt a painful premonition of impending tragedy. Her deep-set eyes seemed to have a hopeless staring look, and her voice sounded hollow, without vibration.

The next morning her concierge said as I arrived, "Oh, Mademoiselle— something terrible has happened to Mlle. O'Donnell!" I ran up the stairs to my friend's studio. The concierge followed me inside the door and clutched my arm. The studio was empty. "Oh, Mademoiselle," she groaned, "I smelled gas in the hallway and tried to get into her studio, but it was locked. I ran for help, and they broke open the door and found Mademoiselle lying dead on the floor, the gas tube tied over her mouth with a towel. They took her away!" Here, indeed, I was approaching *"les choses terribles."*

During the winter of 1912, Mother and I attended the opening of the Rodin Collection at the Metropolitan Museum in New York. I wrote an account of it to Rodin that seemed to please him, for he answered: ". . . Your description of the day made it a happy one for me; because they opened my exhibition, and because you were there to send me this note about it . . . *mes souvenirs de grande sympathie.* . . . Aug. Rodin."

He asked me to send him photographs of my work and keep him informed about my studies. After receiving them he wrote: ". . . Ma chère Malvina, chère élève: Votre travail est béni, parce que vous travaillez avec votre cœur. Vous avez le sentiment, vous êtes d'un pays énergique. . . . Vous avez de belles armures. . . ."*

How such simple words could give new courage and patience to his pupil in New York! And again the words of wisdom written after hearing that I had been ill and exhausted and obliged to stop work and go to the country:

"Ma chère Malvina: La lassitude que vous ressentez est toujours la compagne des efforts que vous faites. Ne vous effrayez pas. . . . Modérez vos productions à vos forces . . . permettez-vous un repos chaque fois à la campagne, et jouissez du bonheur de vivre! Votre Maître et ami . . . Aug. Rodin."†

From Roquebrune-Cap-Martin, where he had gone after a severe attack of influenza, he wrote me: ". . . Je vous félicite d'avoir vendu un groupe en bronze. Votre ardeur au travail est récompensé déjà, maintenant il ne faut pas quitter ce sentiment de vigueur . . . l'équilibre de la santé est la base pour avoir la force de produire de l'art. . . ."‡

---

* *My dear Malvina, dear pupil: Your work is blessed because you work with your heart. You have sensibility, you are from a vigorous country. . . . You have fine equipment.*

† *My dear Malvina: The fatigue you feel always accompanies the efforts you make. Don't be frightened. . . . Adjust your output to your energy . . . allow yourself a rest each time in the country, and enjoy living! Your Master and friend . . . Aug. Rodin.*

‡ *I congratulate you on having sold a bronze group. Your eagerness to work is already rewarded, now don't give up this sense of power . . . stability of health is basic if you are to have the strength to produce art. . . .*

My first stay in Paris had been for about sixteen months; twice later I returned for the summer only, always working under Rodin's direction. During these summers the Sunday visits to Meudon continued, and during my second summer Sam sometimes accompanied me. I had mentioned Sam to Rodin, and asked if he was fond of music. He said that when there was a good interpretative playing of Mozart or Bach, he enjoyed it. So it was arranged that Sam should come and bring his violin.

We made the little journey by one of the Seine boats that travel up and down the river. Rodin greeted Sam warmly and took him on a preliminary tour of his studio, showing him both his own work and his collection of antique sculpture. Then he brought Rose Beuret into the studio to listen to Sam play. Both he and Rose seemed genuinely moved, and later he wrote out the following statement:

> At last I have found an artist who can play and understand the classics. I can perceive the trace of ancient art in his fingers, the echoes of another time in his interpretation. In him I find the elements of a great artist. He is bound to succeed, but perhaps not at once, as the public is hardly accustomed to this refinement and purity of style. Many great modern artists have played for me these same things of Bach and Mozart, but never as Grimson has done today, never with such reverence and supreme understanding.

He said to Sam in one of his typical bursts of advice: "Ah, my young friend, you are on the right road, but you must not be discouraged if the way is long. Have courage and patience; you will win in the end. Let nothing tempt you to deviate from this chosen path, even if at first you do not find the appreciation you deserve. The public must be led and convinced; after that, the world is yours. You have the reserve of the great masters. Your art is warm, vibrant, and healthy. Of all the players who have come to me, I have never asked one to return, but if you will come again and let me listen to you, I will be grateful."

Rodin removed his velvet cap, and taking Sam's hand in his, he said, "Si mon pauvre opinion vous vaut quelque chose, le voilà et je vous donne les félicitations de tout mon cœur."*

This generous outgoingness was typical of my experience with Rodin. And it manifested itself not only during my summers when I worked directly with him, but even during the winters when I was away.

In July, 1914, while in Sussex, England, with my mother, and shortly after the news flashed around the world that the Archduke of Austria had been assassinated in Sarajevo—the torch that was to set off global conflagration—I received a cable from Rodin. He told me that he had expected to arrange and attend an exhibit of his works at the Duke of Westminster's house in London, that he had been taken suddenly ill and would not be able to come from Paris.

---

* If you value my poor opinion somewhat, there it is, and I congratulate you with all my heart.

. . . He therefore requested that I go at once to London and supervise the placing of his bronzes and marbles, and then, with the Comtesse de Greffühle, that I attend the formal opening as his representative.

This request was to me nothing short of a command. Mother and I packed our bags and left Sussex for London. Presenting my telegram to those in charge at the Duke's mansion, I began to direct the unpacking of the cases and placing the groups with the aid of skilled workmen. On the second day one or two titled ladies of high position appeared, fancied that they would like to place the things differently, and tried to crowd me into a corner. I held on, however, at the sacrifice of my popularity. Finally, at noon, I sank exhausted into a chair, two hours before the Queen and a few royal guests were to arrive and open the exhibit.

To my utter amazement the first person to arrive as I was resting in the hallway with the movers was Rodin on the arm of the Comtesse de Greffühle. He was bundled up in a shawl and heavy muffler, and waved me a greeting, explaining that the Comtesse had kidnapped him from Paris and that he was too weak to resist. He asked me if I had carried out all his instructions. I asked him to look over the rooms and change whatever displeased him. The grand ladies were disappointed when he smilingly approved of everything and made no change.

"Well done," he said, "and now let us go!" He bade adieu to all and asked Mr. Hatchard, the Duke's secretary, to call a hansom cab. When it came, he bade me get in and tell the driver to go to my own exhibition at the Leicester Galleries. I had told Rodin before leaving Paris that I was going to London for the opening of this event. He knew very well how much it would mean to me to have him see this first attempt of mine to show my work in a foreign city; surprisingly, he remembered that my show was closing that very afternoon. Even though it was so close to closing, he rebuked the manager for not making more adequate pedestals, and had him rearrange my bronzes in the window! The manager and I were both silenced by the innate authority of this distinguished visitor whose orders were promptly followed.

The Queen and her ladies in waiting attended the private opening of Rodin's exhibit which began at two o'clock. Rodin escorted Her Majesty through the galleries. I was with Mother, and too shy to accept Rodin's suggestion that I should join him in the first gallery where he said he would present me to the Queen. Mother and I discreetly stayed in a small room adjoining his exhibit where we enjoyed gazing at Gainsborough's "The Blue Boy." (Later, it came to America, and I saw it in its new home at the Huntington Library in Pasadena.)

When the Queen and her ladies in waiting left the exhibit, Rodin asked Mr. Hatchard if he knew what had become of me, and Mr. Hatchard disclosed our hiding place. Rodin reprimanded me, saying he felt I should not have missed such a rare occasion to meet Her Majesty under quiet circumstances. Only because the Court was in mourning for Sarajevo had the opening been private.

He handed me a slip of paper with an address, saying he would be attending a tea party and he would expect me to call for him there at six thirty.

This I did, much to the annoyance of all the guests, for he demanded, then and there in their presence, that I supply him with a tree, a garden, and a quiet supper out of doors, or he would perish from the social pressure of London! This was a large order, but I said, "Oui, Maître, ça y est!"—it can be done—and he came out, followed by one of the ladies of the reception committee. Her motor was at the door, and Rodin told me to get in and give the chauffeur directions. I shall never forget her look of astonishment as I gave her the address of St. Dunstan's in Regent's Park, or the heated argument that ensued, for she had been carefully deputized to see that Rodin attended a formal dinner that evening in London. Her words were useless; Rodin had by this time wound his gray worsted muffler entirely about his head, and declined to speak at all, merely indicating with his hand to proceed toward Regent's Park.

As we approached this splendid estate in the heart of London, my courage began to waver. What if my friend Mrs. Otto Kahn, who owned St. Dunstan's, were not at home? We rolled up to the front door, and to my relief the butler said that Mrs. Kahn was upstairs in her room. I bounded up the stairs, two at a time, and pantingly submitted my request—for a tree, a garden, and a dinner for Rodin! Knowing me well, she merely laughed at my impetuosity and said she was dining out and going to the opera, but that I could go ahead and show Rodin onto the terrace and that she would give orders to the butler.

The lady accompanying us had expressed keen disappointment at Rodin's refusal to attend the dinner and the opening of Covent Garden Opera following the banquet. She had not the courage to attend it without him, nor to join the other guests in their box at the opera. I asked Mrs. Kahn if she had any unused tickets for the performance that night, and she at once handed over two splendid ones. Feeling like a highway robber, I ran downstairs and presented the tickets as if it were a matter of course to produce such things at will; the lady accepted the seats with thanks, and drove away.

I then showed Rodin across the terrace to a magnificent tree and garden, where after an hour an excellent dinner with fine red wine was served. . . . "Sorry I cannot stay with you, Hoff!" Mrs. Kahn called to us as she left for her dinner in town.

It was a memorable evening, and we lingered on the terrace until nine o'clock, when I called a taxi and drove Rodin to his hotel in Piccadilly, rested and calmed after his fatiguing day of exhibitions, royalty, and tea parties.

The following day I conducted him to the railway station and saw him off to Paris, wiring our good friend Giselle Bunau-Varilla to meet him and motor him to Meudon. It was a great relief to receive her cable the next morning reporting that the Maître, although very weary, reached his home safely.

Mother and I were living in an apartment on the Boulevard Montparnasse in Paris that summer of 1914, an apartment we had rented for an indefinite period—just how indefinite (the war was soon to evacuate us and send us home) we never suspected! Rodin asked me to assist him in sorting and cataloguing his collection of drawings. As I worked with him, I was greatly encouraged by his constant interest in my studies; quite frequently I would carry in a basket whatever I had in progress, if it was small enough, for his wise criticism, which I would note carefully in my diary. One day as I was about to show him a draped figure of a dancer in plaster, it fell on the floor. The head, one arm, and one leg were broken off.

Rodin quickly picked up the one-legged torso and, turning it slowly in his hand, set it on a table. "Dry your tears, my dear, let me show you that what remains intact is quite sufficient to express your meaning. This fragment suggests the rhythm of the dance and balance of the whole figure. You must learn from this that one must capture the accident and transform it into science!"

At another time we were discussing decorative sculpture for gardens or interiors. He looked at me and pointed his finger warningly. "Promise me, Malvina, that you will never do sculpture to please anyone or to amuse—always be serious, thoughtful, responsible, for this is an art not to be played with!"

A few weeks later came the calamitous news that any day war might be declared. I was still helping Rodin sort his drawings (I urged him to sign many of them) and place certain marbles in the halls and rooms of the Hôtel Biron. He had, not without encountering bureaucratic resistance, given his entire collection of art to the French Government, which in turn had given him the Hôtel Biron for a permanent museum.

About five o'clock, August 2nd, the concierge brought Rodin a cable from England saying they dared not ship back across the Channel the cases containing his work, which had been at Dorchester House. War was too near; everyone was under a cloud of apprehension. Rodin handed me the cable, saying "There it is—War!"

When I asked the concierge how things were going in the streets, and if Paris seemed aware of the cataclysm, he urged Rodin to start for Meudon at once, as he lived seven miles from the city, and if war was declared before he reached the gates the motor that had been loaned to him might be seized by the authorities. So we gathered up some drawings and papers and put Rodin in the car with his faithful plaster caster to accompany him in case of trouble.

I walked all the way home along the Boulevard Montparnasse and saw in the expressions of all who passed that the dreaded monster WAR was at large—indeed, had his fangs deep in the hearts of every living soul. Soldiers were pasting great placards in huge letters on the walls: "Mobilization—ce n'est pas la guerre, citoyens . . . il faut nous préparer contre la menace de nos ennemis!"

The next day a letter from Rodin was delivered to me by his exhausted companion who, though lame, had walked all the way from Meudon to bring it to me and to bring me news of the Maître. Our concern over his safe return to Meudon the day before had been all too well founded. Mobilization had been declared before Rodin's motor passed the gates of Paris, and the soldiers requisitioned the car, forcing Rodin to walk. He and his lame plaster caster started on their weary way and were finally given a lift by a passing peasant's cart. At Meudon, he found that his only horse had been seized, and his workmen called to the colors. Every means of travel had been cut off. In his note to me he enclosed a military telegram that ordered him to remove all his works of art at the Hôtel Biron to the cellar within forty-eight hours!

This was a chance to render my master a real service, for he was literally helpless. His influential friends understandably had their own safety at heart and could not be reached for assistance in this emergency. So I spent about six hours with my friend Giselle, securing necessary police passes; and her father, Colonel Bunau-Varilla, lent us his motorcar to bring Rodin from Meudon to Paris. He gave the necessary orders to the movers, and we spent the next day with six strong men, moving all the bronzes and marbles from the carefully selected positions in the galleries to the storeroom in the basement. This peremptory order was a bitter experience to Rodin. In his old age, at this tragic crisis of history, he was made to feel subservient and abandoned.

Rose Beuret, who had so faithfully served him since girlhood, was aged and feeble. Her story in itself is pathetic and touching. She had come to pose for Rodin, a beautiful girl of nineteen who earned a meager living making artificial flowers. They fell in love and lived together most of their lives. Rodin would often travel to Italy or England and leave Rose for weeks or months at a time; but in spite of his changing moods, volcanic tempers, and love of adventure, he always returned to Meudon to find his devoted slave keeping his home in order, ready to continue her career of self-effacement. She was a peasant by birth, very primitive and instinctive, very jealous, never permitting a servant to enter the house, even as a cook or helper, for the hard cleaning and washing.

August and September, 1914, were two months of frenetic existence, broken dreams, and difficult situations for all of us. Mother was not well, and with the dangerous war front so near, the doctor urged me to take her to America. This meant saying good-bye to Rodin just at the moment when I might be of most use to him. It was he, however, who, after seeing my mother, told me my way led to America without delay. Rodin recognized my mother's rare quality, for he said to me with solemnity one day when I was worried about her: "Your mother is one of the saints; you must care for her with much tenderness . . . her love is a gift from God!"

Rodin and I continued our friendship in occasional letters, and through them I learned that as the war continued and air raids made life at Meudon unlivable, he and Rose went to England for a time. While in London, Rodin, who used to watch the British regiments march past his window, decided, in token of his gratitude to his English brothers who offered their lives to fight with his own French boys, to present to England the entire collection of twenty masterpieces that had been shown at Westminster House and were still detained at the storage docks.

Returning to France, he faced a winter of cold hardship. He realized his health was failing, and decided to marry Rose. They had been partners in youth and age, and after many storms and struggles of poverty, labor, and gradual success, at the height of his fame, these two friends were married at Meudon. Her sufferings seem to have been effaced by this act, for in spite of fragile health her delight and pride were such that all who witnessed the ceremony were moved to tears. Her smile was radiant as Rodin kissed her hand and presented her to his friends like a young bride. Two weeks after the wedding Madame Rodin died. Until the very end she was elated and full of gratitude to her *"soleil,"* as she called him, often speaking of herself as his *"ombre."* She was seventy-six years old.

In 1915 Rodin went to Rome to make a portrait of the Pope, and was happy to find there his friend Ivan Mestrovic, for whose work he had a profound admiration and who lent him a stand, clay, and tools needed for work in the Vatican. Rodin wrote to me: ". . . Je suis à Rome où forcément la beauté de la ville immortelle vous soulage et vous fait du bien. Sa Sainteté ne m'a donné que trois séances. J'ai fait une esquisse. . . ."*

Later in the same year I received a long letter containing the following lines: ". . . l'art, chère amie, c'est si beau, et vous le sentez si bien, le travail qui fait la vie de l'artiste un dieu . . . et la vieillesse est encore heureuse avec . . ."† and again: ". . . après cette guerre, et c'est là la vraie gloire, nous seront plus vrais . . . moins négociant, et espérons que les artistes seront plus vrais. . . . Je vous sens vraie, . . . Rodin."‡

These precious words of friendship and interest in the endeavors of a young artist attest to the simplicity of a great man. Let other critics write as they may; it was a privilege, an honor, to have known Rodin as a friend and Master!

The war dragged on, and Rodin was feeling the strain of the world's misery added to his own burden of advancing years.

It was in 1917, after the hardship of a winter without fuel, that his great spirit folded its wings and was at rest. He was seventy-eight when he died. He and his wife are buried side by side in his little garden at Meudon; a great bronze of "The Thinker" was placed on a granite boulder over the graves, and broods there in solitude.

The man, the student, the sculptor, all complete the story; if one were privileged to know every side of this titanic character one could perhaps evolve the total concept. The sad part of it is that few people did know or study him from many sides. It is the general opinion, I find, that he was a great artist, untamed and violent. He certainly broke the bonds of tradition and gave new freedom to the art of sculpture.

During the years of friendship, when discussing art I never heard him speak lightly of any phase of it. His attitude was that of a passionate student of nature, trying to penetrate into her secrets and willing to sacrifice everything in life for the power to learn the truth of things, and be able to reveal it through his art.

* *I am in Rome where inevitably the beauty of the Eternal City solaces you and does you good. His Holiness has given me only three sittings. I made a sketch.*

† *. . . art, dear friend, is so beautiful, and you feel it so well, the work that makes the life of the artist [like that of] a god . . . and old age is still happy with [it] . . .*

‡ *. . . after this war, and this is the true glory, we shall be truer . . . less mercenary, and let's hope the artists will be truer. . . . I know you are true, . . . Rodin.*

Rodin, MH, Mme. Vivier, and Rose Beuret

Often he was ferocious and volcanic, his emotions were hard to control, and argument was impossible, but there was always a vulnerable spot, and if one could but find it he was helpless. His sense of the beautiful was so keen that at any moment his rage would subside if he could be brought to realize that his words or actions were ugly.

Though basically simple as a child, he was forever experimenting, searching in all the byways for richer color, for more violent contrasts of emotional experience. In spite of his speed and facility in grasping a line or form, he would work for weeks or months at a single figure, struggling to reproduce its true values. To beauty, either in nature or in the human body, he was an abject slave.

His original plaster casts illuminate his careful study of detail and form. Every surface and plane is studied and certain; afterward they were put in marble, often greatly enlarged, and he would sometimes leave places in the stone uncut and vague, but purposeful. This was taken to be a mannerism or weakness, often causing the casual critic to say that it was a pity Rodin never carved his marbles to a finish, or that he never learned to model hands or feet.

No sculptor's collection comprises so many careful and finished studies of hands and feet as Rodin's. I have sorted nearly two thousand of his drawings myself, and although the later ones are often a single line to catch a motion or continuance of form like the swift thrust of a rapier, the early drawings made on menus, billheads, or laundry lists are as direct and powerful as Michelangelo's.

It is true that many sculptors worked with him and helped him carve his marbles. Is there a sculptor who ever created such a world of marble who did not avail himself of extra hands? Rodin's brain was so teeming with ideas that not even three or four carvers could keep up with his fertile vision.

His constant concern for the welfare of those in whom he had confidence was remarkable. I, among others, can bear witness to many instances of his encouragement and to his understanding of the times of stress through which an artist with an honest conscience is bound to have to fight his way.

It is often thought that art is a form of recreation, indulged in by those who shun hardship. The true artist is never at rest, and such a giant as Rodin labors at his work with passionate devotion, from early morning until dark; indeed, after daylight fades, the dreaming muse begins to torment the mind until it can plunge again into manual expression.

The principles on which art is built are fundamentally the same as those of life itself. Sincerity of soul, accuracy of the outward and inward eye, constancy and patience are indispensable to any real accomplishment, be it art or merely living, perhaps the greatest art of all.

CHAPTER TWELVE

SEVERAL SCARES

DURING OUR first year in Paris, in 1910, Mother and I seemed to whirl in a vortex of excitement. One of our more dramatic moments involved as chief actors the poet D'Annunzio and a French actress. "La Comtesse," as she was known, had noticed sympathetically my insatiable desire to study French poetry. She often spent an evening with us reciting poems or declaiming the part she was studying in a play by D'Annunzio, called *La Femme malade de toutes les fièvres*. It was all very stimulating and new to me, and Mother enjoyed the recitations, and could in turn recite verses from Victor Hugo, De Musset, and other favorites.

Suddenly the Comtesse was taken ill, and telephoned to ask if Mother and I would come at once to her apartment. We hurried off, Mother with her usual foresight taking a hot-water bottle, ice bag, and thermometer. We found the door to our friend's apartment ajar; she was in bed.

Her maid had gone away for the weekend, and she was evidently alarmed and almost delirious, at moments reciting lines from her *Femme malade* and at other moments thrashing about on the pillows. Mother took her temperature and found it to be 104 degrees. We were afraid to ask who her doctor was (how might she react?), so I was sent off to the nearest restaurant to buy ice, and hurried back with it. The ice bag was put behind her neck and cold cloths applied to her forehead, and Mother gradually calmed her patient and told me to stand guard in the next room and see to it that no visitors were admitted.

As it was Sunday afternoon, many interesting people appeared, but when I explained the situation they expressed their sympathy politely and departed. I felt I was doing very well as a French maid, when the bell rang sharply and, the moment I opened it a crack, I was brushed unceremoniously aside. The man who entered tossed his hat on the table and removed his coat. "But, Monsieur," I said (I had recognized D'Annunzio), "Madame is very ill with high fever and cannot receive you today." D'Annunzio gave me a disdainful look. "This does not concern you, Mademoiselle. I shall go in!" and in he went.

130

Mother had left her patient to refill the ice bag in the kitchen, so I watched through the French doors leading to the bedroom and saw D'Annunzio standing at the foot of the bed, peering like Svengali at the hypnotized Comtesse. "It is good that you have a high fever today!" he said loudly. "Now recite your lines, and we will get a true interpretation . . . the best, the only way that this part can be understood and well acted!"

There was absolutely nothing we could do. Two artists were on fire, and Mother and I decided we had better keep out of the way. So we stayed in the kitchen. We could hear the hysterical voice of the patient reciting vehemently and passionately, and the occasional commands and criticisms of the Italian poet spurring her on; after an hour there was silence and we heard the outer door at the end of the hall slam. He had gone—after reducing La Comtesse to a state of complete collapse. Mother again soothed and quieted her and replaced the ice bag. We stayed until late evening when the maid returned and took charge, and we made our way across the city in the last tram to the Montparnasse corner of our street.

"Well, Malvina," said Mother, "now you have seen 'the way of a man with a maid,' and 'the way of a serpent upon a rock'! There is often cruelty and pain mixed with love!"

It was not surprising that living under constant emotional tension would prove more than my physique could endure.

One of the exasperating symptoms of my illness was a constant hunger, and to placate it I had been indulging in too many cups of coffee and brioches snatched up at any sidewalk café and relished like some secret vice. My ravenous appetite was the more inconvenient as we were practicing the strictest economy. Just at this time, and at the height of my strange condition, my sister Helen and her husband Dr. Draper were due in Paris, although Mother and I did not know exactly on what day they would appear. One evening Mother prepared a fine supper complete to what she called "a filling dessert"—all of which instantly vanished—when the bell rang. "If this happens to be someone who wants to take me out to dinner, please, Mother, don't say that we've eaten!" I ran to the door, and there stood Helen and Will, wreathed in smiles. "We've just arrived and have come to take you both out to dinner tonight to celebrate." I gave Mother a meaningful glance and said, "Wonderful, we'd love to go to a good restaurant, *hurrah!*" Mother was obviously nonplussed, but ever resourceful said, "Malvina would love to go, but I had an early supper and have a lot of mending to do; you all go out and enjoy yourselves, and come and lunch with us tomorrow."

Somehow I felt I had overshot my mark, but off we went, and no one could have enjoyed a spree more than I did that night. Having heard much about the culinary art of Marguery's, I was at a high pitch of excitement when we reached the restaurant, and the delicious sole Marguery more than lived up to its reputation—to say nothing of the crêpes Suzette prepared out of a flaming chafing dish and ceremoniously wheeled up by the maître d'hôtel.

To top off the evening we went to a play, and during intermission I suggested that we wander in the foyers where I knew refreshments were served. We had hot chocolate and whipped cream, a treat popular at the time. Will seemed to be watching me somewhat suspiciously, but merely mentioned that although I seemed to have a very good appetite I looked too thin and pale to suit him. I felt the sword of Damocles hanging over my guilty head. The following morning it fell, and I was soundly taken to task for overworking—going to drawing classes at night and overliving during the days—all resulting in a severe case of anemia. Will called in another doctor for consultation, and together they ordered me to leave Paris with Mother and go to an obsolutely quiet place where I must follow a strict regime of rest and diet.

This decision was in a way a tremendous relief to me, after an uphill struggle of weeks, afraid to say how ill and unfit I felt. So I confessed that I had resorted to raw eggs and brandy to keep up my strength. My Daemon had been driving me along on what was left of my nervous energy; the days and nights were too short for the endless studies I had embarked upon; acute dramatic situations burned all about me with a fascinating incandescence. So it was decided that we should go to the forest of Loches where we had rooms in a little *auberge* at the edge of the woods, quiet, far from Paris's electric turmoil.

Notes from Mother's diary: ". . . We must go back now a few centuries to Charles VII and Louis XI. On the tomb of Agnès Sorel is her effigy with her little feet against two tiny ewe lambs; the stairs connecting the apartments are narrow and winding; the old chestnut tree in the courtyard was planted by Francis I, the last monarch who inhabited the château."

Carved over the portal is a poem by Voltaire to Agnès Sorel.

Under the flickering of a rusty lantern we were guided by a lighthearted young girl with peach-bloom cheeks and a glittering smile into the chilly blackness of the vault where Sforza was caged for ten years; and when he was told he was to be released he fell dead. Little wonder after such hell! His only excitement was to see his fellow prisoners dragged into the antechamber from which they were pitched headlong into a bottomless pit with jagged blades projecting all the way down, their shrieks and moans intensifying his misery.

"In the next cell the father of Diane of Poitiers was held for three years. Her one ambition was to liberate her father and make up to him for years of imprisonment." To do this, the story goes, she became the mistress of Francis I, but actually her husband's influence unlocked the jail.

Each day we drove along different roads in the forest, the great trees restoring us by their dignity and quietude.

In those days boar hunting was in full swing in the forest. One day a white boar had been killed, and the dogs and horsemen came rushing from all directions to the clearing where Mother and I, in our peasant equipage, had halted for a rest. With gallantry typical of the grand seigneur, the leading huntsman rode up to us and asked if we would like to join the party and return with them to his château of Montrésor and witness the ceremony of dividing the boar, inviting us to be his guests at the hunt breakfast. We accepted with alacrity, and our own amusement at the way we looked, in our primitive cart with a colossal white horse, helped to make the expedition informal and full of laughter. The Duc de Montrésor must have had a sense of humor to include us in his triumphant entry to the château courtyard, with the white boar carried on four spears ahead of him.

On our return to the inn a letter from Paris notified me that my plaster portrait of Father, which had been sent to my first Salon exhibit, had received First Honorable Mention. This provided a strong tonic to hasten my recovery.

Returning to Paris, restored and ready for life again, I began going to the informal evenings of music and recitations at Janet Scudder's studio. Two sensitive Danish musicians whom we called the "Great Danes"—Eva Mudocci and Belle Edwards—played violin and piano duets, and each time I would have the desperate, almost crazed awareness that I could never hear Father's music again.

One evening an exotic-looking little woman who claimed to be a Buddhist came swathed in veils and scarlet robes. It was suggested that I serve as the recording medium for an evening of automatic writing. It proved to be a hair-raising message from the ghost that had haunted Janet in Florence when I was there—the planchette wrote swiftly, and I found it difficult to keep up with my secretarial duties as sometimes the ghost spoke in French and then in English, claiming that she had lived in the villa now occupied by Mabel Dodge, and had been murdered by one of the former owners. Janet, who of course was at the seance, was mentioned as the recipient of this message and ordered to go to Florence and trace any possible clue to the whereabouts of the ghost's child: "Madame M is being cared for by the peasants of Tuscana, but you must go and find her." Now we asked the board where this child was; we asked from every angle: questions as to where Janet could find her, in what street, who would know this person, but no usable information was forthcoming.

The experience was rather an eerie initiation into spiritualistic phenomena. Janet was so shaken by it that, in spite of the lack of definite information, she promptly packed and went back to Florence. After a week of futile hunting and questionings, she returned, calmed and convinced that since she had carried out her mission the ghost would not return to disrupt her life, and I don't think she was tormented again.

A strange episode occurred now that might be called "Kidnapped in Paris." It followed a literary tea at Mildred Aldrich's, author of *Hilltop on the Marne*. Many writers and artists were at the party, but one very *chic dame* attracted my attention by her pallid masklike countenance and beautiful clothes. She came up to me and began a pleasant conversation, saying that she had heard of my studies of Russian Ballet and that she knew many of the dancers themselves, and if I enjoyed the theatre she would like to take me to the Odéon or to the Opéra-Comique. Naturally, I was happy to accept. After a time the lady left our gathering, and I stayed on with the others.

When I finally descended the four flights of stairs, it was dark outside and had started to rain. I noticed a fine motorcar at the curb—they were rare in those days—the door of the car opened and with a quick gesture my acquaintance of the pale mask called to me to get in and said she would drive me home.

Utterly unsuspecting, I accepted. She asked my address and gave a rapid order in Italian to the chauffeur. As it was quite dark I could not see anything that looked familiar, then gradually began to sense that we were speeding into a quarter entirely unknown to me. Was it possible that I was being kidnapped by this undeniably alluring person? My furtive glances roused her awareness to my unspoken thought. "Be not alarmed, my dear; I just wanted to show you where I live before leaving you at home, and here we are; I will show you some interesting pictures of your friends the dancers, and many other great artists as well!" She held my wrist as we mounted the wide stone entrance steps. The door swung open, and a Chinese servant in a long silken mandarin coat bowed as we entered the hall. The pale lady said that I was to be shown into the reception room.

The door was shut immediately, and I found to my dismay that it was locked. There was nothing I could do but look about at the many signed photographs hanging on the walls, inscribed by Sarah Bernhardt, D'Annunzio, Duse, and many other notables of the stage. Incense was burning in a bronze bowl in one corner of the room. I drew the curtain aside and found that the windows were heavily barred. Apparently the scene was set for a new act of student life in Paris!

Before I could think things over, the door opened and the Chinese servant said that Madame la Comtesse was waiting for me upstairs. My heart was beating hard and I tried to devise an escape without making a scene. On my way up the wide carpeted stairway—beautiful tapestries hung on the walls—I noted the distance from the front door. The butler knocked on a door and showed me into a softly lighted, spacious bedroom. Madame la Comtesse was in a wide four-poster bed with rosy pillows piled about her. The air was filled with subtle perfume. The pale face of my hostess looked beautiful, framed in the soft cushions, and her dark luminous eyes followed me as I drew up a chair between the bed and the door. I knew I was trapped, but when she said she had ordered a little supper for us to be served in her room I felt there would be a moment when I could escape. She spoke softly at first, but there was smoldering emotion in her words, and we knew we were engaged in combat—not with drawn swords, but with deep inner conflicts that were not of our making.

"The heart hath reasons of which reason knoweth nothing." At last she rang for the supper. When the butler entered carrying a heavily laden silver tray, he left the door ajar. As he crossed the room to the little table on the far side of the bed, something snapped in my head—swifter than the mind could act, I fled. Running down the stairs, hardly touching them, like a flash I reached the front door, managed to unlock it, and ran into the cold dark night with my heart pounding wildly.

I was free—I do not remember the streets I ran through, turning corners and finally hailing a passing taxi that carried me home—bewildered and unhappy.

I was learning the ways of a strange new world, but the story was as old as time itself. It was I who had been newly initiated.

CHAPTER THIRTEEN

STUDIO ON
THIRTY-FOURTH STREET

AFTER SOME sixteen months in Europe, in late July, 1911, our budget of one thousand dollars had been exhausted and I knew we were obliged to return to New York. During my last days in Paris, I felt as if the streets and windows became fogged. I wrote in my diary: "The past is slipping away from the present—slipping, slipping—and I am full of tears and aching." The day of leave-taking, I walked the streets for hours, took photographs of the great gate and courtyard at 77 rue Varenne (the Hôtel Biron), and returned to our "Chambres Meublées, 2ème à droite."

On the boat going home I wrote: "What has been is now a memory."

I brought back the small bronzes I had made in Paris. My arrival was quiet. There was the happiness of being with Sam and telling him face to face, in full, what I had written him about from abroad. I told him I had made a start, but I had much work to do here. I was to do dissection, museum drawing, perspective: Rodin had offered his advice and had requested that I keep him informed of my progress and send him photographs of new pieces. I had determined to study sculpture as a whole, not just a few facets of it. For some years yet it would be a complete giving of myself to technical and artistic training. Sam understood that perfectly. He was similarly busy. He had concert engagements, and constantly practiced to keep himself ready for any unexpected call.

I told him about my experiences with Mamma's arthritis in Rome and Paris. In those days it was called "inflammatory rheumatism," and it was a frightening illness. Mamma probably would need me more as time went on.

Sam and I picked up easily where we had left off, with old friendships and associations. We saw much of the Drapers, all branches of the family, and all dear to us. Around Macdougal Alley were Mrs. Whitney, James Fraser, Victor Salvatore—and when I saw them, it was with the fun of my now being somewhat Europeanized.

Immediately after I came back, though, I spent a few weeks at Mount Kisco. I had to "chase" the bronze of the "Russian Dancers" that I had taken from the foundry in Paris before the men there had had time to finish it. I was curious to find out whether my lessons with Rosales in Paris could be put to practice on my first bronze. A worktable and heavy wooden vise made it easy to hold the figures securely. To cut off the little vents and pins and to hammer the surface smooth gave me a satisfying sense of know-how; then I patined it with acids, following carefully the instructions written out for such work by Père Limet in Paris. He had been Rodin's *patineur* for many years and had given me many receipts and let me experiment in his workshop at 65 Boulevard Arago.

The patining went well, but mine was just a summer workshop, and the lure of riding horseback frequently tempted me to leave the studio and dash away through the woods and lanes.

The winter of hard work came all too swiftly. If I was to be a practical sculptor now, I had to have a studio. The one I actually found was a fourth-floor rear in an unprepossessing house in East Thirty-fourth Street, over a florist shop. On the same floor, in the front studio, Edmond Quinn had made the bronze figure of Edwin Booth for Gramercy Park. Quinn was a retiring, hard-working sculptor, with a strong streak of melancholy that in the end drove him to suicide.

Since Mother and I had to have a place to live, we found an apartment across the street from my studio, on the third floor of a building next to the Armory. It was a comfortable enough place with three bedrooms, and here my brother Charles, who was still a bachelor at that time, came to live with us. Charles was the wonderful person he had always been, kind, unfailingly thoughtful, always ready to do any favor asked of him if he could. He worked for a Wall Street brokerage house and went often to the Racquet Club to which he belonged, saying he did more business there than he did during office hours. An anchor of the household, he took a steady interest in what I was doing.

FIRST MEETING WITH PAVLOVA

By now my top-floor studio across the street was in operation. My only furnishings were one chair, two boxes, two modeling stands, and the dreams I brought with me from Paris. I also had my bronze group of Pavlova and Mordkin, my "Mort Exquise" (a marble group), a small study of a shivering girl ("La Frileuse"), and a portfolio of sketches. Pavlova was then dancing in New York at the Metropolitan Opera House, and Mrs. Otto Kahn, aware of my interest in her, arranged that I should meet her, telling me to bring my little group along. I had seen Pavlova from a distance; now, eye met eye with under-

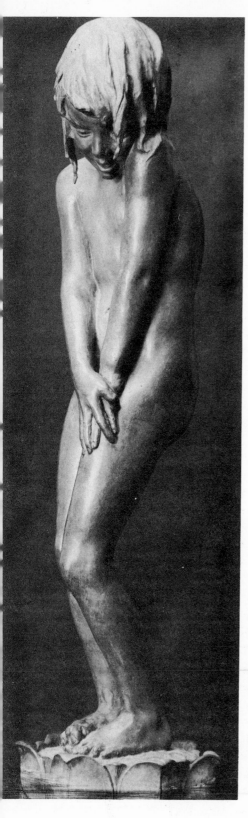

"A FRILEUSE," FOUNTAIN FIGURE (© MH)　　　　　"MORT EXQUISE"

standing and sympathy. She was touched by what I had managed to do even under the difficulties I faced, and wanted at once, impulsively, to help me. She said that she would arrange for me to have a permanent pass to the wings where I could draw without being under any pressure. This opened an important and vital period in my life. I was soon preparing to model a new study of her (the "Gavotte"). She liked a sketch I made of her with her head thrown back, and suggested to her manager that it be used as a poster, a "stick-up" as they called it. I did a special version of it in strong black and white, with touches of red added in her hair and drapery. That led to a series of posters for the Ballet Russe.

Following that, I started a portrait of Roger Wolff Kahn, then aged five. This commission took me to Morristown where I stayed with Mrs. Kahn. I almost gave up the struggle to model the boy, who quite naturally foiled my efforts to keep him quiet. We finally became good comrades, however, and after many weeks the portrait was completed. I then carved it in marble and made a replica in terra cotta.

All this time Mother's selfless devotion to my interests had relieved me of outside responsibilities, and I was free to work at my art from morning until night.

In the little studio in Thirty-fourth Street I had encouraging visits from Adolph Ochs, the owner and publisher of *The New York Times*. He asked me to make studies and do research covering a project for a Peace Monument on Lookout Mountain in Tennessee. The plan was so vast that the idea of working on it made me quite dizzy. (Unfortunately, the scheme was later abandoned, because of the war in 1914.)

High spots during those months were the midday luncheons at the Times Building. Mr. Ochs would invite me to report on the progress of my work, and there I would listen with amazement to the opinions of world affairs tossed from one side of the table to the other by the editors, visiting foreigners, and leading educators. From time to time Mr. Ochs would draw me into the conversation with some question about my studies in Paris with Rodin. His kindly smile of reassurance helped me to speak on my own subject, then gladly resume the role of listener.

In a short time the studio was filled with work. The landlady warned me that I must look for another place; there was too much weight on the floor. My friends suggested that I hold a little exhibition before I move, so I engaged an empty room one flight up in the same building and, with the loan of a few stands and a case or two, set up the bronzes and marbles that were my entire stock. By good luck a number of people came, and I made four or five sales, among them a bronze to Mrs. E. H. Harriman, who seemed pleased, in fact enthusiastic. This encouraged me. Henry Frick came also and commissioned me to do a portrait of his daughter Helen. "Come and look at the Houdons in my collections; it might be suitable to do my daughter in the eighteenth century French manner!" Rather abashed, though I had copied Houdons in Paris, I looked at his Houdons. Like that sculptor's other work, they had a very definite style, a particular approach to the subject's eyes (very alive), and a delicate

PAVLOWA
RED CROSS
BENEFIT
Metropolitan Opera House
Tuesday Eve. Nov. 24.
TICKETS NOW ON SALE AT BOX OFFICE
AND MUSIC LEAGUE OF AMERICA, AEOLIAN B'LDG. W. 42nd ST.

MH drawing Anna Pavlova for poster

grace of drapery and detailed treatment of the hair. I did my best to carry it out as he intended, and he appeared pleased with the final result in marble. All the time I was scrutinizing his face—he was so sympathetic and unhurried, I felt it inevitable that I would one day do his portrait.

In those days of high-voltage activity before the First World War, we used to play with the same enthusiasm with which we worked. When Mr. Borglum told me that I might have a party in his enormous studio, and gave me free rein, as he was going to the country, I asked Sam, John Alexander, and Herbert Adams to help me plan a fancy dress ball. With the additional help of Charles Dana Gibson, Victor Salvatore, and a group of artists, musicians, and architects, we arranged a series of tableaux. Sam particularly was creative in his ideas for these and in the arrangement of sequences, continuity, and costumes for the whole party.

For his own costume and that of a musician friend, Teddy Flint, he painted on voluminous white Pierrot suits a series of musical notes from the Glazunov "Autumn Bacchanale." It was like the careless music of an accompaniment: half notes, quavers, treble and bass signs. Those who knew and could read music especially enjoyed these costumes drawn from Pavlova's dance.

Our method for the tableaux was to stretch black cheesecloth across a wide gilded frame, with, behind it, a background of black velvet against which we posed models selected for their beauty and ability to stand absolutely still. They held their breath for the few moments a curtain was drawn aside. The models were pipeclayed pure white. For Venus de Milo, Miss Anderson, a favorite with all the sculptors, posed with black velvet bags over her arms and with the drapery arranged exactly like that of the statue. By a clever effect of side lighting behind the black cheesecloth, such illusion was created that no one in the audience could detect the velvet bags, and the arms appeared broken off as in the original marble.

The finale was a special divertissement for Pavlova and members of her company. As the orchestra struck the first bars of the "Bacchanale," Paul Reimers, disguised as Mordkin in a tawny union suit and a leopard skin, with vine leaves in his hair, and I, in Pavlova's wig of curls and red chiffon polka-dotted costume, rushed in holding a scarf over our heads and performed the dance, which we had rehearsed for weeks under Pavlova's direction. Until far past daylight, Mr. Borglum's lofty skylight tossed back the echoes of our music and laughter.

At the 1913 exhibition at the New York City Armory, modern art made its first entry into the United States on a big scale. The press was on hand, each paper trying to outdo its competitors in coverage, with full pages of pictures and criticisms. The headlines featured Marcel Duchamp's "Nude Descending a Staircase" and Constantin Brancusi's "Mademoiselle Pogany," with the critics crying, "Is it an egg or is it a woman?"

The violence of the rejections and cheers disturbed me, and I couldn't make up my mind how I felt. I thought it might possibly be years before I knew my true reaction. But I was very much aware of the Brancusi head; I recognized that it had its effect even without any features, and my sympathy for it helped me later when I interviewed him in Paris. His courage in slashing away all details was self-evident, and the Armory Show as a whole was presented with an authority that was convincing: Duchamp was an entirely new revelation of art-calculation-like-mathematical-calculation, and I could see that he must have learned much to do even that one picture. But some of the other work in the exhibition seemed false, and I resented any touch of falseness because I was terribly honest in my own point of view, and to me art seemed like love, something that should not be profaned. I thought, Classic work has endured, and there must be a reason. And even what is "modern" isn't altogether new. In Spain I was to discover Hieronymus Bosch. Some of his work is available in France, but I became aware of it only in Spain. It has power; it is a valid representation of one part of human experience. But such experimentation and extremism are only a minor tendency in the art of the past, and at the Armory they were the whole show.

And so I decided that I would take my time in evaluating what I had seen. Years later, Margaret French Cresson wrote in a *New York Times* article (in 1949), "It is Modern, but is it Art? That is the pertinent question!" Time alone will give the full answer.

Sometimes (as in 1913) I wondered if it might not be a defect in me not to have experimented more—not to have been more curious, let's say—so that I could develop a personal style. When I saw Brancusi's work in Paris and felt its intent and sincerity as I talked with him, I sensed that I could benefit by his example if I wanted to. But I wasn't sufficiently impelled. I did do what every sculptor does at times: I looked at my model in a mirror, because that often obliterates the nonessentials, especially when you're trying to simplify and eliminate details. But I never believed that such things gave one a "style"— in fact, I used to make Rodin laugh because I said, in a French equivalent: "Nobody'd ever be able to see from what I do, whodunit, because my style changes with the people I do." Whatever guides me is some subconscious impression from the subject, whether it's young Thoreau or my mother or Father Teilhard de Chardin—that's what influences me, each person's individuality. But of course one does get a range of technique, and certain discoveries remain deep in the mind, like Rodin's caution about respecting the accidental.

But mainly one works. One awaits, as Rilke said, "the awakening of stones."

MH AT SNIFFEN COURT ENTRANCE TO STUDIO AT 157 (*Underwood & Underwood Studios*)

CHAPTER FOURTEEN

NUMBER 157: A DREAM BECOMES A REALITY

MY NEED for ground-floor space was urgent. Sniffen Court, the picturesque alley off Thirty-sixth Street, had lured me with its ten attractive buildings, but they were small, and I wanted size for a permanent home. Still, I tried to draw up practical plans for doing over the Henry Clews Stable at Number 9. The idea interested Mrs. E. H. Harriman, and we tried to get an option on the property. After weeks of delay and many false hopes, we finally cut the inevitable red tape, only to find that the building had been sold to Mrs. Lanier.

Then, in desperation, I found that the 157 East Thirty-fifth Street stable could be bought, and Mrs. Harriman lost no time in acquiring it. She told me to do it over into three studios and rent them for her to reliable tenants, myself on the ground floor as one of them, Edward McCartan the sculptor upstairs, and his pupil Marjorie Curtis, later Mrs. Thomas Chadbourne, in the smaller studio next to his. This stable had previously belonged to Mrs. Morris K. Jesup, and then to Mrs. Morgan Hamilton, well-known residents of this Murray Hill district when fine horses and carriages were in vogue.

That there were seven horse stalls in the rear, and a cumbersome elevator that had broken down and lay in the middle of the floor, did not daunt me. The old-fashioned carriage room in front, lined with heavy wooden harness cases, was another sizable obstacle to overcome. But to the young, nothing seems impossible, and the space—25 by 100 feet—was tempting to anyone confronted with "dispossess papers" as I was.

We drew up various plans, and wreckers were engaged to dismantle the heavy machinery for the cumbersome carriage elevator and remove this, as well as the horse stalls and harness cases. Then builders came and cut away most

143

of the hayloft, leaving a section in the rear studio as a balcony, to which a stair-case was added. The upper part of the rear wall had three windows; these were taken out and the brick was torn down as far as the second-floor level. As this wall faced north, it was ideal for a skylight, which was set at an angle and the roof cut back three feet for the purpose.

The rear open courtyard, where formerly the horses had been washed, was roofed over with another north skylight; the box stall off this was removed, and the heavy Dutch door to it was reset in the retaining wall that formed the end of Sniffen Court by permission of all the owners of the eight little buildings in the alley. Subsequently, when 157 was completed, the appearance of this end wall was enhanced by two plaster panels of the Parthenon frieze and a gay blue door. Other Sniffen Court stables were made over into studios and charming houses by those who had the imagination to see the possibilities of creating a really picturesque quarter in the heart of the East Side Murray Hill district.

As the building progressed we gained courage and, by using the old bricks from the rear wall and a few new ones, we built an open fireplace and chimney on the east wall of the rear studio. The concrete floor was covered with wood flooring, and the wide carriage entrance doors on Thirty-fifth Street were removed and a large ribbed glass window was put in their place.

The second floor, which had served as coachman's living quarters, still remained to be done over. Partitions were ripped out, and the ceiling was heightened to admit two north skylights for the two studios. Two bathrooms and a kitchen were installed on the floor.

Finally all was in order and the painted walls were dry. We invited the owner, Mrs. Harriman, to come and examine the result, and we were happy when she expressed her satisfaction.

When my belongings were moved from Thirty-fourth Street to Thirty-fifth Street, my pieces of sculpture that had seemed too big for the first studio shrank into insignificance in the vast new space of 157. I felt a bit awed, and the saying came to my mind: "It's better to have big ideas in a small place than to have small ones in a big place!" I thought a great deal about this. To the little Thirty-fourth Street top-floor studio, with its spare furnishings, I had brought my dreams from Paris, and there the immortal Pavlova had posed for me for long, exciting hours while I drew her billboard posters and program covers, and modeled the "Gavotte." She would ring the bell at the street entrance, giving her private signal, which affected my whole being as directly as an electric spark. Heart, brain, spirit, every fiber tingled with aliveness; as she tripped lightly up the stairs she would call up to me, "Malvinoush—ka!" and by the time she had reached the third floor where I met her she would have taken off her hat, gloves, and scarves and tossed them to me in her childlike playfulness. Once inside the studio she would disrobe and reappear "in costume," as she insisted on calling it, in less time than it takes to write of it—a snug little suggestion of short tights, long-heeled golden slippers, and the famous yellow poke bonnet with long streamers.

Pavlova and MH at 157

She insisted upon my catching the airy lightness of her pose, by holding her breath as if in flight, and this was contagious enough to cause me to hold mine quite unconsciously until we both felt faint. Then she would say, "Where is Mamma's sherry wine?" Many were the glasses we consumed during these breathless, happy sessions.

The diaphanous clinging yellow satin dress, which I added as drapery after the nude figure was completed, served to accentuate the grace and rhythmic silhouette of her figure.

Pavlova herself had a lively interest in modeling, and while she practiced steps before my long mirror, we both studied the motions of her hands and arms and the position of her feet. First I drew them, and then we both tried them out on a series of small flexible armatures about eight inches high. This mutual enthusiasm in the work reached out in many directions. I attended morning rehearsals of the members of the ballet, a revelation of Samurai discipline and technical training. Pavlova would watch the girls and then, suddenly throwing off her shawl, she would spring onto the center of the floor, call for the music to be repeated, and electrify all of us by a brilliant tour de force as in staccato, well-aimed words, sometimes in Russian, often in English (for many of the girls were from England or America), she would indicate where they had failed, broken the line of motion, or danced only with their feet. "You must dance with your head and hands and body, and *always* with the heart, my dears . . . not only with the feet!"

She demonstrated many little tricks to me—how to rise up and down on the toes with arms outspread and head erect "to strengthen the muscles and to hold your balance, Malvinoushka. . . . Do it every day, and then slowly bend your knees up and down, but do not hurry; and when you put on your stockings, stand this way on one foot, and put on one stocking; change to the other foot and pull on the other. . . . Do not cheat by leaning against the wall or anything else. . . . Just learn balance, and you will have strong legs and feet."

When I originally gave the "Gavotte" for casting, I found that I couldn't resist trying to convey to the workmen some sense of its airy weightlessness. I urged special care with it.

The "Gavotte" is small. Often, in looking at it, I think that many things that are done small have a more direct response to the emotion that went into them. Sometimes they are later enlarged. I've never done this with the "Gavotte," liking it as it was. To enlarge a statue, to get a full-size or heroic-size version of the same idea, many artists think that all they have to do is to have it enlarged mechanically. It would be too easy if that were the case. There are many times when even a single figure can be ruined just by enlarging it. You may have to work over it for weeks to get it merely as good as it was in the beginning, and yet the enlargement is what the public knows and judges the sculptor by. Perhaps if they could see the first flush of the idea in its smaller form, they would acknowledge its winning quality. But in common practice, a workman is hired to make an enlarged statuette, which is what it actually is. True heroic sculpture

"LA GAVOTTE" (*Cecil Beaton*)

is not statuette sculpture enlarged. Too much is missed along the way. Recognizing the possible loss, the devoted sculptor does the necessary work of remodeling, to bring the sculpture back to its original thrust.

The "Gavotte" was much liked. Mrs. Robert Woods Bliss took a colored-wax copy by hand to the museum in Stockholm, wanting to offer Sweden this recognition of their graciousness to her and her husband while he was Ambassador there. Copies of the "Gavotte" are in the Carnegie Institute in Pittsburgh, in the Corcoran Gallery in Washington, and in the Metropolitan in New York (where it has been in and out of storage), and Pavlova added it to her London collection of interpretations of her work by sculptors and painters. She always had a particular feeling for it because, she said, she could never forget the posing and that special airy lightness we had tried to get into it.

PAVLOVA'S BIRTHDAY PARTY

When life began to swing into rhythm in the new 157 studio, my friends insisted that I stage another fancy dress party, and include the neighbors in Sniffen Court. Pavlova's birthday gave us the occasion. When I asked these neighbors if they could join in and let me rope off the whole alley from the street, they enthusiastically agreed to open the ground floors of their houses, and the police gave us permission to stretch a great blue curtain across the end of the court. We set up green iron tables and colored umbrellas and strung round orange paper lanterns from opposite windows across the alley.

This gave extra space for refreshments and cool air, for the party was held in May and there were over two hundred guests in costume, many taking a share in the long program of stunts: Japanese jujitsu demonstrations, wrestling and solo dancers, and classical Greek, Russian, East-Indian, and African numbers. The studio had been transformed into oriental splendor by red and gold hangings, satins and brocades all loaned by the fabulous Mr. Miller of Louis the XIV Antique Shop fame. For Pavlova's birthday his cooperation knew no limits. Forty thousand dollars' worth of hangings covered the walls and balcony railings. Dancers appeared in his rare masks and costumes dripping with semiprecious jewels.

When all was in readiness, about 8:00 P.M., and the first guests began to arrive, I discerned Mr. Miller, of rotund shape, with his ever-smoldering cigar, disguised as a Maharaja of India, his high turban and black silken costume bedecked with strings of pearls. He pulled more strings of pearls out of his pockets and put them around my neck, then slipped a set of gold and jeweled bracelets on my arms and said not to worry—they were covered by insurance.

There were musical numbers; then a poet, Helen Gerry, recited verses of her own in an effect of moonlight, the darkened room now illumined by a single shaft of pale light that fell on the young girl, draped in diaphanous white chiffon. "Klinks," as we called her, was known to many artists and had posed for all the tenants of 157, and also for Peggy Cresson, daughter of Daniel Chester French, who made a fine marble portrait of her.

PAVLOVA IN ICON AT HER BIRTHDAY PARTY AT 157, SAM IN PIERROT COSTUME AT FAR RIGHT

For another act, Sam and René Gimpel, the brother-in-law of Sir Joseph Duveen, who were great friends and were about the same height and looked rather alike, made up as the Fratellini Brothers, the great French circus clowns with whom both Sam and René were familiar. Both enjoyed the art of makeup and made themselves unrecognizable, and then they had to be hid in the boiler room until their moment came to run out and do their act, the famous act of the Trained Flea. Sam had a tripod and camera and draped a black cloth over his head and waved to René to pose for his picture, and René struck a histrionic pose and the camera blew up and everybody was terribly scared. But as he and Sam cleared away the wreckage, it was clear that they were all right and they had given the party quite a sensation.

The climax came at midnight. A huge gilded icon frame with closed doors had been mounted high in the corner of the room. Behind this we had led Pavlova, covered by a long veil, and she had taken the pose of the Byzantine Madonna, her hands held together, fingertips touching as in prayer. The decorative headdress was set on her head, and the signal was given for the doors of the icon to open as the gong struck twelve. Pavlova remained immovable as a procession of guests walked up before her. I was the last in line, carrying her birthday cake with lighted candles. The audience applauded wildly, and then gasped in delight when Pavlova smiled.

Oukrainsky, Swirzkaia, and Pavley, members of Pavlova's Ballet, often spent hours in the studio, generously affording me opportunity to make drawings of their dances. These I first drew on three-inch-thick lithograph stones, then hand-printed them on Japanese rice paper under the guidance of a lithographer who stayed after hours in his workshop in Hudson Street and taught me how to apply the ink and use the handpresses there.

Serge Oukrainsky was associated in my mind with good fortune. First, his own. He had been a contestant in six-day bicycle races and had developed a phenomenal strength and control of his foot muscles that helped him in ballet. One night his chance came as he stood in the wings watching a solo dancer who by mischance sprained his ankle. Oukrainsky told Pavlova that he had practiced this same dance and could do all the toe-point steps in his bare feet. She decided to give him a chance. His first performance won him thunderous applause and started him on his way to stardom.

He is also associated with good fortune of my own. I made a bronze of him which I called "The Incense Burner." Previous to this, Mr. Bertelli of the Roman Bronze Works had cast six bronzes of my "Gavotte" on speculation, and I had then sold them over a six-month period. Now, with "The Incense Burner," I ventured to have a bronze made on my own responsibility before I had an order. It sold. I made another and that sold too, and so I gained the confidence to help myself in this way. In later years, Oukrainsky and I haven't met personally, but we keep in touch by corresponding at odd intervals. He has directed a school for dancing in Los Angeles for many years.

Pavlova and Novikoff, Volinine, and Stowitz posed for the groups "Les

"La Péri"

Orientales" and "La Péri," and for many panels in the reliefs Pavlova insisted that I make.

"La Péri" charmed me. It's about a man who is told by the Fairy Queen that he can have the girl he loves provided he does not give in to the temptation of giving her a kiss. Finally she's dancing with him and holding a lily in her hand. She bends backward in his arms, and he leans over and inevitably kisses her; as he does so, she sinks down and the lily falls on the ground.

When Pavlova and a partner would come over to pose for this, there would be an argument, whether to let people see that he actually did kiss her or whether she could just be sinking down as he bent over her. Of course, whatever male partner was there would say, "No, why should I give up the pleasure of giving her a kiss?" for any man who wasn't a fool would think that it was absolutely necessary to give Pavlova a kiss.

But the dance appealed to me because I felt in its symbolism the unexpressed beauty of the ballet, something so delicate and fragile, represented by Pavlova, that it should be free from any earthly desecration. You would infringe on the laws of immortality by kissing her; you would destroy an imperishable image.

But the main undertaking with Pavlova and the male members of her group who posed for me was a frieze of twenty-six panels—fifty-two figures—representing her in just one dance, the "Bacchanale." This was the dance in which she had made her reputation, and she wanted to record it. She had tried recording it in the movies, but that hadn't come out so well in her own opinion. It was very hard for her to dance within the chalked-out limits of a moving-picture performance. They drew circles on the floor and she was required to dance inside them, but she found herself unable to think about the dance and those circles at the same time and she had a tendency to jump over them or go past them. She did convey the intensity of her purpose, though. That came through even in the film. But, not satisfied, she still had the determination to record the "Bacchanale," and so she worked with me over a period of five years, whenever her tours happened to bring her to New York, London, or Paris where I could continue the series. When all the panels were completed, we hoped some day to place them in an academy of the dance that might be directed by Pavlova whether in New York or in London.

Alas, this dream never materialized. Another plan evolved, however, which was to include the panels of the frieze—four feet high—in a music auditorium in Cleveland. In this case, after two years were spent making all the enlarged panels to fit the architectural setting, the whole project collapsed. The donor became bankrupt, and the sculptor, as is often the case, was left "holding the bag," in this instance twenty-six four-foot panels in plaster for which Pavlova and her partners had given many hours of time. The sculptor was also left with a considerable debt plus a pretty serious heartbreak.

Later (1937) the panels were exhibited in the Richmond, Virginia, Museum during a larger showing of my work. They just fitted the big gallery there, the three sides and over the doors. It wasn't necessary to cut down even a single panel; everything just happened to fit. The frieze then appealed to a group of donors, who asked to have it left another month or two while they tried to make arrangements for having it there permanently, but eventually there wasn't enough interest and it was shipped home to me. I finally had to get the frieze up out of the way by hanging it on my own walls, no small project in itself with the weight of over two dozen four-foot-square panels—not to mention some weight of frustration—and there they still hang, gathering flowers of dust. Nevertheless, the record is made. There Pavlova still floats in the ivory transports of her first dance, free, rapturous, undying.

Other commissions came along, and work possessed me. There never was a question of giving up or of letting discouragement turn my energies aside. To learn to cut marble or wood and to understand anatomy and the world around one was enough to keep anyone busy and hopeful.

The first figure I built in 157 was that of a young bacchus holding a panther cub in his arm and crushing a bunch of grapes with his uplifted right hand. Water was piped to these grapes from inside the life-size bronze figure, which later was set in a pool on Paul Warburg's estate in Hartsdale. Frequent trips to the zoo were needed to make studies of the panther cub, and from then on I returned to model some of the infinite variety of wild animals.

Elephants came next. I asked Mr. Carl Akeley to introduce me to Hattie, his pet elephant at the Central Park Zoo. After this formality I started to model a little elephant, placing my stand close to the bars of Hattie's pen. After two hours Hattie became bored and, gathering up in her trunk whatever water there was in her trough, she suddenly loosed a well-aimed blast, blowing my little model across the hall and flattening it on the opposite wall. I was more watchful on my second attempt, and managed to complete my work without further accident.

Music

Good music, of all antidotes and stimulants, was the best tonic to replenish the springs of the spirit. The aching silence when my father's music ceased did not grow easier to bear—too long a spell without someone to play—and melancholy settled upon me. So I blessed the musicians who came and went each season, many of whom played for me on Father's old Chickering piano. Something about a spacious room seems to awaken the imagination, and many were the hours that Schumann, Chopin, Beethoven, Brahms, and Bach were heard and practiced within these high walls. Under the spell of music new ideas would spring into being; and the pianists, lost in their own world, would ignore me so I could draw or model in the studio for hours at a time—each of us immersed in that impersonal world of dreams where we slip off personality and become the selfless messengers of our daemons.

PANELS OF THE "BACCHANALE"

Leonard Borwick, the English pianist, was one of the first to give me the treat of his music; indeed, he looked and played so much like my father that it was extraordinary.

Ernest Schelling knew so well my craving for music that he frequently came by at teatime and, without a word of suggestion, would lift the piano top, settle his long body into a special curve, and let his very long fingers wander over the keys until the sudden moment came when he would plunge into the "Carnaval" and play its capricious, gay, tragic, wistful variations like a creature possessed. In these informal and unselfconscious hours I was able to hear a better performance by many players than I ever heard at a public appearance.

In those early days we had occasional string quartets and trios as well as piano. Felix Kahn had his own quartet in which he played the Second Violin or Viola and Sam played First Violin. He equipped my four music desks with light reflectors, and when these were plugged into the wall and the players settled, the other lights would be turned off and the music would have its best effect.

In the summer of 1914, Sam wrote to me in Paris (where Mother and I had gone in the spring) to tell me excitedly that he was bringing to completion an invention that had engrossed his attention for months. He called it the "Rhythmikon"—a magic box enclosing a simple mechanical device operating a clicking marker and a bell. By inserting a perforated card, one could make the marker click off any selected rhythm within the bars of music of a composition, and the bell would ring at the downbeat beginning of every bar, thus identifying the bars. Unlike the metronome, which merely gave varied speeds of evenly divided time, like stately syllables, the Rhythmikon divided time into complexes of rhythm. Sam had been working at this invention in a rented laboratory cubicle he called his "playroom." He had an oily-looking bench, and access to machine tools, lathes, and whatever he needed for his experiments. It wasn't long now before he perfected the Rhythmikon. The marker glided over the square-cut perforations, making its clicking sound, and an instrument was now available that could clarify for pupils and players in orchestras the subtle and often difficult rhythms in the compositions presented to them for the first time.

Sam demonstrated the invention to many eminent musicians and teachers, who were unanimous in their praise and gladly endorsed the importance of this new device. Especially enthusiastic letters were sent by Toscanini, Kreisler, Joseph Hofmann, and Pavlova, and a host of other professionals gave their tributes.

Alas, the upheaval of war was to delay and finally annul Sam's efforts to put the Rhythmikon on the market. Someday, perhaps, interest may be revived in this invention, which was patented and the models for which still exist.

CHAPTER FIFTEEN

THE WAR

MY WAR EXPERIENCE was largely associated with the Red Cross. Early in the first winter of the war, Pavlova started her season with a tremendous Red Cross Benefit at the Metropolitan Opera House. She and her partners spent many hours in my studio planning for this, since I had assumed the responsibility of assembling a committee that would sell out the house—which it did, making many thousands of dollars for the Red Cross.

Pavlova had been of inestimable service to me just a few weeks previously, helping Mother and me get back from Europe when all the Atlantic steamers were booked up. She liked to joke with me about it. Mother and I, at Rodin's urging, had tried to get booking from France. Impossible. Desperate, we went with light luggage to London and there found Pavlova and her manager, who schemed that I be put in charge of delivering artists' drawings and new stage settings to their New York offices. In this way we were able to get a cabin—Mother and I—and after a rough voyage (many passengers slept on mattresses in the ship's hallways), we arrived safely home.

The Red Cross became intensely active as the war progressed, and as my sister Helen Draper was at the helm in the New York chapter, I felt the urge to join her. So, giving up most of my days, I worked at the Red Cross office on Fifth Avenue and Thirty-sixth Street. Helen wanted me to take over a department where a speaking knowledge of French and German was needed, a Bureau of Communications through which people wrote their relatives in foreign countries. This letter-writing service had to be organized carefully to help those who deserved to be helped, while preventing any coded communications from reaching the enemy. I found that a tall, dignified, self-contained person named Louisa Frith was a kind of genius at detecting coded letters or any hints of suspicious behavior, and she tipped the police off to several spies.

At this Red Cross office I also had working with me Marie-Louise Emmet. Her father was some relative of Robert Emmet, the Irish patriot. I called her

157

Sauvage because she was untrained, untrammeled, and undisciplined and obviously didn't fit the name Marie-Louise; after I started calling her Sauvage, everybody did. Among her other talents, she ran a car very well and would go anywhere at any time—on a dark night, for example, to meet a boat. She was husky and strong and smiling, and had short, straight-cropped hair, a bellhop cut with a bang across her forehead. She was so wonderfully loyal and helpful that I thought of her when I needed someone later, after the war, to accompany me on my mission to Yugoslavia.

In the late afternoons and evenings I myself went to a driving school to gain familiarity with the different makes of cars and to be taught what to do in case of breakdowns and emergencies. My lifelong interest in mechanics tempted me to stay long hours and work harder than necessary. With the Red Cross one never knew what make of car one might be asked to drive in an emergency, so at the school we were really tossed about without warning and might even be told to drive a truck that the teacher knew would not hold out. This assignment might cause us to dismount in some abandoned spot and really get down to changing tires or mending something inaccessible and difficult. It was a rugged introduction to driving, and after I passed the examination I was given a certificate by the National League for Woman's Service—Automobile Section—stating that I was competent to drive, care for, and handle an automobile in government service.

Although I worked very hard at the Red Cross, between times I consoled myself at 157 by composing a group of two kneeling figures, known as "The Offering." It was an attempt to interpret Verlaine's poem "Offrande":

> ... Voici des fruits, des fleurs, des feuilles et des branches
> Et puis voici mon cœur qui ne bat que pour vous,
> Ne le déchirez pas avec vos deux mains blanches,
> Et qu'a vos yeux si beaux l'humble présent soit doux. ...*

It made me happy that when this group in bronze was exhibited in Philadelphia it was given the George Widener Gold Medal, and, later at the National Academy in New York, the Helen Foster Barnett Prize. Later on, I carved it in marble. This was so fragile that I never sent it out to be exhibited.

SAM IN THE WAR

Early in the war, Sam's brother Harold, a fine violinist, was killed. He had been among the first to join the British Army, and was killed a few months later. This tragic loss had a powerful impact on Sam. He determined to volunteer for his country's armed forces.

He was to survive the war, but not unscathed. After training in England, he was sent with an artillery unit to fight in the Italian Alps. There, a few months later, he was in one of several lorries going along a mountain road,

---

* *Here are fruits, flowers, leaves, and branches,/And here, too, is my heart, which beats only for you./Don't tear it with your two white hands,/And may the modest gift be pleasing to your lovely eyes.*

MH and Sam at the end of the First World War

carrying ammunition to an advanced post. He had just taken off his steel helmet to wipe his forehead when an exploding German bomb drove the helmet into his side, almost cutting his spleen in two, and he was hurled head-over-heels down the mountainside into a stream below, spraining the tendons of his wrists as he fell. Revived by the shock of the cold water of the stream, he put up his hand and discovered that his scalp had been pulled half off. Somehow he managed to crawl back up to the road, and blacked out and only came to in a hospital in Ventimiglia.

There it was discovered that he had broken ribs and a fractured skull. Tetanus set in, and he was taken to Queen Alexandra's Hospital in London. He had tetanus cramps, called arc cramps because, as if with irresistible compulsion, the body forms an upraised arc from head to feet. Sam's hands, along with the rest of his body, became frighteningly rigid. He exercised and retrained his hands, but was never to regain sufficient flexibility to play the violin at concert level. He did recover from the tetanus and was nursed back to health after many months of expert care.

Early in 1919, his friend Lieutenant Hugh Lofting wrote me about a visit to him at the Convalescent Home in Lymington: "I only saw Sam for a couple of hours during my Christmas leave. . . . [He] was his old jolly self—full of confidence in the future of *others*. He looks of course pulled down but nothing so bad as one would have expected to see him after the awful time he went through."

Once recovered, Sam reenlisted and stayed in the army until nearly a year after the armistice!

In the meantime, I had continued my work at the foreign department of the Red Cross in New York which brought me in touch with people from many countries. Among these the Serbians seemed in most dire need of our assistance. At the beginning of the war they had been defeated and driven back over their mountains. Village after village was lost; the winter added cold and starvation to their suffering until the staggering remnants of their ragged army took refuge on the Island of Corfu. From there one of their patriots, Colonel Milan Pribicevic, came to America. His burning desire was to collect here ten thousand volunteers and lead them back over the defeated area to regain the captured villages.

The colonel was presented to my sister and me, and we were asked to advise and help him in what then appeared an impossible task. During his first visit to the studio he laid his plans before me and showed me harrowing photographs of his martyred compatriots and starving soldiers. His haggard face was illumined by penetrating deep-set brown eyes. They seemed to smolder and burn with the intensity of his patriotic fervor.

Meetings with his trusted friends were arranged and, with the protection of our Department of Justice in Washington, a secret campaign was begun. My mother agreed to give him a little office in our apartment where he might write and store his papers. Before he started on his travels to collect volunteers, he posed for his portrait in a knitted helmet, like the chain mail of the crusader's armor. Now in the Metropolitan Museum, this portrait is labeled "Modern Crusader." Besides his facial structure and likeness, I felt I must in some lasting way record the heroic idealist whose faith alone sustained him against the hordes of opponents, a man whose honor and integrity burned like a torch in darkness.

After some months his hopes were realized, and many thousands of Slavs joined his ranks. When America declared war, he donned his uniform, and our Red Cross gave him and his brave men a heartening send-off from the 71st Regiment Armory on East Thirty-fourth Street in New York. They joined the Allied forces in Salonika and, before the armistice, won back every mile of their country. On that day the victorious army lifted Colonel Pribicevic on their shoulders and marched into Zagreb, the capital of Croatia. He was able to liberate from prison his three brothers, who had been condemned to death.

A quite different occasion that stays in my mind from these years was a ball given to Edward, Prince of Wales, who later, as King Edward VIII, abdicated his kingly crown to marry an American. This reception and dinner dance was given by Mr. and Mrs. Henry P. Davison at the old Waldorf-Astoria, then at Fifth Avenue and Thirty-fourth Street. My sister Helen Draper was a leading spirit in every Red Cross activity, and was well acquainted with Mr. Davison, who was then president of the organization. He invited her to the ball as one of the honored guests, and in her reflected glory I was also invited to attend. I wore the same pink brocade gown to the Prince's Ball as did my grandmother Elizabeth Lamson in 1860 to the ball given for Edward VII when he was Prince of Wales. I carried a similar rosebud bouquet.

When my turn in the line came to be presented to the Prince of Wales, Mr. Davison told him the story of the ball gown and its first appearance. The three full flounces of the stiff brocaded gown stood out and waved at every step and the pointed bodice was laced so tightly that I scarcely dared to take a deep breath. The prince expressed great interest, and graciously offered me his arm to walk about for a few moments so that the gown could be admired. I was delighted, and enjoyed a rare and happy evening.

One of the major efforts I made during the war was for the Appui aux Artistes (Aid to Artists). The Appui asked me to form an American Committee to raise funds to keep five canteens running for the families of artists in Paris. The men were called to the army, and they had no time to arrange life for their wives to carry on without their support.

In 1915 Giselle Bunau-Varilla, a fellow student in sculpture and a most capable member of the Appui, came to America to help me organize more groups in other cities. Her first appeal was made at a meeting at 157, and many architects, painters, and sculptors joined our group. Ernest Peixotto, the illustrator and etcher, was our secretary, and with the help of fine committees we were able to keep the five canteens running for five years and with enough money left over to buy bonds, the income from which was given as yearly prizes to needy, talented French artists. This expression of our gratitude to the City of Light and romance and to her immortal artists and poets has been a treasured symbol, a strong bond of Franco-American friendship.

GRANADOS

It was my personal privilege to experience the bond of friendship in another area of the arts. In the year 1916 there was given at the Metropolitan Opera House the first performance of the opera *Goyescas* composed by the Spanish musician Enrique Granados. He and his wife were invited to come over for the event, and during their stay in New York Ernest Schelling, who was their devoted friend, brought them to my studio.

Granados was a short, swarthy little man with such oversized black eyes they seemed out of all proportion to his face, and a drooping black moustache that reminded one of a walrus. Luckily we could talk together in French, for Granados and his wife spoke no English. They were living in a small hotel room, and when Granados saw the piano in the big studio, he flung out his arms and asked if he might practice there. We placed a screen around the piano, so that he would not be distracted; and hearing Spanish music played by such an artist was one of the great events of my life. The romantic lyrical melodies of the intermezzo of *Goyescas*—which Granados composed and added to the score of his opera just before the premiere—seemed to embody the essence of his Catalonian spirit. The song of "The Maid and the Nightingale" pervaded the very space within my studio, and I frequently still find myself listening to that palpitating, heartbroken music. Schelling studied all Granados's music with him, and certainly played it more in the spirit and rhythm of the composer than any other pianist I have since heard. After hours of playing, Granados would look around the screen to see what I was up to, and with some delicious swift arabesque on the keys, he would give me the signal that work was over and he was ready for lunch. After that, he would fling himself laughing on the huge divan, calling it the *"monument du repos"*! I would cover him with a big fur robe and promise to call him in two hour's time.

When the opera was presented and his American visit came to its end, a purse with $1,000 in gold was given to him by a group of admirers and friends. The night before the Granadoses were to sail, he called me by telephone, saying in a nervous voice that his wife had had a premonition of death and that he too was certain he would never reach home or see his children again. He wanted to tell me this and say a final good-bye and thank me for letting him feel that my studio was his home in America. He asked, in case any of his children ever came to New York, if I would show them the *"monument du repos"* and tell them about our wonderful musical mornings.

There seemed to be no way to calm his fears or suggest that he might be suffering from the result of strain and fatigue. "No, Malvina, this is the end; you will see I am not mistaken. . . ."

MACDOUGAL ALLEY BOOTH FOR APPUI AUX ARTISTES. IN BOOTH, LEFT TO RIGHT, LESLIE EMMET, SAM, RUTH DRAPER, EDWARD MCCARTAN, ROSE CUMMINGS, MH, NISSEN (© *Paul Thompson*)

The ship reached England safely, and from there Granados and his wife took the ill-fated *Sussex* to cross the Channel to France. It was torpedoed by a German submarine. The blast blew off a section of the ship, and fifty-five passengers were drowned, among them my two friends. The bodies of other victims were recovered, but in spite of a long search no trace was ever found either of Granados or of his wife.

When the news reached his friends in America, a benefit concert was given at the Metropolitan Opera House by Paderewski, Kreisler, Casals, and others. Their wives sold costume dolls in the lobby, and the total receipts were $11,000. Ernest Schelling, who was playing in Spokane that night, sent a check for $1,000. All this was sent for the care of the six Granados orphans.

Twenty-six years passed, and no word came from any member of the Granados family. Of course, I had written to them after the tragedy.

One wintry afternoon, with snow and wind swirling against the windows, I was sitting by the fire waiting for tea when I heard a strange voice, and there in the doorway stood a tall, dark-eyed, haggard-looking man in a thin overcoat, collar turned up, snow still covering his shoulders and dripping from a felt hat that he held in his hand. His unmistakably Spanish appearance and the somber lines etched into his face made me instantly sure.

"Are you not the son of Granados?" I asked.

"Yes, I am Victor, and only now have I found out that this was where my father practiced when he was in New York. I was so young when we lost our parents; we were so destroyed by the tragedy, and my older brother never told me who it was that wrote him all about my father's visit here. Yesterday Mrs. Schelling gave me your address. I came from Barcelona after the terrible revolution there. I have lost my wife and my home, and my children are with the Catholic Sisters, and with relatives. I have been very sick since coming to America. . . ."

He sank into an armchair and warmed his hands at the fire. When I had given him two or three cups of tea, I told him of his father's visits, and how much beautiful music he had composed and played on my father's piano, and then I spoke of the last telephone message of premonition and how I had put away his father's key, promising him that if any of his children needed a friend they would find one right here in this same house.

Victor agreed to stay in the second-floor apartment. He was obviously very ill, so he was put to bed and I sent for my doctor, who found that Victor had pneumonia and called in a trained nurse to take care of him. This visit turned into a year and a half's residence at 157, during which time Victor seemed to be followed by "disasters," as he called them. It was evident he suffered from a shattered nervous system. In spite of everything, however, he managed to compose the major part of a Spanish ballet, and two sets of an opera called *Oceania* —a madrigal, which he gave to Mme. Lucrezia Bori after she had arranged to get word to and from his children in Spain.

We were able to recover his old cello, then in pawn, and I kept urging

MONUMENT DE REPOS

him to practice. He had a fine, natural tone. By good fortune we obtained a scholarship for him to spend a summer at Mrs. MacDowell's Artists' Colony in Peterboro, New Hampshire. He did good work there in orchestrating his compositions, and enjoyed the companionship of his fellow artists, especially Lucas Foss, whose talent and skill made a deep impression on all who knew him there.

Later Victor was persuaded to move to Hollywood and join Spanish friends, and he has remained there since.

Mrs. Harriman

The continuity of my life at 157 throughout the rather tumultuous early years and even later depended on the strong, steady hand of Mrs. E. H. Harriman, who had bought the building and rented the studio to me. Just as she helped me, her sense of responsibility went out to other artists, and she had a special talent for straightening out confused situations. I could always go to her with problems and expect understanding exactly fitted to my need, and her interest didn't stop there. She would frequently appear at the studio and ask how things were going.

At one point she decided to have me make a portrait of her and carve it in marble. She wished it placed in "Arden House," and I persuaded her to pose in her "opera best"—a brocaded gown, fur cloak over one shoulder, and her beautiful pearls. Having studied with admiration the portraits by Houdon and Carpeaux, I was filled with a secret desire to make a portrait of a "grande dame," and here certainly was the opportunity.

Some valuable training in the study of Houdon had been a chance in Paris to copy in marble his four famous busts, Washington, Lafayette, Paul Jones, and Benjamin Franklin. I had also tried my hand when I did the portrait of Helen Frick. Now I felt courageous enough to attempt difficult problems. As I look back to those days, they seem to be so much longer than the short sharp daylight hours of today! Mrs. Harriman would appear promptly at ten o'clock, dressed in her low-necked gown, and her white hair perfectly coiffured. "The time we spend together here, Malvina, must be put to good use. You must do your work, and I must be a good model; in most things it takes two to ensure a successful result, and surely in this one!" How often do I recall with gratitude her patience and good sportsmanship during this difficult commission. She gave me many wise counsels, and insisted that I should consider the future in all my planning. "Make a frame for your life, Malvina; see that it is built with solid, honest foundations, so that later on you will have some place where you can rest and read, and have a fireplace—it is important—don't think such things drop into your lap . . . we have to plan and work hard for them, and always remember that with any kind of home atmosphere, it must be shared with others who may not have either a place to rest or a fire before which they may find warmth and companionship. . . . For most people, you will discover, possessions are not as valuable as are good friends."

BUST OF MRS. E. H. HARRIMAN
(Peter A. Juley & Son)

ERNEST SCHELLING AND ENRIQUE GRANADOS

I think she sensed my deep appreciation even when she was very exacting. For I did try to follow many of her suggestions, and we had many happy days together. A sense of security and mutual trust blessed our friendship. Luckily, Mrs. Harriman thought I could progress with the portrait by going to the opera in her box and watching her there. The wonderful Saturday matinees in Box 9 still linger in my memory; fortunately, the invitations continued for many years after the portrait had been completed, during the "Golden Age" of our operatic history.

When the marble portrait was approaching completion, Mrs. Harriman would come in and watch the carving. One day she noticed the difficulty of carving the pearls. "Aren't those pearls a little larger than my own necklace?" she asked, smiling.

"Perhaps," I answered, "but posterity will never check on the size; maybe my sense of self-preservation made me make them larger—the larger, the fewer to carve, you know, and please remember—if my chisel slips and I tap off one of these there's no way of putting it back!"

She was silent for some time; then, as she left, she said: "I wonder why more people don't visit studios and find out for themselves how difficult it is to be an artist. Most of them have no conception what labor and tense concentration go into the work."

Mrs. Harriman often took me with her to her home place at Arden, New York, where we boarded a funicular railway for a one-mile lift to the level of the stone house on top of a high plateau. I remember a long talk by the fire; we were alone and she talked to me most affectionately, offering her guidance and friendship. I wrote the words in my diary: ". . . Malvina, I want you to know that I stand ready to help you in any way I can. You have earned the right to ask of me any favor without feeling indebtedness. We are not put on this earth to live alone; we need one another, and the only real happiness comes from within the heart, and we must try to share it with those we love. . . . Keep your heart straight and your head will follow it!"

The words echoed her lifelong philosophy, but as a personal token of loyalty and interest, they were a strong armament.

I made a statuette portrait of Mrs. Harriman's daughter Carol in a fancy dress costume. It was cast in silver and decorated with gold leaf. This was shown at my exhibit at Mrs. Whitney's Gallery in West Eighth Street. One day, about lunchtime, I went in to see the director about the show and noticed that there were only two demure-looking ladies in the gallery; they were dressed in fur coats and carried muffs.

I passed through the rooms to the office at the rear, and after ten minutes returned toward the front door. Finding the gallery empty, I noticed that one of the stands was also "empty"—for the silver statuette had been stolen; one of the harmless-looking ladies had obviously tucked it into her muff and made off with it as soon as she found herself alone and able to leave without being observed, the guard having gone out to lunch. The statuette was attached by piano wires to the stand, but these had been cut with sharp pliers.

This was only one of a series of thefts that took place six or seven times in different galleries during the following years. A group of two dancers in bronze once shown in a gallery window on the street level in Fifty-seventh Street was stolen on a rainy day by a man holding an umbrella. Standing in front of the window, he cut a square in the glass with a diamond ring on his right hand, reached in and pulled out the group in less time than it takes to tell and, slipping it under his ample raincoat, walked quickly toward Seventh Avenue. One of my friends who happened to live across the street watched the operation spellbound, but by the time he had run down two flights of stairs and dashed through traffic, the thief had disappeared. My friend examined the window with the square of glass pushed inside and saw that the group had been within reach of a long arm. He reported it at once to the police. The gallery was closed, as it was Sunday, so it was reported to the manager the next morning, but nothing was ever found. The cool expertness of such a trick struck me as unusual, and I almost felt flattered that anyone would want a piece of my sculpture badly enough to take such a chance. Three or four of my small "Incense Burner" bronzes were also stolen within three years.

In June, 1916, my brother Charles Lamson Hoffman married Lillian Holmes Crimmins. A group of his friends gave him a resplendent dinner and presented him with an old English loving cup. I wept as I helped him pack his trunk for the last time and realized that I would not be able again to knock on his door and say: "Chass, your bath is ready. . . ." for he had been a devoted and beloved member of our family for a long, long time and a tower of strength in time of need. Mother and I felt bereft when he left the home nest, but fortunately his wife and two sons brought him great happiness until his untimely death in 1929, at the age of forty-nine. When his first son, Richard 3rd, was a year old I made a portrait of him. This boy was killed in a motor accident when he was eighteen years old.

In 1917 I had an exhibit at the Brooks Reed Gallery in Boston. At the opening I was introduced to Mrs. Jack Gardner whose Venetian Palace museum I had been privileged to visit. During that visit I had been much struck by John Sargent's "La Carmencita," with its flamboyant colors that reminded me of the watercolors I had seen in his studio in London. Now the presence of Mrs. Gardner at my exhibit aroused my curiosity. Why should she come to see the work of a mere beginner like me? She wandered about by herself, then came up to me and asked the price of one of my lithographs of the Russian dancer Oukrainsky. "I'll take that one home with me," she said, and lifting her rather full skirt to the knee, pulled a roll of bills from the top of her stocking, counted out the amount, and put back the balance. She walked up to the wall, took down the framed drawing, and walked out with it under her arm. I was not the only one to register an expression of astonishment, but her original and forceful manner seemed to touch off a spark, and a number of other visitors followed her example by purchasing quite a number of these drawings, leaving them on the walls, however, until the exhibit closed.

BILL

This exhibit was one of the evidences of acceptance that began to give me courage. A much more important one was my acceptance by the studio-cleaner Bill. This tall lanky Slovak who had chosen a job and glorified it into an art was the finest of workmen, a perfectionist.

He had worked for the "big shots," as he called them—Saint-Gaudens, MacMonnies, Childe Hassam, Daniel French, Herbert Adams—and he was selective about his clients. Saint-Gaudens he worshiped. "The Saint had the stuff it takes!" Bill would say in a voice that suddenly became shy and reverential when he spoke of the days when he lived in Saint-Gaudens's place at Cornish and cleaned his studio. "He wasn't given to passin' out compliments, but if you did a job extra well, he'd smile and say, 'That's better than good,' and somehow I figgered that if you take on a job, even if it is a mean one, you can get a powerful load o' satisfaction out o' knowin' it's extra well done!"

At the end of his life, Saint-Gaudens was carried by Bill in his arms from the house to the studio and home again.

"He never gave up, Lady Hoff, and never whimpered; I tell you the Saint had what it takes!"

When I first achieved the eminence of a key on Bill's ring, he was working for Herbert Adams, and living on the top floor of his house. Every Christmas morning he came into Mr. Adams's studio with a box of cigars that the "Saint" had once given him. With great ceremony he would open the lid and invite Mr. Adams to take a whiff. Not one had been smoked, although Bill's passion for good cigars was a legend among his artist friends. Then Bill would take a long whiff himself and close the lid tightly, smiling and enjoying the gift all over again.

Once I asked him how I had been chosen for his key ring, and Bill told me that he had kept an eye on me ever since I broke the ice on Fifth Avenue, with my "Roosian Dancers" in Marcus's jewelry store window. "One day when I was working for Edward McCartan upstairs at 157," he added, "I looked you and the place over, and I decided I'd better start." I didn't tell him I'd dreamed of having somebody like him since Herbert Adams had told me about him.

What a joy Bill was and how he reveled in a job well done—the brasses and doorknobs shining, every stand scraped and rubbed with wax, every tool clean and in its place. What this means to a sculptor nobody who is not one will realize, for modeling and carving are dirty jobs, at the best, with marble dust or lumps of clay everywhere underfoot and tools to be continually cleaned and sharpened. To start the day's work with everything in readiness is one of a sculptor's dreams.

When Bill cleaned the floor, he pushed all the stands and chairs to the center of the room and worked along the wall edge and baseboards, moving about on his knees, his reach so wide that his long arms covered a great area with a single stroke. With his left hand he rubbed hard with a bit of cloth soaked in a secret liquid; then he followed with the right-hand cloth saturated in another special mixture. He worked back toward the center until he had cleaned a wide band all around the room. There was an easy rhythm in his movements, no waste effort. After the stands were scraped and oiled, these were pushed to the wall and left on the cleaned floor surface. If any part showed a blemish, Bill carefully removed it; then he tied wads of woolen cloth over his feet and, pressing hard, "skated" for an hour or so over the entire floor. When all was finished, he would stretch his lanky body, light a cigarette, and gloatingly survey his work.

There was only one possible man when the inside of the high studio skylight needed to be cleaned—Bill. He set up an eighteen-foot ladder, onto the top of which he had fastened a soapbox precariously with two thumbscrews. Pail and rags in hand, he mounted to the top rung and reached his prehensile free arm upward until his fingertips would touch the glass to give him what he called "a Christian Science sense of balance." When he saw me stop work and watch him with alarm, he would call out: "Maybe if you brought me the daily newssheet, Lady, I could slip it under my dogs and raise my estimation of myself a bit. Don't worry, go take a walk around the block, and when you come back I'll have the tops clean, or I'll be dead. How's that for a fair offer?"

"O.K., Bill," I would say, and then I would go out for a couple of hours, for it took Bill as long as that—no shortcuts for him!

Another skylight, in the studio at 159, produced a sufficiently shocking incident. The roof of this studio was accessible from adjacent buildings, and some of the rougher element among the boys of the neighborhood molded themselves some cement balls for ammunition and proceeded to fight with them across the roof. One of these balls crashed through the skylight when Bill was washing the floor. Glass showered down, and one large sliver struck the floor like a poignard and remained riveted there. Both Bill and I stared at it, fascinated, thinking the same thought: What if either of us had been under it? I notified the police, and they rounded up the boys responsible and read them the riot act, but I decided to take no further chances. I put heavy wiring both over and under the glass when it had been replaced in the skylight.

Bill had a leaning toward artistry. The statements he made out for his work and purchases, always meticulous and definite, were presented invariably on large sheets of yellow paper with the lettering carefully spaced so that it looked like print. He had held a drafting job once in an architect's office in Chicago, but his lively imagination had been his undoing. "They gave me a drawing of a porch to copy," he told me, "and I got interested in it and added a couple of owls on top of the entrance. I thought it was a swell addition, but next day the boss eased me out, and said that if I wanted to draw birds I'd better go to the zoo!"

Occasionally he added entertaining explanations to his expenditures. When our winter coal had been carried into the cellar by two down-and-outers, Bill itemized part of the charge as "extra greasing of the palms—them guys need a surprise like that once in a while!"

Always, laying a bill on my desk, he would strike an attitude in the doorway and watch me write out the check; then we would smile at each other and say in unison: "It's a pleasure, I'm sure!" and bow formally.

One day while he was working I asked him what had started him on his long career of helping sculptors.

"I'll figger that out for you when I'm not so busy," he answered. "Just now I'm rubbing hell out of this floor!"

The next day Bill appeared with a bundle of newspapers and an armful of photographs and portfolios. Tossing them all onto the model stand, he said: "Here it is, Lady, you asked for it; that is the story of my misspent life!" He opened the portfolios. "Here are my early attempts at drawing cartoons and caricatures. Made them all at Pratt Institute. Thought I was going to be a real artist."

Most of the drawings were done in the nineties during the period of Bill's dandyism when he sported a cane, spats, a high white collar, and a gray fedora worn at a sporty angle, topped off with a monocle attached to a long black ribbon. Many of the drawings were clever portraits of himself and of types he had noted in Greenwich Village. A number of them were biting caricatures, some of which had been reproduced in *Life* and *Judge*. Instead of blowing his first check from *Life* on a celebration (it was for $10), he framed and hung it in his room. Among the published drawings was one of a group of little children, delicately and sensitively done, an astonishing feat, I thought, when I looked at the massive left hand in which he held a pencil.

"But it's good, Bill," I commented.

"No," he stated firmly, "not good *enough*. It didn't take me long to know my work was second class, maybe third, maybe steerage, and it made me sick. I wanted tops or nothing, so I decided to work in some artists' studios to help them out, posing and kneading their clay and cleaning floors, studying all the time to see what the heck art was all about. When I fix up the clay into nice fat little sausages, just the right consistency, I says to meself—If ye can't do it yerself, at least you can grease the wheels for the other guy and help him to climb to dizzy heights!"

When I suggested that he ought to break in a young assistant to carry on "the Bill technique," he shouted at me, "Hell, Lady, none of the kids today know what work means and they don't plan to find out, either. I tell you it's sweat and elbow grease and love o' beauty in me own special way that got me where I am. The kids today try to get by, leavin' out all they can, so maybe the boss won't see behind things or around the corner. But I start off with the bad corners and back o' things, so I know when the furniture is pushed back it's setting on clean ground. That gives me a kick. To hell whether the boss sees it. A good boss will notice just that sort of performance, and if he doesn't, well, I'll damn well drag him over one day and make him look behind things, and he'll say, 'Bill, it's beautiful,' and on my way home I'll feel so lighthearted I'll blow the first poor guy I meet to a beer!"

After we had finished the portfolio, Bill spread his clippings on the floor and began sorting them, sitting in his favorite position, first on one and then the other of his big feet. This, he used to say, rested his knees, and his shoes were so big that they served as a stool and saved him the bother of carrying one around. After years of this he had acquired a peculiar walk that I have seen only in the most primitive people whose feet turn in from sitting in that special manner, and from climbing trees.

The clippings were all about the artists for whom he had worked. It pleased me that he had kept one about a bronze of mine. "Bill Working" I called it, and it was Bill sprawling over the floor in his old running shirt, a cigarette butt hanging from his lips, a scraper in his hip pocket, even his patched shoes worn full of holes. The familiar little curl of hair stuck up from the back of his head like the tip of a Chinaman's cap, and in front of his enormous hands were his bucket and rags. The bronze had just been bought by the Jeu de Paume Museum in Paris.

"It sure does show me down to the ground," Bill said, regarding the photograph with pride. "I'm real happy to be set permanent in Paris. That's a real town! I looked it over with all its dames the time I walked from London to Madrid. Yes, that's the truth; my 'dogs' are so big, and my legs so long, that they carried me all the way, except for the boat ride, and a few good lifts on trucks. I looked at all the masterpieces I'd heard about. After that, I had no more doubts, thinking I could be a real artist on my own steam, but I was going to choose who I'd work for, and I'd always tell 'em the truth, good or bad, whether they wanted it or not!" Bill was pleased with the idea; he threw back his head, and laughed.

If I was entertaining a guest, Bill might choose that moment to appear in the studio after cleaning the roof, carrying a broom and shovel over his shoulder, the shattered brim of a felt hat on the back of his head (he had torn the crown out), and I would introduce this gigantic scarecrow (he used to say that he had posed for almost every statue of Lincoln in the United States) brandishing a bucketful of cinders.

"Pleased to meet you," he would say, bowing to my guest. "We meet 'most everybody in this joint. You'll pardon my observing that our great Mr. Edison may have brains for inventions, but his plants over there on Thirty-ninth Street and the river generate a hell of a lot of cinders and hard labor, along with their electric juice. So long, visitor, and come again when I can stay longer!"

Once he came to the studio in a fine new overcoat that someone had given him. As I was about to admire his appearance, he took the coat off and flung it on the modeling stand.

"That's the first and the last time I'll risk walking through the streets of this town with this coat. I thought I would save some money by walking up here today, but instead of that I looked down and saw how shabby my shoes looked compared to my fancy overcoat, so I stopped and had myself a shine. While I was sitting there, I happened to look at myself in the mirror and noticed how badly I needed a shave and a haircut. When I got through paying for all that and started up this way, guys kept walking up beside me, saying, 'Brother, can't you lend me a dime?' so of course I lends him a dime, but when I get to this street and an old fellow comes up to me at the corner, I just gives up and says, 'Lay off, brother, you have made a mistake; I work this side of the street myself!' That overcoat cost me a dollar forty, and I thought I was saving carfare! Now I begin to feel sorry for how the other half lives, and I give this coat away tonight!"—and he did.

There was nothing one could do about Bill. One winter he began to fail, and the faded green-black overcoat with the upturned collar, held together by four-inch horse-blanket safety pins hung limper than ever on his gaunt frame. How he hated to give up and see another man called in to help! His pride was shaken, and he began to talk about old age and death and "what can a man leave behind him!" Then suddenly he vanished. When my postal cards did not produce results, I thought he must be really ill. Then I learned that he was in a hospital with a serious infection. I found him in a crowded ward (it was at the time of a pneumonia epidemic) where there was merely room enough to stand between the beds.

At a glance I knew Bill was doomed. His sunken, burning eyes stared beyond the limits of this world; his head rolled sideways on his emaciated shoulders; his huge frame seemed stripped to the bone; and attacks of delirium were fogging his mind. I put my hand on his arm.

"Oh, Gawd, Lady Hoff," he gasped, "I didn't want you to see me like this. I'm on the skids now for the last ride, and nobody can help me, nobody, not even you. So long, Lady Hoff, lean over a bit. I got no wind left. Gee, the skids are steep, like a ski jump ye never seen before. . . ." He choked, and closed his eyes and waved at me slowly, as if from a great distance.

Jean-Julien Lemordant

One day in March, 1917, a hotel messenger brought me a letter from a friend in Paris, Monsieur Léonce Bénédite, Director of the Luxembourg Museum. He had known me during my student years, just before the war, when we had both worked with Rodin, helping to sort hundreds of drawings and making an inventory of his collection. The war had driven us apart, but we had kept in touch by letter; I now read this note in French:

> Malvina, you have wanted so much to help us in this war, and you feel so far away, I am sending the war to you! The man who takes this letter to America is the symbol of the best we have in France. His name is Lemordant and he is a great painter. He volunteered at the outbreak of war, fought bravely, was terribly wounded, was taken as a prisoner to Germany, and was later exchanged. Now we send him as our messenger to America. He is going to New Haven and other places to lecture. I know you will care for him, and be his friend. . . .

I wrote an answer in French, saying I would come to the hotel in half an hour, and gave it to the messenger. Arriving at the desk, I sent up my name,

HEAD OF JEAN-JULIEN LEMORDANT

"BILL" (©MH)

saying I would wait for Monsieur Lemordant to come down. The clerk looked puzzled.

"But, Miss, do you know that this man is crippled, and can get about only with two canes, and his head is bound up in a bandage . . ."

My heart sank. "What should I do, then?" I asked.

"He left word for Miss Hoffman to come directly to his room, fifteen o one."

I went up. The door was ajar and I knocked.

"Who is it?" came the deep-voiced question.

"Malvina Hoffman," I said.

Then, in French, he said, "Oh, come in. Sit down there next to me," and he held out his hand. The room was in semidarkness. A white bandage was bound around his head, covering his eyes. He is blind, I realized, with a shock. There was a long moment of silence between us.

Then he said: "Our friend in Paris has told me all about you and your friendship with him and Rodin, and how you worked with the Master until the outbreak of the war. But you know nothing about me except what he has said in his letter to you. I can well imagine what you must feel to find that the man he sent into your care is both blind and crippled. But if you will give me the time now at our first meeting to tell you my story, we will not have to refer to it again, for there is so much that I must accomplish during my short visit to America."

I assured him that he could take his time and that I would listen carefully.

Then he began his story. "In August, 1914, I was spending the summer, as usual, climbing about the rocks in Saint-Guénolé in Brittany, where I have a studio and where I loved to paint the people and the sky and the radiant colors of the country. Then war was declared and, although I was beyond the age that would be called upon to serve, I wiped the paints from my palette and hung it on the wall of my studio. I turned my pictures toward the wall and hung my only pair of extra shoes on a nail.

"I trekked to the office of army enlistments and applied for active service. In the 41st Regiment of the Infantry I obtained my baptism of war. The struggle broke over us like a tidal wave. In one engagement, I was charging up over a little hill with the other men when something in my knee cracked; a bullet had struck it, and one of the soldiers had to use his bayonet as a splint and bind me up before we could go on. Over the top we went, but there we found ourselves very close to a line of Germans who had hidden in a ditch, and a volley from their revolvers at close range cut us down. One of their bullets struck me here. . . ." and he pointed to the bandage around his head.

The Germans captured him; but he was repatriated in an exchange of prisoners. Though blind, he then prepared himself to give lectures on the art and sculpture of France. As he went about with two canes, lecturing, he was thrilled by the news that he was to be sent to America to receive the Howland Prize at Yale University. "It was this honor that gave me the chance to come to this country of yours," he said to me. "Although I have wished all my life to see it, I must now content myself with feeling it. I am to go to New Haven in June to deliver the graduation address to the students.

"The recent operation, one of many I have had on my head, was to try to prevent the splinters of the bone from growing inward, because if that happens it might pierce the envelope of the brain; that would be the end. There is unfortunately a possibility that I may get worse over here, as there are signs of an abscess on the brain. It is necessary for me to travel lying down, and if possible with two mattresses to prevent the jarring on my hips and spine, as this causes me terrible pain."

At this point he held out his hand, and I grasped it; I assured him that I would do all in my power to make such a difficult journey possible for him. His traveling companion, a young Frenchman, would be in charge for the first week; after that, a group of friends would help, including Miss Helen Frick.

One of the trips that I took with him was to Pittsburgh where he spoke to a crowded auditorium at the Carnegie Institute. The evening after the lecture was spent at the house of Miss Frick who had invited Dr. John Alfred Brashear the astronomer, to meet Lemordant. The aged scientist and lens grinder related the story of his life, how after many years of labor and study he was able to make his own lenses and telescope by which he could bring man closer to the wonders of the stars and moon. I translated the story as he told it to Lemordant, and it was evident that the latter was deeply moved. He would often stretch forward his hand to grasp Dr. Brashear's, and one could feel the bond of friendship that was being forged between them.

Lemordant in turn told the story of his own life, how in his youth he had studied the coastline and the skies at Saint-Malo, and how later he had spent years climbing over the rocks of Brittany, settling at last at Saint-Guénolé. He had built a little studio there facing the Atlantic, which at this point of the coast rolls across in full sweep and breaks its gigantic waves against the cliff at Finistère. In this little fishing village Lemordant had grown to maturity, beloved by the fishing folk for his simple honest ways, and for his colorful painting. His figure, carrying an easel and a canvas, was a familiar sight to the natives along that coast. He would go out at sunrise and often return late. During the days of the "Pardons," Lemordant painted the crowds of fisherfolk, the women dressed in black with their starched white coifs tied tightly under the chin with fluttering ribbons, the men in black felt low-crowned hats with black ribbons, and golden embroidered vests; all trudging along the sands under the blue magnificence of the Brittany sky, the endless, changing patterns of the billowing clouds forming iridescent reflections in the pools of water on the sands.

When the time came for him to deliver the lecture at Yale, after his last appearance in New York—a lecture at the home of Samuel Lewisohn—the doctors warned him that his condition was serious and that he would have to sail for Europe immediately after the Yale engagement. After this successful climax to his trip, Dr. Carrel and I bade him bon voyage with apprehension and anxiety, realizing that he was in a much-weakened condition.

The next news we had of him was a short note telling us that the abscess in his head had burst during the voyage and that he had to have an operation on arrival at the Military Hospital. During this operation something had gone wrong, and he had lost the power of speech, his left arm had been paralyzed, and he was lying on a board, unable to move.

The long years that followed were a never-ending battle against darkness and hopelessness, but he amazed his friends by his independence and his zest for work. He concentrated his energies on learning how to speak again, and how to memorize what was read to him. He obtained a mechanical device that cut wax records, and to this he would make whatever sounds he *could*, noting the words he was *trying* to speak; and the next day his secretary read those words to him again, and he would listen to the records and try once more to make sounds that resembled more what he was trying to say. By this tedious process he finally achieved the impossible; he regained his voice and his vocabulary to such an extent that he could give lectures, bringing large audiences under the spell of his inspiring words. He could sing the old songs of corsairs, sailors, and fishermen, and never forgot the lines he had locked away in memory.

Having studied architecture in his youth, he now turned to architectural problems, and fabricated a scale model of a house; to a cardboard plan he attached sections of cardboard to mark the elevations, and instructed his friends how to cut these with a sense of accuracy that astonished them.

By the good fortune of selling some of his paintings to various museums and art collectors in America, he was able to buy, after several years, a little piece of property on the Avenue du Parc Montsouris in Paris. This land was listed as unsuitable for a building of any kind, owing to the steep declivity of the bank, which ended in a retaining wall of the avenue. Perhaps it was the very impossibility of this project that challenged Lemordant to overcome what to another architect might have been an unsurmountable problem. After months of experimenting with his scale models and conferring with builders and contractors, the work was started, and when the house was finished, to the astonishment of all, he had constructed a completely modern type of dwelling, original in form and detail, although such architecture was almost unheard of when Lemordant became blind in 1915. He had, of course, had many articles read to him describing this recent evolution, but it was startling to see how his mind had grasped the new ideas of horizontal lines and simple, flat surfaces. In 1932 he moved into his new home.

In 1935 he was in a taxicab driving across Paris when it collided with a truck, and turned completely over. In the accident, his head struck against the pavement, reopening the old wound in his forehead. He took advantage of his misfortune by authorizing the doctors to explore the sinus cavities and see if by any chance the optic nerve might not be released from pressure, which he himself had believed caused his blindness. He assumed full responsibility for the operation, which he had never before been able to persuade them to undertake.

After some time the doctors decided to remove the bandages from his eyes and test his sight. They put him in a small dark room, flashed a strong light from one side and Lemordant cried out, "I see light—too much light!" He was then bandaged up again, and remained in the hospital for more treatment for several weeks longer. The news of the miraculous, though only partial, return of his sight was flashed around the world, for his case had become known and his reputation as a soldier and lecturer had been publicized in many countries. He was overwhelmed by the letters and telegrams he received rejoicing with him in the possibility of regaining his vision.

When I returned to France in the following year, we met at Saint-Guénolé in his little stone house on the rocks. It was evening, and after supper we went down to the beach for a walk along the sands. It was low tide, and the miles of sand gleamed in the moonlight. We had hardly dared mention what had befallen him, but now he said: "At last, Malvina, I can tell you that the waves are breaking, for not only do I hear them; I can see the moonlight shining on their white crests!"

Turning to go home, we were facing the lighthouse of Eckmühl. As the shafts of light from the beacon swept over the sea, it also enveloped us for a fleeting moment in its powerful rays. I saw Lemordant put his hands up to his eyes and then pull down his hat over his face, saying: "Is it not wonderful? The rays from my beloved lighthouse are really too strong for me now; they almost strike me down with their power. Let us face the sea for a moment and here under the stars give thanks for this miracle that has happened to me, that I have come from utter darkness into partial light!"

Unveiling of the "Bacchanale." Left to right: Sam, Marie-Louise Emmet, Léonce Bénédite, MH, William Astor Chanler

PART III

CHAPTER SIXTEEN

MY FIRST "BIG JOB"

DURING THE war years, each summer Mother and I took a holiday in August and spent a few weeks at Little Boar's Head, New Hampshire. One of these is memorable to me, for I was given the chance to try my wings. Abraham Garfield, architect from Cleveland, had seen my group of Pavlova and Mordkin in the "Bacchanale," in small size. He was looking for a big group in bronze for a client's garden, and one day, while on the beach, he suddenly turned and said, "Do you think you could model your group of dancers over-life-size and have it cast in bronze within a year and a half?" That an architect could actually be willing to take a chance on a young sculptor almost took my breath away. "My client wants something gay and decorative, and somehow I think you could pull this off."

Such an opportunity stirred my imagination, and my hopes knew no bounds. The group was completed, cast, and delivered to Cleveland on time, and I had the pleasure of seeing it installed with the planting and setting just as the client, architect, and the sculptor wanted it.

It so happened that the next winter a group of French critics and museum representatives visited Cleveland and wrote to me to say that they would like to acquire a bronze replica of this group if the owner would permit another cast to be made, and that it would be given a place in the Luxembourg Gardens in Paris. It would be hard to describe my feelings in reading such news. Mr. Dalton, the owner, was gratified by the thought that a copy of his group was wanted for a setting as ideal as the Luxembourg Gardens. He not only enthusiastically gave his consent but also offered to pay the cost of the second bronze as his way of expressing his admiration for France.

I arrived in Paris in May, 1919, by invitation of Monsieur Bénédite, curator of the Musée du Luxembourg and Musée Rodin. He offered me the choice of two or three pedestals in different sections of the gardens. When we came to the one near the Medici Fountain, I hardly dared ask if this would be a possible choice. Monsieur Bénédite gave me a quizzical glance. "I kept the best for the last, Malvina." My eyes filled with tears of happiness. Is there any artist who has spent his student days in Paris and has wandered at sunset in these gardens who does not cherish fond memories of this secluded rendezvous of romance, the rectangular pool bordered by ivy-garlanded chains, and at the end of which is placed the marble group of dreaming lovers quite oblivious of Father Time, who hovers over them kneeling on a marble cloud.

So, in my innocence I felt that one of my children would be in this enchanted garden forever and ever. . . . Had immortality touched me with its wing?

After the Second World War, twenty-nine years later, in 1948, I went to Paris again. News had reached me that the Nazis in their occupation of Paris had stolen and melted down many bronze statues, among others my group of dancers. So, one afternoon I walked across the gardens and came to the Medici Fountain and gave thanks that this at least was intact and just as it had always been; the lovers were still sleeping unharmed. *Eros omnia vincit.* A German bomb that had fallen in the pool below them did not go off and did not disturb them.

I wandered nearer the site of my group. . . . There was no trace of it left —not even the pedestal—nothing but the pang of memory! The dream of immortality had been totally effaced.

When I had arrived in Paris in May, 1919, at the invitation of Monsieur Benédite, I went at once to Giselle Bunau-Varilla, who welcomed me to her home at 71 rue Notre-Dame-des-Champs. The green room with casement windows looking out on the garden was to be called mine, and once again I could rejoice in my familiar old "quartier," living in a beloved friend's home.

I found Monsieur Bénédite trying to reinstall Rodin's collection in the Musée Rodin. He asked if I could assist in finding certain pieces that had been hidden for safety during the war. When I entered the Hôtel Biron in the rue de Varenne, I was choked with emotion, and thankful to be permitted to express my debt to my Master by working there, washing and cleaning his marbles and helping Monsieur Bénédite place them in the galleries as I had helped Rodin himself just before the outbreak of the war. We found the missing bronzes where they had been buried by trusted friends.

At the completion of this work, and as a great surprise to me, I was made an Officier de l'Instruction Publique in Paris, and it was gratifying to be welcomed into a group of eminent artists and citizens, who all had a common interest in the art movement of the day, as well as in the background and tradition of the past.

As directors of the canteens of the Appui aux Artistes, which had been active during the entire war and for a year afterward, a group of us were given a party by the artists of Montmartre; the stage setting was the Place du Tertre—the moon was full and red, there were flowers and speeches, and dozens of little tables were set out for us on the Place—it was like a scene in the opera *Louise*. The painter Neumont opened his studio for the occasion, poets recited their verses, and the *patron* of one of the restaurants opened his wine cellar to the guests, handing me the keys, so that champagne and French wine flowed throughout the evening.

After this celebration I reported to the American Red Cross and to the League of Red Cross Societies, concerning my forthcoming trip to Yugoslavia, and had the good fortune to meet General Sir David Henderson, Director of the League. I was struck by his finely chiseled features and sad, thoughtful eyes, and was gratified when he gave me the opportunity of designing a badge for the League. He also promised me that if he should come to New York, and had the time, he would pose for a portrait, and we parted with high hopes, but not sure that we would ever meet again.

Although I was working with the Red Cross Communications Department at the time, I was unable to find out anything about Sam from whom I had had no news for nearly five months. But finally, in June, I got word from him that he would have three days' leave. We were able to arrange a meeting in Paris, and he was present at the unveiling of my large bronze group of Pavlova and Mordkin in the Luxembourg Gardens. It was an ecstatic and memorable day for both of us.

The first Sunday that I could free myself from duties I spent at Meudon, just as I had done so many times with Rodin years ago, wandering about in the garden, communing with his spirit, and again marveling at the hundreds of plaster casts and expressions of his genius, stored in endless cases and drawers in his studios.

July 14th of that same year, 1919, was the *Jour de Gloire*. Sam was able to join me again in Paris for this happy celebration, when a victory parade was staged on the Champs-Elysées; the victorious armies marching down the Avenue de la Grande-Armée, through the Arc de Triomphe, and curving around the Place de la Concorde. Once again good fortune came our way, for my sister Helen and Sam and I were invited to see the parade from the balcony of the Hôtel Crillon with Mr. Henry White, Member of the American Commission to Negotiate Peace. Although we started out very early in the morning, when we came to the Avenue des Champs-Elysées the crowd was already so solid that for the only time in my life I crossed that wide thoroughfare without touching my foot to the ground! As I was thin and light, I found myself lifted by the pressure of people, and thus suspended I never touched the pavement again until I reached the sidewalk in front of the hotel.

The finale of that great day was fireworks all over Paris, which we watched, with our fellow artists, from the roof garden over Neumont's studio on the Place du Tertre where we had a magnificent view of the entire city.

By now Sauvage (Marie-Louise Emmet), my friend of the New York Red Cross, was with me, preparing to accompany me to Yugoslavia. She was at the evening celebration with Sam and me, and afterward she and I took Sam to the Gare du Nord to see him off, as he was to return to army service for an indefinite period. After leaving Sam, and finding the streets too crowded for normal traffic, Sauvage and I decided to walk back to Giselle's rather than risk taking a cab; in fact, we saw cabs bounced and pushed over in the streets, and found it safer to keep afoot.

My next duty was to confer with Mr. Herbert Hoover, then Director of the American Relief Commission, and talk over the proposed trip to Yugoslavia. I had been active in this work in New York, and had been requested to go to that country to inspect the twenty-five child-feeding stations and bring back a report. Mr. Hoover now sent for Sauvage and me to receive our passports and to be thoroughly briefed by his secretary, Mr. Lewis Strauss, for the trip. He showed us the map of the Balkans on his wall, punctuated by red and white pins. "These are the places I want you to visit; the red ones are epidemic areas —typhus, malaria . . ." Before we left his office, Mr. Hoover gave us this very brief, but definite, instruction: "Do not forget that you are wearing a uniform of the United States. Do not get shot, for that might make complications for your government, and do not get sick, because that will delay your return. Everyone else I have sent to that area has fallen sick and is in the hospital— and this time I want better results!" His smile was kind, however, and we were fortunate enough to carry out the order to return, in spite of the fact that we were indeed very ill, both of us, on the trip. But we did succeed in getting a full report, and many pictures and data, which we delivered to Mr. Hoover on time. He made selections from my account, and arranged for the story to be published, with many of my drawings and photographs, in the magazine *Survey*. Another version, with illustrations, was published in *Travel*. A complete copy of the report was given to the State Department.

CHAPTER SEVENTEEN

THE BALKAN ADVENTURE

THE BALKAN TRIP began in Paris, and when we boarded the night train, the Orient Express, to go to Trieste as our first stop, Sauvage and I felt we were embarking into the unknown. We had been warned of many hazards and existing epidemics, but we were young and healthy, and keen for adventure. I was standing on the platform of the car as the train was about to start. A military delegation came alongside and saluted two British officers, who quickly boarded the train with their orderlies. The whistle blew and we pulled out.

To my surprise one of the officers was General Sir David Henderson, who was going to Geneva. I could scarcely believe my eyes. Only a few days before I had met him at the Red Cross office, surrounded by his official aura of authority. Now we were on the same train, and he joined us in our compartment, where we talked over all aspects of our trip as the hours sped past. There was no edge to the horizon of our thoughts. A sudden newness attached itself to the most ordinary remarks. It is by such accidental circumstances that a lasting friendship may come into being. Speeding through the darkness into dim regions of unfamiliar territory, not knowing if there would ever be another meeting, sensing the dangers ahead and the probability that my journey might well terminate in some pest-ridden village in Macedonia, every moment seemed charged with significance.

I went out to the platform to smoke a cigarette, when the other British officer, who was a stranger to me, came through from the next car. "Temperley is my name," he said in a deep British voice. "I was told by my orderly that you two ladies were going on a trip through the Balkans—orderlies know everything that is going on, you know!" he smiled. "I'm on a similar errand myself," he continued, "but I've traveled that country many times before; they call me the 'Balkan Dog,' but I'm really just a harmless historian. How far do you go on this train?"

COLONEL PRIBICEVICH AND MH IN UNIFORM IN THE BALKANS IN 1919

"We get off at Trieste," I answered, "and from there we go by motor or by whatever means of transport we can find."

"I go through to Belgrade," said the major, "and from there down through Albania if I'm lucky. There's a lot of fighting still going on down there. You must be careful about that, and about your health too. Watch out for lice and long-legged malaria mosquitoes—and never drink water without disinfecting it."

"Nice holiday resort!" I remarked, "but why worry—it may not happen!"

"If I can be of use to you, and if our paths ever cross again, here is my card," said the major.

"If you ever come to Cambridge," he added, "come to see me there at Peterhouse. We'll have lots to talk about after you visit these Balkan countries. Good luck, and au revoir!"

Sauvage and I traveled for seven weeks after our arrival in Trieste. In Athens I fell a prey to sunstroke, trying to study the wonders of the Acropolis in the scorching heat of midday; but this was my only time free from Red Cross duties and I felt it was worth the risk. Shortly after my recovery, at Salonika, which was our next stop, Sauvage found herself in the hospital with "sand-flea fever," a jolly sort of disease that can cause such swelling of the face and glands that one would think the victim had been bitten by a dragon rather than a flea. We were finally well enough to start northward by train. The heat was gross, and the dusty air quivered in the blistering glare, as we stopped at the dingy station of Skoplje. We were carrying ten bags of ice from Salonika to the Red Cross Hospital for diphtheria patients, and although much had melted on the way there was enough left to be of some help.

On the station platform, to our amazement, was Major Temperley surrounded by many sick and sallow malaria victims. He looked more unkempt and exhausted than anyone we had seen on the way. When he caught sight of us, he jumped to his feet. "My word, girls, what a piece of good luck! Cheerio, and how are you?"

We were ordered off the train to change to another string of baggage and cattle cars going to Nis. Ducks, pigs, and chickens were being unloaded by the peasants, and then we were told to get on board at once and the Major and his orderly jumped on with us. The cars were filthy beyond words. The wood benches had served merely to separate the cattle and the pigs. No glass was left in the windows and there were no screens; Major Temperley gave the place one look. . . . "Clear out, girls; we'll have this place swept and disinfected before you come inside!" We sat listlessly on the steps of the car, so hot and weary after our long journey that nothing mattered; but we were grateful for the major's precautions.

All that day and through the night we rattled along in this odoriferous cattle car. But the wonder of that journey was that this dusty worn-out Cambridge professor was able to keep me so interested in his tales of Balkan heroism and history that I was actually sorry when we neared the jumping-off depot at Nis. The poems and lyrics he recited on that trip revealed a wealth and accuracy of memory that dumbfounded me. I shall always remember the lines he recited after telling me that an artist must ride Pegasus with a light hand. "Never let the weight of Life get you down. . . . Remember these lines by Tennyson, Malvina:

> "There came a rider to the castle gate.
> The night was stormy and the hour late,
> The horse had wings and would have flown
> But that his heavy rider held him down. . . ."

These were his parting words as we climbed down the steps to the platform at Nis. He went on to Belgrade and then back to London. Another friendship born in a railroad car.

Many years later, Major Temperley came to Harvard as "Exchange Professor," and at that time he often visited my New York studio. We found that, like wine, our friendship had ripened with the years.

While I was abroad on the Yugoslavian trip, Mother was in the care of a fine, capable nurse, Mrs. Norma Beckford, and when the weather was warm she took Mamma up to a house she had in New London, Connecticut, on the water's edge. After my return, still feeling the effects of my heat prostration at Athens, I went up to see Mamma, and she said: "I'm all right; you don't have to worry about me. It's cool here by the water, and I'm being spoiled and having a lovely time, but I don't see why you don't take a holiday yourself." Urged by Mamma, at the end of August Sam and I and Sauvage and Ed McCartan decided that my car Peewee would navigate well enough to take us up to the St. Lawrence River for a two-week outing. As we left, I said, "We must stop on the way and see Mother, because she'll laugh at this car that's still running." We decided Peewee ran on air and water—that's about all we ever put in—still, it got us to the Thousand Islands, and there we rented twin cabins with a little porch in front. Ed and Sam were in one and Sauvage and I in the other, and we went paddling, canoeing, fishing, picnicking, and wandering around in the woods. I have never been back there since, and so the memory of that carefree, magical holiday remains unchangeable in my mind.

DR. FRAENKEL

As my mother's health continued to fail, one of the great comforts to her and to me was Dr. Joseph Fraenkel, a rare friend I made in those difficult years. He was a Viennese Jew, in brilliance and wisdom so far ahead of his time that he was considered a fanatic (Gehirne mit zwei Beinen—a brain with two legs!). But to those who appreciated him, he gave unreservedly of his knowledge and perceptiveness in medicine and philosophy, and influenced the few doctors who dared to blaze the trail for new treatments of physical and mental ailments.

His eyes were frightening. They protruded from under his bushy eyebrows and blazed with a ferocity that pierced falsehood or bluff. He searched the depths and was not afraid of exposing what he found. At the top of his house he had a library and working laboratory where, after his crowded days of caring for the sick, he would continue his indefatigable searching. A celestial and terrestrial globe stood at each end of a big table; books in many languages lined the walls and were piled on the floor beside his desk chair.

By some stroke of fortune I was admitted to his inner sanctum. When I first saw him in this study, it was as if I had entered another world. He had been engaged for years in translating the Latin works of certain scholars into English. Everything that Swedenborg had written he had thoroughly read and absorbed. Rows of books on Oriental religions and philosophy were among his treasures. The best translation he could find of the Vedic writings in Sanskrit were his constant companions. Fabre and his revelations of animal life, the Bible, the poets of Germany and France, philosophical treatises from many minds in many lands—this world of wisdom and spiritual understanding was all stored here. It was at night that he withdrew to his workroom, and it was there he took the time to initiate his pupils into secrets that were at that time thought to be out of reach or reason. We would turn the wooden sphere slowly, while he explained the course of planets and stars as if they were his close friends. "Read, Malvina, read always. Search out the ancient Oriental truth of things. They knew so much more than modern man. Ages of laziness and worldly-minded men have forgotten that Asia was old and wise before Europe was born!"

His devotion to my mother was extraordinary. As her health failed, he sensed the unspoken fears that racked my heart. His own health was broken, and his time on earth was limited, but to the very end he would come to comfort us when he should have been in his bed. Sometimes at night he would appear, uncalled, sure of how much he was wanted. I had constant evidence of his psychic powers and supersensitiveness, as well as of his human understanding. His incisive criticisms of my work in the studio would shake me into new awareness. ". . . Look for the best, Malvina. Die Menschen verheimlichen sich!" After a few moments of talk about how to read and study the masters of old, he would draw a book out of his pocket and put it on the table, saying: "Read it thoughtfully, Malvina, and try to remember it!" Once it was Fabre d'Olivet's *Hermeneutic Origin of the Social State of Man*. "It sounds formidable, but it is good for you. When you have finished reading it, bring it with you, and we will discuss it." Without another word he would be gone. Another time it was the Golden Verses of Pythagoras that he gave me, and I still treasure the hours we spent reading these, and commentaries that filled a large volume. He it was who first revealed to me the mind and writings of Édouard Schuré, whose book *Les Grands Initiés* went with me on most of my travels. If there were only more teachers like this man, who could touch off the smoldering embers in the minds of their pupils!

One night after my mother had been especially restless and I was unable to sleep, I went to the telephone in a moment of weakness and thought, I must call Dr. Fraenkel. Before I could call the number, the telephone started ringing. I answered at once and heard my friend's unmistakable voice: "I think tonight you and your mamma are having a hard time. I come in a few moments. . . ." He hung up. There was nothing to do but to marvel at this experience, and in twenty minutes there was a soft knock at our door and there he stood, wrapped in a white muffler and heavy overcoat. "I go to Mamma first," he said, as he passed and put his hand on my arm. "You wait here."

He came back before long. "She is asleep now, and will rest. And you must learn also to sleep. It is an art, when the mind is troubled to learn how to rest—otherwise you will get insomnia—that would be bad. But do not tell me I should not have come tonight. I know very well my own sickness. I sent the nurse to get a prescription for me; she will be coming back soon. I go now, and she will never know I came out. The younger doctors insist they can save me by operating. I know that they cannot, but in a few days I will let them have their way. Otherwise they will always say, 'We could have saved him!' I do not wish to be saved. Life is such a sensitive, wonderful introduction, but it is only a beginning. Keep your fires burning, and always listen by way of the heart, not the words, and always you will be filled with wonder!"

About a week later some friends persuaded me to go to dinner with them at l'Aiglon Restaurant. I was not in the mood to be gay, but forced myself to go in spite of a sense of impending sorrow. Groups of young people were enjoying themselves all about us. My soul was gripped with a sudden overpowering emotion. Voices grew faint. . . . The next thing of which I was conscious was a cold wet compress being put on my forehead. I was lying in the rest room, having fainted at the table.

When consciousness returned, I asked my hostess for permission immediately to make a telephone call. I was able to get to the booth, and I asked for Dr. Fraenkel's nurse. I was so sure he had gone to the hospital that I had memorized the number to call later that evening. When I asked for a report on my friend's condition, the nurse replied, "Dr. Fraenkel died ten minutes ago."

"Did they operate?" I asked. "Yes," she said, "but they found his condition hopeless."

A strange quietude came over me. I bade my hostess good night and said I could drive home alone, that I felt quite able to go and preferred that no one accompany me. Reluctantly she acquiesced.

The following morning, in that suspended moment of dawn, I felt suddenly the presence of someone standing at the door of my room. It was Dr. Fraenkel who appeared clearly before me. He put his hand forward, and I felt it pressing my brow. "It is all right now, Malvina. I am with God!"

"THE SACRIFICE"

In 1920 when I was in France, I purchased a ten-ton block of Caen stone and had it shipped to my stone carver Robert Baillie in New Jersey. The year before, Robert Bacon, in my studio in New York, had expressed his interest in

"THE SACRIFICE"

the study for a memorial group I was planning. Very soon after, in France, I was saddened to hear that this fine and valued friend had died. Mrs. Bacon telegraphed me that his last wish had been to have me make the group, "The Sacrifice," in French Caen stone, and she confirmed the commission and said she would present the group to Harvard as a memorial for World War I.

On my return after the stone had been shipped, we began work. When the heavy masses of excess stone had been cut off and the group reduced to about six tons and ready to finish, we moved it on a truck to 157. There we took out the big front window of the erstwhile harness room and built a ramp of two steel rails on supports made of railroad ties and so managed to get the rough-cut stone in.

For fifteen months Baillie and I carved this group. If I had known ahead of time what work was involved in carving a full suit of chain armor in stone, I think I would never have started such a medieval labor of love. Since we could not use a mallet for fear of lifting off the stone links, we had to carve them with hand pressure and sharp chisels. However, it strengthened my arm and tested my patience and won me the friendly help of Mr. Bashford Dean, Curator of Arms and Armor at the Metropolitan Museum. When the group was finally finished, he gave me a rare gauntlet and a piece of chain mail, saying it was because I worked like a medieval craftsman.

During the last months of work on this group, I offered the use of my car to the New York Red Cross. I was sent on numberless errands, including meeting the steamers bringing Red Cross workers to New York. One of the most distinguished visitors I was sent to welcome was General Sir David Henderson who in Paris had agreed to let me model a portrait of him if he ever came to America. Between the dock and his destination in New York we made the appointment for the sittings and, since his time was limited, I built up the head from memory so that we got off to a good start. He was one of those aristocratic Britishers whose definite clean-cut features are a delight to sculptors. I noted new lines of suffering on his face and found that since our last meeting he had lost his only son in an airplane accident.

Sir David showed interest in the figures of my stone group, and I confessed to him it was difficult to find the type I wanted for the young crusader. He drew a photo from his uniform pocket and said it was the last one taken of his aviator son. The serene strength of the face struck me, and I begged leave to borrow the picture and use it as my guide. Sir David agreed, and before he left assured me that the crusader was very like his son. When the portrait of Sir David was completed, a deep and abiding friendship had been formed between us. I gave him a little bronze he liked as a souvenir when he left, for somehow we both had the presentiment that we would never meet again.

He went to Geneva, and from there I had news that he had been taken ill. I remember still how earnestly I prayed for his recovery, hoping the waves of thought might be strong enough to reach Him. . . . At last a letter came for me, postmarked Geneva. Mother asked me to stay with her while I read it. It was from Lady Henderson: "David received your letter, but was too ill to write you. He died yesterday. He had your letter beside him. He spoke often of the portrait you made of him in America. I am wondering if it could go to the Imperial War Museum in London?" The following spring I went to see Lady Henderson in London and arranged to carry out her wishes.

When the stone group of "The Sacrifice" was almost completed, an incident occurred that I make no effort to explain, but these are the facts:

One morning I awoke from a dream in which there had appeared to me the figure of a man walking toward me. His face was clearly defined as he came quite near, and he said, "What are *you* going to do about this?" I was so startled at the emphatic question that I woke up wondering who the man might be and what it all meant.

At breakfast I related the dream to Mother, who, having heard of my dreams many times before, dismissed the matter with a smile. Just then I took up the morning paper and noticed the headlines describing a terrible accident that had occurred in Boston Back Bay station. Gervase Elwes, the English tenor, had missed his step when getting off the train just as it started to move. He was being met by a delegation of friends and admirers, and before anyone could realize what had happened, his body fell between the platform and the train and he was killed.

"Mother," I cried out, "I feel sure this is the man who spoke to me in my dreams!" I read aloud the story and tried to quiet the pounding in my head. Something strange had certainly shaken my equilibrium, for, although I had never met Gervase Elwes, try as I might the message kept repeating itself. But I said no more about it.

Two weeks later, Ernest Schelling asked if he might bring a friend to see the "Sacrifice" group and if I would permit this lady to stay in the studio alone, as she had recently suffered deep tragedy and did not want to meet anyone. The hour was arranged, and when the heavily veiled lady had spent the desired time in the studio she asked to speak to me. It was Lady Elwes.

She asked if I had known her husband, who had recently been killed in an accident. I hardly knew what to answer, but I said, "Perhaps!" She went on to ask me if I ever made portraits from a death mask and photographs. I replied that I had occasionally been able to do this if I could obtain enough accurate data, and she said that she could collect various photographs. Then I could no longer keep silent about my dream, and I told her what had happened. "If your photographs show me the profiles of the same man whom I saw in my dream I am sure I can make his portrait." In the dream I had seen only his front face.

When the pictures came, I was dumbfounded. It was the same man. Lady Elwes had planned to return to England in ten days' time. I promised to work as rapidly as possible. In fact, I was driven as if by a supernatural force. Elwes seemed to appear before me in a certain place in the studio, and I would talk to him and ask him to turn so that I could see his profile and I worked exactly as if a living model was posing for me. It was somewhat like the experience I had had doing my drawing of Keats in Rome.

After four days of work, I developed a high fever and had to have the clay head taken to my home as I was too ill to go to the studio. When Lady Elwes came to see the portrait two days before sailing, she brought a priest with her who had known her husband well. I could not get up to receive the visitors, so Mother acted as hostess. They were left alone for a while in the front parlor where the portrait was. Then Lady Elwes came to see me in my room and expressed astonishment at the accuracy of the likeness, and especially the expression, which she said was not in any of the photographs and was evident only when her husband was singing.

Naturally I was somewhat overcome, for it had been an exhausting and feverish experience. The head was cast in plaster, and Lady Elwes took it to England where a committee of her friends who had other portraits submitted as a memorial decided to select mine. So it was cast in bronze and placed as his memorial in a niche built into the wall of Queen's Hall, London. During the London Blitz in the Second World War, the hall and everything in it were completely destroyed.

There are mysterious moments in life that we cannot explain, but the sequence of unpredictable events relating to this portrait was certainly more than coincidental.

The "Sacrifice" was completed, and the time came for moving the group up to the Cathedral of St. John the Divine, where it would stay for a while until it could be sent to Cambridge. Once again we took out the big front window and backed an open truck up to the wall of 157. Three marble carvers and I went along with the stone group and directed the unloading and placing in the Chapel of Ansgarius. Brick piers had been set up to hold the block, and, extending beyond it, a wooden base and steps. A stone base could not be used in the chapel as we were warned that the beams under the floor were not strong enough to support the weight. I designed two tall Gothic candlesticks to stand at the head on either side of the group. These were always lighted when the verger noted visitors going into the chapel to pray. A high stained-glass window shed its light over the carved figures. The setting was ideal.

The group was later moved to Cambridge, Massachusetts, and permanently placed in the Memorial Chapel at Harvard University.

GERVASE ELWES

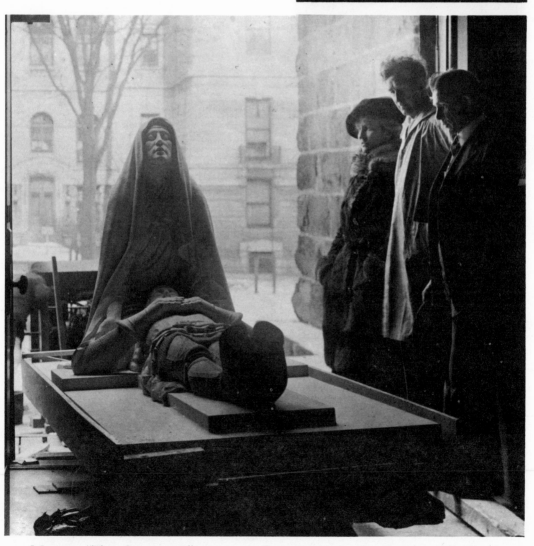

MOVING "THE SACRIFICE" INTO THE CATHEDRAL OF ST. JOHN THE DIVINE

CHAPTER EIGHTEEN

DISCOVERY OF
FINISTÈRE—LAND'S END

In 1920, the same year I began "The Sacrifice," I made a trip to the far end of southern Brittany, called Saint-Guénolé. In an old guidebook it was described as a place "unfrequented by tourists, swept by storms and high winds."

As I drove south from Quimper in a rattling old omnibus, the vegetation became more and more scant and the rocky fields and bent-over scrub, with a few distorted cedars still fighting against the wind, corresponded with the description in the guidebook, but there came a strong salt tang of the sea air; and the first glimpse of the dunes and massive coast convinced me with irresistible magnetism that I had found the place that I needed and had somehow been looking for all my life. It was a compelling experience, pulling at the roots of my being—a sort of blood-and-bone sense of identification.

The days and evenings were filled with surprise and revival. The vast spacious sky, the dramatic masses of amethyst cloud forms reflected in the shallow pools, the primitive stalwart types of fisherfolk wearing rust-colored sailors' suits with pink patches on knees and elbows, or darker blue suits with pale blue patches—every glimpse was a temptation to the artist—even to the snug little gray stone houses tucked into the edges of rocks, with pale blue fishnets waving in the breeze or hung from windows or spread on the ground to dry between the fishermen's homes.

These "land's end" people of recent years, alas, have had too many contacts with tourists. They have also taken to touring themselves, the growing motor facilities having made travel possible for many who until the present time were satisfied to stay in their stone houses and let the rest of the world wear itself out with futile complications. Such changes have destroyed the sense of remoteness

196

that had been the charm of this *coin perdu* of Brittany. Only at the far corners where rocks and tempestuous seas still wage their eternal war can we find the silent type of fisherman whose physiognomy reflects the strain of combat against the elements, and that strength of character one finds clearly marked in men who "go down to the sea in ships."

In the peninsula of Penmarch I have for many years studied the Bretons. The farmer type differs in appearance from the fisherman, but there is an archaic force in both. The women in their black bodices and spotless white coifs add character to the picturesque landscape, and the few valiant trees that withstand the winter winds bend toward the land eastward, their crests forever bowed by the long strain of the ocean storms. An occasional wooden windmill breaks the outline of the horizon as one crosses the country leading to Finistère. When one reaches the coast at night, the great revolving shafts of light from the lighthouse of Eckmühl warn of perils beneath the surface. No wonder that the sailors pray for protection of their fragile boats threading a course between the Île de Sein and the Pointe du Raz. Even on the clearest and bluest of summer days a *lame de fond,* or tidal wave, a gathering together of the waves in a united mass, is a frequent occurrence, arising without warning near the shore, sweeping over cliffs and beaches, taking its toll of any living creature who may have ventured too near the water's treacherous edge.

As I traveled inland, I noticed that the faces of the people appeared less rugged; the eyes, less watchful, were deeply shadowed by square, furrowed brows. The coifs changed in their design in each successive village. Dainty white lace bonnets denoted Audierne, and the stiffly pleated ruffles worn on the shoulders as a wide collar, Fouesnant near Beg-Meil.

Threading my way along the south coast, I found the Carnac ruins of Druidic times, the mammoth granitic menhirs aligned in endless rows, all leading, according to scientific conjecture, to the rising sun. In Morbihan and other places I found the dolmens, stone tables and sacrificial rocks, evocative of an ancient race that once inhabited this area.

The Bretons are a quiet, self-assured people who make friends slowly and carefully. Having met the newcomer, they wait patiently, allowing no familiarities, and only after a period of intense examination and testing of his trustworthiness may he hope to be admitted as a friend and share their hospitality. Touch their hearts, become their friend, however, and there is no race more loyal, devoted, or trustful.

I made a number of charcoal and pastel drawings of the fisherfolk; one of them was of Guillaume Tanneau, my constant companion and a member of the Charlot family who owned the *Malvina,* a rugged fishing boat of Saint-Guénolé which they had named for me.

After I returned to America from Brittany, Mother and I visited the valley of Tyringham, near Stockbridge, Massachusetts—Mother in Miss Cannon's "bo'din'house" and I in a rented barn in a nearby field. It was here that I tethered the old pony that was offered to me for the season if I could manage to get a

"Breton Wrestlers"

MH and crew of the *Malvina*, St. Guénolé harbor

halter over his head. He had been turned out to graze back of Richard Watson Gilder's house. Enjoying his freedom to the full, he would wait until I almost reached him, then wheel about, fling his heels up, and dash off into the woods around the edge of a swamp. Not to be easily deterred from the rare opportunity of riding, I decided to keep on each day, trying a new set of tricks to lure the polo pony to my side and then be quick enough to get a rope around his neck. At last fresh grass and sugar won out. Once captured, the pony renounced his mischievous ways and let me lead him to the barn, where I saddled and mounted him and rode home to show off my catch to Mother.

We soon made a pet of the pony, and he ate his oats and feed from a box beside my own rustic lunch table in the barn. He posed for his full-length portrait, about fourteen inches high, and since I had him near at all times I could observe his equine points at close range. Sam, who came up for a couple of long weekends and stayed in the bo'din'house with Mamma wasn't too happy about my riding the pony, and considered that I was risking my neck. Perhaps his fears had some slight justification, for the pony had been trained to play polo, and when I rode him he would occasionally start off at a fast pace and take some inadvertent motion of my knee or hand for a signal to turn; before I knew what had happened, I would find myself on the ground, watching a startled pony who gradually slowed down and came to see what had happened to me.

Tethered under the rear porch at night, he seemed quiet enough until we had a sudden thunderstorm. The lightning was zigzagging through the cracks of the barn walls as the rain fell in sheets. After a sharp flash and clap of thunder, I heard him thrashing about; I peered through the wallboards and saw the frightened pony, dragging a post and a section of the porch floor, trying to force his way through the trees. Nothing for it but to dash out into the rain, untangle the ropes and odd pieces of wood, quiet down the trembling animal, and lead him back inside the barn where we could better face the frightening storm together, and both get a rubdown.

Living rather like a gypsy, in and out of the woods dense and damp in their shadowy coolness, I felt free that summer and in tune with the voices of the earth around me.

SAM AND MOTHER

Mother, who had had a stroke and that fall and winter was obliged to get about in a wheelchair, pressed Sam to come to our apartment in East Thirty-fourth Street where her wonderful nurse Mrs. Beckford agreed to care for two invalids instead of one. Sam was just recovering from a severe attack of pneumonia. It is quite possible that my brother-in-law Dr. Draper had saved his life. He had taken immediate drastic steps, having Sam hospitalized, and having him undergo a serum treatment, just then being innovated by Dr. Russell L. Cecil. The serum caused terrible reactions resembling convulsions, but it finally won its therapeutic battle. I visited Sam every day, and just before Christmas he was permitted to leave the hospital.

Sam had been back from Europe less than a year. When he had still been in the service and I too had been abroad, he was asked to attend a large dinner given to reunite the patients of Queen Alexandra's Hospital who had recovered from their severe injuries. Each could invite a member of his family or a friend to attend the ceremony, and I was glad to be with Sam on that memorable occasion.

The chief surgeon who had treated Sam asked me to visit his office the following day. I had told him we were engaged to be married, and he wished me to know and understand certain things in regard to Sam's injuries, so that I might be ready in case of future emergencies. He warned me that there might be recurrent periods of melancholia. His concern and honesty impressed me, and I assured him of my willingness to assume any responsibility or sacrifice that might be entailed, and expressed my gratitude for his advice.

When Sam was discharged from the Army and returned to the United States, it was to find that the ordinary life of the West had hardly been affected by the war, and his engagements might have continued immediately. It was a very disturbing thing to know, but we talked the situation over with his agent and, realizing that Sam would not be able to play concerts again and that it was best to face it and get it over with, the agent insisted on an immediate clean break.

It was not a help in this situation when Sam now had a severe attack of pneumonia. It meant much to both of us that Mother invited him to stay with us. She was kindness itself, and happy to feel she could still be of use by such a gesture of hospitality and friendship.

One could not be with my mother and not feel the spell of her unshakable faith and the endless love that overflowed from her heart. Her philosophy was born of lonely hours filled with prayers. She had a gentle grace and saintlike smile that had only to be experienced to convey a sense of blessing. Her way of guidance was so sure that time has not dimmed her wisely chosen words or tone of voice. I recall with what sagacity she counseled me: "Sometimes, my dear, although it is hard, one must be swiftly cruel to be truly kind."

During the last years of her life she had posed ever so patiently that I might model and then carve her portrait in marble. Love filled my heart as I endeavored to express all my feelings.

Whenever Mother and I went to church together, I found myself listening to her while she made the responses and repeated the prayers. It had struck me that she was always silent during the recitation of certain parts of the Lord's Prayer: ". . . Give us this day our daily bread. And forgive us our trespasses as we forgive those who trespass against us. And lead us not into temptation . . ." These words she never spoke, but quite audibly ended the prayer, "For Thine is the kingdom, and the power, and the glory, for ever and ever, Amen."

The last time my mother was able to visit the studio before her final months of illness, we lighted two tall candles in bronze standards at each side of the stone figure of the woman who was kneeling by her dead crusader. Mother was

MOTHER IN MARBLE

deeply moved when she looked at the group illuminated in the candlelight in the otherwise darkened room. "What will you call this?" she asked.

"Sorrow is the mother of Beauty," I answered.

She placed her delicate hand on the arm of the recumbent knight in armor and, looking up at the woman's face, she said quietly, as if she were speaking only to her, "Leave there thy gift upon the altar and go thy way."

During her long illness we often read the Bible together; finally I summoned courage to ask her why she invariably omitted certain lines in the Lord's Prayer.

"My child," she whispered, for she was very weak, "I've tried never to ask God any favors, only praying for His guidance; I think we should earn our daily bread in some way, not ask Him to give it to us. And if we do forgive the trespasses of others, we know He will forgive us our own failings, and as for temptation . . . I think life would be very dull without a little temptation, and surely if we did not ever feel tempted we could never develop our own power of resistance!"

Then followed long hard months when the Angel of Death hovered about us day and night. Many times after the evening performances Pavlova would come to our apartment. Her love for my mother was deep and genuine. She would take off her coat and the scarf that covered her head and walk ever so gently along the corridor to Mother's room. She would kneel on the floor beside the bed and hold Mother's hand in both of hers and lay her cheek against it. There were no audible words spoken; love communicates in silence.

Try as we may to steel ourselves for the ceasing of mortality, no warning, no preparation can lessen the blow. On the day of her death Mother recited her own version of the Lord's Prayer. I was kneeling beside the bed, holding her pale hands in mine. I watched her, wondering if she would have even the strength to finish. She smiled and seemed to whisper a few words; then the silence came.

The weeks of slow adjustment followed; the inescapable final problems had to be faced. The little laces and shawls were folded and put away. Some of our furniture was given away, the rest of it sold, and the apartment closed. I felt suspended in a vacuum. There is the immutable law beyond our ken. We must learn to endure, and believe in things unseen. We may come close to the veil that hides from us the great mystery, but we must not try to draw it aside. When we accept the omnipotence of death there is a fusion of spirit—as in that semiconscious state between sleep and waking—when complete understanding between two human beings goes far beyond the power of words to express. Occasionally in a dream of someone very dear there comes the flash of love and recognition, fusing fire . . . everything earthly consumed away in its path . . . only essence remaining.

After Ma's death, Sam tried to comfort me, but he was sorely stricken himself. He had been close to Mother during those long, final terrible months, and understood my despair. I was so bereft that it was a constant mental battle for me to find out how I could adjust my life without her. My work and Sam's comforting saved my reason. Driving myself, I turned to carving; then, in June, near collapse, I took refuge in France.

My loving friend Giselle Bunau-Varilla arranged to have me stay with her and a group of friends on the Mediterranean island of Port-Cros. There were French, American, English, Danish, and Russian artists—left-wingers and rightists, aristocrats, rich and poor, male and female, as varied a group as you would be likely to find. Among them was Alexandras Jacovleff, a young Russian artist whom I had previously met in Paris, at the close of the war, when he had just returned from China after two years of study on a traveling scholarship in the Orient.

JACOVLEFF

To earn his daily bread, he had contracted with the *patron* of the restaurant La Biche on the rue des Martyrs in Montmartre to paint in fresco on the walls of his upper dining room an allegorical procession, a chariot drawn by white bulls with gilded horns and a bevy of lovely maidens and youths carrying exotic fruits and flowers. In the entrance lobby and along the stairway walls were to be life-size portraits in sanguine crayon of the chef and the *patron*. There were to be designs of gigantic platters of bright-red lobsters, vegetables, and fruits luring the visitors up to the dining rooms.

Three meals a day and two guests a week, I think, were the allowance represented by his meal ticket, with two years' time in which to complete the decorations. As the work progressed, Jacovleff's reputation spread, and many visitors began to make reservations for tables facing the *grand décor*. La Biche was put on the map as *the* place to lunch or dine and see the fantastic set of paintings. There was always an air of detachment and elegance about Jacovleff. At Port-Cros, after an early breakfast, we would don bathing suits and climb down the cliffs. When we went out in the little sailboats, Sacha or Jaco, as we often called him, would strap on a pair of Japanese diving goggles and tie a handkerchief over his head so the goggles would not shift. Leaning over the rail and scrutinizing the translucent waters for shells and waving plants on the rocky bed of the Mediterranean, he would suddenly give us a signal to stand by, clamp on a sort of nose pin, and his sleek brown body would cleave the air and disappear in a splash of glistening foam. We would strain our eyes, trying to watch him swimming about, twenty or thirty feet below, pulling up tufts of seaweed and twisting mussel shells from their rocky attachment. After what seemed an interminable time underwater, he would appear on the surface and lift his catch to our outstretched hands. When after repeated divings he had collected what he wanted, we would sail back to the pier, and he would bid us adieu, carrying his underwater treasures in a sack over his shoulders, trudging up over the cliffs to his studio in the old fort.

For a week or so no one guessed what he was doing with these sea plants and iridescent mother-of-pearl shells. As the motto of our holiday was "Each one *to* himself and *for* himself," none of us asked any questions. In the evenings we masqueraded and played our parts as reincarnations of the Hyksos tribes, our costumes and masks fantastic inventions designed by Jacovleff.

One day he invited us all to the gala opening of a new dining room for the Hyksos kings. The old fort had endless space, courtyards and rooms and ramparts, and his desire to decorate and transform the blank walls had wide range. To our amazement we saw the walls aglow with mysterious rainbow lighting. Candles hidden behind the iridescent shells had been arranged in a garland of patterns on the walls, and hung among these garlands were oval medallions framed in shells and seaweed, each containing a life-sized portrait in red chalk of a member of our little band. The fantasy and ingenuity of the scheme fascinated me, as did the grotesque masks and costumes he had concocted out of Bristol boards and gaily colored cotton. There seemed to be in him an endless store of world lore ready to be drawn upon at a moment's notice. Legendary characters, Chinese actors, Japanese wrestlers, African wood carvings, Russian icons, scenery and costumes ranging from *Prince Igor* to *Les Sylphides*, frescoes of Pompeii, mathematical cubists, abstracts—anything that had come under his eagle eye had been noted and stored away in his memory. With all this knowledge of the world, he still remained at heart a child of the forest, and his love of nature's magic gave him an exhilarating *joie de vivre*.

While on the island, though I continued the compulsive work that had been my refuge in New York, I began gradually to relax and to find that the outdoor activity and the special tone of fantasy and imagination were helping me. Jacovleff contributed much to my recovery, and became a friend whose further career fascinated me over the years.

When Georges Marie Haardt organized the Citroën Expedition from North to South Africa, Jacovleff agreed to go as the official artist. When the travelers returned, a gigantic exhibition was staged at the Arts Décoratifs in Paris. Jacovleff exhibited more than three hundred pictures painted in tempera or drawn in sanguine and pastel during the long trek across the deserts and jungles that had ended up in Madagascar.

The success of this expedition, "The Black Crusade," gave rise to the plans for another in which writers, scientists, archeologists, and Jacovleff would again set forth under the leadership of Georges Marie Haardt from Paris, this time to cross Asia from Kashmir to Peking.

Just about this time I had contracted with the Field Museum in Chicago to go round the world to model the Races of Man, and I planned with the Citroën group to meet them in Peking. They were to cross the continent of Asia from west to east, and we were to cross America, visit Hawaii and Japan, and reach Peking, in December, 1930.

When we reached China all communication with the French expedition had been cut off. It was impossible to get news through any official channel. Finally, after many weeks of anxious inquiry, we were informed that the members of the expedition were alive and safe, but I was advised to give up the hope

JACOVLEFF SELF-PORTRAIT IN SANGUINE CRAYON

of their arrival for another month. Our little party was obliged to move south-ward to Shanghai. My work then took us by a roundabout route to Calcutta.

The first thing we did on arrival in Calcutta was to inquire at the French consul's for news of our friends, Father Teilhard de Chardin, Jacovleff, and Haardt. We learned that Haardt had just died in Hong Kong, and all further plans for his group had been canceled. To Jacovleff this was the sudden ending to all his dreams and hopes, to lose his devoted friend, the leader who could gal-vanize the mind of an artist to great accomplishments. Rare indeed are such spirits today, and irreparable is their loss. Jacovleff brought his friend's body back to Paris. He searched for anodynes and escape in passionate work, a resource only too familiar to me.

Later he was asked to come to Boston to direct the Museum School of Art; he threw himself wholeheartedly into the work there for two consecutive seasons. His pupils quickly recognized his prodigious skill as a draftsman and painter.

On occasional weekends in New York he would spend the day in my studio drawing and painting; showing me how to mix egg tempera colors, he would then try all sorts of experiments with them. We would talk of the days in Port-Cros that had become a sort of dreamlike memory.

During the last years of his life he was restless and dissatisfied with his work. He felt that as a painter he must search for new means of expression. He worked like a creature possessed . . . he felt his ability grow, and his horizon widen. He resigned from the Boston School to devote all his time to the develop-ment of his new technique.

Not long after this he was stricken with a fatal disease, and died in Paris in 1938. Three days after his death I received a letter from him, written just before his attack: ". . . Now at last I feel free and strong, and my wings will carry me to higher mountains than I have ever been able to reach. It is so wonderful to·feel this new power and happiness in my work! . . ."

PADEREWSKI

After my stay in Port-Cros at the time of Mother's death, I had another restorative experience, that of going to Geneva to be with the Schellings and to make my first studies for the portrait of Paderewski as "The Statesman." Pade-rewski in 1922 was representing Poland at the League of Nations, and as I had a permit to sit where I might see him, I was enabled to study his expressive, sen-sitive face.

He spoke seldom, but his silence was eloquent, and the silhouette of his profile was clear-cut against a dark background. Important as it was to see him in this public capacity, it was also highly helpful that I was able to meet him almost every evening in private life. Either he would come to play bridge with the Schellings or we would go to Morge to spend the evening with him. While he played cards, I was able to make many drawings and note the strong Slavic planes and the record of suffering that gave his face its indefinable quality of majesty.

PADEREWSKI "THE STATESMAN" (© *MH*)   PADEREWSKI "THE FRIEND" (© *MH*)

PADEREWSKI "THE MAN" (© *MH*)   PADEREWSKI "THE ARTIST" (© *MH*)

When we met later on in New York, I had built up the heroic bust of "The Statesman" with the heavy wings of the Eagle of Poland forming the sides of the shoulders and continuing down over the pedestal. He agreed to come to pose for the bust, and gave me a seat in the front row at Carnegie Hall for his first concert, the day before he was to come to the studio.

When he appeared on the stage, the applause was deafening. While he was playing Chopin, I suddenly decided that I must do another portrait of him as the artist. His whole personality seemed to be transformed and uplifted by the music, and at one point as he played a mazurka his thoughts were suddenly revealed to me with such poignancy that I knew it to be the moment I must seize and somehow incorporate in my new interpretation.

Returning to the studio I started to build up the clay on a new armature, possessed by the compelling Daemon and unable to think of anything else. When I had carried the portrait as far as I could, I discovered that it was four o'clock in the morning. As my appointment with him was for 10:30 A.M., I hurriedly covered the head with wet cloths and took an aspirin to go to sleep. When Paderewski appeared, we uncovered "The Statesman" in clay, and I started to work. He posed very quietly, and even tried to relive the days at the League so that his inner emotions might somehow be reflected in his expression.

During the rest period he walked over to the second covered head and, with his uncanny insight, asked if I had tried another version since hearing the concert. "I noticed your seat was empty after I had played the mazurka," he said. This disarmed me and, of course, I confessed. "Let me see it," he said, and I uncovered the clay.

"Did you work all night on this?" he asked.

"Almost," I said. "C'était plus fort que moi—I couldn't help it! Perhaps you would not mind posing for this just once, just a little while . . ." I hesitated.

"Impossible," he said. "This one is finished; it is the portrait of my inner self lost in my music. I could not evoke this mood unless I were playing a certain piece."

"Yes," I agreed, "it was a fleeting expression and I know exactly in which passage of Chopin it occurred."

He looked at me with his extraordinarily keen eyes. "If we go upstairs to your father's piano, I will play the passage for you—write it on a paper here and we shall see if I am correct."

He began improvising; then, gathering himself together into that remote world where the great find their strength, he began to play the Chopin mazurka. When he came to the slow, sobbing refrain that occurs at intervals, he stopped and turned his tragic face toward me—holding his hands on the keys—the pedal sustaining the sound of the chord. . . . "This is the moment in which you discovered me," he said.

I could not speak, my throat closed with emotion, but I nodded. The notes he held under his fingers were those I had written down.

"Come now, Malvina, we will sit down together and I will tell you the story behind that moment." We went over to the big couch and he began his tale:

his youth, his struggles, discouragements, his study with Leschetizky when he had practiced every evening until late at night and how his short fingers had forced him to do hours of stretching exercises because at first they could barely strike an octave with any sense of security. Then he spoke of the love he felt for his first wife, their stark poverty, their only son a cripple never able to walk, his wife's terrible illness and the need of better care for her than he could find or afford before her tragic death . . . words that fell like stones in a pool of tears. "Il faut accepter ta souffrance pour être poussé vers ton ascension. . . ."* He laid his hands on mine.

When the two portraits were finally cast in bronze, the heroic-sized "Statesman" mounted on a black-and-gold marble shaft, it was decided to exhibit them at Knoedler's in Fifty-seventh Street. Paderewski attended the opening day, and as his friends gathered and asked him which interpretation he preferred he smilingly patted the eagle wing framing the "Statesman" and said, "Ceci est le portrait de ma personalité—l'autre est moi-même!"† He was never at a loss for the *mot juste*.

About a year or so later, on Christmas morning, we were fixing up Number 157 for a gathering of friends; I was perched on a ladder tacking up garlands when the bell rang, and to my amazement who should come in carrying a long white box, but Paderewski. . . . I dropped the hammer in surprise and climbed hurriedly down. "This is Christmas, Malvina; why shouldn't I bring flowers and celebrate, too?" We spent a never-to-be-forgotten hour, and he ended the visit by playing the Chopin mazurka from beginning to end.

When the last vibration had faded, he turned and took me by the hand, for I was standing beside him. "Artists have to fight many battles that others never suspect; life around us is too active, too violent. . . . We must often be alone; otherwise our best thoughts will hide themselves. Deep down in our hearts there is peace if we take the time and the silence to find it. . . ." I listened and said nothing, but the lines of the poet Samain crossed my mind:

> La parole a des notes d'or,
> Le silence est plus doux encore
> Quand les cœurs sont pleins jusqu'au bord . . .‡

The silence was charged with a sense of eternity. Time was suspended; one heard the heartbeat that is more potent than language.

Suddenly I noted a change of expression in Paderewski's face—a gentle relaxation, a warmth and kindliness as if indeed he had withdrawn into that blessed land of silence where he had for a fleeting moment found peace. And so it was that another side of this complex personality was revealed to me, and I knew that I must try again to capture in my sculpture something of this revelation. We did not see each other again for some weeks, but when Paderewski

* *Thou must accept thy suffering in order to be urged on toward thy ascent.*
† *This is the portrait of my personality—the other is myself!*
‡ *Speech has notes of gold,/Silence is sweeter still/when hearts are full to overflowing . . .*

came to the studio the next time he found there a new portrait, almost finished. He smiled as he examined it, and without a word mounted the model stand, and I worked in silence. In about an hour I said, "The doors have closed now; I cannot go further." We both agreed that this was the most sympathetic version and that it would be called "The Friend."

Before I had it cast into bronze, the original plaster of this portrait was stolen together with a number of other objects; the house had been temporarily closed, and when I returned it was to find traces of wholesale robbery.

Fortunately, I had photographed this portrait, so there was at least a visible record.

When the Second World War loomed over Europe, and Poland was again torn asunder, Paderewski's titanic strength succumbed. His last weeks in a New York hotel reflected his anguish.

I shall never forget the look of elsewhere and remoteness that clouded his eyes as his fingers would rest immobile on the surface of a table before him. The sharp Slavic characteristics were intensified, and the sufferings of his people and of his own heart were graven deeply on his countenance.

This was indeed the Last Phase, reflected in my last portrait of him, completed after his death, a bronze of which was placed on a Polish ship, built in America and named the S.S. *Paderewski*. Alas, this ship met with disaster; soon after its launching it was bombed and sunk in the Caribbean Sea. All aboard were lost.

CHAPTER NINETEEN

A NEW HOME

IN THE AUTUMN of 1922, after my work with Paderewski and the restoring months abroad, I returned to New York to a problem that proved a rude brush with reality: finding a place to live and making a home for myself. I explored the nearby neighborhood of Murray Hill, but with no results, and the only solution seemed to be to use the roof space over my big studio and build a penthouse apartment. With this in mind, and helped by Sam, I drew up a set of plans that included a large sitting room, bedroom and bath, and armed with this and some general estimates of costs I went to consult Mrs. Harriman. I had been able to save enough from the sale of sculpture to guarantee her a regular rental, which financially, of course, was no bonanza for her, but would yield a small percentage on the proposed investment. I would have to be responsible for the rent of the entire building, as our tenant Edward McCartan had moved to Sixty-seventh Street and his other studio at 157 would have to be turned into my dining room. The rest of the space on the second floor would become a kitchen, bedroom, and bath.

Mrs. Harriman took the plans and said she would consult her office and let me know her decision. "Think it over carefully, Malvina. It's a pretty big burden to assume, and you will have to stay here all summer and oversee the builders yourself . . . house building includes endless details and takes a great deal of patience!"

In two weeks she gave me her approval; the following months were crowded with new responsibilities. Despite numerous obstacles and differences of opinion concerning the plans, we managed to keep within the city building laws—no easy task. Sam and I discussed carefully where to have the stairs, working this and other details out directly with the builders, for we had no actual architect. At last the construction was done, and we undertook the plastering of the ceiling, walls, and high, wide chimney front of the living room. I insisted that the walls and ceiling be finished with a rough surface in varying tones of light buff.

211

When we ran the templates for the mantel, the masons were quite sure I was touched in the head, but as we all seemed to be having fun and the results were my headaches, not theirs, they kept on until the place was completed. One day, while passing a fire sale on Lexington Avenue, I picked up four plaster columns of twisted spirals, two for the ends of the mantel; the other two we set in the alcove and ran a plaster arch between them, coloring them to look like wood. Then came the problem of casting a rope molding for the curved doorframes and for the bookcases sunk into and flush with the walls. When the room was finished, even the skeptical workmen agreed that the effect was restful and "different" from that of any other place in the city.

Later that autumn all was in readiness. The sixteen-foot-high walls of the living room and a balcony gave a spacious feeling and afforded very good accoustics, for it somehow removed all echoes. Music was still Sam's life; and although he could no longer play the violin at concert level, he liked to play in quartets, where he felt covered by the sweep of the other players. He would get cramps at times if he played too long and he never knew when these cramps would come upon him, but with his characteristic courage he continued his active role and the living room was planned for music. Its focus would be Father's Chickering grand piano, and Sam's one worry was how we would get it moved up from the ground-floor studio. Neither of us cared if we had any other furniture so long as we had the piano. There was no possibility of moving it through the house, the turns being too narrow. Finally we obtained permission to haul it up by block and tackle to the next-door roof and, using boards to distribute the weight, we rolled it over to a French door in our living room that opened above the roof there, and raised the piano and brought it in through this door. The big divan (the *"monument de repos"*) came the same way, and that and the piano and a desk constituted the furnishing when I moved in. As a housewarming gift, Mestrovic gave me a bas-relief of a pietà and cemented it into the rough plaster wall himself.

A cherished mascot is the eighteenth-century singing bird in a gilded cage (about fifteen inches high) set on a carved wood base. This feathered songster moves his head, opens his beak, and flutters his tail while singing a nightingale aria. The sound is so true to nature that visitors are convinced it is a living bird. He was discovered in an old shop in Paris, and the perfection of the mechanism has kept the little bird singing happily ever since.

CHAPTER TWENTY

MARRIAGE

IT WAS EVIDENT that the time had come when Sam and I should be married and unite our hard-working and totally sympathetic lives in our own home. After his readjustment to the loss of his concert career, Sam had turned to a useful allied profession, that of restoring rare old musical instruments.

This he would continue, and so far as I could I would help him, and he would help me in my own projects, for we already had good evidence of our ability to share our interests and our hopes.

So on June 6, 1924, Sam and I were married in the chapel of St. Ansgarius in the Cathedral of St. John the Divine, the ceremony being performed by Dean Howard Robbins. We wished the ceremony to be simple. Sam and I entered the chapel together, and my brother Charles gave me in marriage. Sam's best man was Dr. Frederick Gay, Professor of Bacteriology in the College of Physicians and Surgeons of Columbia University. There were no ushers or bridal attendants, and only a few very close friends and relatives were present.

It made Sam and me happy that, at the time, my stone group, "The Sacrifice," was on temporary display in the chapel.

After the service, Sam and I motored up to a country inn near Mount Kisco where we spent five blissful days and then returned to New York and our new home at 157. There I continued work on the two large figures destined for the Bush Building in London.

For the summer months the Paul Warburgs loaned us a little house in Hartsdale, including a garden and a remodeled barn for a studio. "All this and heaven too" made us feel that Fate was smiling upon us, and our hearts were filled with gratitude and boundless faith in the future.

MH and Sam on the steps of the Cathedral after their marriage

CHAPTER TWENTY-ONE

BUSH HOUSE

MOST OF THE time spent in the studio during 1923, 1924, and 1925 was devoted to the development of a sculptural group to be placed over the entrance of Bush House, Kingsway, London. This nine-story modern office building was designed by Harvey Corbett, well-known New York architect.

Irving T. Bush, who controlled the vast activities of the Bush Terminal in Brooklyn, was a curious type of hard-hitting businessman and dreamer. He asked me to work with him on his plan to make his big building in London a symbol of American and English friendship.

It was my first chance at heroic stone sculpture that must fit into an architectural scheme. The design was to be kept simple, but was to interpret the concept of England and America holding a torch over a Celtic altar, with this inscription carved along the base: "Dedicated to the Friendship of English-Speaking Peoples."

When Mr. Bush and Mr. Corbett came to see the small models, they accepted the design and I was told to make a quarter-size model of the group. When completed, this was photographed and the prints were blown up to two sizes, one in which the men's figures were twelve feet high, another where they were fifteen feet.

In the spring of 1923 Mr. Corbett and I met in London, and the enlarged photographs were mounted on three-ply wood, cut out, and set in position on the stone plinth that was to support the group. Under this plinth were two huge columns rising from the street level eighty feet below. First we set up the twelve-foot size, and very early in the morning, before the Londoners were on Kingsway, we appraised the effect and agreed that the figures were too small. The next day the larger "cutout" was set up and "the boys" looked more in scale with their surroundings. We left them well secured from the back for another day, studying them at different hours, and noted the amazing fact that pedestrians would look up and see the figures and say to one another, "Blimey, there

215

are two statues up there today, and yesterday there weren't a sign of 'em!" At a distance the illusion of stone was certainly very surprising.

On my return to New York, I built up half-size models, each figure seven and a half feet, and these were turned over to stone carvers in Closter, New Jersey. Six sections of Indiana limestone were measured and roughed out by twelve men, two working on each block.

Sam used to come out with me often to see the progress of the work, and was very friendly and helpful with the carvers. I could ask Sam a thousand questions because he was a very practical person. He would get answers for me if he didn't have them. During the final weeks I spent a great deal of time at the carving studio, and when the carving was almost done, thirty or forty of my friends came out to see an advanced assemblage of the group. Soon after that, the figures were finished, crated, and taken to be loaded into the hold of a steamer, and this proved to be no simple operation.

When the first big section was lifted from the dock, we heard an ominous creaking of the deck boards on the ship, and the captain megaphoned down that we would have to stop and lower the piece back onto the dock instead of into his ship. The deck-lifting machinery was unable to take the weight. That meant we would have to get some kind of outside hoist that would haul up the pieces and lower them directly into the hold. We consulted with the Brooklyn Navy Yard, and at great expense engaged a tug with hoisting equipment that was ordinarily used for raising and lowering locomotives. This tug slowly lifted the pieces of stone and set them into the hold, all of us meanwhile anxiously waiting and watching. When the pieces were safely in place, the captain put dozens of sacks of potatoes around them to steady them against any possible motion. Only then were we permitted to leave, assured that our cargo had a good chance of reaching its destination.

A few days later I set sail for London and Bush House, but disembarked at Liverpool with the purpose of exploring the vast new cathedral being built there by Sir Giles Scott, the British architect. At the end of a long afternoon inside the great structure, making notes and sketches of special details, I became aware that light had faded and I was in semidarkness. When I tried the big door by which I had entered, I found it locked, as were the several side doors.

Discovering a half-open doorway at the base of one of the huge stone pillars and the beginning of a spiral iron stairway inside, I began climbing. When I reached what seemed in the darkness rather a dizzy altitude, I heard a great burst of organ notes and noticed a crack of light just ahead in a doorway leading from the stairway. To my delight and relief, I found myself in the organ loft, face to face with a surprised organist who was just starting to play. Apologizing for my unceremonious appearance, I explained my predicament. The organist very kindly edged along on the bench and beckoned me to sit down beside him. This accidental meeting became a musical interlude of pure delight for me. The organ had only just been installed, and the organist permitted me to listen to a program of Bach and some splendid choral works that filled the vast cathedral with their glory and my heart with wonderment.

Between selections he would ask me where I came from and why I was in Liverpool. When I told him of my father's musical career, starting off by mentioning his unfortunate mishap while playing the organ in Manchester at the age of twelve, the organist became very friendly, and it was late in the evening when we wound our spiral way down to earth again.

I asked him where I could find Sir Giles Scott, and he gave me his address in London. I called on him there in his quaint old office in the Temple. He received me graciously and, after I had expressed my enthusiasm for the cathedral, I asked what other building he had designed before winning this difficult commission. He smiled and pointed to the wall: "Do you see that pipe rack? That was my only piece of architectural construction until I won the Liverpool competition. I made the pipe rack for my father. I was twenty-five at that time, and it has taken me twenty-five years to learn how to build a cathedral. I'll come to Bush House one day and visit you on your scaffolding!" To my delight he did come, climbing the eighty-foot perpendicular ladder inside the tubular cage all the way to my high perch.

On my arrival at Bush House the big stones were hauled up into place by a hand-turned windlass and single cable. Perhaps I should not have been overcome with anxiety, but as I knew some of the blocks of stone weighed six tons and others eight tons I was in a constant state of apprehension as I stood on the opposite corner and watched the heavy load rising into the air. One day just as an eight-ton block reached the level of the plinth, the men stopped winding, and the block dangled perilously on its cable. The men quite calmly locked the windlass rachet and walked away to crawl through the aperture in the wall of the building that gave access to the plinth and upper scaffolding.

I ran into Bush House and took the elevator to the eighth floor, where I met the workmen. "What happened?" I gasped.

"Why, lady, it's teatime," was the laconic answer. "We'll pull it into place before we leave today, don't you worry!"

After the pieces were assembled, my task was to complete carving the head on the figure of England. We had been forced to ship the stones before this was finished, and because there was no sunlight to accentuate details we were obliged to deepen many of the accents on the faces and shields. To do this work I had to sit astride the shoulders of the big figure and be given a strong boost by my assistant carver to enable me to reach my perilous perch ninety feet above the street. The winds added difficulties, for my hands were stiff with cold and it took all the courage I could muster to finish this task. Just to write about it many years later chills my blood. One does, however, get used to almost anything save hanging, they say, and after the first few days and nights I managed to control my fears, indeed, almost to enjoy the danger of my position.

When the figures and shield were finished and had been washed down with endless pails of strong tea to make them match the color of the rest of the building, we had a formal celebration at the unveiling. Mr. and Mrs. Bush and Sam and Helen joined me a few days before the party. Lord Balfour pulled a cord that released a curtain of flags, a Scottish band played "God Save the King,"

MH WORKING NINETY FEET ABOVE THE STREET AT BUSH HOUSE (*Pacific and Atlantic Studios*)

FAÇADE OF BUSH HOUSE (*Brown Brothers*)

and traffic on Kingsway and Aldwich was stopped for half an hour. The crowds gave a cheer, and shivers ran up and down my spine and tears suddenly filled my eyes. It was a thrilling experience.

During the Second World War one of the last "doodlebugs," or "buzz bombs," that fell in London struck off the right arm of the figure representing America in this group—but England kept calm, and held the torch alone. I was glad I was not called upon to replace America's forearm, for the memories of the five weeks I spent perched ninety feet above the ground were anything but tranquil.

RETURN TO NEW YORK, 1926

In pleasant contrast with this London commission was a request from the firm of Goodhue Associates to carve a memorial design on the stone pulpit in the Church of the Heavenly Rest in New York. The rough stones were already in place, as well as the pulpit steps, so my carvers and I had the rare privilege of actually working in the church and feeling that what we carved was an integral and permanent part of the structure. At last I was given the opportunity of carving into stone my favorite phrase from the Bible: "Where There Is No Vision, the People Perish."

Adding to our dedication during those peaceful days, the organist would play hymns and practice the music of Bach until the walls of stone reverberated and the whole outside world was forgotten. When the time came for carving the inscription around the top of the pulpit, I gave the Italian carver the long strip of tracing paper on which the words were drawn in six-inch letters. I told him to paste it on carefully between the indicated lines and *not* to start cutting until I returned from lunch.

When I came back and examined the lettering, to my consternation and dismay I found that he had started pasting the strip *from the end of the inscription* and, by stretching and flattening the damp paper, he found that there was one letter too many at the starting point, so he had calmly cut it off and was sharpening his chisel to start cutting. The words, meaning nothing to him, now read: "Here There Is No Vision, the People Perish"!

At just that moment Dr. Henry Darlington, the Rector, appeared on the chancel steps and, noting my expression and emphatic gestures, asked what had happened. "Read this!" I said, pointing to the inscription, and then told him how close we had come to making a disastrous blunder. His surprise was genuine; then he laughed, but I doubt if he ever passed this carving without remembering the challenge of these prophetic words.

The Châtelet Harpsichord

CHAPTER TWENTY-TWO

FINDING THE DU CHÂTELET HARPSICHORD

WHILE SAM and I were in Paris in 1926, Sam made a spectacular musical find. He had spent many hours wandering the streets in search of rare old musical instruments, especially a famous harpsichord supposed to have been lost or destroyed. He was thoroughly informed on the subject; besides, he was familiar with the history and construction of all manner of instruments and he had become expert at detecting their value even if they were covered with dust and hidden behind other antiques.

In a little shop in a side street leading up toward Montmartre, he recognized the unmistakable remains of the Châtelet harpsichord that he had been hunting for. A prolonged visit, with a few glasses of cognac, finally achieved the desired result. As a student of eighteenth-century music, Sam told the shopkeeper he would like the chance to rebuild an old instrument and see if he could restore the sound. So the broken and grimy harpsichord was purchased, and directions for shipment were left with the dealer.

Sam was to stop on the way to the steamer the following day and bring the money for a deposit, and it was on this visit that I saw the instrument for the first time and fell under its spell. Originally built in Antwerp, it was rebuilt in 1770, during the reign of Louis XV, by Pascal Taskin (pupil of E. Blanchet), famous in the records of rare instruments. When Sam found it, it was, as might be surmised, in a state of dilapidation, covered with grime and filled with the

221

strips of the broken sounding board and the black and white keys that had been thrown inside as they became detached.

Back in New York at 157, Sam took almost sixteen months to do the difficult and exacting work of restoration, but each step of the way was encouraging, for in proportion as the grime was removed, the richness of the painting was revealed, and when the strips of the sounding board were pieced together, a lovely painted rosette was found with this inscription:

Pascal Taskin
Luthier de Louis XV.

At the back end of each key were carved the initials P. T.

The black keys were of ebony, the white ones covered with ivory, but their relation to one another was the opposite of those of our pianos, sharps and flats on the harpsichord being white. Finally the quills for plucking the strings were reset (they were made of boar whiskers), the felts were renewed, and the stops adjusted. There were hand couplings for combining the two manuals (keyboards) or for changing the tones of the notes plucked.

When the work was completed, the instrument was carried carefully upstairs to the music room above the studio, and there tuned half a note lower than today's concert pitch to reduce the tension on the strings.

With the installation of this "temptation to music," many of our musical friends enjoyed trying their skill at playing Bach, Scarlatti, and other seventeenth- and eighteenth-century composers.

A certain historian who came to see the harpsichord established the fact that the painting on the inside of the cover tallied with pictures he had seen of the Château de Cirey, in the Vosges Mountains, and the wing that had been added to the original edifice at the time Voltaire was the reigning influence not only in the life of the Marquise du Châtelet but in the literary and political world of that time. This clue to the origin of the instrument inspired us to plan our next trip to France to include a search for the château. To make the quest more difficult, we found there were three places named Cirey, but all within easy motoring distance of one another. Armed with a portfolio of large photographs of the instrument both inside and out, a camera, and 16-mm. moving-picture equipment, Sam and I started off, in June, 1927, toward Nancy and the Vosges Mountains, and there searched in local bookshops for anything concerning Cirey, Voltaire, or the Marquise du Châtelet. The search was rewarding, and we read late into the night about the characters of our "eighteenth-century romance."

The next day, with the help of maps and much questioning, we came to Cirey Number 1, as yet with no trace of the château. We continued to Cirey Number 2, where the road marked on the map led to an enormous compost heap beside a peasant's farm—dead end!

The afternoon saw us motoring along the river Blaise toward Cirey Number 3 with a certain apprehension of failure; coming out of a wooded section of the valley, we found a river on the left side of the road, and as I stopped the car to scan the opposite hills my eyes caught the silhouette of the château, as painted on the inside of the cover of the harpsichord. Pointing to the distant hillside, I watched the expression of delight and surprise on Sam's face. There it was—unmistakably—we opened the portfolio to check it with the big photographs.

But running between the object of our search and our road was a river with no bridge in sight! We continued at higher speed, and at last reached the little village of Cirey 3. Fortunately, there we found a bridge and, turning back on the other side of the river, we pulled up at the stone gatehouse of the château estate. The owners were away hunting, but an English lady housekeeper was in residence and, as Sam was English, she was persuaded to let us in, soon sharing in the excitement of our adventure, intensified by the evidence of our photographs. Most graciously she admitted us to the Voltaire Wing, where we read the inscription over the doorway: Deus nobis hace otis fecit.

In the great room leading to the garden terrace, we were shown where the famous "lost instrument" had once stood. Great thick candles on the mantel had collected pyramids of wax almost a foot high about the bases. These were lighted for us. Then we went into the secret garden where Voltaire retired each morning to do his writing, under trees whose old trunks were covered with ivy and moss.

We were permitted the next morning to take movies and stills and to wander about the place with freedom, so our quest was rewarded. A four-leaf clover and ivy leaf came back with us as mementos.

Voltaire described Cirey in a poem:

> Asile des Beaux Arts, solitude, où mon cœur
> Est toujours demeuré dans une paix profonde . . .
> C'est vous qui donnez le bonheur
> Que promettait en vain le monde. . . .*

No doubt the music of this rare instrument must have added to the enjoyment of all who were privileged to hear it under Cirey's hospitable roof.

One of the renowned romances of the eighteenth century was that between Voltaire and the Marquise du Châtelet. Although the many accounts of it were widely divergent, it seems clear that there was a bond of common interests and mutual admiration, and that on both sides there was a passionate love of life and learning. It is not surprising that stories of the relationship have been biased; they were often drawn from unscrupulous or politically jealous contemporary informants. No outspoken satirist like Voltaire could hope to escape intrigue and vitriolic criticism. His power and influence were felt in many countries, but his human qualities were often ignored.

The Marquise, a woman of rare wit and erudition, lived with her husband and children in the Château de Cirey. Here this exciting hostess gathered together eminent artists, writers, musicians, and philosophers of her time. She was

* *Refuge of the Fine Arts, solitude, where my heart/Has always dwelt in deep peace . . ./It is you who gives the happiness/That the world promised in vain.*

the "bluestocking" *grande dame* who engaged the best craftsmen to transmute her fancies into form, whether ideas for houses, gardens, or harpsichord. At the time when Voltaire lived there, a great room was added to the château where the coterie gathered by candlelight and matched wits. The harpsichord of exotic beauty was placed there. On the underside of the cover Le Sueur painted the Marquise, the château, and the gardens. The sides, end, and back of the case were ornamented by Vernis Martin medallions representing the arts and crafts to which La Marquise, or "La Divine Émilie" as she was called, had given her patronage. There was a double keyboard, with a locking mechanism, so that an octave was sounded by striking a single key—a chef-d'œuvre of craftsmanship.

As to Voltaire's relationship with the Marquise, his own letters and reliable documents of the period give unquestionable evidence that *les convenances* were strictly observed at all times. Voltaire often directed the literary and theatrical evenings at the château. He projected slides from a magic lantern, and accompanied these with caustic and amusing commentaries. To this varied entertainment by one of the great showmen of his time, the harpsichord contributed its delicate and lovely background.

THE DRAPERS

In 1926, at the beginning of the year, my beloved brother-in-law Dr. William K. Draper died. Since he and his father had bequeathed their medical books to the Columbia University College of Physicians and Surgeons, I later made a memorial plaque, with both their portraits on it, for the College library.

The Draper family had always been close to us. William, of course, had seemed to me like a wonderful friend when he came courting Helen, and Paul and Ruth were my childhood playmates. As Paul grew up, he developed a tenor voice and a musical talent of rare charm, singing German and French songs. In 1910 Mother and I visited him and his wife Muriel in Florence. The story of his fabulous life in London after he won the Irish Sweepstakes is vividly described in Muriel's book, *Music at Midnight*. Their son Paul inherited his father's musical talent and became famous as a brilliant tap dancer.

But it was Ruth who was especially close to me. After her remarkable talent for monologues made itself evident (it began in her teens), she would sometimes try the effect of a number in my studio before giving it in public, and this private tryout always gave me a thrill. At the first public performance I would watch the reactions of the audience and join in their enthusiastic applause.

During both the First and Second World wars, she contributed generously of her time and talent to war relief, and helped my Appui aux Artistes fund by repeated presentations of her great monologue *Vive la France*. In 1951 the universities of Edinburgh and Cambridge conferred upon her the Honorary Degree of Doctor of Law, and the title of Commander of the British Empire was given to her by King George VI. Her wonderful virtuoso acting continued for many years. In 1956 she undertook a short season of monologues in New York. She seemed at the top of her form, and the audience gave her unstinted applause.

PAUL DRAPER AND HIS SON
PAUL, AGED ONE YEAR

RUTH DRAPER AS A DALMATIAN PEASANT (*Nicholas Muray*)

Alas, her career suddenly ended, for during the night after her sixth performance she died in her sleep—the final curtain had fallen.

MUSIC IN THE BIG ROOM

The atmosphere of certain rooms may sometimes reflect the personalities
of those who have lived in them. If living has been intense enough, something
of its essence remains—of the emotional experiences, music, the comparing of
adventure, tragedy, drama, secret confessions! The big open fires of crackling
logs that have lent a glow of warmth have had their special part in establishing
the character of the spacious living room over my studio. The old grand piano
whose strings have resounded for nearly ninety years to the techniques of masters
could tell many a tale of midnight melody, long hours of my father's faithful
practicing, and afternoons of chamber music with Father, Sam, and others playing together in pulsating trios and sonatas. On Sunday evenings singers would
lean against the ebony case and, with my father at the keyboard would sing
passages from operas and songs of Brahms, Strauss, Reynaldo Hahn, Fauré,
Debussy, and many others. No need of notes, for these artists knew their beloved
songs by heart, and my father knew the accompaniments. For more than forty
years this same piano stood in the front parlor of our house in West Forty-third
Street. Then it was moved to East Thirty-sixth Street, where Father played on
it every day until the end of his life. Then it came with Mother and me to the
apartment in East Thirty-fourth Street, and finally, when the stable at 157 East
Thirty-fifth Street was remodeled, it lived in the studio on the ground floor.
When the living room was built upstairs, it was hoisted up there and placed in
a corner position where it remains to this day.

The high ceiling and general acoustics of the room usually tempt artists
to raise the lid and do full justice to the fine instrument.

The same is true of Sam's harpsichord. Madame Wanda Landowska, whom
we had known in Paris, came to tea one day and enjoyed playing on the harpsichord, finding that the sonority of the long base strings and delicately pure treble
notes were of an exceptional richness.

Miss Yella Pessl, another harpsichordist, who had given many recitals on
the concert stage and radio, came frequently to practice, and she used every art
of persuasion to borrow it for her public appearances. But the risk of moving
such a fragile case and possibly throwing the whole mechanism out of order
made the loan impossible.

An extraordinary display of musical virtuosity followed an informal tea
party given to our devoted friend Mrs. E. H. Harriman. Josef Hofmann, whom
we had known for many years and whose daughter Josefa was studying sculpture
with me, asked me to invite George Gershwin to the party as he wished to discuss with him certain rhythmic problems of jazz which he felt that he himself
had never mastered.

When George with his ram-shaped head, gay blue shirt, and strong cigar
appeared and caught sight of the harpsichord, he at once sat down before it,

tipped the chair back, and started off with some passages from Bach. It was not long before he gave up in despair, for his restless nature could not adapt itself to the reversed color of the keys, or the primitive method of coupling keyboards for greater volume, and the absence of pedals.

Hofmann was standing beside George as he struggled with the harpsichord. Then he took him by the hand, led him across the room to the Chickering piano, raised the top, and said: "My dear young man, you should be happy in your own form of music; you have created American rhythms of extraordinary originality; they are beautiful, and they are *you*—why do you want to play the classics, and why do you beg me to show you *how* classical music should be played! You have your own idiom—develop it! Now I shall try to play some jazz for you, just to prove that I really cannot do it; because for me it is not the natural way in which to express myself. It is superimposed and sounds false; with you it rings true and sounds authentic—but don't try to play on a harpsichord!"

They continued their discussion, and each would show the other how certain passages should be played. Then Mrs. Harriman asked Hofmann to play some complete and uninterrupted composition on the piano. The square, powerfully muscled hands began to wander over the keys—suddenly he plunged into a Chopin "Polonaise," wringing such a wealth of resonance from the old piano and pounding on it with such force that we could hear the strings cry out in pain or delirium, whichever it was.

After these pianistic fireworks Hofmann left, promising to go with us to the new Gershwin operetta that was to open the following week. When he had left, George sat down at the piano rather dejectedly, and we urged him to sing and play the lyrics of his operetta, which he did with delightful ease. Despite the cigar held between the fingers of his right hand most of the time he was playing, the syncopated, unpredictable turns and twists flowing fluently from his fingers proved beyond question that his music was indeed an outpouring of himself and of no other, and his gloomy mood vanished.

Another delight was a recital given by a young and gifted Italian violinist named Giorgio Ciompi, with Miss Pessl accompanying him on the harpsichord. Their selections of seventeenth- and eighteenth-century music were many of them unknown to us, and the novel beauty of this combination of instruments was quite a revelation.

In 1930 I attended a recital by José Iturbi at Carnegie Hall. He had played many of my favorite compositions, and after the concert I went to the Green Room to express my gratitude and admiration. He had heard of the harpsichord, and suggested that we drive to 157 so that he might see it.

When we climbed the second flight of stairs and lighted the lamps in the big room, he was genuinely surprised to find himself in an atmosphere unsuspected from outside these high walls.

When I opened the harpsichord and the light was turned on it, he exclaimed in delight, sat down, and let his fingers feel out the strange new sounds of the plucked strings. I showed him how the couplings were used and, after an interval of experimenting with different effects, he played a difficult Bach fugue, then Scarlatti and Gluck, on and on, bewitched by the unfamiliar sounds he was controlling. Dignity, style, and the suggestion of romance and aristocracy seemed to vibrate from the strings; it was as if this instrument still held the power to evoke the spirit of a lost period.

This harpsichord is today in the Museum of Musical Instruments at Yale University. How often of a winter evening do I spend long hours alone by the fire, recalling with nostalgic delight both this instrument and the beauty of the music that came to life in this room!

CHAPTER TWENTY-THREE

NIGHT WORK AFTER THE BALLET AND MOVING PICTURES

ASSOCIATION WITH the Pavlova Ballet Company brought me many new friends of the stage. After the evening performances the dancers would frequently come to my house for a reviving snack; then they seemed to gather energy and be quite ready to pose! These midnight sessions had a rather special quality; we were sure of no interruptions, and the hush of a sleeping city is somehow conducive to study. The musicians would try out themes and new ideas for ballets, while dancers who were not posing would practice their steps and exchange opinions in rapid Russian, so that presently I had acquired a fragmentary knowledge of that language, enough at least to enable me to get the gist of the meaning: *"Spasibo! Ochen horosho"*—Thanks, everything all right. . . . What a joy it was to work with these beautiful strong bodies, leaping and dancing about!

Among the scenic designers who formed part of this group was Boris Anisfeld. He had escaped from Russia with his wife and baby at the time of the anticzarist revolution. They had trekked their way across Siberia to the coast where a vessel brought them to America. A huge roll of canvasses and a few bags of clothing constituted their worldly belongings.

The first important exhibit of Anisfeld's work was arranged by the Brooklyn Museum. Boris had a thick shock of black hair, a heavy pointed beard, dark brown eyes, and a sallow complexion—a typical Russian.

He posed for me to model his portrait, and he painted one of me that now is part of the collection of the National Academy of Design. He would bring sketches for the scenery at the Metropolitan Opera, and we took a keen interest in each other's professional struggles. He eventually gave me the original sketch for a scene in Maeterlinck's opera *The Blue Bird* as a souvenir of the many happy hours we had worked and played together at 157.

Later on, he moved to Chicago where he has for many years been an instructor of painting at the Art Institute.

One day Sir Joseph Duveen came to call at my studio. I could hardly guess the purpose of his errand; he scanned the various pieces that stood about the studio and then focused on the marble portrait I was carving of Anna Pavlova in a pensive and rather sad mood, with hands folded across her breast. She and I had enjoyed the contrast of quietude after all the poses of vigorous action in the dance that we had interpreted together.

Sir Joseph asked me what I intended to do with the marble. I said: "If and when I ever finish it, my responsibility ceases; Fate must take charge. The work belongs to the sculptor only during the period of creation."

"Why not send it to London and exhibit it? I should like to buy it and present it to the Tate Gallery," he said. Three months later, Knoedler's in London exhibited it. Unfortunately, Sir Joseph had been taken very ill and had gone to the Continent for a cure. Only a short time after his return to England, he died. I was deeply disappointed that the bust was not seen by him in its finished state and presented to the Tate Gallery.

The marble portrait eventually was shipped to Paris, and in 1961 I brought it home to 157. Expert packing ensured its safety. To receive it unhurt was something of a miracle, and I confess to a deep sense of relief when it was finally placed on its own pedestal in my studio.

DESHA AND TONY

When the ballet season was ended and the studio was no longer filled with dancers, there was time to concentrate on other matters. Without warning came a request from an electric research bureau that I help in making some colored moving pictures of dancing subjects with music accompaniment. This certainly was a "change of trouble." Fortunately, as always, Sam was there with his practicality and infinite resourcefulness. With his help, I plunged into the new and totally different problems of training dancers for slow-motion shots. Sam arranged the music and made a record of it to fit in with the dance and made a notation of all the poses for the dancers' guidance. We installed the necessary Victrola and stretched a huge blue curtain across the studio as a backdrop. Desha, a young Yugoslav dancer, was to film her hit "Bubble Dance," tossing colored balloons into the air to the rhythm of a Brahms waltz. We tried out all kinds of lighting and timing in deciding how to build up a stage set of a grape arbor on which clusters of balloons simulated four-foot bunches of grapes. Sam tirelessly helped me rehearse the dance.

MARBLE BUST OF PAVLOVA

Desha and Tony Sansone then worked up a dance in which they suggested by pantomime Debussy's *L'Après-midi d'un faune*. With his mechanical aptitude, Sam backed up my suggestion about doing something then considered impossible: to have the figures photographed in shadow on a screen. Experimentally we placed the lightly clothed dancers between a three-layer gauze curtain and the camera, and had light thrown from behind the curtain so that the figures became silhouettes moving in scenery shadowed on the screen from behind. Sam was quite at home with the 4,000-watt lamp and could show the men just what was necessary to get the shadow sharp, but not so sharp that it destroyed the illusion (of water flowing in a stream, for example, which we simulated by making it flow from a hose over corrugated tin). Amazing effects were produced, and the studio became a wilderness of branches, Spanish moss, weeping willows, and electric wires. After weeks of trial and error and endless rehearsals, we were authorized to build the full-size stage sets in a movie studio in the Bronx that was rented for a huge sum for one day only.

Desha, Tony, Sam, and I started off at 7:00 A.M. in a taxi and went first to a movie studio in Astoria where they were shooting jungle scenes for *The Emperor Jones*. The taxi driver was told of our plan, and he helped us collect all manner of moss and foliage and branches that were not actually being used in the O'Neill stage set. We piled the taxi full, tied the rest on the roof, and drove off to the Bronx studio. There the expert stagehands seemed to enjoy the apparent madness of our scheme. Entering into it, they showed appreciation of our shadow effects on the screen, and the illusion of moonlight on a stream appeared on the curtain with no suggestion of the absurd props used to achieve the optical effect. By two o'clock we had taken two pictures of *L'Après-midi d'un faune* with sound-track accompaniment. Then we had to demolish everything and build up the grape arbor for the "Bubble Dance."

There were so many balloons to blow up into six-inch grapes that we nearly blew ourselves inside out. Frequently they would explode and leave us faint and frustrated. Then Sam had the idea of getting a tank of compressed air. Our awareness of how much the studio was costing per hour made us accomplish the impossible. By four o'clock the Brahms waltz started and Desha performed her dance. She plucked the balloon grapes successfully from the vine-covered arbor and caught them on the musical beat. When the gong rang at five o'clock, we had finished two pictures.

We were so tired that I cannot recall anything further, but the films were shown here and in London, and the "Bubble Dance" met with special praise. The effects of shadows and slow-motion shots then gave me the thought that by taking out certain frames from these filmstrips a dramatic series of still slides could be made. If Desha and Tony studied these on the studio screen, they could recapture dynamic patterns they had been totally unconscious of while dancing. We fitted a series of these poses into sequence and evolved a slow-motion dance to waltz music, and off they went to try it on Broadway with great success.

Of course, the almost nude figures had to be of exceptionally fine proportions, and the male dancer had to be powerfully built, with a sense of balance to give assurance to his partner and to the audience. It was far more difficult for them to do the slow-motion patterns than to dance to a quicker tempo.

In August, 1929, while I was in Paris arranging the shipment to America of a large exhibition of over a hundred of my sculptures, I was suddenly interrupted in my studio by a visit from Monsieur Arsène Alexandre. My inherent weakness of forgetting names afforded this gentleman a surprise, for I was quite unaware of his important position in the world of art, and could not understand why he felt it necessary for me to drop everything immediately and turn my attention solely to him. A truck had been backed up to the studio into which were being loaded many wooden cases containing my bronzes and marbles. About twenty pieces were still outside in my garden ready to be packed; these Monsieur Alexandre explained to me, he would examine, as he had been asked to write a criticism of my work for the magazine *Renaissance de l'Art*. This gave me as much of a surprise as I had given him, for I had never had a one-man show in Paris, or sought any publicity, and could not account for this sudden recognition at a moment when most of my work was boxed and ready to go to America.

However, after a half hour we reached a friendly basis of understanding. I was forced to explain to him that I would have to cut the visit short as I had an appointment to finish a portrait of Giovanni Boldini, the portrait painter. Monsieur Alexandre was incredulous, saying that he had known Boldini many years, that he had never known him to be willing to pose for anyone, that he had not in fact been known to go out of his studio in the daytime for the past five years, living a very retired existence because of his advanced age of eighty-six years. Seeing that Monsieur Alexandre did not really believe that I was making this portrait, I asked him if I could give him a lift in my car. He said, "Yes, to the office of *Figaro,* of which I am the art critic, as you should have known without my telling you!"—and he shook his finger at me in admonition. I smiled and said, "But, Monsieur Alexandre, perhaps you will believe me when I show you the portrait, which I hope you will recognize as your friend Monsieur Boldini." When I lifted the clay head to put it into the car Monsieur Alexandre put his hand on my shoulder and smiled in a very kindly and forgiving fashion . . ."C'est lui, c'est bien lui!"—It's he, it is indeed he!—and from that moment on, our drive across Paris was a delightful one. He confessed that it was the first time he had met an artist who had lived so long in his city without asking a favor of him, and he wished me well in my difficult undertaking of completing the portrait of Boldini, adding that although he himself was now rather advanced in years, he was determined to make a thorough study of my work and would write a monograph on the subject during the coming year. He seemed familiar with my previous activities and, tremendously pleased, I went over to model Boldini with renewed courage.

He received me as he had on the two previous sittings, wearing a bowler hat pulled over one eye and flourishing a black cane. The sittings alternated between animated talk and complete silence, for after vehemently expressing his views on a variety of subjects Boldini would suddenly doze off in his chair, still wearing the bowler hat. I was accordingly free to concentrate on my work without interruption or self-consciousness. In four sittings the portrait was completed to his satisfaction, rather a feat, I thought, as his face was full of subtle expressions reflecting a complex nature. When I said good-bye, I asked Monsieur Boldini what he would like to have done with this portrait; it had been made at the request of his great friend (I might say "muse") Mrs. Philip Lydig, of whom he had made a dozen portraits. She had insisted vehemently that he break down his Chinese wall of isolation and, because of his long friendship and admiration for her, he told me that he had agreed to admit me under protest. He asked that one copy in bronze be presented to the Brooklyn Museum, on condition that it be placed next to his portrait of Whistler, which he considered his best piece of work. I promised that this would be done, and I made the gift later that year. Another replica was presented to him for his own collection.

Mrs. Lydig was delighted with the results of our common efforts, and said: "Now, Malvina, you must make a portrait of me in Egyptian alabaster—I know just how I would like to have it done!" I had seen Rita frequently in New York, and had heard her praises sung by Ignacio Zuloaga, the Spanish painter. She had the rare gift of drawing out in her friends their individual qualities, disarming them by her repartee and true feminine charm. She personified for many of them the essence of style and the rapidly disappearing art du salon. At dinner in her house each person at the magnificently set table was tactfully drawn into the conversation, so that, though there were twenty guests, by the end of the banquet, each one was left with a vivid impression of all the others. Her sensitiveness and love of beauty were a constant stimulant to her artist friends who realized that she expected the best they could produce, in conversation, personal appearance, or, in the case of professionals, art.

After a serious operation and long illness at a hospital, so strong was her spirit that, to my amazement, a few weeks later there came a knock at my studio door, and there stood Rita Lydig, the "Alabaster Lady," in a Spanish lace blouse with high collar, black velvet skirt, African gold bracelets, and diamond and platinum chain from which hung a beautiful lorgnette, her head held high and her face radiant. We started in at once to make her portrait, and although she was so ill that frequently during the sittings she had to resort to periods of rest before resuming her characteristic pose, her patience and courage never flagged. When finally the portrait was finished and carved in alabaster, we exhibited it at the Grand Central Art Gallery, and on the opening day Rita came and stood beside it.

It was a very short time after this that she was taken back to the hospital for her last and fatal illness.

Because of the fragility of the material, the alabaster portrait was never sent out again to another exhibit. In 1961 it was acquired by the Rosenbach Foundation in Philadelphia.

CHAPTER TWENTY-FOUR

IVAN MESTROVIC

It was by a rather fortunate chance that I became acquainted with Ivan Mestrovic in 1925, the year the art world here vibrated to the shock of his first American exhibit, consisting of one hundred pieces of sculpture.

The Brooklyn Museum was the institution with sufficient vision and enterprise to organize this huge show and send it about the country to other museums. Other museum directors were intelligent and courageous enough to wish the public to see what magnificent marbles and bronzes were being made by a Yugoslav. Mestrovic, although famous in Europe, had seldom been heard of in this country, his very name (correctly pronounced Meshtravich) suffering under American approximations.

It was because of my Yugoslav Relief trip that Mestrovic was brought to my studio on his arrival. As I was familiar with his work through photographs and books, he felt at home in 157, and we became close friends. I offered him use of the place until he could find a studio of his own, and what I learned from watching this Titan at work was more than anyone could learn from books or even perhaps from many of the best sculptors. His touch was infallible. "Never put on a piece of clay," he used to say, "unless you have thought out beforehand just where and why it should be added."

When Mestrovic asked me to pose for him to make a three-quarter-length portrait, we pulled out the clay barrel; he threw together a rugged wooden frame on a low stand and wired a piece of lead pipe to a central post.

"Let's start," he said without more ado, and I stopped working on my own clay model of the moment. "Stay just as you are, holding the tool, and turning your head toward me." That seemed simple, so there I stood, watching him pull great wads of clay out of the barrel, place them methodically on the frame, and, as the figure began to take form, tap each piece with the side of his hand. "Be-

235

MH in front of her over-life-sized bronze of Mestrovic

cause my wrist was broken and badly set, Malvina, I find I can push the clay better this way when the pieces are large." Then came the finishing surface of little pellets pushed firmly with his thumb. Only occasionally did he pick up a flat wooden tool and cut the lines of the drapery or divide the masses of the hair. Almost all of the modeling was done without the aid of any tool; the details of the face were built up with smaller pellets so rapidly and with so little correction or wasted effort that in three mornings I supposed the whole finished. Suddenly he decided he had not caught the character he wanted, so, without warning, he cut off face and hand and began throwing great chunks into the barrel.

"Let's do another," he said, "just a head this time. . . . I'm finding out what I want as I study you." I leaned against the wall rather discouraged, and threw my head back. "That's it, hold it!" he said, and lighting up his ever-smoldering cigarette, he plunged into the new problem with a still fiercer determination. The pose was hard to hold, and I had to rest often, but in four hours it was finished, and he was satisfied. "This gives me a new idea," he said, "and I'll make it here next week, so you may watch without having to pose at the same time.

"Now, let's see," said Mestro (this had become his nickname at 157), "if you can make a life-size charcoal drawing of me in less than two hours; that will be a good way for you to find out about *me* and for me to find out if you know how to draw!"

"If I succeed, would you be willing to pose for me to let me try to make *your* portrait in clay?" I asked, frightened, but so excited as to be ready to risk anything for the chance to learn.

"We'll see," and as he smiled, I knew I was being put to a severe test.

There is something life-giving about jumping off the deep end, and finding that it is not really so bad as you had feared. Had I had time to think it over, I doubt if I would have dared do many of the things that have filled my life with adventure and unusual memories.

The charcoal drawing came off better than either of us expected, one of those happy accidents—and Mestro agreed to pose. "Begin tomorrow morning," he said with a twinkle in his eyes, "but you do just the head—yes?"

"We will see!" I answered, and he caught the echo of his own words.

During the night (the best time to work on something difficult) I built up the head, leaving plenty of clay, however, for shoulders, just in case. . . . It was certainly the crucial test, this task I had set myself, and the sittings were fierce battles to maintain a determination stronger than the doubts that beset me constantly.

"Only two wooden tools, Malvina, and give me a lump of clay to play with while I'm posing." So we started off. After three sittings we had a visit from Zuloaga, the painter, who was holding a comprehensive exhibit of his work in New York. He had known Mestrovic a long time, and was an ardent admirer of his work. He seemed happy about my portrait and urged Mestrovic to give me all the time I needed. They went off to lunch together, leaving me exhausted, but happy.

That evening Zuloaga stopped again at the studio, and we had tea by the fire while he told me tales of his own experiences with portraits. "You must take advantage of your sitters' moods," he said. "Some days they want to ask questions all the time, and other days they will sulk and squirm and have you on the rack. Then suddenly they will begin to talk and tell you the most amusing things about themselves. You keep right on working as if nothing else mattered. . . ."

"And now," he said, jumping up and crossing the room to a ladder against the wall, "this is just what I need!" He took up a brush that had been left in a can of red paint, and started up the ladder. High up on the brick wall he painted in large letters OSEZ! "You say, Malvina, that you dare not ask Mestrovic to pose for a full-length figure! There is my answer—DARE!" and he waved good-bye and was gone.

That night I built up the whole figure from the floor to where the clay bust was set on a stand, the three-legged stand consequently serving as armature. Mestro's heavy corduroy trousers and linen smock made a massive support for the bust I had started, well over life size, and the third leg of the stand held up the clay for the trunk of a tree against which he was braced.

When Mestro came the next morning, he gave one look at the big figure in the middle of the floor, and laughed: "Your back must ache, Malvina! What an idea to make a figure on the floor! You cannot turn it and you will have terrible troubles, but never mind . . . the worst is over, for the head and shoulders fit well on this figure, and I will be a good model. . . . That will help more than anything else!"

Then he caught sight of the red paint on the wall. "That was the message your friend Zuloaga left for me yesterday, when he came back to see me," I said, and we both had a good laugh.

The figure turned out well. A group of friends came to the studio to see it, and to my delight two of them, Mr. Felix Warburg and Mr. Edward C. Blum, purchased it and presented it to the Brooklyn Museum.

That year, 1925, Mestrovic went to Chicago and received the commission to make two colossal Indians on horseback for the Michigan Avenue bridge. He made endless drawings in red chalk, using the side of the crayon for the shadows and the sharp edges for defining outlines.

On his return to New York he found a studio in Washington Mews where he built up small-scale models for this project.

One day he and his good friends Sir John and Lady Lavery took me to lunch at the Lafayette. Mestro suggested that Sir John might pose for his portrait after lunch and that we would all meet at the studio again at six and dine together. Sir John agreed with enthusiasm, and at the appointed hour Lady Lavery and I arrived and, seeing the amazing likeness completely finished now in clay, we both cheered. Lady Lavery said: "I always told John I could hang a wee

MH by Mestrovic (*Frick Art Reference Library*)

Mestrovic by MH

kettle on his nose because the end of it turns up so suddenly and now you, Ivan, have proved that I was right!"

The happy hours spent with these friends resulted in the following arrangement: when I went to Europe to spend the summer and winter there, the Laverys with daughter and secretary moved into 157, and Sir John painted many portraits there, including one of His Eminence Cardinal Hayes.

Sir John was one of the quaintest, most lovable Irishmen I ever knew. His wit and warmheartedness radiated an atmosphere of good cheer wherever he went.

Never were tenants so enjoyed by their landlord as these two gay creatures. The stories they wrote me about parties at 157 made me regret the distance between us, and when they left, the whole house and studio were enriched by new cushions, gay curtains, boxes of heavenly paint brushes, a fine easel, and—gift beyond price—packets of gold and silver leaf that have been treasured ever since and used whenever I need a special gilding or silver finish. Generosity seemed to emanate from Sir John. He told me he felt he never could repay the world for his own good fortune. He was a foundling who had never known his own birthday—"Sure, my friends give me a birthday party whenever we meet!" and then he would add, wistfully, "The beauty of my wife, Hazel, did you notice her amethyst eyes? Could I ever be thankful enough for such a gift as that from the good Lord Himself?"

His delightful home in London and his big studios were the gathering places for many notables in literature and painting, and speaking of luncheons, I recall the scintillating repartee at one special luncheon Lord Reading gave for Bernard Shaw on his seventieth birthday; Irish wits were matched and sparks flew. I found it breathtaking to hear such linguistic thrusts and parries, and the ladies kept very quiet except for laughter and occasional words of admiration and amusement.

CHAPTER TWENTY-FIVE

MY PARIS HOUSE

THERE SEEMED to be a strange force at work shaping events that directed my fate. The work I had managed to collect in Paris during the many summers I had spent there forced me to look about and find a place where we could live and feel at home, not in hotels, and where I could also store the plaster models.

Catching one's breath after a long race is as essential as the actual drive and throb of creating. This is true even though there is a rhythm and balance in work that makes of creation the re-creation of its own forces.

Near the Paris studio that I had rented for several years was a vacant lot terminating the dead end of the Villa Chauvelot. By persuasion and with the invaluable assistance of a bottle of Dubonnet and the guidance of Monsieur H. Crocé-Spinelli, architect and man of affairs, I managed to buy this lot in 1927 on the last night of my summer visit to Paris that year. Part of the site was originally the entrance to one of the catacombs. The great hole had been filled in with paving stones, and six shafts of concrete had been set on the solid stone foundation and these projected above the ground and determined the size of what I might build on with safety. The rest of the plot I made into a garden.

While I was planning for this house, many of my friends doubted and disapproved and even thought I was quite mad, but my good friend Lemordant encouraged me. If he was able to plan his own house with incredible handicaps— unable to see, unable to measure—just by using cardboard cutouts, certainly I could be my own architect. His boost to my morale was one more bridge of sympathy between us.

When my plans were drawn up, I made arrangements for forwarding them from New York (to which I had in the meantime returned), and my new friend and adviser Monsieur Crocé-Spinelli engaged a builder in my Paris *quartier* to go forward with the work there. By a magic which, in my experience, is not often forthcoming, the house was built and ready for occupancy the following June,

"VILLA ASTI," MY PARIS HOUSE (*Mildred Capron*)

A GARDEN CORNER OF VILLA ASTI, WITH MH's "ORPHEUS AND EURYDICE" GROUP

1928. I went over toward the end of April to supervise the painting, and bought the absolute essentials for furnishing the house. Sam joined me in June and was astonished at finding it so nearly completed. We called it Villa Asti, deriving again from that sparkling Italian wine that had given me my nickname. The address was 25 Villa Chauvelot, which at that time was a little dirt street leading off the Boulevard Chauvelot. Later, when the city paved the "boulevard" and changed the name to rue Santos-Dumont, the Post Office registered the house as 25 Villa Santos-Dumont.

It was a solid happiness to move all my plasters here to our own house and to have a permanent home and studio in Paris. The Villa Asti was actually a fairly large three-story building, but seen at the end of the street, with only part of the front showing, it seemed deceptively small. The ground floor had a garage (under one end of the house), a furnace room, and a comfortably large studio with a concrete floor. Off the studio was a door to a staircase going up to the second floor, which had a kitchen, dining room, and two bedrooms and a bath. The third floor had a large living room with a big northern window (it was used as a painter's studio by some later tenants), a bedroom with bath, and a large storeroom. Altogether there was generous space for both living quarters and work. Behind the house was an area of walled ground where we soon made a garden and brought ivy plants from Fontainebleau—which grew up to twenty feet in height and entirely covered the hollow-brick wall.

All that summer Sam and I added to the house furnishings. In the nearby rue de la Convention, shops sold Brittany and Normandie furniture, and we were enthusiastic patrons. We had a grand piano. We were soon to have zebra hides and other exotic items from Africa. We painted the walls warm bright colors to go with our furnishings and our moods, and gradually we evolved the life-giving home that was to sustain us for many years to come.

On the same street with us were tradespeople and artisans who not only helped us establish our home but later assisted me professionally. There was an upholsterer; there were a wood-carver and frame-carver who made very handsome baroque-looking picture frames, a house painter, a draftsman and model-maker for architects—they were all useful and skilled workmen. One was a Breton granite-carver who was very kind and shared space with me when the Hall of Man work was simultaneously crowding me out of two studios. These kindly neighbors would lend me things I didn't have, like extra-long ladders or extra-heavy ropes. It proved to be one of the happy choices of my life that I had decided to make my home in this street.

Not long after I built my house, Monsieur Alexandre completed his book about me, in French, illustrated by pictures of about sixty pieces of my work. This constituted a résumé of about twenty years of professional struggle. No parties in daylight hours, few holidays, and no exhibitions—I seem to have been an addict to hard work that constantly, even with its desperation and daily discouragement, turned to joy. There was never a time when I was not glad and eager to get to work at once, day after day. As soon as I had an idea, I thought only of how soon I could try to carry it out and express it. I worked not from any

LIVING ROOM UPSTAIRS WITH SAM AT THE PIANO AND MH READING

sense of duty or feeling of obligation, but always to gratify this inner passion to express something. It was something stronger than I was, something I just followed. It never let me alone. If I didn't have a commission, it was all right; I had time to do something else that I wanted to do that didn't yet belong anywhere. If I did have a commission, I worked at it conscientiously, to make it right for where it would belong. But my true center of work was not commissions; it was an enormous capacity for falling in love with everything around me: every person, every man on the street, and every woman and child and cat and dog or any queer thing that happened in my path and became a sculptural idea. So as I had in New York with Bill, I collected a group of varied types in Paris: as examples, the coal man, the mattress maker, and a "witch" who lived on the other side of my high garden wall.

My Neighbor

It was well known in the *quartier* that she didn't come out in daylight. Therefore she was known there locally as "the witch." One evening I trailed her as she was carrying home a *filet* (a net shopping bag) of potatoes. The bag slipped and the potatoes rolled on the ground, and when I helped her pick them up, she was dumbfounded to have anybody speak to her. After this incident, she became more amenable. I would see her peering out of the door of her garden gate onto the little Alley Chauvelot where I was walking. I could stop and speak to her for a few moments if she didn't shut the door in my face, and we became quite friendly on that basis. I asked her if she wouldn't come in to see my garden and studio which adjoined her place. I said, "Out of sheer curiosity, wouldn't you like to see what's on the other side of your wall?"

I had a purpose in this. During my talks with her, I had tried to memorize her head, and had modeled it life-size in clay; in fact, I had built up two clay heads, one of her peering out of her door with defiance in her eye and a great guard of self-defense, but the other one with just the bony structure and general aspects of her head, left that way deliberately because I hoped, when she came to see me, there might be a new expression, a new attitude of mind I could catch. And that's how it was. She did come, and was intrigued by all the things she saw. She was surprised when I told her I wanted to do her portrait, and when I said, "Let me show you what I've already done from memory and then maybe you'll come just for a time or two and that's all I'll need to finish it." Then I showed her something that revealed to her her own cross, witchlike self with the door up against the side of her face. "Ah," she said, "but this is *désagréable,* and I'd like to have a more pleasant portrait." "I plan to do that too," I said, and showed her the second head. A little doubtful, but getting up her courage, she agreed to pose for me, and that was how I came to do these two heads of this neighbor of mine.

It was typical of my involvement everywhere, of my daily eagerness to remake the world around me in new forms. Every human being was a worthy subject, an idea, a means of continuing my incessant work. I was chained, but I was a willing prisoner.

THE "WITCH WOMAN" AT HER DOOR

THE PLEASANT VERSION OF THE SAME WOMAN

JARRY THE JOCKEY

An iron gateway near my house led into a dingy little courtyard just wide enough to hold a two-wheeled cart—beyond were two horse stalls. In one stood a drooping old mare of rusty hue, sagging first on one side and then on the other, ready to lay her ears back and nip anyone who dared disturb her. In the next stall a younger but uncouth-looking horse stood endlessly nibbling at his acrid straw bedding—sparse enough at best to cover the hard damp earth floor. Above these two stalls boards were laid across rough beams, and on these the straw and hay were stored. This supply was reached by a ladder from which various rungs were broken and hanging at odd angles. The hayloft was covered and walled on three sides but open in front to the four winds of heaven. This was Jarry's bedroom and home.

Jarry was a spare person of sixty years or so, with finely chiseled features, sunken eyes, hollow cheeks indicating the absence of teeth, and the sallow color of a ravaged existence. He arose at 5:00 A.M. from his night in the straw under a ragged horse blanket. He reached for his faithful bottle of red wine—a long drink, a stretch, and a yawn—and he shook himself like a dog and crawled out and down the ladder. He drew two pails of water from the tap, then pushed aside the sleepy horses and put their hay into the manger. Oats were expensive, and so were given only once a week as a delicacy. He talked to his equine friends, conversing with them continually while he cleaned out the stall—only one, for in the other lay the old mare who never went out any more, and the thick flooring of manure made a warmer bed under the sparse straw for her rheumatic legs.

With a friendly "À ce soir, mes amis!" Jarry pushed open the creaking iron gates and wandered off in the bleak dawn, winding his muffler around his neck as he went on his long journey of an hour and a half to reach the place where he worked from 7:00 A.M. until 5:00 P.M. delivering packages and carrying mail to the Central Post Office. "A position of great responsibility!" he would say with pride.

As a newcomer in this remote corner of Paris, I was mystified by this emaciated neighbor, but shy about asking too many questions. Occasionally I noticed bunches of carrot greens hanging out of his pockets, and at last I had the courage to ask him what he did with them. "Ah, ma petite dame, c'est le déjeuner de mes petits lapins. Voudriez-vous les voir?" (Ah, my little lady, it's lunch for my little rabbits. Would you like to see them?) He led me through the garden gate of my opposite neighbor, Paynot the cripple, who owned the two horses and who dragged himself on heavy crutches as far as the curbstone where by superhuman effort he would lift his great helpless body into the two-wheeled cart, gather up the reins in his left hand, for the right was useless, and drive off around the corner of the alley and disappear.

Jarry opened the wire door of a little box and put in the carrot greens. The rabbits pounced upon them with ferocity. One little fellow always seemed to be pushed away from the feast by his strong rivals. I watched Jarry. He knelt down and began talking to him as if he were a child: "Va, mon petit chou, n'aies pas peur; faut se battre pour vivre . . . vas-y . . . courage!" (Come, my darling, don't be afraid; one must fight in order to live . . . Come on . . . courage!) But the little bunny hung one limp ear and crouched in his corner disconsolate. Jarry opened the wire door, put in his hand, and picked up the little bundle of furry discouragement. I watched him feed the wee rabbit until its fears subsided, and then he put it into his pocket to nibble what was left, and there it fell asleep while Jarry went about his business.

One autumn he came to me in my studio carrying a rabbit in his arms and asked if I ever modeled animals. As it happened, I was making a statue of St. Francis with his wolf and birds about him. Jarry's emaciated sad face lit up with a smile of delight when he saw the group I was making.

"Did not St. Francis love animals too?" he asked.

"Yes," I said, "he did. Will you pose for me with your little gray bunny this morning?" He agreed at once, and I included the little visitor in my group.

While posing, Jarry seemed to grow garrulous and in response to my questions related how he had started life as a jockey for a wealthy racehorse owner in Passy. He had ridden in many races and had won many a good prize and high tips. Later he had become a groom in these same racing stables; then, through temptation and bad habits, he had taken to drink, spent all his money, and lost his job. His self-respect vanished, but his love of horses survived. From bad to worse he sank to the depths of the horse market. There he met Paynot who eventually brought him to the Villa as keeper of the old black mare, the brown horse, the rabbits, and the dogs, and in exchange gave him his lodging in the hayloft and a few francs a day.

Jarry agreed to pose for his portrait as soon as he had finished building a brick wall for my garden, which he did after his hours of work. He had learned the trade during his early years. One evening I said to him, "I will make you as a brickmason. Give me a few of your bricks." I took these to a chemist craftsman who ground them up and mixed them with a binding liquid. Then we cast the portrait in this unusual material. I liked the color and consistency resulting from this experiment, and mounted the portrait on two hollow bricks as a base.

A few weeks later when I returned from a journey I learned that Jarry had been taken to the hospital very ill and not expected to live. I went at once to the hospital and found a specter on a narrow iron bed in a long line of pallid sufferers.

He opened his eyes and recognized me. A wan smile . . . "How is this? Is it you? I did not expect to see you again. I miss my animals—they do not understand this. . . . But tell me, are they getting along well?" A fit of coughing stopped his feverish words. Tuberculosis had taken its deadly toll. I left him some fruit and a few flowers and promised to come again soon with news of his beloved animals. His starry eyes reflected his thoughts. As he lay there, no longer noticing me, I wondered from what race of aristocrats this derelict of humanity had sprung. The ashen skin was drawn now so tightly over the sensitive, delicate

"The Mattress Mender

"Jarry"

features that the traces of breeding and fine bones were the more unmistakable.

Three days later the news came . . . Jarry was dead—Jarry the Jockey, the groom, the bricklayer, the vagrant, the drunken aristocrat, the kind lover of animals—my St. Francis of the Villa Chauvelot. . . .

THE MATTRESS MAKER

In another part of my *arrondissement* lived a weary, frail little woman who made over mattresses. She carried a wooden frame and a big bag of equipment on her stooped shoulders. When a client called to her from a window or doorway, she would stop and listen to a bill of complaints about an old mattress that was worn through in some places and had lumps in others. The mattress maker would smile and offer to do what she could to restore the mattress and make it comfortable. Then she set up her frame, unfolded the camp stool that hung on her arm, and climbed the stairs, sometimes many flights, pulled the mattress off the bed, lifted it over her head, and carried it down to the street. There her work began. Her nimble fingers would rip the seams and pull out all the stuffing. A cloud of fluff and dust enveloped her, and one could hear her coughing and singing a little refrain over and over again.

At noontime, the sacred hour of *midi,* she would put down her needle or scissors, straighten up, shake off her apron, and take a few long weary breaths. She would unwrap a little bundle and break off a section of bread, and in ten minutes she had finished and wiped her hands and face with a coarse white handkerchief. Working steadily until six o'clock, she would complete her task, put away her tools, sweep up the sidewalk, putting all the debris into a newspaper carried along for the purpose. Then, with the remade mattress hoisted onto her head she trudged up the stairs to deliver it to its owner. Once replaced upon the bed, she would pat it lovingly all over, call attention to the new white tufting and the even surface. "Oh, you will rest well on this now!" she would say as the owner carefully counted the coins into her palms.

One day when she had finished her work in front of my neighbor's house, I asked if I might walk along with her. She seemed a little startled, and began coughing, but then she smiled and nodded assent, and we started off. "You know," I said, "I have been watching you at your work; even last spring I noticed you when you came into my little alley. Your face and expression interest me— you see, I am an artist. May I help you carry any of your heavy burden?"

"No, thank you, Mademoiselle, I am used to it, and the weight is well balanced, and the distance to my house is not far." We followed the main street and turned into another alley. "There is my door," she said, pointing to a dingy entrance.

"Do you live here alone?" I ventured to ask.

"Oh, no, Mademoiselle, I live with my sister, on the fourth floor. She is an invalid, poor soul, but she can sew a little. She has not been out of our room for three years. Now I must leave my frame and tools here and go to the store to buy food for our supper."

We retraced our steps to the corner and entered a little shop. When she had counted out the sous for bread and coffee, she tied up the few remaining coins in her handkerchief.

As we walked slowly, I said: "You do such fine work, I wonder if you would do over some mattresses for some friends who live in the next *quartier*. They would pay you well, and give you a good lunch, too."

"Oh, but no, Mademoiselle, I couldn't do that, thank you just the same. You see, I have never left my own *arrondissement*—never!" She was coughing again.

"Someone told me that," I said, "but I could hardly believe it, and could not guess the reason."

"Well, you see, I have been here a long time, and my neighbors know me. They all work very hard, and they are poor, but they depend on me. They need a comfortable mattress at night after their long hard day's work." As she spoke, I was struck by the beauty of her expression, and we walked along in silence for a while.

"Also, Mademoiselle, I cannot walk very far; my lungs are weak, and I must be within call if my sister has a bad *crise* of the heart; our concierge can come and tell me quickly. I always tell her in which street I shall be working."

"Do you have plenty of work?" I asked.

"Oh, yes, my neighbors keep me busy enough; and, really, Mademoiselle, don't look so worried; is it not enough to have found a way to be useful to others? It makes me forget myself."

"Indeed, yes," I answered, "but it is not an easy fight for you. May I tell you that I admire the way you work, very much. There are many ways of working, but you obviously love your work, and this helps you to be patient and careful of every detail. It must indeed be a consolation to you to know that when you have done a good job, other tired people will find their rest through your labors." Her eyes filled with tears and a light seemed to shine out from her very soul.

"Would you come some day soon, and instead of making over a mattress, may I engage you to pose for your portrait in my studio? You see, I *do live* in your *quartier*, and I want so much to do your head. You can just sit still, rest for a few hours, talk to me if you like, and I will be very grateful." After a little shy hesitation she agreed.

On the appointed day, she appeared at the studio door. She seemed nervous, and kept clasping and unclasping her hands. I led her to the armchair, set out the model stand, and asked her to make herself at home. Her cough bothered her, and she tried hard to repress the paroxysms that sounded so ominous. Her cavernous dark eyes roamed about the studio and, after a long silence she said: "What can you see in my poor thin face, Mademoiselle, that can interest you? There must be so many lines and hollows."

"Well," I said, "Nature has a way of recording our thoughts in the face, and what I see in yours is beauty and patience and fortitude. Is that not enough?"

There was no reply, but when I next dared to look at her, I noticed there were tears running down her cheeks and falling on her thin clasped hands.

CHAPTER TWENTY-SIX

FIRST EXHIBITION

IN THE summer of 1929, as I mentioned in connection with my first meeting with Arsène Alexandre, I was busy collecting all the finished work I had done in Europe and shipping it in bond to my New York studio. There the cases were piled up on the floor of 157, and for days the customs officials and I examined the contents, they seeing to it that I was not bringing in wholesale drugs or other "forbidden goods" camouflaged as ART.

Before long the sculpture was ready to exhibit, the first exhibit for which I had so long prepared. Then came the ordeal of hanging oneself on the public line—"to be or not to be" passed or panned by the critics. There were one hundred and five subjects in sculpture in sixteen different materials, and many life-size crayon portraits. The exhibit at the Grand Central Art Gallery drew unexpected crowds, and many pieces were sold. The Brooklyn Museum had started the ball rolling before the exhibit opened by buying the two heroic black marble heads of a Senegalese Soldier and a Martinique Dancer.

My big family of "brain children" traveled around to the different museums throughout the country and did not return to my studio for five years. Each museum cooperated with the next and took over the task of installation, publicity, and transport. Such a tactful and generous "assist" saved me from being overwhelmed by my own output, and such encouragement to an artist was certainly of inestimable value. I had gambled for big stakes entailing all my time and strength as well as a costly outlay in materials.

While all this was going on, and in addition to my regular sculptural activities, I had discovered a new kind of work to keep me busy. One of my doctor friends, Dr. Henry McMahon Painter, urged me to make a series of medical drawings and prepare some illustrations for a book on embryology. He was a shaggy, gruff individual who dressed in homespun. He looked like an oversized

252

sheep dog; his big heart and boundless kindness endeared him to all his patients and friends.

This subject interested me intensely, and I continued to study it long after the requested drawings were completed. And my interest in medicine was not to stop with this.

Dr. Harvey Cushing

The summers I did not go abroad were generally spent on the seacoast of New Hampshire at Little Boar's Head. Dr. Harvey Cushing, renowned for his brain surgery, had a cottage there on Ocean Road, and he and his family lived there for many summers.

He and I were walking on the beach one day when he suddenly said: "I have a great idea in my head that I want to have carried out in sculpture on a big scale. There *must* be a symbolic monument of some sort at Togo Circle in Cambridge facing the green plaza between the gray stone buildings of the Medical School. We doctors work all our lives trying to find cures for disease and how to reduce human suffering, but we need something symbolic of the Spirit to arouse people to the fact that science is no cold, utilitarian profession. Here are these massive gray buildings where science and medicine are being studied, but there is nothing to suggest beauty or inspiration of the soul. I want you to go to Togo Circle with me, and we will look at this splendid site together. It is worth fighting for, and I will help you if you're ready to gamble on a big idea!" I had gambled many times before and have since—I gladly made the appointment, and we met at his hospital and went to the proposed site.

We sat on a curbstone, staring at the great buildings. Dr. Cushing was in a serious, thoughtful mood. "What would you think," I said, "of the Four Horsemen of the Apocalypse—War, Pestilence, Famine, Death—and above them the Angel commanding them to spare those who have the sign of God on their foreheads? It is these forces of destruction that you doctors are fighting, isn't it?"

Dr. Cushing gripped my hand so tightly that it hurt. He asked me what I could do about it, and I said, "Make a small-scale model, and then ask the angels to help us realize our hopes."

"Then go to work, Malvina, on 'The Four Horsemen,' and I'll hunt up the angels!"

That following winter, the winter after I built my house in Paris, I took a trip to North Africa and Italy to study monumental sculpture, and then went to Zagreb to study with Mestrovic in preparation for work on "The Four Horsemen." Mestrovic himself at that moment was working on horses, since he was still on his lakefront Chicago commission and was at the stage of making twenty-six-foot models. He offered me one of his studios and supervised my modeling of horses in relief and my work on a small model of an Arab stallion at a nearby horse farm.

Often he would call me into his studio to help the two or three other students build up one of his own big clay horses on its wood and iron armature.

The group of "The Four Horsemen of the Apocalypse"

HEAD OF DR. HARVEY CUSHING BY MH

BAS-RELIEF FIGURE OF DEATH FOR THE SERIES ON
"THE FOUR HORSEMEN OF THE APOCALYPSE"

After a while he would mount the scaffolding and start the surface modeling while we tossed him lumps of soft wet clay.

One day shortly after I had arrived, he said I was in for a severe examination. He went to a shelf and lifted off a heavy plaster cast of the famous horse's head by Phidias, from the Parthenon. "Now copy this as exactly as you can in the same size, and after two days I will come and check it with the original," he said. When he came back, he noted the errors I had made, told me to correct them, and without further warning said I was to start all over again the following morning and make the same head from memory in his studio. There would be no model to refer to. Another lesson in memory and observation, reminding me of the time Rodin had told me to make a half-life-size head of one of *his* portraits after studying it for fifteen minutes. Such lessons are without doubt the most valuable kind of instruction, and are remembered for a lifetime by the terrified student.

So Mestrovic trained and helped me, and when our stint was over he would lock the studio door and we would cross the courtyard to his house and have a cup of tea with his wife, Olga.

I owe it to Mestrovic that he found an Austrian professor of architecture and perspective to give me lessons in drafting and making drawings to show my scheme of the horsemen from all points of view. These lessons proved useful to me on many occasions, but were made more difficult by the fact that the professor spoke only German, and technical German presents problems.

Still training myself, in Paris that summer I continued the study of monuments and horses, for I was near the horse markets and could tie the animals to a post outside my studio in its little dead-end alley.

I made the scale model of the groups on my return to New York, and when they were ready Dr. Cushing came to see them at the studio. It was a year and a half after our consultation at Togo Circle. The place was filled with horses and angels and archangels in the round and in reliefs. He seemed acutely conscious of the amount of work I had devoted to the project and moved by the significance of the biblical lines which I had tried to interpret. We read aloud the verses from the Book of Revelation:

> . . . behold a white horse [Pestilence]: and he that sat on him had a bow; and a crown was given unto him: and he went forth conquering, and to conquer. . . .
> And there went out another horse that was red [War]: and power was given to him that sat thereon to take peace from the earth, and that they should kill one another: and there was given unto him a great sword.
> . . . And I beheld, and lo a black horse [Famine]; and he that sat on him had a pair of balances in his hand.
> . . . and behold a pale horse: and his name that sat on him was Death. . . .
> And I saw another angel ascending from the east, having the seal of the living God: and he cried with a loud voice to the four angels, to whom it was given to hurt the earth and the sea, saying: Hurt not the earth, neither

the sea, nor the trees, till we have sealed the servants of our God in their
foreheads.

. . . What are these which are arrayed in white robes? and whence came they?
. . . These are they which came out of great tribulation, and have washed
their robes, and made them white in the blood of the Lamb. Therefore are
they before the throne of God. . . .

They shall hunger no more, neither thirst any more. . . . For the Lamb
which is in the midst of the throne shall feed them, and shall lead them unto
living fountains of waters: and God shall wipe away all tears from their eyes.

Dr. Cushing went back to Boston with high hopes, and with the plans and
photographs carefully packed in his briefcase. "Now we shall see, Malvina, if
there is any possible way I can get this plan supported and carried through!"

"Well," I said, "I was working for the angels, even if *you* don't find any!"
He did not, despite many efforts. He was almost as disappointed as I was, and
this common attempt and poignant ending cemented our friendship.

A few years later I remember spending a weekend with the Cushings in
New Haven. Dr. Cushing had complained of feeling ill, and appeared apprehensive when we had met in Paris in November. Now, in April, he wrote me
that he had suffered a great deal with an infected foot, and had had an operation
on it which he himself supervised under local anesthesia.

He met me at the New Haven station, standing at the top of the long
stairway and waving to me with one of his crutches. His good humor and unconcern about himself were significant features of his character. We spent what to
me were memorable hours in his library, studying his rare books on anatomy,
chief among which were large books of plates of the Vesalius collection of
anatomical charts and studies and Dr. Cushing's own notebooks filled with brilliant drawings. He recovered from his foot ailment and had several years of
good health, and then, one day in October, 1939, he lifted one of the heavy
Vesalius folios and noticed a bad aftereffect. He was sent to the hospital and
put in an oxygen tent, about which he characteristically complained that it cut
off his vision, and he carefully and cheerfully kept track of his diagnosis. A few
days later, without pain, he died of a heart block. In his will were detailed
instructions for leaving his rare medical library to Yale University.

Some years after his death I made a portrait of this wonderful friend, which
I am glad to say met with the approval of his wife, his collaborators, and members of the faculty. This group of friends had it cast in bronze and placed in
his Memorial Library near the precious books he so loved. I had most helpful
criticism from Mr. Dean Keller, who had made a fine crayon portrait of Dr.
Cushing from life, and from Dr. John Fulton, who had written a most complete
and revealing biography and had worked closely with Dr. Cushing for many
years. Photographs loaned to me by the surgeons who knew Harvey Cushing in
Peter Bent Brigham Hospital and had taken many snapshots while he was working there were also of inestimable assistance.

The most definite impression that my friend made upon me, still clear to
the inner eye and helping me, was when I saw him in a brief rest period during

one of his famous brain-tumor operations. I had stopped over in Boston to visit him on my way to Little Boar's Head. He came into his office in his high-collared surgeon's coat; his face was tense with lines deeply graven; his finely shaped jaw had a stern rigidity. He sat down behind his desk, lighted a cigarette, and peered at me without saying a word. After a brief moment or two of relaxation he said: "This business of having a man's life in your hands is exhausting; the one I am trying to save now is so close to death that I haven't much hope, but it is his only chance. Now let's talk about 'The Four Horsemen' and our big idea for placing them in Togo Circle, so that people can see in symbols that scientists do fight for humanity!"

We had only a brief moment or two, but they branded themselves upon my mind. I had seen the man in the grip of his own Daemon, trying to save another's life.

CHAPTER TWENTY-SEVEN

OUT OF THE BLUE:
THE HURRICANE YEARS

THE MOST challenging and comprehensive project I ever undertook came from the Field Museum of Chicago's startling offer to have me "travel around the world and make a hundred or more life-size models of the Living Races of Man."

For the sake of continuity in this account of my life, I shall attempt to retell this transglobal story (told elsewhere in *Heads and Tales*) so that the reader may follow me through the busy years that led me to distant lands and enabled me to study the myriad types of our human family in their own habitats, a rare opportunity and a test of strength and perseverance. My experience revealed as nothing else could have done that we are indeed all members of the same great household and that when wars are not raging and tearing life apart, there is the possibility of brotherhood and friendly understanding among the races.

After the contract was signed in Chicago in 1929, and before Sam and I embarked for Europe and farther points, I agreed to make two life-size full-length figures in my New York studio, the "Nordic Male" and a Plains Indian chief named Long Lance. These were examined by the president of the museum, Mr. Stanley Field, by Dr. Berthold Laufer, and by members of the staff. The figures seemed to give them confidence that I could proceed to Europe for further work in Paris.

That summer the splendid Colonial Exhibition was in full swing in the Bois de Vincennes, an auspicious circumstance because it had assembled numberless native tribes from Africa, Indo-China, Java, Bali, and other colonies. An introduction to the director of the exhibition made it possible for me to motor to the park early in the morning to "borrow" for the day the special types I needed. I would drive the natives to my house and we would work all day in the studio, then, at four-thirty, I was to drive them back to the exhibit and get a signed receipt and another permit to return in a day or so and repeat the performance. In this way I obtained splendid models for the group of "Dutch East Indies" and for a "Senegalese Drummer" and other important sculptures. The models enjoyed their outings, for the drive enabled them to see many parts of Paris, and our picnic lunches in my garden seemed to be a real adventure for them.

In 1930 Sam and I went to northern Spain on the first short trip for the collection of racial types. At San Sebastian we came upon a Basque peasant driving a pair of white oxen along the road and decided to use him as a type. We persuaded him to come and pose for a life-size bust which I modeled in our hotel room. Fortunately, the room overlooked the beach where he had tethered his oxen so he could keep a watchful eye on them as I worked.

During our stay we had the great pleasure of visiting Señor Enrique Fernández Arbós and his wife. He was the eminent Spanish conductor who had conducted symphony concerts in America the preceding year. We also saw the painter Zuloaga in his enchanting home Zumaya, about an hour's drive south of San Sebastian and recalled his great OSEZ written on my studio wall. There was a folk festival in full swing at the time, so that we could see all the costumes and dances of the different parts of Spain and hear their folk music.

When five figures for the Field Museum were completed and cast into plaster, I decided to do a bit of gambling. My contract had stipulated that the final material was to be painted plaster. I was determined to change this condition, and I knew this matter must be handled with care, for my secret idea was to have all the figures cast in bronze with three or four of the heads to be carved in stone or marble.

So I engaged the Rudier foundry to cast two of the African figures into bronze. These I set out in my garden, leaving the other plasters in my studio next door. I then cabled to Chicago that I was ready for inspection, and Mr. Field and his wife came to Paris. My feelings may be imagined, for I was putting my faith in my own conviction, with no idea of what Mr. Field might decide about changing the contract from colored plaster to bronze.

The gods were on my side, and the two African figures glittered in the sunlight of the garden as the Fields arrived. There was a moment of suspense when Mr. Field tapped the figures with his seal ring. "What does this mean, Malvina? These are in bronze—and you were told to put them in plaster!"

"Oh, I took the risk!" I said. "The others are in plaster in the studio; in this way you can easily judge the effect of the materials for a permanent collection."

The die was cast. Mr. Field cabled and consulted with his trustees and with Marshall Field, who generously offered to donate toward the additional cost involved. Later Mr. and Mrs. Stanley Field, Mrs. Charles Schweppe, and others also contributed funds with enthusiasm. My hopes soared, and the long journey was decided.

A trip to London enabled me to meet the Most Noble Marquis of Reading, who had been Viceroy to India, and his able secretary Stella Charnaud, later to be his wife. Lord Reading's wholehearted interest in the plan was of inestimable help, for he presented me to a number of Maharajas of India who were in London at the time, attending a Council of Princes. Armed with letters of introduction and valuable guidance and advice, I was in an auspicious position for the work I was to undertake in India, the Malay jungles, and Ceylon. Stella Charnaud's help was of the greatest value, and our friendship has been a rare blessing to me ever since.

While in London I went one day with Henry Field, the anthropologist, to the Wellcome Historical Museum, which I had discovered in 1910, and enjoyed a most enlightening two-hour visit personally conducted by Dr. Wellcome. When he heard that we were leaving soon for a trip around the world, he said that he would prepare a medical kit for us and bring it to Paris so that he could teach us just how to use all the medicaments, antidotes, and instruments. We also carried another medical kit given to us by our own Dr. Simard, and thanks to their invaluable professional advice and equipment, we found ourselves ready for every emergency.

An American by birth, born in Wisconsin, Dr. Wellcome often told me stories of how, even as a little boy, he was interested in medicine and wanted to become a doctor. In the old days his father and other citizens of the town were obliged to build strong wooden blockades and stand off attacking Indian tribes. After some of these combats, young Henry would assist the surgeons, who happened to be the Mayo brothers, as they operated on the victims of tomahawk and arrow. He would hold the basin and unroll the gauze for Dr. Mayo and, by watching carefully, became more and more expert in his ministrations.

As a young man he went into partnership with Mr. Burroughs, another American, and together they perfected a method of converting many medicines into dry form, such as pills, tablets, and compressed bandages. The idea possessed his mind that for travelers and explorers, especially in the tropics or disease-ridden areas, these supplies would be of special value. He tried to introduce the idea in America, but was not successful.

They went to Canada where on a modest scale they were given encouragement to develop their drug business. It was in England, however, that their first real effort was supported, and it was generously encouraged in British Africa, India, and Australia. Enormous quantities of these specially prepared drugs were shipped by the British Government. In return for this encouragement Dr. Wellcome made an agreement that if he made a fortune—which seemed probable— he would devote it entirely to forming a great collection of Medical History and present it to the British Government in recognition of its help. He then became a British subject, was knighted by the King, and lived for the rest of his life in London.

When he died in 1934, he left a legacy to the British Crown of $5,000,000 and a stone building for a museum in which his entire collection might be displayed.

Gretchen Green was engaged to be our secretary-companion for the trip. She had lived for years in India and China and knew many helpful and influential people.

She went directly to the Far East to prepare the way for our arrival, making sure that the American Express Company would carefully store our shipments in the various ports to which we had sent them from Paris.

In a few weeks we closed the little villa in Paris and sailed for New York where Sam and I stayed with my sister Helen Draper; then we bade farewell and entrained for Chicago.

At the Field Museum we were given our final briefing by Dr. Laufer, whose long experience in China and Japan gave us indispensable guidance. His parting remark I shall always remember: "Don't try to hustle the East. Try to listen and learn the lessons of their ancient wisdom."

We sailed from San Francisco into the misnamed Pacific Ocean, and reached Honolulu after a rough and gale-blown voyage. There I modeled the Polynesian type of a Hawaiian surfboard rider, preparing myself by watching for hours as the glistening brown "ricers" balanced their magnificent bodies on boards that carried them on the crests of the powerful breakers.

After this we went to Japan, and through one of Dr. Laufer's letters of introduction were met offshore and escorted through the customs to our hotel in Tokyo by a special envoy from Count Hyashi, a member of the Emperor's council.

We were soon visited by Count Hyashi himself, who discussed with us a difficult request that Dr. Laufer had prepared him for. We were asking for permission to visit the Sakhalin Island of Hokkaido where the race known as the Ainus was kept under Japanese authority. No travelers were allowed to go to northern Japan in those days prior to the Second World War, so we were asking a very special favor in the name of Anthropology to study the physical aspect and way of life of this little-known race.

When we promised to follow all instructions, the permits were issued. We had to proceeed with utmost secrecy, with the warning that we would be met at our destination and be under constant surveillance.

The almost insurmountable obstacles were gradually overcome, and our trip was accomplished without mishap if we pass over a few earthquakes, blizzards, and raging storms.

The Ainus do not resemble the Japanese. They have heavy foreheads and straight eyebrows and look more like the Russian muzhik type. As they were shy and retiring, it seemed lucky to us that our local guide was herself an Ainu girl. Yai spoke fluent English, having been adopted and educated by a British missionary who had lived in Sapporo, the capital of Hokkaido, and she gladly introduced us to her relatives in the Ainu village and enabled us to take movies of some of their typical activities—building huts, fishing, and bear hunting. Their bleak existence was confined to a limited area of barren seacoast, and they were not permitted to travel about or leave their reservations.

We enticed two adults into letting me model them. The man posed for a

full-length figure, the woman for her head and shoulders. I made another portrait of a younger Ainu whose beard was still rather short, and so I was able
to see the character of his jawbone, a rare sight indeed, for they never shave
or cut their hair.

The two weeks we spent in Hokkaido produced results that delighted the
museum, in fact surpassed all expectations, for it had seemed dubious that we
could get permits allowing us to study the nude figures of a race that has the
odd habit of never removing clothing and rarely washing, a cause of permanent
skin sores. These skin sores gave us the idea of urging the models to come to
a dispensary near us where they submitted to being disrobed and washed with
healing medication. This enabled me to measure their proportions and model
the figure in the nude. The treatments gave relief, so the Ainus willingly
returned and the good news quickly spread. We were dressed in doctors' robes
and obtained valuable photographs of their physical conformation.

Returning to Tokyo, we showed Count Hyashi the photographs and plaster
casts of our elusive Ainus, and he expressed great interest and approval.

I then found Dr. Rudolf Teusler, in charge of St. Luke's International
Hospital, and confessed to him that I had a very painful left arm, which was
swollen and apparently infected. He called his chief surgeon, a Japanese, who
had studied X-ray technique with Dr. Alexis Carrel in New York. He diagnosed
my ailment immediately and said that if I would submit to heroic treatment,
he would try to save the arm. My heart missed a few beats at this announcement.
I agreed to come to his X-ray laboratory every morning at nine o'clock. The first
two mornings I fainted when the doctor opened the infected area. He refused
to give me an anesthetic as it would retard the normal circulation of blood. He
then directed the X ray for five minutes onto my arm, which was open to
the bone.

After five days he assured me that the infection was arrested but that I
must continue to have my arm held up by a padded sling and my hand bound
up to my neck. If anything could make my daily task of sculpture more difficult
this was it. Despite these threats and anxieties I managed not to lose any time
and finished my Japanese Woman's portrait bust so that we caught our steamer,
and sailed over to Tientsin, the port by which we entered China.

For six weeks we lived in Peiping, and a studio was put at my disposition
in the basement of the Peiping Union Medical College, between the Mouse
House and the Morgue. Every morning a stalwart young coolie trotted me in
his ricksha over the icy streets from the hotel to the college. And my models
came there to pose. The coolie was the one I chose for a full-length figure. I
also made the portrait of Dr. Wong Wen Hau, and modeled other types of
North, West, and South China. Sam made a great number of valuable photographs of types, front, side, and back, with accompanying anthropological data
for each subject.

Life in Peiping was intense and exciting. Mei Lan Fang, the eminent actor,
took me to see theatrical performances. Dr. Hu Shih, the leading scholar of
China, gave us a tea at the Returned Students Club where he gathered a throng

of artists, writers, and actors. Some of the young students we met there offered to guide us to museums and shops of special interest.

The winter temperature was 26 degrees below zero, which was rather a threat to our health. My arm was still in a sling, and the frigid ricksha trips every day finally overcame my resistance. I succumbed to a case of Peiping pneumonia, with acute sinus and antrum infection. Luckily an American doctor ordered me to bed, where I remained about ten days. When I recovered, it behooved me to make up lost time, modeling the types selected by the local anthropologists.

The heavy responsibilities of the trip and successive physical threats began to tell on my nerves. Gretchen Green, who had traveled from Paris in the opposite direction from ours, rejoined us in Peiping despite overwhelming obstacles. She took the last postal plane from Shanghai, cramped among the mail sacks and more or less smuggled into Peiping, which was at that time under martial law.

Our next stop was Shanghai, where I modeled a few types, and by good fortune found Dr. Hu Shih at our hotel. He had fled from Peiping in disguise, and never went out in daylight, as the Kuomintang had set a price ($200,000 in American currency) for his capture, dead or alive.

A group of Japanese insurgents were staging a series of attacks, and to the accompaniment of machine-gun fire against the foreign section of Shanghai I made the life-size portrait in clay of Dr. Hu Shih. This was a more exciting experience than it might seem in this abbreviated account. He urged us to pack up, cast the plaster mold of his portrait, and get off without a day's delay. This seemed a next-to-impossible task, but we accomplished it, and the night after we left, our hotel in Shanghai was looted and set afire.

We found Hong Kong a lively place with crowded streets and a busy harbor. The great number of houseboats and every conceivable form of sailing and fishing craft gave the impression that the city had overflowed its limit and the inhabitants had taken over the water for living purposes. At night it became a sparkling scene of myriad lights and their reflections. Lanterns of all shapes and sizes hung in festoons on the decks, and from a distance the harbor was transformed into a fairylike spectacle.

I was still weak from my illness in Peiping, so we decided to stay in a quiet hotel at Repulse Beach across the mountains from Hong Kong, overlooking the beautiful bay dotted with islands.

One moonlit night I walked along the glistening sands, watching the incoming tide. With a cane I drew the outlines of huge elephants on the clean flat beach. My nerves had been on edge, and suddenly seemed to snap. A sense of acute depression swept over me and I felt detached from life, as if cut adrift and unable to make any effort of will. I wanted oblivion and that only. As I look back over a distance of nearly forty years, I can still feel the tremor of icy fear that overpowered me. By unaccountable means, perhaps by response to prayer, we recoil from the lethal threat. A mighty struggle follows before we

"Chinese Coolie"   Aristocratic Chinese lady

can bury our anguish and build up a new mask behind which we continue to act our multiple lives.

I set to work again and modeled the "Woman Carrying a Basket of Mud" (for the road menders). Her stoicism gave me renewed strength.

The steamer trip to the Philippines took us to a tropical zone where we were forced to buy thin clothes and adjust ourselves to a violent change of temperature.

The port of Manila looked like an outpost of American activity, crowded with United States sailors and officers in their white summer uniforms.

Our quest for a type of Igorot headhunter began by our consulting a group of missionaries who had lived among these tribes in the mountains. They advised caution and agreed to help us. After a few days studying the problem and meeting the local authorities, we were told that a fine specimen of this race would be willing to let us photograph him and that he agreed to pose for his portrait. Through interpreters we were able to establish friendly relations, and reimbursed him with presents for himself and his tribe: certain foodstuffs, salt, tobacco, and colored bead necklaces for the women.

From Manila we sailed southward by way of Borneo and Macassar to Bali and Java where, for a number of weeks, we collected data, batiks, and moving pictures, and I modeled dancers and types of natives working in the paddy fields.

The island of Bali remains in my memory as the epitome of natural enticement. The natives rejoiced in their own physical beauty, and the continual sound of gamelon orchestras and the glittering radiance of the landscape combined to ensnare any artist or sensitive traveler who had eyes to see and ears to hear.

My outdoor studio, when I was modeling the figure of a Bali girl, was a walled courtyard of an ancient temple, the façade of which was covered with sandstone carvings of warm rosy pink. The children with their tawny strong bodies gathered about us, but behaved quietly and decorously.

Toward evening I generally worked in the courtyard back of our rambling old hotel. There my only audience was the invalid proprietor, who lay on a bamboo couch and regaled me with local gossip.

The people of Java and Bali were so friendly that I found it difficult to say good-bye to them, but we felt we should keep to our schedule.

The group in the Hall of Man that represents the Dutch East Indies consists of four figures: two young boys with their fighting cocks crouching by the roadside, a familiar sight in any of the islands; standing behind them a girl from Bali carrying a pyramid of fruit in a colorful and gilded wooden container balanced upon her head; and a little boy from Java eating a banana while he too watches the cocks being baited against each another, but firmly held back by the hands of their respective owners.

The Javanese seemed far more sophisticated in their manners than the ingenuous and often childlike Balinese. Their batik industry was developed on a large scale, and their life reflected the influence of Dutch colonization to a marked degree. The magnificent carvings on the Borobodour Temple were the high spot of our sight-seeing in Java.

We sailed to Singapore, where the harbor was seething with shipping and the docks were crowded with cargoes being loaded and unloaded, the air pungent with aromas of coffee, saffron, and strong spices. We made the renowned Raffles Hotel our headquarters, and with the aid of the local museum director plotted our journey through the Malay jungle to model and photograph the three tribes known as the Jakuns, the Sakais, and the Semang pigmies.

An experienced Malayan chauffeur and a British interpreter were placed at our disposal and we started off in a Ford car, to follow the trail marked out for us on a map. As the tribes were nomadic, word was wired ahead to the Jungle Police to locate them and then guide us from the nearest "rest house" or overnight stopping place.

The weather was torrid, but when we went on foot, frequent showers cooled us off temporarily until the sun reappeared to dry our clothing and test our endurance. One thing that enabled us to survive was to wear wet palm leaves inside our pith helmets or double white-felt, wide-brimmed hats.

Despite warnings to wear high snake boots that were far too hot and heavy for me to manage, I resorted to tennis shoes and socks, trusting to my guardian angel to keep the serpents out of my path. The jungles were lively with monkeys, elephants, crocodiles, and occasional black panthers. Many a low tree branch had a sleepy boa constrictor hanging like a festoon or stretched out to full length, and at night the air was aflutter with weird sounds: croaking frogs, the hum of insects, and sharp barks of small wild animals.

As I look back upon this trip, I realize how fraught with danger it often was, but at the time the excitement of the search and the intensity of work under such primitive conditions completely obliterated any sense of fear.

A certain ritual was strictly followed by these so-called "savages." They generally stipulated that I must send away, out of sight and earshot, all the other members of our group, sometimes three or four, including the British interpreter, while I remained alone with my chosen model for an hour. Then we would send a messenger to bring them back. This certainly imposed a deadline for the modeling of a life-size head. The head, when finished, had to be transported to the nearest town or port where water was obtainable for plaster casting, which would be done only after the clay model had been approved by the resident anthropologist.

On the last lap of our drive to Penang, we had the unexpected thrill of seeing a sleek black panther jump off a high boulder, landing across the road thirty feet ahead of our car! The car preceding ours by a half hour had disturbed the same animal, but was not as fortunate, for the panther had jumped directly onto the canvas top and hung on by his claws until the driver by swift and desperate zigzags finally threw him off. When we examined the shredded top of that car in the hotel clearing, we all realized what a close call we had had.

From Penang we sailed in a coastal steamer by way of the Andaman Islands

VEDDA, SOUTH INDIA TYPE FROM THE HALL OF MAN

"SICILIAN FISHERMAN" FROM THE HALL OF MAN

to Calcutta, watching the black-skinned natives of the Islands, expert rowers, shoot their long canoes through the water at incredible speed.

The heat in India was fiercely cruel. The sunrays cut our necks like a knife, and we were forced to hang wet kerchiefs or big wet leaves under our helmets to protect our necks and shoulders. To work under these conditions at first seemed unfeasible, but the museum director, who was kindness itself, set apart a room facing north where I could study and model the types already selected by him and his anthropological colleagues. The cooperation of all those who had known of our expedition and its objective was truly remarkable. Their understanding gave me endless encouragement.

Our trip through India carried us from south to north, east to west. The memories of temples, carvings, burning pyres along the Ganges, flaming sunsets, jungle trails, and the wild criminal tribes dancing and performing incredible feats of athletics and acrobatics—all crowd themselves into a dramatic panorama far too extensive for this abridged account.

Near Madras I made the figure of a southern type of coconut-tree climber. He worked his way up and down the towering tree trunk like a jumping-jack toy, jerking upward, grasping the rough bark between his hands and his tough prehensile feet. After two hours of work, about midday, my eyes suddenly saw a cloud of black spots, a thin sharp pain encircled my head, and I fainted from sunstroke.

My resourceful model cut off the top of a coconut, poured the cool liquid over my head and, opening my mouth, poured the refreshing milk down my throat. Although it caused me to cough violently, the treatment brought me back to consciousness—to find him squatting beside me on his heels and holding his glistening heavy knife across his knee. After a rest we went home, and continued our posing and modeling the next day at six o'clock in the morning before the sun became too lambent.

As a respite and revival, we decided to stay a week in Ceylon before the long voyage through the Red Sea and Mediterranean to France. There we were startled to find lush green vegetation with moss and shady woods. It seemed like a corner of Paradise after the parched and scorching areas of India. We made trips to the Temple of Buddha's Tooth and to the mountains above Kandy where we watched the tamed elephants being scrubbed by their young mahouts, and then set to their task of carrying tree trunks to the lumber camps.

The Devil Dancers performed for us so that Sam could take movies, and they tried to persuade us to bring them with us to England and America!

Returning to France in the spring, we felt a keen awareness of the blessings of Nature. Life seemed suddenly so relaxed. The fields were aglow with flowers, the breezes laden with perfume. All was well with the world.

The Dutch East Indies group

CHAPTER TWENTY-EIGHT

LIFE GOES ON

REACHING PARIS, we found many of our shipments already stored in the custom-house, awaiting our arrival for examination. Having packed about forty cases of plaster heads and one-third life-size figures and endless other objects collected on the trip, I was a bit apprehensive as to whether they would be broken en route. Tissue paper or excelsior was never available, and we had to have recourse to a strange collection of each country's newspapers and the straw covers on mineral-water bottles to bind the plaster casts. To the amazement of the examiners at the customs in Paris, and to my great relief, everything arrived intact, not a crack or a break except one finger on one of the casts.

The following weeks were charged with frenetic activity. I rented two additional studios near my own, and had the one-third life-size figures enlarged and built up from the original small models by pantographic machines to assure accuracy. Sam was busily engaged in editing his films and cataloguing over two thousand photographs.

Eugene Rudier, the master founder, agreed to put his best craftsmen to work at once, casting the heads and busts into bronze. His foundry was only a ten-minute drive from my studio; I had known Monsieur Rudier ever since my student days in 1910 when Rodin took me to the foundry and asked the workmen to instruct me in the technical maze of sand-mold bronze casting, chasing, and patining. There were about sixty craftsmen whose expert knowledge produced almost all the bronzes in the Hall of Man. Only a few were cast in America by the "lost wax" method.

The work necessitated daily visits to the foundry, and I often would spend the mornings supervising the chasing and final coloring, for it was essential to have variety of tone so that the regrouping of many figures would not give a monotonous effect.

When all the figures and heads were at last finished in Paris, they were exhibited in a huge empty studio at the Rudier foundry.

MH and Rudier in his Paris foundry with a number of bronze figures for the Hall of Man

Many of the consulting scientists and museum directors had followed the work with interest, and it was decided to invite me to show all the small originals —one-third life-size—and some of the full-size figures—at the Trocadéro Museum in Paris, then in the large circular building that was later transformed into the Palais de Chaillot.

It was rather a Herculean task, but with the cheering cooperation of my French pals, *copains*, it was undertaken with pleasure, and their companionship was a stimulating experience. After hard work and penetrating damp weather came happy evenings with friends, music on Schuré's piano in the big room at the top of the villa, and crackling open fires. Father Teilhard de Chardin and the Abbé Breuil, both renowned paleontologists; Pat Kelly, the latter's assistant; Henri Rivière, the "bloodhound of folklore," who could sit at the piano and play for hours and keep everyone alert by his intransigent, often caustic observations; Marcel Griaule, the African explorer and authority on ancient history and languages of Abyssinia and the Sahara Dogon Tribes; and Ernest Schelling, who would often come to practice his concert programs, making the big wooden rafters ring when the piano top was opened and he would give us a Chopin polonaise or the Schumann "Carnaval." Dr. Harvey Cushing, Mrs. William Hooper, my cousin Herbert Haseltine, Frances Rich, Madame Emma Eames, and many others often came to visit us.

Mrs. Adolph Spreckels of San Francisco gave us a party at the Ritz after the opening of the Trocadéro exhibition.

It was an interim between world wars; life was not so frustrating and uncertain as it is today.

When Paderewski came to lunch at the villa, there was always a special effort made, for I knew his gourmet tastes and how scornful he was of poor wines. Once I recall when Marie was to pass the bottle of wine I told her beforehand to say: Vaugirard 36–37, which sounded rather like a vintage label, and to our astonishment Paderewski recognized it instantly as my telephone number and, bowing his head in affirmation answered, "Oui, à Paris c'est une bonne marque, mais à New York je préfère Murray Hill 2–3931" (Yes, that's a good brand in Paris, but in New York I prefer Murray Hill 2–3931), which actually had been my unlisted number when we had met there two years earlier. His lightning responses and accuracy of memory often staggered me, and somehow he always made me feel that he had really enjoyed his visit and the simplicity of our hospitality. Over the coffee by the open fire there was no sense of haste or preoccupation. He could concentrate his whole attention on what he was saying—the rest of life was erased, canceled out, and complete rapport seemed established—one sensed the miracle of spiritual communion.

KIKI

Kiki, my Siamese cat, was my mascot on many trips across the Atlantic and a constant source of diversion at the studio. His azure eyes and tawny coat were admired by all who made his haughty and distinguished acquaintance. He traveled so far and with so many different members of his own family that we decided that he should have his own passport. This home-made document, which looked exactly like his owners' only reduced in size, the good-natured custom officials enjoyed stamping as a harmless joke on his various crossings.

When at home in the studio he posed patiently for me to model him, sitting up as still and stately as only a princely cat can. He had many names and had no preference which you used. He paid no attention to any of them or to you except when he felt he was being neglected or forgotten; then he would either rub against your foot or bite you ever so gently on the ankle. At mealtime, however, he demanded his share of meat in no uncertain manner, and if this was not forthcoming he emitted such primordial howls that nothing could be done until the call of the wild was answered and his appetite assuaged.

He almost lived on Sam's shoulder. He became so much a part of Sam and was so quiet that Sam would almost forget he was there; then somebody would scream because this immovable, unnoticed object would leap off wildly and dash at something, flashing his strange, intense blue eyes and switching his tail.

During a cold and damp winter in Paris, Kiki fell ill with pneumonia and a sort of brain fever. His devoted French Dr. Méry was so alarmed one night by the serious condition of Kiki's lungs, which seemed to be closing and causing him great distress, that he motored to his clinic to fetch a little oxygen tank. When he returned, Kiki was almost unconscious; the doctor inserted a tubular needle under the furry skin and pumped in oxygen. Kiki began to revive; his body was inflated, the skin making a crackling noise when he moved. For hours the doctor worked over him—ice bags packed around his head, flaxseed poultices on his chest; Kiki's eyes opened at last, and gradually his breathing became normal—the crisis was past.

He responded with patience and gratitude to our care, and in two weeks was restored to health and again able to enjoy his pranks and games. He traveled with me back to New York, adding another customhouse stamp to his passport collection.

The next year in Paris I summoned the doctor again, who found that Kiki had an abscess in his salivary gland, under the lower jaw. This was opened and disinfected and bound up. Daily dressings were necessary, with injections by hypodermic needle. I would lay him on his back on a table, telling him to keep perfectly quiet. He let me unwind the bandage; then, to my amazement, he would remain absolutely still, rolling his eyes at me, switching his tail, but never moving his neck. I could wash out the wound, go across the room, prepare the needle, return to the table, and he would make no move to escape, even when the needle was inserted. A new bandage was securely wrapped around his neck, and I lifted him up and patted him, saying, "All over now. Off you go!" With a wild leap he would dash out into the garden and tear around the little plot of grass to vent his feelings.

He kept well and active for two years or more after that. Then one day a sudden coughing spell, and the matting of the sleek tawny fur warned me that Kiki had caught a serious germ. His bright eyes lost their sparkle, and he moved

MH and Kiki in the garden of the Paris house

about the house slowly and wearily. While lapping his bowl of milk he would stop and turn his head, questioning me in his eloquent way—and slowly walk away from his supper, coming up and rubbing himself against my ankle. This time I knew it was his last illness. Despite the best care, nothing could be done to save him. He had a miniature four-poster bed with red pillows and a fur coverlet. He was content to lie in this in a little knitted sweater, and seemed to realize that there was no more fight left in him, but to the very end he purred and accepted his fate as a Prince of Siam should do.

In 1933, timed for the opening of the great Chicago Century of Progress Exhibition, the Field Museum opened the Hall of Man, at last completed except for the American Indian types that were added a little later.

At this period, back in the States, I was frequently ill and had to endure a great deal of physical pain, as well as emotional strain. I felt rather like a living ghost, and nothing seemed to matter.

In spite of my poor health and many problems, I managed during the following months to make a memorial fountain for St. Mark's School, and also the Gardiner Memorial, a symbolic bas-relief in marble, for the chapel at Groton School, Massachusetts.

In the autumn of 1935 Anne Morgan and I met the Izcue sisters in Paris. They were gifted young Peruvians who had learned many secrets from the ancient Aztec dyes used in the famous cloths such as the Paracas woven materials, and they were adapting these old patterns to modern fabrics for Rodier, Schiaparelli, and other French textile experts. Miss Morgan generously invited the two young girls to come to America, where she supplied them with a little apartment. They learned English while helping us organize the first exhibition of Pre-Columbian art in New York. This exhibit was held at a gallery in East Fifty-seventh Street and aroused spontaneous interest and enthusiasm both in the textile and art worlds. Three or four museums cooperated in lending us cases and groups of their collections so that we could show a very varied lot of terra cotta and early stone carvings, as well as the gold and precious objects found in the excavations of tombs. Many of these were loaned to us from the Larco Herrera Museum outside Lima, and sent up to our show by airplane.

In April of 1936 Helen accompanied me to Nevada and stayed with me there on a ranch outside Reno for two weeks, until she felt sure I could fight out the rest of the time on my own. The reason for this journey was an unhappy one. The gathering clouds had overshadowed me for months. Sam had had many attacks of depression, and his doctors had insisted that he should live alone and try to find new fields of interest. His most desperate sadness still was being unable to play the violin. Such readjustment to life was a constant psychological battle. He seemed forced to withdraw into himself and for some time had felt unable to see any of our friends or live a normal life. He had plunged into study of science and optics, worked in a laboratory, and produced new and complex techniques in unexpected fields. For two years he stayed in a tiny apartment uptown. Finally he and his doctors decided that our married life must end.

I was so stricken by this decision that my life seemed a total shipwreck. I was racked with the emotional battle, and felt so ill and heartbroken that I consented to Sam's decision. He, too, was desperately unhappy, but seemed forced by a hopeless despondency to take this step of a formal divorce.

My experience in Reno can best be described as hell framed in a splendor of vast scenery. I rode horseback over the plains, a way to be alone and avoid social activity.

At the end of my enforced residence there Marie-Louise Emmet, who at that time was living in California, came to fetch me, an act of loyalty and understanding, and we drove in her car all the way to Beverly Hills in a single day. There I met Anne Morgan, another devoted and never-failing friend. After a few days of rest and readjustment, we flew home over the Rockies, high over the snow-capped peaks from Los Angeles. Aimed straight at the full moon, I stayed awake to watch the day fade into the velvety darkness of the starlit night. Then, after the long hours, came the miracle of a glowing green light surrounding the entire horizon, spreading into gold and reddish rays. This was indeed the radiant dawn of a new day, such as I had never witnessed before. In my desolate heart I felt as if there could never be a new dawn. . . . My inner light had been blotted out.

CHAPTER TWENTY-NINE

NEW ARTS

THAT YEAR opened a new phase of my life that seemed to me, if not consoling, at least adventurous: the publication of a book. Its origin goes back to the time when I had just finished the long strain of travel and constant work that went with my trip around the world. The Ernest Schellings invited me to visit them in Céligny on Lake Geneva. Piano music and the strains of the Flonzaley Quartet filled the air, and Paderewski, as was his custom, came often to visit my hosts. I had been writing something about the last stage of my work for the Hall of Man, *Our Aboriginal Brothers* and *The End of It All*. His surprising verdict was that these pages were the *end of a book* and that I must start at once to write the beginning! He advised me to concentrate daily on the project of writing down the whole account of my journey. I must consecrate certain hours each day to the task, and he promised to come to read the manuscript in Paris in the autumn.

Unfortunately, I was taken ill and advised by Dr. Klebs, who lived nearby at Nyon, to return at once to Paris and to prepare for a long siege. A severe infection moved in on my fatigued bloodstream and nervous system and I spent most of the fall and winter in bed, with a streptococcic attack culminating in a sciatica that doubled me up like a jackknife. That my constitution was able to withstand this twofold affliction is mostly owing to the expert care and constant watchfulness of Dr. Albert Simard. His understanding of an artist's temperament enabled him to control and protect me not only during that serious crisis but ever since, on many occasions.

In spite of sickness, I kept my promise to Paderewski to work daily at writing. I wrote regardless of pain or fever, and I probably managed by this work to save my reason. At any rate, I accumulated voluminous pages of manuscript, which my secretary Guldie struggled to type up when she wasn't acting as nurse.

During this time, by a curious coincidence, I became still more deeply involved in the literary life. Just before I had left for France the preceding summer, I had had an unexpected visit from Mr. Richard Walsh and Pearl Buck.

Mr. Walsh had been in Asia for a year and had met many people there, introduced by letters from my traveling companion Miss Gretchen Green, and he wanted to talk to me about them. It was my first meeting with him and with Mrs. Buck, whose novel *The Good Earth* I had read and admired. So we celebrated with a glass of Dubonnet in the studio. Mrs. Buck expressed a desire to explore the house; we went upstairs, and on our way down again she said: "This is exactly the kind of house I am looking for, where I could feel the urge to work and think creatively. Do you know any similar place I could rent?"

"Why not rent this one?" I said.

The deal was closed and the papers signed the same day, and I sailed for Europe, happy that such gifted tenants were to be in my house. The walls of 157 must have pricked up their ears, curious to know how a writer really arranged her domestic life to ensure the necessary uninterrupted hours. I was, however, across the ocean, and unable to hear any overtones of the literary compositions being brought to life under my roof. The biography of Mrs. Buck's father, *Fighting Angel*, many articles, and doubtless a host of other works were written there.

In the meantime I kept on with my own writing, helped, encouraged, and guided by Maxwell Perkins and Wallace Meyer, finally producing the book *Heads and Tales*, which was published by Scribner's in 1936. Prepublication sales gave evidence to the editors and author that our labors had not been in vain. In fact, I think all concerned were happily surprised, and I was tremendously relieved; this first venture into a new field of art had its doubts and fears for one whose life had been dedicated to the wordless art of sculpture. Up to now I had been satisfied with three-dimensional silence, believing that the artist can make even stone, wood, and the clay of the earth become eloquent. The sculptor at least can express his feelings without footnotes or index. With today's haste, the chances are that only a limited few will ever pause long enough before a piece of sculpture to search for its inner meaning or grasp its evident significance, but still . . .

ANOTHER BOOK

In the spring following the publication of *Heads and Tales*, Olga Samaroff, the pianist, gave a dinner party to which I was invited, and there I met the publisher W. W. Norton. Having so recently been initiated into the field of writing and feeling genuinely shy in the presence of publishers, I was unprepared for the high-pressure technique of W. W. N. He started in at once to convince me that I must write a second book and let him publish it, that it should be entirely different from my first book, and that it should be built up on the lines of a textbook for students and laymen and should include chapters on the contemporary scene in the plastic arts in at least fifteen countries! Further, it was to be ready for publication in ten months and was to include 260 illustrations.

Knowing little about authors' contracts, I suggested that he consult with Max Perkins at Scribner's to see if he had any objections to my working for another publisher. W. W. N. reported that he had had a satisfactory consultation with Mr. Perkins and that the latter was interested only in my writing, at some later date, a longer biography that would be in no way a textbook.

"It is all inside your head now, Malvina. All I'm asking is for you to pull it out and write it down! This is a way you can make a real contribution to the teaching of art. . . . When *I publish a book it lives,* and don't you forget this!"

I sailed for Europe the following day and brought back the manuscript and pictures for the book in November.

When the manuscript was finally approved and the illustrations selected, Mr. Norton insisted that I write a last page or two as a finale for the book.

This ultimatum had to be met, but for some reason I could not seem to think of an appropriate "declivity towards the exit," a device recommended by Mark Twain to which all visitors should be led, or pushed, as soon as they got up and started saying good-bye.

In desperation I went to W. W. N.'s office and asked if I might try to find some ideas by working in literary surroundings. . . . He led me into the reading room and shut the door.

On the table before me I noticed sheets of manuscripts in German and English. I read the following lines by Rainer Maria Rilke which touched off my imagination:

> And you wait, are awaiting the one thing
> that will infinitely increase your life;
> the powerful, the uncommon,
> the Awakening of stones,
> depths turned towards you
>
> .   .   .   .   .
>
> And you know all at once: That was it.
> You arise, and before you stands
> a bygone year's
> anguish and form and prayer. . . .

Feeling stirred, I wrote a page or two to lead to this quote and went into W. W. N.'s office again and said: "These lines subsume everything I've tried to say in my book. Why not print them on the last page?"

He read what I had written and then called his wife on the telephone. "Malvina wishes to quote Rilke's poem as a finale to her book. As your translation is not yet published, have you any objection?" He read the lines to her. . . . She agreed. "Thanks a lot," he said, and hung up the receiver, shook my hands, and told me the book was finished.

Sculpture Inside and Out was printed and put on sale in April, 1939, as planned.

With the publication of two books within a short space of time, I had a new and most interesting experience: fan mail began coming in from all parts of the country and, in fact, of the world. Letters about *Heads and Tales* came in from places I had never dreamed of, most surprising expressions of appreciation. Invalids would write to say that they had always hoped to travel but that now they were bedridden or "shut-in" and that the pages of my book had carried their minds to faraway lands and made them forget their prison walls. Boys in school or college would write wishing to buy copies of the various illustrations. Their selections were always different from what one might have expected.

People I had never seen wished to thank me for expressing their own inner thoughts. . . . It was a revelation to me to think that my first attempt in the literary field could result in so many pleasant repercussions.

During the Second World War the book was placed in a number of libraries on troop transport vessels, and a series of letters resulted from G.I. Joes. Of course, I answered all these letters, and very often correspondence continued between us. In one instance an army officer wrote me about the little bronze I had made for my "Column of Life." This was a study of what is known in the Tantrik lore of India as the Kundalini Yoga—in my statue, a flame rising between two figures symbolizing the perfect union of the male and female principles. This study had meant a great deal to me. I had made the first sketch for it in 1914, only six inches high. In 1919 I carved it in marble about three feet high. Another version, in bronze, was mounted on a column-like pedestal in a series of reliefs representing the Six Centers of Kundalini, all bound together by the coils of the serpent Kundalini and topped by the inverted lotus flower.

But my officer-correspondent wanted to buy the little bronze study illustrated in my book, and if I would send it to him he would transmit the money by postal order. I wrote him the price and received the amount, plus two dollars for insurance and airmail postage! The little packet started on its journey to Guam, via the Postmaster in San Francisco. By the time it reached Guam, the officer had moved on to another landing base in the Pacific. The box was forwarded to him; again airmail delays caused it to arrive after he had been transferred to the forces of occupation in Korea.

In the meantime he wrote that he was afraid it had been lost and that he despaired of ever receiving his "mascot." "I did so want to carry it with me as a symbol of beauty to counteract the hell I've been living in!"

I wrote to the Postmaster in San Francisco and told him the story. "We never call anything lost, or start searching until a year has elapsed from the date it was originally shipped!" was the answer. This message I passed on to my fan-mail friend and told him not to give up hope. Then came the word from the officer that he would soon be returning to the United States and would I prepare another copy of the bronze? Two days after the receipt of this good news, a little worn-out package was delivered by post to my studio, with so many stamps and official forwarding directions that it was hard even to find the original name and address.

The "Column of Life"

Of course, I recognized it as the little box containing the bronze sent eight months earlier. While I was examining it, the doorbell rang, and who should appear but the actual officer to whom we had shipped the parcel! He stood there smiling, in his smart uniform, young and handsome, with flashing white teeth and more ribbons and medals than I had ever seen on one soldier. We had a happy meeting, and then he said, "Where, oh, where do you suppose my little bronze could be?"

"Look beside you on the table," I said.

After reading my second book, *Sculpture Inside and Out*, a man in Allentown, Pennsylvania, Mr. Leverett H. Cutten, wrote me that he had decided at the age of sixty-one to take up the study of sculpture and teach himself from my book.

He had a son in the service and had made a life-size portrait of him, which he wanted very much to submit by photographs for my criticism. He could then make the necessary corrections and changes when the boy had his next leave before going overseas. I told him to take photographs of the boy and of the bust from the same points of view and send them to me. With these I could check the likeness and make specific suggestions for improving the construction of the head. These he followed carefully and achieved a very creditable portrait. He learned from the book how to cast it in plaster himself. During our long correspondence he told me of his interest in silversmith work, a craft he taught.

Six months after the portrait was completed, my fan-mail pupil appeared at the studio in person. He brought me a set of lovely silver coffee spoons, which he had made and marked with my initials, simple and distinguished in design and as beautifully balanced as an Indian's paddle.

About a year after I had received the gift of these spoons, my friend Frances Healey in Hampton Falls, New Hampshire, asked me if I would care to design a silver chalice in memory of her father, to be given to the tiny chapel, the "Little Gate to the City of Gladness."

When the design had been approved, and the inscription drawn on the base, it was suggested that I incorporate on the stem of the chalice a gold wedding ring that had belonged to Fanny's mother. I thought at once of my fan-mail friend Mr. Cutten, whose craftsmanship and ideology had so impressed me. He procured the necessary silver, made a model, including the ring set into the stem, and brought it for my approval. By long hours of labor and dedication he completed the chalice and paten, and made a beautiful wooden case, lined with velvet-covered partitions to hold all securely in place. The silver hinges and clasps were wrought with the same care for design and detail that he had given to hammering the form of the chalice itself.

The Dance International

Such are the direct and indirect results of publication. Shortly after my first excitements in this new area, I was to have a climactic experience with my long-standing passion, the dance. Motoring back from the 1937 exhibit of my sculpture at the museum in Richmond, Virginia, Louise Branch and I concocted the plot for the first Dance International. It seemed to us the psycohological moment to make a tremendous effort for international goodwill by way of the arts, and we laid out our work for the summer months, collecting dance-film sequences and art objects connected with the dance from many countries and art museums. From all of the persons concerned we received enthusiastic cooperation.

Surely the outstanding popularity of the Dance International with the New York public during its six weeks of exposition at Radio City the following winter was proof that such an enterprise could find adequate support. The press cooperated, and free publicity was lavished upon the project. The showing of dance films from fifty-two countries drew a continuous attendance from 10:00 A.M. to 10:00 P.M. daily during the entire period. The heavy responsibilities assumed by our group in exhibiting two thousand objects of art—paintings, sculpture, and mural decorations—along with the film sequences can hardly be realized by those who have not actually accepted such a challenge.

One of the outstanding dancers in the Rainbow Room series was Frank Roberts. When this six-foot-three black Liberian stepped into the arena, everyone felt his unique quality of selflessness and integrity. The dancer was transformed into a Pagan Pilgrim dragging himself toward the carved black idol in the center of the floor. He dropped his cloak, then laid on the ground his staff and curious straw headdress. There was no musical accompaniment, and everyone was awed by his prayerful intensity as he prostrated himself before his idol.

At the end of his performance I asked him to pose for me in the attitude of supplication that was the climax of this dance. We were both completely exhausted at the end of eight seances. When I asked him what impelled him to try so hard to help me interpret this pose, he said simply: "My people are poor. We need God's help. Though I'm interpreting a pagan supplication, I am a Christian and I believe in prayer. My own prayers will die when I die, but if this prayer of mine is cast into your bronze figure, it will go on and will bring help to my people."

"DANCE IS THE ART OF SPEECH BY MEANS OF GESTURE."—PLATO

"A savage does not preach his religion—he dances it." If we go back as far as the rock paintings of paleolithic times, we find representations of women dancing around a nude male. One of these paintings was found in the Cogul Cave, and Abbé Breuil permitted me to reproduce his drawing of it. These dances were no doubt ceremonials, and of phallic significance. From early times down to the present, the African tribes cultivated the art of dancing, and nowhere was the role of drum rhythm better understood as an accompaniment driving the celebrants into a frenzied and ecstatic climax. The paintings of the earliest female dancers in Africa showed wasplike waists that seemed to resemble the Minoans of Crete.

A number of superb dancers over the years gave up time to me and permitted me to attend rehearsals, which for my study of rhythm and line were even more instructive than the finished public performance. My natural interest

A Dance International group onstage at Radio City. Central figure: Louise Branch. To her right, Ruth St. Denis and Martha Graham. To her left, Paul Whiteman and Doris Humphrey

in far-off countries and peoples also led me to study books on primitive and religious ceremonial dancing. Although our knowledge in this area remains fragmentary, it is likely to contribute some new channels of approach to a subject that seems to me more and more one of the strongest links of understanding between one race and another.

To watch models whose training gave them dynamic control of their bodies was a privilege to me in my profession. Obviously, to be able to draw the muscular coordination of perfectly balanced, evenly developed young bodies—primitive or not—was one of the great opportunities of my career.

Pavlova the incomparable and Nijinsky in his barbaric perfection took the audience by storm. Pavlova could create a world of fairy lightness before our eyes, and in a flash could change her mood into one of poignant pathos or savage abandon. Technically exquisite and resourceful in a way that has never been surpassed, she regretted constantly the lack of new, talented pupils to whom she might impart her inspired secrets. "Oh, Malvinoushka!" she would cry after long and arduous practice with her troupe, "why are there so many dancers who think they can dance only with their feet! If I could find one who dances with her head and her heart and her whole body!" and she would wrap her frail shoulders in a little shawl and stamp her tiny toe slipper and ask them to repeat, for the nth time, the phrase, the position, the mood of a certain strain of music.

Schools of Russian dancing were opened in many European cities, as well as in New York and Chicago.

The great hope that Pavlova cherished and shared with me was that of founding an Institute of the Dance in New York—an aim affording ever new incentive toward extending the interpretations of her art and preserving records of it. Her motion-picture attempts were not too successful. As I have described, they came before the days of modern camera technique that can shoot from any angle and at any speed. She encouraged me to capture the rhythm of motion, and I continued in that close communion with her that would have allowed us to carry through many of her hopes and plans if her life had not been cut short by her untimely death.

In 1931 she was preparing herself for a trip to The Hague, where she was to perform for the Queen. Realizing how fatigued she was, I begged her to rest for twenty-four hours before taking the train. But her sense of responsibility drove her to desperate efforts. She was ill when she started off; fever gave her eyes an alarming brilliance, and when she reached The Hague she was unable to leave her room. Three or four days later she died of a severe case of pneumonia. Her husband, Victor Dandré, telephoned me the news of her death. As I attended her funeral service in the Russian Church in London, I realized that her passing would leave an irreparable gap in the remaining years of my life, for Pavlova had been not only my muse in every sense of the word, but a beloved friend and constant *inspiratrice*.

CHAPTER THIRTY

NEW YORK WORLD'S FAIR

DURING THE first months of 1937, a group of New York civic leaders organized a campaign for a $125,000,000 project, "The World of Tomorrow," raising funds and preparing architectural and landscape plans for the general layout of the fairgrounds at Flushing Meadows. A $60,000,000 mile-long mall, with novel water and light effects and decorated with colossal sculpture, was to be the main feature.

Tests were made by engineers to find the means to solidify this new ground adequately, to support the buildings and the great Perisphere and Trylon, the theme symbols of the Fair.

A forest of great tree trunks—twenty miles of poles, each ninety-five feet long—was driven into the ground, upside down. On these was poured a flooring of concrete, and on this the steel construction of the Sphere and Trylon was riveted. Like magic did this unbelievable cage of steel grow into the Perisphere's skeleton. The great three-sided Trylon armature sprang up beside it. Buildings and towers seemed to emerge from the new ground like castles in a fairy tale. Flowers and fountains decorated the walks, and on May 1st, 1938, a preview of gigantic scale was staged, with a motorcade of military units and international floats, displays of fireworks, and a dancing festival.

In the latter spectacle four hundred dancers from fifty-four nations in national costume participated. Many of these were groups organized and drilled for the International Folk Dance recitals at Rockefeller Center, under the direction of our Dance International.

During the winter of 1938, painters, sculptors, and designers who had been selected to work for the Fair executed their quarter-size models after their original one-inch-to-the-foot models had been accepted by the Board of Design. The artists who had been chosen were immediately immersed in activity, all having been told that the Fair could not pay for work commensurately, but each was asked to contribute his best. My subject was a circular cutout relief of dancers from seven countries, set in the center of a round pool. The figures were 16 feet high.

In 1939 Père Teilhard de Chardin returned to New York from a trip to South Africa. Late on a June afternoon he arrived at my studio without a word of warning, just as I was about to start out to spend the evening exploring the Fair. I asked him to come along. Miss Morgan had left me a packet of tickets enabling us to board a speed launch that left a dock at East Fifty-second Street at frequent intervals to carry a few passengers to the boat landing in Flushing Bay.

We had to pass through a very swanky cocktail lounge to reach the steps leading down to the water. Père Teilhard was not in the least fazed by the obviously startled expression of the gay and rather noisy young socialites at seeing a Jesuit priest and myself going directly to the river door and boarding the boat. The captain collected our tickets and said: "You'll be smart to take the seats just behind the glass front, for the rest of the passengers will get plenty of spray; it's a bit windy going near Hell Gate." Père Teilhard laughed heartily at this, and we were happy to be so sheltered. In about ten minutes the other passengers piled in, and the speedy launch tossed plenty of wet and windy spray over all of them. We kept dry, however, and Father Teilhard thought it was a great joke.

The climax of the trip was the grand finale at the lakeside, where thousands of watchers gathered to see the truly magnificent display of fireworks. Everyone joined in singing the National Anthem—young and old, rich and poor, black and white and yellow shoulder to shoulder—the whole world seemed to be in the mass of people welded together for this dramatic moment of unity.

"Oh, that this moment might last!" was Father Teilhard's remark. "The brotherhood of man must be galvanized into such an emotion to be the blessing of all men!"

Then the battle of getting to the subway and home—for we were now miles from the boat landing, and Father Teilhard wanted to feel a part of seething humanity. He got his wish.

When the Fair closed, five of us sculptors were told to take our work in sections and store them for a year during which time the Board would try to interest the museums and the public in raising the necessary funds to put our models into permanent materials and set them up in a park on the Fair site.

Then came the ominous threat of another war—omens of destruction! We were told to vacate the big storehouse in twenty-four hours, destroy and remove the plaster models—"or else"! There was no alternative. So a wrecking crew was

Fountain of Dancers set in the Spiral Garden at the World's Fair, 1938

engaged, and my dancing figures were reduced to fragments and made into land as an entrance to a nearby cemetery. To say that this was a devastating event is something of an understatement.

When the Fair closed, five of us sculptors were told to take our work in responsible for reviving my passion for medicine. One day in Paris, in 1937, I received a letter from Dr. Robert L. Dickinson in New York, a well-known doctor in the field of obstetrics. On my return to New York we met, and it was not long before our combined enthusiasms produced a comprehensive plan of demonstrating to the general public at the World's Fair Building of Science and Health a series of sculptured models that would be in every way scientifically correct and artistically sound, revealing varying stages of the development of the human embryo from the first moment of conception to the completed nine-months baby. This miraculous first span of life had not been presented in sculptural form as we felt it could be, so together we worked out just how these models were to be made and how many of them would be necessary to portray graphically the vital stages of prenatal growth.

Abram Belskie was engaged to model the various panels and sculptured models under the constant direction of Dr. Dickinson at the Academy of Medicine. As consultant and collaborator I became more and more interested in the plan, and made many studies of the stereoscopic X-ray photographs taken of pelvic formation and various stages of embryo development. From these photographs and other data, a series of models were devised in monochrome plaster with the color and texture of pale terra cotta.

When completed, this series was put on view, repeated objections having been overcome, despite warnings from a few religious institutions that the series would probably have to be withdrawn. A continuous crowd of all ages, men, women, and children, passed before this theatre of life in amazement, and without one adverse criticism. Over a million people saw this exhibit, and endless requests, letters, and inquiries were received as a result.

Orders for the complete series came from maternity centers, hospitals, and elsewhere, and a public-spirited citizen, Mr. Charles Schweppe of Chicago, provided funds to give the Field Museum not only the first complete set but also a model of a newborn baby. His funds further financed experimentation needed to make a flexible articulated model of a three-weeks baby for teaching parents the care of children in maternity centers. An important result of this financing was that Dr. Dickinson was able to make master molds of the teaching material.

This work led me into other channels of activity supplementary to medicine. Especially interesting was the problem presented by Dr. W. E. Caldwell and Dr. Howard C. Moloy of the Sloane Hospital for Women in New York. Dr. Caldwell submitted as a problem the difficulty of teaching students the intricate technique of obstetrics without adequate three-dimensional models. In exploring the field, I found to my amazement that up to the present time the most dreadful-looking leather or papier-mâché mannequins were the only ones obtainable. I was shocked by their unnatural, repellent aspect. Feeling that the impression upon a medical student or trained nurse or any other normal human being must be similar, I offered to try to solve the problem by going to Bellevue Hospital and making studies of newborn babies. They pose well, being asleep most of the time.

Dr. Caldwell, a noted obstetrician, arranged a demonstration at the Sloane Hospital of casting with Negacoll, an applied rubbery liquid that hardens as it sets, so that the doctors interested in making casts and keeping records of valuable head formations might be able to do the work themselves.

With the first series of embryological models as a starting point, the Field Museum was encouraged to build up their full exhibit of human biology, for which I was later commissioned to carve, in pink marble, a three-weeks-old baby asleep on a pillow as a consolation "happy ending" to the nine-months-of-pregnancy series.

MH in Red Cross uniform, Second World War

CHAPTER THIRTY-ONE

AGAIN, WAR

159—MURRAY HILL WORKSHOP

Some years after I bought 157, the old place next door at 159 came on the market and I was able to buy it. It was something of a hazard, for, once a stable like 157, it had been used in recent years as a garage and was soaked in gasoline and was highly inflammable: unless I could make it safe again, it would be condemned. The cellar had to be made fireproof and vaulted with firebricks and provided with an iron staircase. Along with this renovation, I took out the second floor and made the whole structure into a high studio like 157. I had to get men from New Jersey to put up strong rigging, the kind used on docks or in mines, to get the unmanageable beams out. I had no architect, and planning the work took a great deal of time and tied my mind in knots.

When I was finished, though, I had a handsome additional space and a safe building next to me. Then one thing led to another. Many students had been coming to me, asking for instruction, and with room now to handle them, and seeing their genuine eagerness, I let myself be tempted to start a demonstration workshop where the complex processes of plaster casting, marble pointing, and bronze casting in wax and sand might be shown in various stages.

In the rear studio at 159, I had a machine set up to do half-size reductions with the models set on turntables so that students could grasp how the machine functioned. I demonstrated the enlargement of models on the big pointing machine set up on the opposite side of the room. Marshall Field encouraged the plan, and Frederick Keppel of the Carnegie Foundation gave helpful advice in arranging the explanatory labels. We also had evening lectures in which plaster casters and founders demonstrated the techniques of their craft.

During the winter we steadily scheduled groups of students, sometimes fifty a week, who would spend two hours looking about and asking questions, which various assistants and I endeavored to answer. Classes from Pittsburgh and from the Temple School of Art in Philadelphia came at their holiday time, and groups from the New York Public High School of Music and Art seemed to enjoy this informal and painless way of learning how to deal with the practical problems that confront the sculptor. Groups from Barnard College and Cooper Union also came to study.

Upstairs at 159 I showed examples of native carvings in wood and stone, and a costume carved in human bones, from Tibet. As a result of my wanderings over the globe, I had picked up many odd examples of "instinctive" arts and crafts and, alternating with the sculpture, we hung vivid dynamic paintings, on cotton, of the Balinese theatre, or the dyed tappa-cloth designs of Hawaii and Samoa.

The response to my efforts was more than gratifying, but too exhausting for me to continue. As one does with so many "castles in Spain," I was forced to give up the enterprise, owing to the greater need for "war essentials." Art became a luxury item; our materials were cut off; and the workmen were taken into plants for manufacturing explosives and vehicles of army transport.

With the coming of possible air raids, and the call for civilian defense workers, I closed the "159—Murray Hill Workshop," packed the contents in cases, and then joined the Red Cross First Aid Corps and assumed the duty in my precinct of an air-raid warden. The Metropolitan Museum offered to set up the contents of the demonstration cases as an art educational exhibit for students for the duration of the war. They included examples of my own sculpture in various materials, such as stone, wood, terra cotta, *simili pierre*, brick, and alabaster. The bronzes were shown in the progressive stages from the plaster models; gelatin molds, lost-wax and sand processes, and the way the bronze appears when the metal channels are removed. The surface chasing and final patining by acids were explained, and the varied colors obtained by different methods were shown.

In 1948 I replaced all these teaching models in my studio at 159.

REFLECTIONS

Dreams and carefully planned programs to make them realities are suddenly disrupted and forced into the background by war. But something of all this effort survives, and sooner or later dreams are reborn and coming generations carry them along.

History lists the daylight battles of war and war's suffering, struggles, speeches, and accomplishments, but where must one seek the record of the battles fought in darkness, the breaking of human hearts, the truth about all those whose contributions are anonymous?

Many undergoing such experiences may have had qualities of greatness. There would be a never-ending list of unknown saints and sinners who have spent their lives wrestling with the daemons of the night, and who at last by some blinding revelations have been caught up into the Divine rhythm and been transformed—others who by their quiet, selfless fortitude and patience have found their own path to Peace.

It is in the deep still pools that we can see the reflections of heaven. It is in the dark silences that we may rediscover that invisible essence that lives on forever, re-creating Beauty—both visible and invisible, yet dazzling in its purity when it reflects God's Spirit. It may shine from the humblest as well as from those in power; it is like the "quality of mercy" unstrained and free, becoming a "monarch better than his crown," but more often found in nameless hearts and in quiet lives.

To believe that the recording angels make notes of such unwritten dramas would be a consolation. Perhaps they file the letters one never dared to post, fearing to intrude, the impulses held back and reconsidered, and then found to be "too late." The gifts we made of real sacrifice and which left us with a sense of depletion—all these and more that form the core of a personality may have their own means of survival in the infinite scheme.

The sages tell us that no good deed is wasted, but there is undeniably a great fund of human expenditure that goes unrecognized. "We must see with the heart," says the French aviator-author Saint-Exupéry, "not only with the eyes." There are many who look, but do not see or discern the motive under the surface, do not see the depth of useful, uneventful lives, do not see what raises some to the ranks of the "indispensables." These are forever remembered by those whom they have served and by those who recognize the quality that can bind the heart, mind, and hands of man in the service of his fellowmen.

Such a New Year's Party at 157 and 159!—thanks to the unpredictable Gretchen Green, once more "Shepherd of the Flock of All the World"! After days of planning, pushing away sculpture, and transforming the drawing tables into refreshment counters, we finally staged a shortwave broadcast to thirty-two countries under the auspices of the Office of War Information.

The evening started at seven o'clock, when stray sailors and merchant seamen from the far corners of the world arrived. Coatracks were arranged in the front room and along the hallways, even into the cellar room. Having had previous experience with parties—although this one started with a list of 60, which grew to 125 people—we knew we should probably have to prepare for 250, as was the case.

Thirty-two nations were to be greeted on the shortwave radio. Sixty-four men, two from each country, were stationed in a long double row in 159. The other guests and mariners from East and West were asked to observe silence in 157—this may sound simple but it was not! The microphone was set up in the 159 laboratory, with technical men tucked in between statues, shouting orders and testing loudspeakers in both houses so that any sound effect of group singing, or mandolin, piano, or pipes, could be picked up at will, to give a background similitude of crowds speaking many tongues, of clinking glasses, and snatches of national folk music.

I roamed about in ARC uniform to help the guests identify their hostess, and frequently blew my air-raid whistle to get attention for the peremptory instructions from the technicians: "Stop 'em yodeling in there; we need 'Auld Lang Syne' and a bit of Scotch heather in this section!"

Then the dark-skinned Indians from Calcutta and Bombay were rounded up; their black, deep-set eyes glistened and their white teeth flashed as we urged them to sing typical Hindustani music. . . .

"You boys from New Zealand, you got your chance early, because you are leaving tonight, and here's your hometown now, waiting for you to say, 'Happy New Year to the South Pacific, and don't forget Pearl Harbor. . . .'"

All the while there came crowding in more and more seamen and their friends, Chinese and Canadians, Javanese and South Africans, blond blue-eyed Scandinavians and huge ebony giants from Dakar and Liberia. The air was thick with cigarette smoke and laughter in all keys; trays of red mulled wine and cakes were continually being passed and consumed.

Occasionally the center of the floor was cleared, and the audience motioned back toward the walls; solo dances, tricks, mind readers, and accordion players provided diversion or roused the company to song.

A few policemen from the station house opposite 157 stopped in to see what might be going on, having noticed the throngs of varicolored visitors. When the show was over, they assisted us in rounding up the sailors and seamen who were reluctant to say good-bye to their companions, and at the door we waved them on their many ways to the far corners of the world.

Another program of the OWI was broadcast to France in November, 1944, to mark the anniversary of Auguste Rodin's birth in 1840. (At the time of the centenary, 1940, the Voice of America had not come into existence.) The announcer was Amédée Ozenfant, the well-known French painter who directed an art school in New York. He opened the broadcast with remarks addressed to Rodin:

"At the start of our careers we hailed you as the Master. We recognized you as a genius and your sculpture as a permanent treasure. Modern in one sense, but not the modernism of a passing hour. Audacity marked your work; your style was an innovation because it was original and authentic." He continued with a summary of Rodin's career, and then said:

"To offer homage to the memory of Rodin I have asked three sculptors to join us today: Malvina Hoffman, his pupil and an American sculptor—her group in bronze, 'the Bacchanale,' is placed in our Luxembourg Gardens; Jacques Lipchitz, representing the modern school of sculpture; and Alexander Calder, an American who lived six years in Paris, artist of the *avant-garde*—composer of 'mobiles' in metal. I will ask Miss Hoffman to tell us a few things about Rodin. . . . When did you first meet him?"

"In 1910 I became his pupil, and what a master! Then in 1914 I was sorting his drawings with him, and we spent weeks placing his bronzes and marbles in the galleries of the Hôtel Biron. When the war was declared, he was stunned, and when the Government ordered all his sculpture cleared out and stored in the cellar, Rodin remarked: 'Civilization is a coat of paint that washes off when it rains!' The following autumn, when I left for America, I recall Rodin saying to me, 'To live is nothing, but to sacrifice life for an ideal is what gives to man his veritable quality.' "

Then Calder spoke: "Rodin created sculpture as no one else had ever done —that's what I love about him."

Lipchitz added: "I prefer Rodin to Michelangelo as I prefer Cézanne to Rembrandt, because they are nearer to us and to the preoccupations of humanity of our own times. Rodin was one who contributed to the emancipation of man. I consider him to be an immense genius!"

Ozenfant concluded the broadcast: ". . . et vive Rodin."

This recording was rebroadcast many times, to various countries.

On the first of December, 1942, an order came through from Headquarters that every air-raid warden who had signed for active duty would be required to enroll for the standard course of First Aid Training.

East Thirty-fifth Street happens to be in the 15th Precinct, and the station house was far too small to hold the crowd of wardens from this sector. There were about 250 of us waiting in the street. Finally the officers were able to herd us into groups, and drove us like sheep to the space that had been donated by Mrs. Alice McLean in the headquarters of the American Women's Voluntary Service, at 40 East Forty-first Street.

I had completed the Instructors' Training Course at the New York Chapter of the American Red Cross. Teaching a cross section of one's neighborhood afforded most enlightening glimpses into human psychology. My pupils ranged from actors, professional musicians, and landowners to Italian-American ice dealers, plumbers, and housewives. No longer were social standards of any importance. This was an experiment in street democracy, and the question in the Bible, "Am I my brother's keeper?" was answered with a resounding affirmative.

A gathering in the studio at 157 included sector wardens and senior wardens of the precinct as well as presidents of the principal women's clubs in New York, and certain wardens from large buildings on Fifty-seventh Street, Sutton Place, and along the East River, including Bellevue Hospital—even several members of the Museum of the City of New York.

I called this meeting together to introduce Rudolf Haybrook, the eminent British painter and stage designer. He had been a volunteer fireman in London throughout the war, and had served in the British Army in the First World War. He showed on a screen colored slides of the paintings that had been made by members of the auxiliary fire force in London during actual blitz attacks. Each painting was made by a fireman who had actually taken part in and witnessed the handling of a conflagration that he afterward depicted. These paintings were of such historic and artistic interest that the audience was deeply moved.

In commenting on a picture that showed the remains of a firehouse in flames, Mr. Haybrook told of a number of firemen who were caught under the debris of this burning building. One happened to be himself, and he had been able to see out through a crack and watch the rescuers lifting the weight with a long beam as shown in this painting. When he was dragged out and laid on the ground, he saw the scene from another point of view, and it was from this latter angle that he had painted the extraordinary picture from memory. He was the only man rescued from the building alive. This incident, described quite imper-personally by Mr. Haybrook, brought cold sweat out on one's forehead and, in-cidentally, possibly his own, for he had left the hospital only the day before, where he had been for eleven days, recovering from nerve collapse, fatigue, and a painful thrombosis in his leg.

When he had recovered enough to resume his activities, he asked me if I would mind if he staged a real fire in the courtyard back of my studio, as a demonstration to the wardens. When he asked me if I trusted him to put it out, I smiled and said that if he could not put it out I doubted if anyone else could and that it would be good practical experience for all of us. So rags and papers were soaked in kerosene, and bits of clothing were scattered about. He then called for volunteers, one for the stirrup pump and one to replenish the water, and instructed me to watch the hose line to see that it did not kink, and to blow my warden whistle for a total blackout. The audience was agog with excitement, and apparently very concerned lest the house burn down, though to tell the truth I had not the slightest concern. A blast from the whistle, the lights went out, and a match was thrown into the kerosene. The flames shot into the air and Haybrook said, "Imagine this to be an incendiary bomb that has actually caught fire!" He flung himself full length on the ground, seizing first the end of the stirrup-pump hose in his right hand, and the cover of a tin ash-barrel in his left. This cover he held as a shield in front of his face as he crawled toward the fire, spraying it lightly, putting it out on the walls and floor with a heavier spray from the hose, calling back over his shoulder the directions to the wardens, who were by this time all standing up and crowding about him.

This was the first time after his arrival in America that he had felt in a position to give such a demonstration. Until we were attacked at Pearl Harbor, such procedure might have been considered British propaganda. "But now," he said triumphantly, as he washed his hands, and we coiled the hose away, "now we can fight for both England and America, and that means we will fight to the finish, and fight to win!"

I felt privileged to have been able to lend my premises for so dramatic a service. By men of such stuff as this, the blitz fires of London were put out be-fore morning, and Hitler's demoniacal activities crushed during the terrible win-ter of 1941.

HEAD OF CHRIST

"Have you forgotten, all ye who pass by?"

There seemed to be a question haunting me—day and night! It had re-peated itself so often, so insistently through the past weeks that, finally, one

HEAD OF CHRIST

evening after my class of First Aid pupils had folded their bandages, packed their kits, and gone home, I returned slowly from the 159 studio, alone, and stopped in front of the row of barrels containing clay. "How long, O Lord?" I heard my own voice asking; the world of art had been put aside for many weeks, with all my time and energy devoted to teaching First Aid, or equipping ambulances and canteens, or making forms for bomb shovels, fire helmets, asbestos aprons, and stretchers-that-could-roll-on-two-wheels, or to endless other air-raid activities.

My question was like a cry in the wilderness. Suddenly in answer the other question came: "Have you forgotten . . . ?" and I knew there was no time to lose. I pulled the clay barrel into the studio, found a stand, and rigged up an old pipe-and-wood armature, and, like one possessed, began throwing wads of clay together. The mass grew so heavy as to demand more supports. I drove nails into strips of board and braced them against the inner framework.

On and on went the rough masses of clay, seemingly without shape or meaning, until gradually there emerged a great face of Christ with cavernous eyes, and lips apart asking the eternal question: "Have you forgotten . . . ?" The brows were heavy, and deep furrows cut across the forms; strong cheekbones jutted out like ledges, and the nostrils quivered; the head was bowed; the crown of thorns seemed to weave itself about the matted hair and drive its thorns into the flesh—sweat streamed from the tangled meshes, and seemed to fall over eyebrows and temples. When the class returned to the studio two nights later, they saw the unfinished clay head and asked to stay on and watch for an hour while I worked.

I was driven so violently by an inner power that I could not even release myself long enough to cross the room to find a few tools. I managed to bring the chaotic forms together until at last I saw the tragic face that had been asking the question . . . only then did my mind grow quiet, and I felt at peace. Such a complete dedication is impossible to describe, but as an experience it was overwhelming. All my fatigue had washed away. I felt liberated as I stopped work and turned off the lights. It was 3:00 A.M.

WENDELL WILLKIE PORTRAITS

Shortly after the death of Wendell Willkie in 1944, the publishers of his very successful book, *One World,* wished to pay tribute to his memory by commissioning a bust of him to be placed in the Corcoran Gallery in Washington. I had done a previous portrait head and was therefore asked to do the new one. My previous head of Mr. Willkie had been commissioned by Helen Frick, and I had done it from memory after being one of a lunch party with Mr. Willkie at Mr. Adolph Ochs's house in White Plains. I had sat opposite him, and later he had come and sat beside me on a bench so that I could observe him well from three-quarters and from the side. With concentrated mental notes, I came straight home and worked till perhaps one or two o'clock in the morning, to give substance to my impressions while my memory was accurate and dependable.

Two heads of Wendell Willkie (*profile, Philippe Halsman*)

The problem now was to do something expressive of his trip around the world that had so stirred his imagination with thoughts of human brotherhood. Fortunately, miles of film had been made of him on this trip, and 20th Century-Fox in one of their New York projection rooms ran all these reels off for me. A man sitting next to me gave a signal to the projectionist, who nipped the reels at the places where I wanted sections taken out. Hundreds of such brief but revealing flashes of Willkie character were spliced together for me into a film about twenty-five minutes long. I was provided with a projector of my own and a screen, and in my studio I managed to do something that was almost a contradiction in terms: model from a motion picture. A motion picture requires darkness, while modeling requires light. What I had to do was model by twilight. It was winter and would get almost dark at around five in the afternoon, but there would be enough light from the fading daylight and the light reflected from the screen for me to work. Now repeating a shot over and over, I obtained convincing, lifelike impressions of Mr. Willkie, particularly as he got off the plane and looked around and had that expression of surprise and amazement at the world he was seeing in all its variety and attractiveness—that was the expression I recorded. The publishers liked it, and asked me to carve it in Indiana limestone (stone from Willkie's native state) for the museum in Washington.

With both heads available, the new one and the earlier one done for Helen Frick, I tried an experiment. I put them at opposite ends of a corridor in a gallery where it was impossible to look at them both at the same time. At one end I placed the man listening and smiling, practically in conversation with somebody, and at the other end I placed this head looking up at the world in astonishment and amazement, and then I asked Mrs. Willkie and her son please to tell me which one was more convincing to them. Mrs. Willkie said, "I can't see them together," and I said, "I know. That's done with intention on my part." They were unable to make up their minds. That I took to mean that the two heads were both good likenesses. A bronze of the Corcoran Gallery head was later given to the New York Willkie House. Mrs. Willkie was given a bronze of the earlier head commissioned by Helen Frick, and a bronze of it was given to the University of Indiana.

CHAPTER THIRTY-TWO

RETURN TO FRANCE

IN MAY, 1948, with the war over, I prepared to go to Paris after a ten-year absence, taking with me a large shipment of household supplies, as well as clothing and gifts for friends and neighbors.

The evening before I sailed, guests for an impromptu farewell tea party gathered in the studio. Our sociability was interrupted by the sudden entrance of two policemen who called as they ran through the studio that there was a manhunt in progress on my roof! I continued serving tea while we awaited developments.

After a few minutes detectives appeared to report that a burglar was caught trying to pry open the metal grille on my penthouse window, and would I please come to the front door and try to identify him? This I declined to do, as I had not seen him. The burglar's explanation was simple—he was so thirsty that he thought he would try his luck at breaking in to find a bottle, or "something he could hock for the price of a drink!"

This was the third entry by burglars within a few years, so I asked the police to keep an eye on my abode while I was in Europe. The station house being directly across the street, it might seem odd that 157 should have such a record. The first two "visitors" had removed about everything of value in the house, so that there was only sculpture and furniture left. Sculptors have hard work to make sculpture, and harder work to sell it, and even burglars apparently shy away from bronze and stone, recognizing it as a liability!

The voyage in the *Queen Mary* was chiefly sleeping, eating, and reading. A blessed rest from city turmoil, telephone calls, and interrupted work. After the landing, Beth Hamm, a traveling companion, joined me on the railroad platform, and together with Guldie, my secretary, we undertook to load our bags and valises onto the train, heaving them through the windows with never a porter to help. Passengers, swearing in every language as they waited for service, finally had to follow our example and lift their own goods and chattels inside. Times had obviously changed, but there remained the long lines of French poplars and cultivated fields that soon calmed our upset emotions. We were again in our beloved France, and nothing else mattered.

The shocking war destruction was tragically evident as we neared Caen with its broken walls and houses now empty shells without roofs or windows.

The sounds and sights of Paris were a familiar welcome. Friends were on hand to greet us at the station, and one of them, Monsieur Crocé-Spinelli, brought a little bouquet of roses in a lacy paper holder—just as his late father had done for so many years before the war. We were bundled into the station wagon of the C.A.S.C. (Comité Américain du Secours Civil) with the smiling Alphonse, the chauffeur, to cheer us on our way across the city.

I held my breath as we turned into Villa Santos-Dumont at the end of which was my little house. . . . Would it really be there after ten years? Yes, it was, and what a joy to see the window boxes ablaze with bright red geraniums, just as we had left them in 1938!

Before we could try our key, the door opened, and there stood my faithful Bretonne Marie, smiling through her tears as we fell into each other's arms. Tea and cakes were ready upstairs, nasturtiums and scarlet peonies lending the room their flaming color.

"I remembered," said Marie, "how often Madame would bring home these flowers from the Quai aux Fleurs in the old days . . . so this morning I went there early, at five o'clock, before I went to work, and bought these and the geraniums, so that Madame could have a happy surprise on her arrival!" Such devotion stirred in me a wave of gratitude beyond words to express, but Marie is a Bretonne of terse speech, and she felt my appreciation.

We explored the house, then the garden, now hard to recognize; the bushes and little round-trimmed box trees had grown into a jungle and the privet hedging had become trees reaching the second-story windows. The roof had not leaked, and by some miracle my little house had survived ten years of emptiness with no visible damage. The interior paint was clean, the stair carpet intact, and the African rugs we had carefully rolled up in tar-lined paper were in perfect condition. So was my precious grand piano, which had belonged for many years to Édouard Schuré, the Alsatian philosopher and author, and upon which his friend Gounod had often played.

The metal shutters of all Parisian buildings were streaked with heavy red rust. No painting had been possible, with the lack of supplies and high costs, and the windows of my villa, no exception, added a note of resignation to the general aspect of our alley. Only the defiant gaiety of geraniums in the window boxes were calling, "Cheer up, it's over for the moment!"

After supper that first evening I went upstairs to the big room and found the boxes of records and the phonograph in good order. I threw open the casement windows; the evening sky was a glory over the hills of Paris—the Invalides dome was aglitter. The noises of the day had ceased; the world was resting. A crescent moon was hanging high above the neighbors' red-tiled roofs. Here and there a lighted window framed the silhouette of some silent watcher of the sky.

I slipped the record of a Chopin nocturne into the magic box . . . and Paderewski's playing floated into the evening air . . . then the mazurkas and a polonaise. Through the darkness, window silhouettes began waving their hands to me, and little calls of *"Bis, bis!"* from the neighbors encouraged me . . . a little louder, please! I continued the program for half an hour: Debussy, Ravel, ending with the haunting, romantic melody of Granados's "Maid and a Nightingale." It would seem to be stretching the truth to tell what happened next, but when I reached my bedroom and opened the window on the garden I heard the song of a nightingale, a real one! Not daring to believe my own ears, I called to Guldie, whose room also faced the garden,

"Do you hear what I hear?"

"I certainly do, and isn't it wonderful?"

Echoes of haunting memories . . . where else could such a night of magic come true!

"Fourmillante cité, cité pleine de rêves . . ." (Swarming city, city full of dreams . . .)

Most of our baggage consisted of trunks full of clothing and food to give away; to extract them from the customhouse nevertheless necessitated at least four trips across Paris, and standing in line for hours at a time. We called it the "Battle of Batignolles" after the railroad station where heavy luggage was examined.

Although it was May 15th, rain and cold winds in Paris created a chill that froze the marrow of our bones. The house, not having been heated or dried out for ten years, contributed its own special discomfort, but here we were in the land of heart's desire, and if the French people had stood it for ten years, we certainly could stand it now; we were being afforded the experience of just one of the discomforts of their rationed, austere ways of life. Standing in line for permits to buy food was another salutary lesson. No taxicabs, no car, and mighty few tickets for butter or fats or bread. Luckily we had been warned of these conditions and had ordered many packages sent from America. When these arrived, we had the happy task of distributing them and inviting friends to come and eat American food.

Now along the Seine as evening fell the world became translucent with reflections of peach-bloom roseate skies; a passionate tenderness pervaded the air; one felt like a god observing the wonders of Parnassus. A kind of sacred hush enwrapped the city, and mists rose from the river, hiding the sharper edges of day as the heart remembered similar iridescent evenings long, long ago.

Revisited after such a long absence, Paris now repossessed my heart. I had lived and loved and lost so much since I was here before . . . but the pulse was quickened and the years were canceled as I turned into familiar streets, finding the same old houses, the same courtyards, and by chance the same concierge sitting in the dingy loge, with the cat curled up on the window ledge, sleeping through the centuries. . . .

There are other indelible pictures—the tall bending trees that line the Île St.-Louis—the gold and red lights along the Seine that reflect their gleam in the black river—the ominous shadowy arches of the bridges on a dark night, seen from below as one walks along the water's edge, then, suddenly through those arches, the towers of Notre-Dame!

As I continued my round of visits to neighbors, it was heartwarming to feel their loyalty and pleasure in my unannounced return to the Villa.

Scars of undernourishment and fatigue told their story, but one could sense the old defiant independence flaring up as they would recount incidents of how the Nazis prowled about, listening and keeping watch over all activities, and how after chatting at a café table, some *copain* who had indiscreetly let fall uncomplimentary opinions of the occupying powers would be missed after that evening, and no trace could ever be found.

Two of the little villas that formed part of our "alley" had changed hands; their original owners, known to us for years, had been ordered to a concentration camp and blotted out simply because they were Jews.

Such news as this induced deep thinking and sharpened the edges of the general picture. In daytime people hurried about as usual, but were ill-clad for Parisians; the little touch of style and smartness was lacking. They were game, however, and determined to fight it through, and the younger generation were noticeably stronger and more *sportif*, probably at the cost of parents who had sacrificed their own rations to benefit their growing children.

I never recall seeing so many young children and babies. Even in the old days, before World War I, the Luxembourg Gardens were not so swarming with fat-cheeked *mignon*; it would seem that the laws of nature in this way compensate in postwar years for the tragic losses of the older generation.

I heard tales of collaborationists, some unquestionably substantiated, others based on rumor and hearsay. A definition of this term was "the fellow that collaborated a bit more than you did, and got caught!"

Hunger and poverty, pride and temptation and graft were all mixed together in most of the tales, and those who had withstood the tempting and paid the bitter price of half starving to death, having to hide and live like tracked animals, were countless. They made no show of their survival, but one felt the rapier-like thrusts of scorn directed toward weaklings and profiteers. These had lost their self-assurance, and moved in a ghostly world, shifting eyes and feet in a constant struggle to regain their lost equilibrium.

Revisiting the studio at 65 Boulevard Arago I asked for my friends the Limets, who were the patineurs of Rodin's bronzes and whom I had known since 1910. I found that the father had died; his son Jean was at home, emaciated, all pessimism and frustration; undernourishment and lack of work had taken their toll of his strength, and of that of his valiant daughter Pierrette. She had been a tubercular bent-over victim since childhood, and now that her mother had committed suicide she took care of her father. She went to work at seven-thirty every morning, returning only in time to pick up the rationed food supplies in her little string bag and prepare their evening meal. She told me of our common friends, some of whom, like Angel Zarraga, the Mexican painter, and Soudbinine, the Russian sculptor, had died since my last visit. Lurid, indeed, were the tales recounted by the Limets, and since we were old friends, all barriers were down and they poured out their hearts.

The Teilhard de Chardin Portrait

Now came a thoroughly bad moment that I had been delaying ever since I had landed at Cherbourg. On my trip across, I had been carrying with me a plaster cast of a head of Father Teilhard de Chardin that I had recently done in my New York studio. I had known Père Teilhard over a long period of years, meeting him first in Paris before starting on my trip around the world for the Field Museum in 1929. His illuminating expression coming from his human outlook on many phases of life always fascinated me—above all, his penetrating understanding. His eyes would often smile, and a cluster of tiny lines engraved their hieroglyphs on either side of his face, prolonging the downward slant of the corners of his upper lip and radiating a warm and loving nature.

He had recently returned to New York from a long trip and as we had talked about his coming work with the Wenner-Gren Foundation, I hesitantly asked if I could do his portrait. He kindly offered to pose, and during his hours on the model's stand at 157 he was quick to recognize the struggle I was having to reveal his character. He eased my tension by discussing my craft, a discussion full of wisdom and sympathetic interest. When I was discouraged, he seemed able to restore my confidence and carry my thoughts upward by the force of his own will and faith.

I finally achieved an interpretation; but, not satisfied, I made a plaster cast to take to Paris with me in the hope of doing further work on it. As we landed, a sailor insisted on taking my canvas bag, containing this cast, saying the gangplank was slippery and I would need to hold on with both hands. I warned him about the fragile contents of the bag and that it must be handled with the greatest care. He went to the baggage chute and placed it so that it had a trunk directly in front and another trunk just behind it, and as they slid down to the dock the heavy trunks crashed together. I knew the result, but had been steadily delaying the moment of verifying the disaster. Now I opened the bag.

As I had feared, the plaster was in bits, as forlorn in its many wrappings as only a broken head can look to the sculptor who made it. Recalling how often and how patiently my distinguished sitter had posed for me in my New York studio and how desperately I had tried over and over to catch his elusive, subtle expression and do justice to his aristocratic head, I felt pretty dejected.

Then I remembered how Rodin had said to me, "Capture the accidents in life and turn them into science!" Here was surely a challenge not to be sidestepped. Armed with the weeks of observation and study that had gone into my previous efforts, I decided to get some French clay and start again with a different mood, and a determination of iron.

I called Father Teilhard and told him of the calamity, sensing by his voice how taken aback he was, but I quickly added that if I could just be an observer at a friend's tea party to which we were both invited the next day, I was convinced that I could build up a new and better portrait in clay that would make the one made in New York look like a mere "rehearsal."

The previous one showed his hands clasped and held against his chest. The straight collar and severe black coat seemed to us both to make too formal and clerical an impression.

When I saw him at the tea party, it was on a cold and rainy day and he was wearing a long cape with its collar loosely draped over his shoulders. At once I knew that I must try this effect. It gave an informal and natural frame for the new portrait.

And so it happened that the Jesuit Father came to the villa to find the portrait almost completed. "No more posing," I said. "Just sit down and read aloud from your great-great-uncle Voltaire, and from Ronsard, and if I haven't hit the bull's-eye within an hour and a half, you are authorized to destroy the portrait, and me, at a stroke!"

This daring adventure taught me some deep and terrible things about trying to make a real character portrait, about the importance of constant self-challenging. I cast the bust in Paris; it was far better than the one I had made in New York, and eventually it was purchased by the French Ministry of the Beaux-Arts and placed permanently in the Musée d'Art Contemporain.

I was happy when my Father Teilhard portrait was done. The weather was still cold and threatening, but the crisp Paris sunlight, when it does come, is a bugle call in its clarity, transforming everything to a *joie de vivre* reputedly singular to this corner of the world! The air makes one tingle, and the birds wake one up with a song.

In the public squares and parks of Paris bare pedestals that had supported bronze statues were silent evidence that the enemy had either stolen the monuments for collections of their own or had melted them down for the metal. The heroic bronze figure of Balzac by Rodin and the one of Clemenceau, striding along on his rocky pediment on the Champs-Elysées, were still intact, however.

Not knowing what had befallen the great collections in the Luxembourg Museum, I went one day to revisit the galleries, hoping to find many old favorites in the way of paintings and sculpture. To my dismay the building was closed and empty. I was told that many of the objects had been distributed to smaller museums outside Paris and that the section of recent works was at present housed in the Museum of Contemporary Art where there were vast galleries for sculpture. Comparatively few examples were shown, however, and those mostly of the extreme modern school, mutilated abstracts and gigantic plasters verging on the obscene.

A ceremony of special significance to the art world was the opening of the new Rodin Museum at Meudon. The whole aspect of his home and charming wild garden had undergone a change, resulting in a formal and rather cold effect that caused me a pang of disappointment. The severe lines of the present two-story Musée des Plâtres had obliterated the picturesque stone façade of the old château Rodin had reassembled on the edge of the hill beyond his big studio. This unfamiliar setting for the world of figures, groups, and portraits was something of a shock. Rows of glass cases contained a selection of the hundreds of sketches and studies, but the countless high pedestals and columns with heroic heads and winged figures that gave the old studio a sense of creativeness, of the dynamic torments, questionings, and wild searchings of an elemental spirit —these were missing.

In the days of Rodin the little garden was rustic and untrimmed; the winding paths led to unexpected pools and vistas, or a half-hidden Greek marble. Now the whole scene was obviously public property, and bore the official stamp of state management.

Perhaps in time much more of the vast collection will be added and will better enable students of the future to realize the countless studies and variations that often preceded the final portraits and groups to be seen in bronze or marble in the galleries of the Rodin Museum in the Hôtel Biron, rue de Varennes, in Paris.

THE DE ROUGÉ BAS-RELIEF

I went to Switzerland for a short visit with friends in Geneva, and Bonabés de Rougé, Director of the League of Red Cross Societies, and his wife invited me to motor back to Paris with them. The journey of 575 kilometers, under clear skies and through Wagnerian mountain scenery, was one to remember.

A few days later the De Rougés asked me to join them on a motor trip to Château-Thierry. Their only son, Charles Armand de Rougé, had been killed there in 1940 when he had volunteered to stand guard in his solitary tank at the entrance to the bridge leading into the town, over which came the German army. His companion-in-arms, De Pollès, had also taken part in this heroic stand to hold back and destroy what they could of the enemy crossing the bridge. A Nazi sharpshooter cut off the periscope on the turret of the tank from which De Rougé had swept the bridge with constant fire, each time causing delay in the enemy advance and a need to reassemble before making another crossing. During one of the lulls when De Rougé opened the top of his tank to replace the periscope, a shot rang out and he was fatally wounded.

When De Pollès, who was hidden in a doorway near the tank, saw that his friend was shot and unable to continue tank fire, he touched together the electric wires that were connected to a mass of dynamite he had placed under the bridge. The entire structure was blown to fragments, including high officers and men of the German forces who were again marching in close formation, about to reach the town side of the bridge.

The tragic incident moved me. Out of profound human interest, I took

Charles Armand de Rougé Medallion

Père Teilhard de Chardin

one or two of the photographs De Rougé had of his son, and I began, out of the air, to see if I could get a likeness of him in bas-relief. When I had it done I showed it to the De Rougés, and they were very touched and suggested that it should be put up at the place where he had defended the bridge.

Eight years after the death of the young man, the town held a memorial ceremony at the exact spot where his tank had been stationed. They put my portrait, mounted on a marble plaque, into the wall of a little building nearby, and it was unveiled after a memorial service held in the town church. A solemn crowd of men, women, and children marched through the streets. Veterans of the French Army who had been in action during the 1940 campaign paid special tribute to the dauntless courage of the young soldier who had so gallantly insisted upon defending this dangerous post, well knowing that he could expect no reinforcement, but knowing also that his fire could certainly wipe out a large number of the enemy's forces and that his companion, who had already laid dynamite charges, would carry on if he himself were wounded.

To stand beside his parents as the citations were read and taps sounded by the bugler brought one very close to the tragedy of war—and the broken hearts of the parents whose only child had been sacrificed.

Returning to Paris I found that painters had scraped the rust from the iron shutters of my villa and painted them. These and the fresh Brittany-blue window frames gave color to the end of our alley and seemed to induce a number of neighbors to follow my example. Before the end of July, gay flowers and bright window boxes were decorating many of the little villas nearby.

I invited Maria, the stalwart wife of the captain of the fishing boat *Malvina* in Saint-Guénolé, Brittany, to come to Paris and spend a week with me. As her young son Simon was at work near the city, we had some delightful expeditions together, winding up in Notre-Dame where Maria climbed to the top and saw all Paris, as she proudly reported, for less than it would have cost her to ride all day in buses and then come home exhausted. Dressed in her striking black-velvet Breton bodice and full black skirt, and wearing the high coif of the Bigoudene, she made quite an impression as we walked through the streets and shops.

Maria had lived through so many tragedies that I had feared to find her broken in spirit, but on the contrary her simple faith and philosophy had upheld her and she could still smile and say: "If you have a piece of bread left, you can still share it with someone who has less!"

Early that spring, in New York, I had received an intriguing invitation from my friend, Monsieur Crocé-Spinelli in Paris, to be the guest of honor at a dinner club there known as Les Compagnons de la Belle Table. The date for this was June 18th at the Restaurant de la Reine Christine, near the Place des Grands Augustins, and a reminder was sent me that I would be called for at 7:00 P.M. on that day.

For the first time since my arrival in France, I actually dressed up and tried my wings in a social gathering that proved to be an evening of brilliant repartee, fine speeches, and a menu of the best French cooking that one could taste. Monsieur Georges Villa was master of ceremonies, and one of the forty-eight guests was the well-known "Prince des Gastronomes," Monsieur Chernousky. His critical opinion was sought by the chef, who presented each course for his inspection and who at the end was called from his kitchen to receive the applause and thanks of all the guests. On the specially designed menu was a lithograph by Benno Vigny, who was present. Monsieur Paul Jouve, the animal sculptor, was another guest. After actors, poets, lawyers, musicians, and lay members had each made remarks or recited poems I was called upon to tell them, in French, about my student days with Rodin and the founding of the Appui aux Artistes at the outbreak of the war in 1914 when I was in Paris with my mother. The gods were kind, and the fine French wines revived my long-dormant French, so that I was by some miracle enabled to express myself and convey the sincerity of my emotions about those wonderful few Paris years, beginning in 1910, when the world seemed radiant in its freedom before it was rolled over the edge of the abyss of war, to the end of how many dreams!

PART IV

CHAPTER THIRTY-THREE

ÉPINAL

JUST BEFORE I had embarked for Europe that spring of 1948, my friend Bill Delano had conveyed to me the surprising news that he had submitted my name to the Fine Arts Commission in Washington, D.C., and that I had been accepted as sculptor for the American War Memorial Building, designed by Delano & Aldrich, at Épinal, in the Vosges Mountains in France. Good news, indeed, and an electrifying incentive, as I had known nothing of the project. This was to be a tribute to the twelve thousand American soldiers who fell in the battles near Épinal.

Realizing how important it would be for me to study the actual site and setting for this work, the officers in charge of this project arranged to have me admitted to the cemetery soon after my arrival in Paris, and told me that officers from Nancy would meet me there the following day.

Continual rains during forty-two days had drenched the country so that washouts and flooded streams made the roads at times almost impassable for our automobile. The Moselle River, roaring along almost at street level, splashed ominously against the bridge in front of our hotel.

It was arranged that an aerial photograph and a panoramic view be taken on the first clear day so that the site could be more easily visualized by the architect and those of us concerned with the project.

The water-soaked cemetery was a bleak sight. Hundreds of caskets were piled around the outer borders, all covered with black tarpaulins, and the rows of open graves were half filled with water.

The details of Épinal continued much in my mind during the remainder of my stay in Europe. At the end of three months, the time I had planned for

ARTIST'S RENDITION OF THE ÉPINAL MEMORIAL, AMERICAN CEMETERY, VOSGES MOUNTAINS

Front façade relief, Épinal, left panel

Front façade relief, Épinal, right panel

the trip, I started for home, little suspecting what was to await me there. I had left for Europe much concerned for my sister Helen's health, but I had been receiving constant good reports and cheerful letters from her up to the very last in Paris. All this by no means prepared me for the news I received the morning after my arrival in New York. Helen had suffered a severe cerebral hemorrhage during the night, and I was summoned to her bedside in New Hampshire. The shock left me wondering if it was a nightmare or whether I was awake and facing reality.

Then followed weeks of vigilance and anxiety, trained nurses, relapses, and slight spaces of improvement. In September I brought her home in an ambulance from Little Boar's Head to her apartment at 145 East Thirty-fifth Street, fortunately just up the block from 157. When she knew she was safely back, she was able to relax, and her spirit somehow adjusted to a more regular rhythm and feeling of security. So we had hope for a while, but in October there was another crisis so grave that no one expected her to live more than a few days. She was unconscious, motionless. Day after day the dark angel of death hovered over us. The subconscious prayerful struggle goes on—we fight for life regardless of the price. We cannot learn to accept the omnipotence of death; we watch and pray and move about the house rather like automatons trying to set things in order—we wait, and eternity seems very close.

It was under these conditions that I had to begin work on the responsibility I had accepted, and whose full weight I realized only now—designing and modeling the two large panels and the angel over the altar in the chapel for the Épinal memorial. There was no way of turning aside from this commission. I had accepted it and I had to go on with it. I realized how many months of labor and concentration it would demand of me, with what probable storms ahead, and I started it with foreboding.

It was in these dark hours that the whole design and theme of the composition seemed to take shape in my tormented mind, and with the clarification of my ideas came strength to go forward. I read in Exodus: "I bare you on eagles' wings, and brought you unto myself." From this verse as a beginning, I foresaw and mentally sketched out in its larger forms the memorial as it was to be. I resolved to put aside my fears and do my best. Helen had somewhat improved. The studio immediately took on new life, and from morning until 4:00 P.M. I gave my time and thought once more to the problem of sculpture.

At four every day I went to see Helen, keeping faithfully to the hour so she could look forward then to our being together, and when she felt able and interested enough, I stayed on and had supper with her. But after supper I came back to the studio and put on the artificial light and went ahead with my work, often until midnight. Ideas were coming thick and fast, and I felt under an irresistible compulsion. To get the effects I wanted, I would have to study and comprehend the technique of low incised reliefs as I never had before. My problem was to respect the wall surfaces of the Épinal memorial building, yet embody some convincing message in the compositions to keep the two panels balanced on either side of the entrance and lead the thought upward toward the inscription above.

To represent modern warfare and the apotheosis of battle and its aftermath and to have my designs subject to the scrutiny of military authorities as well as of the National Commission of Fine Arts was obviously to put myself to a severe test. I was willing to face these formidable critics only because I so wanted to do something worthy of the soldiers who lay under the ground at Épinal. Verses from the Bible recurred to me at intervals, and then the last words of Mr. Valiant in *Pilgrim's Progress* came to me as I tried to think what would lift the hearts of those grieving for a loved husband, son, brother, or father buried at Épinal: "I am going to my Father's . . . My sword I give to him that shall succeed me in my pilgrimage, and my courage and skill to him that can get it. My marks and scars I carry with me . . . So he passed over, and all the trumpets sounded for him on the other side."

Trumpets in the sky, angels in the air, wings—wings—and rays of light breaking through darkness. All this subconscious universe kept my mind in a state of turmoil until at last discipline directed the wild currents into a final and inevitable order. It seemed as though Helen's crisis passed, and she began to be better as I went through this waking and sleeping agony of creation. I was comforted, and had renewed hope for her.

When holidays at the University of Syracuse permitted Mestrovic, who was directing the School of Sculpture there, to spend a day or two in New York with his lovely wife, Olga, it was a delight to welcome them. His wise and experienced judgment was of inestimable value to me at this time, for as past master in the art of low reliefs in wood and stone he knew all the "dangerous turns ahead" and the imperious need to guard against any idea not suitable to plastic interpretation. He often said, "It is to *work* and *watch* in sculpture, *not* to *talk*." The truth of this has been demonstrated more often than many care to believe. A rare privilege was to watch Mestrovic carve directly into a big, unevenly broken block of marble the figure of a woman playing a lute—his "Croation Rhapsody." Attacking the marble with hammer and chisel, he proceeded to form the bowed head leaning sideways over the strings of the lute and to bring to life the hands holding and caressing the instrument. The direct and well-aimed strokes never missed their mark as the whole submerged design came to the surface in shorter time than could be believed possible.

Later that autumn my sister had a secondary stroke, and again life seemed to have ebbed out. November 27th was her seventy-seventh birthday, which neither she nor anyone else had thought she would reach. Many remembrances of living friendship greeted her on that day.

The stars came out in a bright, icy sky to remind us that up yonder the rhythms do not change and that, as Baudelaire said, "ce qui est créé par l'esprit est plus vivant que la matière" (that which the spirit creates is more living than material things).

And Helen again began a slow, dauntless recovery. It was too much to expect that she would recuperate everything she had lost. We knew that now, after these several crises, she would go on with diminished ammunition, that she was like an army whose supplies were dwindling. It made for added apprehension, and my heart was filled with anxiety as I began the long process of modeling the quarter-size panels already designed on paper for the Épinal façade. War and Marching Soldiers on one side, and the Angel of Death and the Dying Soldier—"The Trumpets Sounding"—on the other side. In the center over the entrance was an eagle with his wings widespread, and on either side of this were the words from Exodus: "I Bare You On Eagles' Wings And Brought You Unto Myself."

Winter ebbed into spring, and a point came when I needed authentic data to carry through the last stages of my army panel. One day I went to the 71st Regiment Armory on Thirty-fourth Street and enlisted the help of Major Gannon, who offered to lend me guns, helmets, boots, belts, grenades, and so on. He told me that three hundred and ten of their men were buried at Épinal. It was a real assistance, this cooperation from men whose comrades had actually fought there, and I felt at long last that I was tapping a direct source of information. A few days later two soldiers arrived in full battle regalia to pose for me.

A few weeks later the Battle Monuments Commission came. They were surprised to find the studio filled with army equipment. To my relief, they approved of the work done to date and authorized me to take a holiday.

So the working season at the studio came to an end, and on July 1st an ambulette drove Helen, her nurse, and myself to Bedford, New York, where we had rented a house for two months. Summer had successfully started! Bantam chicks and birds gave a touch of farm life to the setting. I rested, read, collected data from diaries of my great-great-grandfather, read them aloud to Helen, and tried to synchronize them as a starting point for my "memoirs." A few weeks of rest seemed to regenerate the fires that overwork had burned out.

On my return to New York in September, the last judgment was still to be pronounced on the quarter-size models for Épinal. The heat was brutal, but the members of the Commission appeared at 157 promptly at ten o'clock one morning. After they had wandered about in the studio studying the models, a final vote was taken. It was one of unanimous approval. Something of a weight was lifted from my mind as they shook my hand and filed out into the red-hot street.

About this time I heard that the sculptor Rudulph Evans wanted to sell five hundred pounds of plastelene, so I went to see it with Russo, my plaster caster, who recognized it as an old friend, having cast many big figures made with this same material and having cleaned it before it was put back into barrels. He assured me that it was in good condition. He said that when he bought it for Mr. Daniel Chester French many years earlier, he paid thirty-six cents a pound for it and it went into the big Lincoln Memorial figure in Washington.

Then it was used by Saint-Gaudens for various figures, then sold to Evans for the Jefferson Memorial. Now, forty years later, I paid seventy cents a pound, and it was considered a bargain! I used it to model the Épinal panels.

An additional responsibility on my horizon was the building up of a full-scale model of a Memorial Flagpole that Mr. Thomas J. Watson had commissioned me to make for his plant at Endicott, New York, to honor the members of the International Business Machines Company who had given their lives in the Second World War. This model was about sixteen feet high. After I submitted the full-size plaster eagles and shields of the five services—Army, Navy, Air, Marines, and Coast Guard—on their architectural pedestal, the model was accepted and sent to the foundry.

Later in the spring I went with Mr. and Mrs. Thomas J. Watson to the Endicott plant to see the finished flagpole in place. The day after our arrival brought the tail end of a tornado with high winds of gale velocity. When it quieted down, we drove over to see the flagpole with Old Glory flying at the top. The steel pole waved a bit, but this was planned for; otherwise it might have given way. The five huge bronze eagles with their wings erect gave an effect of security. These were set on a granite base on which were inscribed the lines of the poet Rupert Brooke: ". . . Into the Night and on, the Strength and Splendour of our Purpose swings . . ."

On my return to New York, the workdays were gradually bringing to completion the sculptural roundels for the Épinal Memorial. The Memorial building would have two rooms, a nonsectarian Chapel on the left and a Military Museum on the right. Midway down a covered colonnade, open at the ends, would be the entrances to these rooms. The roundels, which were five feet in diameter, were to be placed over these entrances at a height of about twenty-five feet in the air. They were in heavy relief, for otherwise they would not have been visible. There would be no light other then the sunlight coming in and hitting the colonnade floor, and that light would be reflected upward so that the roundels had to be modeled in an entirely different way from the two panels and eagle on the front façade of the building where the light would come directly from the sky. The roundels would be stone. The one over the entrance to the Museum would represent the Seal of the United States, and the one over the entrance to the Chapel would include in its circular composition the Lamb of God, the Tablets of Moses, the Star of David, and the Greek Cross.

Another diversion: Thomas Craven, who was promoting the showing of art movies, came to my studio one day. We went over a Rodin film, made in France, and he asked me to cooperate in cutting and editing it. I suggested the idea of a picture of Rodin's hand in plaster holding a small torso of a woman as a background for the title, and offered to let them photograph the one I own. We set it on a revolving stand, which I turned slowly by pulling on a string wound around the turntable. The effect added great interest. The movie had a long run at the Sutton Theatre before going on the road.

Shortly after this digression from sculpture, the Fine Arts Commission arrived to pronounce their judgment on the recent Épinal work. Eugene Savage, the mosaic artist for this same project, came to my studio to set up his model for their inspection. After the Commission had examined both his work and mine, a vote was taken and our models were accepted with enthusiasm. This was the end of an important chapter for me after nearly two years of hard work.

CHAPTER THIRTY-FOUR

TRIBUTE TO HELEN

IT WAS at this time that I first made the acquaintance of Marianne Moore with whose reputation for distinguished but somewhat difficult poetry I was already familiar. Both members of the Academy of Arts and Letters, one day we went together to my studio, had lunch, engaged in some enlightening conversation, and took a kind of introductory survey of each other. Our friendship developed slowly but continued steadily from that time. An inhabitant of Brooklyn, Marianne would often terminate a busy day in Manhattan by having supper with me and talking through the evening. Then I would put her in a cab to return her to her Brooklyn home, arguing with the cabdriver, who would usually protest against going to that far-off place.

I confess that I found her poetry hard to understand, so I would ask her to read one of her poems aloud to me. Then I would say, "I really don't know what that's all about, because of my own ignorance, I'm sure, but just possibly you might explain it to me." She would start explaining it, and then she'd say, "You know, I don't really understand much of it myself," and she'd laugh and say, "Of course, I was convinced I understood it when I wrote it. I'll have to work some more on it," and then there would be jottings in the margin, and revision. She didn't mind my saying what I did—she liked the truth, a mending kind of adhesive to stick over any possible misunderstanding.

She started translating La Fontaine's *Fables*. She read and understood French, but didn't speak it, and she wanted to get a flow, an easy sense of what the *Fables* meant. She would call me up on the phone late at night and ask me to do an unrehearsed, direct translation for her, and I would do it and then she would read me her own translation. I would say, "Is that the same fable?" for her translation would be full of adjuncts and additions and curious new angles and light. But without replying to me, she would ring off and go back to her work.

MH's DRAWING OF MARIANNE MOORE (*Peter A. Juley & Son*)

My friendship with her was a great mental stimulus to me, and I felt a deep tenderness for her. It continues to this day.

It was after finishing the work on Épinal that I went off for relaxation and change of scene to Syracuse to visit Ivan and Olga Mestrovic at their new home. Almost two years had passed since my last visit to them. We went to Ivan's studio and saw his fine recent work, and to his pupils' exhibit, which was most interesting and showed promise. Later we examined his twenty-five religious panels set up around the vestibule and walls of the campus chapel. These biblical subjects deeply impressed the congregation, who stayed on after the church service to examine the bas-reliefs, carved on two-inch-thick walnut planks, some ten feet high, like those of the "Ascension," the "Resurrection," and a long horizontal "Last Supper." These panels were shipped back to Yugoslavia in 1953 and set in place in the Mestrovic chapel at Split on the Adriatic coast. Although all his property, studios, and chapel had been seized by Tito's government, Mestrovic was determined to complete the decorations of his chapel with his own panels.

Also after Épinal, in 1950, I was asked by Swami Nikhilananda, who directs the Vedanta Center in New York, to make the first of the three portraits I did for them. This first portrait was a study of Swami Vivekananda whom I was fortunate in having seen on his visit to America in 1910. I was a young woman at that time, and met him in the dining room of a boardinghouse on West Thirty-eighth Street. I still recall his dark handsome face framed in a saffron turban and his spirit that radiated power through his luminous eyes. I sensed a rare privilege to be speaking with him and to hear the compassionate voice of a holy man from faraway India. This impression of his appearance never faded, and helped me to achieve an authentic likeness, which is now placed at the Vedanta Center in East Ninety-fourth Street.

The next portrait I did for the Center, that of Sri Ramakrishna, was more difficult. I had only inadequate photographs to go on, and though Ramakrishna himself had been filled with spiritual consciousness, his general appearance was more like that of a Roman citizen than like that of an Indian ascetic. Swami Nikhilananda was of great help to me, guiding me and having the power to evoke definite impressions.

I found even that the material of alabaster, in which I was doing the portrait, helped me achieve a spiritual quality, for it retains and reflects the light in a curious way impossible with plaster or clay. Eventually the Center kept a little light always burning below the portrait on the altar, and the flame, being irregular, gave a slight impression of living thought with its changing and nonstatic shadings. With these various, even fortuitous, means—hints in the leader's writings, his effect on his followers and friends, the flicker of a light—you find that you have translated a man's spirit into the modulations of a piece of alabaster.

A few years later I was asked to do the portrait of the Holy Mother of India. It presented much the same problem as that of her husband, Sri Ramakrishna. The Swami Nikhilananda was again helpful because he could frame by a kind

FIGURE OF SWAMI VIVEKANANDA
(Frick Art Reference Library)

psychic sympathy the problem I faced trying to enter imaginatively into the spirit of this holy woman I had never seen. He made the illuminating comment that she had been formed by her husband's philosophy, which she preached. Her husband had been a serene person, and some of that serenity, some of that religious inwardness of character, had been conveyed to his wife, and now she became for me not just a woman with a veil over her head and long, wavy black tresses hanging down, but a woman with a meditative spirit, with enough force to exert the undying influence she seems to have had on thousands of followers. Yet just such serenity and inward power make the subject harder to portray. Most Americans in their mature years have lines and wrinkles, markings of the face that are easy to catch. But the Indian mystic's features tend to be smoothed off, and I had to get at something that would come through that mask of serenity.

With the Swami's help, the portrait of the Holy Mother reached its conclusion, and he was satisfied with the result. One bronze was ordered for his chapel in New York and a second was sent to India for the Centennial Commemoration of the birth of the Holy Mother. The bronze portrait I had made of her husband Sri Ramakrishna (after the alabaster portrait) was also shipped to Belur Math near Calcutta.

It meant much to me to do these portraits. Indians treat an artist as something outside general life. They have the feeling that God has spoken to him and that he is in continuous communication with God, for otherwise he would not go on being an artist. That attitude develops in you a sense of respect and an acceptance of responsibility. I felt both appreciative and dedicated, and I did the best that I could for them.

The summer of the year 1950, when I had begun my Vedanta Center portraits, I took my sister Helen again by ambulette to Bedford, New York, and it was to the same house where we had been the summer before, so everything was comfortably familiar to her. There we had the ramps installed so that I could put her in a wheelchair and get her out of doors. The summer was good for both of us.

Strengthened and encouraged about her, in the early autumn I went off by myself on a short motor holiday to Little Boar's Head. Its spell came over me again, the ever-changing magic of the ocean, the miracle and power of the tides, the healing security of their eternal rhythm. The air soughing in the pines was fragrant with sea breezes. Bathing in the morning and drenching myself in the glorious sunlight, my fatigue lifted and I felt a revival of body and spirit. The sea gulls in their graceful dives were a constant delight, and tempted me to make many drawings and a few watercolors, which, however, never came off the way I hoped they would.

UNITED NATIONS PARTY

In October it was suggested to me that the delegates to the United Nations might enjoy celebrating the fifth birthday of the organization by attending a reception in my studio, with an exhibit of my Races of Mankind. Flags of sixty nations were loaned to me by the U.N. to decorate the studio walls, giving a festive setting, and golden chrysanthemums in big vases and autumn leaves in brass pots imparted a gay appearance to both studios, which were quite transformed as a background for over two hundred subjects in sculpture, including one hundred pieces from the Hall of Man and a wide range of other work, from my head of Keats to the "Frileuse," that little Shiverer (one flicked water at her to see her shiver), and other fountains, and of course dancers—Pavlova, Mordkin, and others—and many portrait heads.

One hundred and thirty United Nations' guests came in the afternoon. Champagne and brandy punch helped the various delegates to enjoy one another's company—India, Pakistan, Thailand, England, France, Argentina, and many other countries were represented. His Royal Highness Prince Wan Waithayakon of Thailand cut the birthday cake, and, like many other delegates who crowded around, wanted to know the meaning of the little wild animals in wax that held the candles and decorated the cake. I smilingly answered that the donor had thought these were suitable symbols for a United Nations party! From then on, informality reigned.

After these festivities and the clearing away of all signs of social activity, I began working on a trophy figure for British Air Marshal Lord Tedder to be presented to the R.A.F. in memory of his son who had lost his life flying. He wanted to have the words "Faith, Courage, and Sportsmanship" engraved on the base. While working, I read the poem written by a young American airman, Hugh G. McGee, Jr., who joined the R.A.F. when he was eighteen years old and was killed over England in 1941:

High Flight

Oh, I have slipped the surly
  bonds of earth,
And danced the skies on laughter-
  silvered wings;
Sunward I've climbed and joined
  the tumbling mirth
Of sun-split clouds—and done a
  hundred things
You have not dreamed of . . .
And, while with silent, lifting
  mind I've trod
The high, untrespassed sanctity
  of space,
Put out my hand and touched
  the face of God!

These lines helped me to suggest the feeling of aspiration in the figure of the aviator.

After her return from Bedford, in the autumn, Helen had another sinking spell, and her strength began ebbing away so that the early winter was very hard for her. She was now at a stage where steadily one could see that she was not going to recover. On Christmas Day she and I listened to the singing of the beautiful carols on the radio. I felt that death was close, and I wondered if I could go on watching the struggle that seemed so unfair, so hopeless. I could not pray for a prolonging of life, knowing that no recovery was possible.

On the last of the year 1950, Helen fell asleep. She did not regain consciousness, and a little after midnight we knew that she was really at rest.

A few years before, she had begun to write an autobiography. Alas, her illness cut this plan off, and the manuscript is left unfinished. What she wrote, however, does tempt me to tell a little of her story.

In the late 1870's, Helen was a friend of Miss Louisa Lee Schuyler in whose home there took shape plans for the Bellevue Training School for Nurses, the first of its kind in America. Helen was interested in this, and she also joined a group of sixty women who volunteered to go to Bellevue Hospital daily to check and report on the rather bad conditions existing there, especially in the departments of nursing and of preparation of food.

When Helen was twenty-three years old, she was asked to become a member of the board of directors of Bellevue Hospital, then under the leadership of Mrs. Whitelaw Reid. This board of outstanding women visited the patients in the hospital wards and arranged for painting and decorating the nurses' rooms. They brought fruit and flowers and clothing and arranged parties and entertainment in the hospital wards. In this work Mrs. Reid gave Helen her devoted friendship and guidance.

In 1901 Helen resigned from the Bellevue Training School and was asked to take the chairmanship of the new advisory board for the Metropolitan Hospital School of Nursing on Welfare Island. In the meantime the United States had challenged Spain in Cuba. The Red Cross immediately organized its relief units, equipped ambulances, and shipped quantities of supplies. Helen applied for a position in the Supply Committee directed by Cleveland H. Dodge. He felt she was too young for the job, but gave her a four-day trial and then told her to stay on, which she did.

Red Cross auxiliaries were formed all over the country to collect the urgently needed supplies, and Mr. Dodge was one of the most active members of the executive committee. Helen became acquainted with his multiple problems. The war experience of this A.R.C. Relief Committee laid the foundation for the present thoroughly equipped Red Cross organization.

The year the war ended, 1899, Helen married Dr. William K. Draper.

When she started her work at the Metropolitan Hospital in 1901, conditions were deplorable, and she at once began to raise funds for a nurses' home, a campaign that lasted many years. At the first graduation exercises of the School for Nurses Helen read this version of the Hippocratic oath:

SANGUINE DRAWING OF HELEN BY JACOVLEFF

You do solemnly swear, each one by whatever she holds most sacred, that you will be loyal to the physicians under whom you shall serve, as a good soldier is loyal to his officers; That you will be just and generous to all worthy members of your profession, aiding them when it shall be in your power so to do; That you will lead your lives and practice your profession in uprightness and honor; That into whatever house you shall enter in, it shall be for the good of the sick to the utmost of your power, and that you will hold yourself aloof from all temptation; That whatsoever you shall hear or see of lives of men and women, whether they be your patients or members of the household, you will keep inviolably secret, whether you are in other households or among your own friends.

In 1909 the nurses moved into a new home, one of the most beautiful and modern residences of its kind in the country. Twenty years later the East Wing was added to give forty new bedrooms. This building was named Draper Hall, and a bronze tablet was later placed there bearing Helen's name. It was the gift of the graduate and student nurses, and of this honor Helen was justly proud. She had served thirty-five years as chairman of the board.

In 1955 the Metropolitan Hospital was moved to New York City at Ninety-eighth Street and First Avenue. Six years later an enlarged new home for nurses was built on the site opposite to the hospital and kept the name of Draper Hall.

Helen was a recognized leader during her years of unfailing devotion to the Red Cross, both the national organization and the local New York Chapter from 1905 to 1944 when because of ill health she resigned as vice chairman of the board.

At that time she was given a testimonial dinner for her four decades of work. At this gathering of some three hundred friends, Red Cross officials, and army personnel, General James G. Harbord referred affectionately to her as a "Pocket Napoleon" indefatigable in her enthusiasm for the cause of the Red Cross.

At the end of World War I she helped in forming the first East Harlem Health Center, which was such a success that thirty other centers were soon organized along the same lines.

Helen's record of public service was recognized by all who worked with her, and was particularly well expressed by Eleanor Belmont, reading the closing words of the resolution of the New York Chapter of the Red Cross at the time of Helen's death: "All the years of her life, modestly, graciously, yet with firmness and unfailing insight, she helped to solve many of the serious problems of her native city; the reward came when her task was well done. The American National Red Cross, the New York Chapter particularly, and the entire community, are better for her having lived and worked among us."

When Mrs. Belmont sent me this resolution, she added in her letter to me: "If what I present seems an understatement, you will realize that I have been influenced by the character of the woman to whom we pay tribute. If the words lack poetry, please remember that the poetry lies in the quantity and the quality of her service."

CHAPTER THIRTY-FIVE

SPAIN AND BEYOND

In May I was stricken by a mysterious sharp pain that seemed to break my back. Getting into bed was an agonizing effort; this was *it*—the climax after a long overstrain of nerves. Agony spasms on both sides of my spine and the sciatic nerve made it impossible for me to move. The next morning, after a night of wakefulness and codeine, I called Dr. Simard, and he and his assistant came at once and gave me morphine and six deep cocaine injections into muscle bundles that were as hard as wood.

I was initiated into a world of pain—so acute that it paralyzed me. What if this immobility were permanent? But the medicos told me to thank God the pain continued, indicating that Nature was fighting on my side. Comforting, if true; I felt no desperation, and had time to learn how to meet a real threat. A week later, still under the influence of codeine, the nerves in my legs were painful and throbbing. The doctor decided that I now had phlebitis and gout added to everything else. After a while I tried to stand on my feet and move around a little. Gradually I learned to walk from the bedroom to the living room, and with that change of scene life began little by little to seem more normal.

In June I moved into a guest cottage that Ned and Louise Bechtel had offered me in Mount Kisco. The peace and fragrance of their adjacent rose garden were restoring; they brought me baskets of flowers and many beguiling books. Wallace Fowlie's *Rimbaud* and Maurice Bowra's criticisms supplied many hours of reading, and I tried each day to wrestle with my own voluminous manuscript. I thought how much more difficult it is to write concisely than at length, and in this mood I reread a poem I had written just before pain had struck me down. I had been led into this experiment by noting (with a side-glance at Wallace Stevens) a typographical error "s" in a novel:

Words . . . words, swords, worlds . . .
One letter more, one less . . . and
She is he and he is she . . .
The juggler of the consonant,
The photofinish of a rhyme
The parallelograms of sound
That make a scaffold
For a poet's life to hang upon, or climb,
Or swing, perhaps?

The poem went on:

reaching
Through darkness to the dawn of things
Arpeggios of dreams that
Skip the measured octaves
Of our space

and eventually recounted the adventures of some summer sheep in "empiric fields of grass." It at least allied me with poets in effort, and perhaps contributed, with sunbaths and complete rest, to my gradual recovery of health.

I began the new year 1952 with the determination to see if I could work six hours a day, and happily found I could. This encouraged me.

The Hall of Fame for Great Americans at New York University asked me to model an over-life-size portrait of Thomas Paine for their collection. I read Paine's *The Age of Reason,* and was deeply impressed by it. I tried to visualize how I could interpret this man in sculpture, and decided to portray him at the time he joined Washington's army, defiant and confident, using his pen as a sword. The portrait was ultimately accepted and placed in the outside rotunda at the Hall of Fame.

SPAIN

During the period of my recovery, I had been continuing my study of the Spanish language at the YWCA. The Spaniard who taught us was intelligent and sympathetic, and he would often walk a little way with me after class and talk to me about his people. From what he said, I began to sense that there existed in Spain a shading of attitude and character profoundly different from any I had yet known. I wanted to find out for myself what it was.

There were other things I wanted to know: the land itself in its immediacy, the art, the feeling for life there.

Late in the spring of 1952, Peggy Cresson (Daniel Chester French's daughter) and I landed at Gibraltar at 9:00 P.M. in a pouring rain, from an over-crowded tender. On shore we read the inevitable sign: "Spain Welcomes You." Our first experience of the country was something short of welcoming. We were herded about like cattle and told to wait for our bags to be sorted alphabetically under a shed. After this lengthy procedure we were hurried into an omnibus with steps so high that most of the passengers had to be hoisted and pushed into it. Not five minutes away, after driving through the dark town, we were ordered out to present our passports. Another short drive, and on the other side of the frontier we were all hauled out again along with our baggage and set before the Spanish examiners whose manner did not seem up to the height of Castilian courtesy. It was midnight before we had dinner, at the Reina Cristina Hotel at Algeciras.

The following morning the weather had cleared, and the travel agent's promise, that we would be in a land of tropical gardens, was kept. The terraces were lined with orange trees aglow with their ripe fruit, and palm trees were waving their glittering plumes. I went down to interview the chauffeur, Gregorio, who had been engaged, with a Ford car, by an AAA letter from New York, and found in him too the generous fulfillment of a promise: gaunt, finely chiseled features, a man who had struggled against hardship but had retained a cheerful determination to make the best of whatever might be his lot.

Just to test my Spanish and Gregorio's resourcefulness, I proposed that we try to purchase a nylon undershirt for myself. In the stores this request produced temporary dismay; then the shopkeepers insisted on showing us what they felt would serve "just as well," including everything from heavy flannel "combinations" to purple petticoats with many flounces. Gregorio's sense of humor saved the situation and provided me with an excellent vocabulary never dreamed of in my many sessions of "Adult Education" at the YWCA.

At Jerez we stopped off to explore the renowned wine and brandy cellars of Gonzáles Byass and were offered frequent small glasses of the oldest brandy and less ancient "Tío Pepe"; these were followed by selected brands of sherries. My friend Peggy looked askance at Gregorio and me while we sipped and enjoyed the novelty of so many free libations. She frowningly warned us that the mountain roads were winding and that the rain had started again. By this time, however, the hard edges of reality had been softened; indeed, quite without any intention to falsify facts, when I came out into the courtyard from the dark cellars I exclaimed, "What a lovely day!" to the dour chill wind and rain.

Gregorio was persuaded to "drive slow," though he politely suggested we go at a quicker pace because "We go like caravan, perhaps I go sleep!" We did get to Seville where, at the wide, shady entrance parkway I was happy to see the equestrian statue of El Cid by our friend Anna Hyatt Huntington. From a double room on a narrow back street where we stayed, above the traffic of passing donkeys, we went, Sunday morning, to the sun-drenched magnificence of the Cathedral, and on the afternoon of this same day I was to gain an indelible insight into what I had come to Spain for, the link between worship and death.

Everywhere in the streets were posters for a bullfight which, if one may believe the repeated claim of posters, was this day to be exceptional. As Peggy pleaded not to go, Gregorio was my escort. We managed to get seats in the *Sombra,* or shaded part of the arena. I must admit that I myself had not lightly made the decision to go, and on our way to our seats I was aching from several hours of painful tension, from the thought that I would have to watch the unfortunate horses of the picadors being gored and tortured by the bulls. This apprehension had troubled me even more, possibly, than the thought of the death of the bulls themselves. I was not too much aware of going to the bullfight to find out about Spain, but when, fifteen minutes before the fight was to start, we were all packed in, row upon row, shoulder to shoulder, thousands of us in the stone seats that encircled that immense pit, I had a shiver of anticipation. This was not a sport, really. These people were very serious, and this anticipatory emotion had some deep, ardent relationship to the Church I had been in that morning.

I felt like an atom lost in a strange world; the dread of being caged in a mob began to overcome me, my heart pounded unevenly, and I wondered what would happen if I were to faint from sheer excitement. Gregorio, sensing my fears, reassured me that we were near an exit stairway and that I would enjoy it as soon as the real fight started, but that I must not stand up or try to escape while the bull was in the ring!

The trumpet blew; the great door on the opposite side of the arena was swung open. Two heraldic horsemen followed by three matadors and their aides on foot, the banderilleros, the picadors on horseback, and four mules with red cockades on their bridles marched across the arena to salute the Mayor in his box. The *cuadrilla* was ready. The Mayor threw the symbolic key into the ring, the signal that the fight could begin.

My relief was great when I saw that the picadors' horses were covered with heavy padded aprons; these hung around the right side of the horse, across the chest, around under his tail. From this moment I breathed more easily, being assured by Gregorio that the bull's horns would not penetrate this protective padding and that since the time of Primo de Rivera the law had insisted on this protection for the horse. Still, during the second round of the corrida, something unquestionably happened that I'm told is not supposed to happen: the bull heaved the horse up, and the momentum dismounted the picador and sent him flying over the fence. There was an instant while the bull balanced the horse on his shoulders and expanded his ribs that gave me my chance to fix the line in my mind—and then he shook the horse off against the bottom of the fence. There was the snap of the picador's shaft breaking like a rifle shot—your ear as well as eye was startled. The bull took a few good lunges at the fallen horse, whose padding had become displaced during the upheaval. Quickly the toreros distracted him and guided him away.

Certainly the courage, agility, and grace of the men were inspiring. Dynamic patterns were fixed into my mind, so open to such impressions. The plastic composition of the various passes—*Verónica; Farol,* standing or on the knees; *Chicuelina; Gaonera; Paso de la muerte*—these and others amazed me and focused my attention on every movement in spite of the conflicting urge to shut my eyes at the crucial moment, especially when the banderillero alone and without protection of any kind stands before the bull with two long darts, raising them high over his head and pointing them downward. Standing opposite the bull, on the balls of his feet, his body taut as a bow, he must judge the instant of the bull's charge, implant the steel darts on either side of the spinal column and, at the same moment, spring backward to escape the points of the horns as the beast plunges.

I managed to stay through the corrida, wanting to be part just once of this passion that has maintained control of all strata of Spanish society for so many centuries. I had read that Julius Caesar participated in bullfights and encouraged the sport, that the bull has been a symbol of religious sacrifice since the days when the blood of bulls was offered in rites of purification. But there was something more. It was the people themselves. It was an emotion and a silence that revealed the characteristic of the race to you. The silence hung over the emotion, and the emotion, that untrammeled roar, hung over the silence. It has to be experienced to be fully understood. Men, women, children all felt it coordinately. Especially at the "moment of truth," you'd see that silence going over the audience like a wave, and it was thick, that silence, it was impenetrable, you couldn't breathe. It was automatic. Nobody said, "Don't breathe. You mustn't speak." It just happened. They all held their breath at that moment. And now if at that moment the man pointing his sword at the bull, the matador, allowed his hand to tremble, if he in any way gave out the sensation that he was afraid, the entire arena would become aware of it instantaneously. And break into hisses. And throw things at him, into the pit.

Evidently it had something, this instantaneous reaction, to do with religion. Before entering the arena, the matador dedicated himself to the Madonna. But his dedication to the Madonna had to be complete. If he was offering his life to Her, what difference would it make whether he was killed in the first five minutes or the last five minutes of the bullfight? How could he at any time withdraw that offering?

This is the question that ran along his sword. And the answer would not be registered so irretrievably if he did not stand there immovable in front of the bull with his sword glittering, the strip of steel extended and cruelly showing any slightest vibration. The blade registered the tremble and ended him as a fighter.

I had learned something about Spaniards that helped me understand the whole country and the people. I felt I was under the skin of the outside. I was inside, able to know—beyond costumes, sounds, colors.

As Gregorio and I left the arena by that exit he had shown me earlier, I was aware that certain moments of the afternoon had made specific impressions on me as if recorded during a trance. I tried to put them down in sketches, but in spite of the awareness I had of an inalterable record in my memory, the sketches were failures. I knew that I would want to translate what I had seen into form, and that meant into sculpture. But I began to understand why the subject had been left to painters. It was difficult enough in two dimensions to capture the lightning of these split-second passes and patterns, these hypnotic compositions. To hope to add a third dimension for once seemed beyond me. And yet I continued seeking and yearning, and in the days that followed I found myself staring into space as if from the air I could recapture my first impressions and on the next attempt achieve more nearly what I was groping for.

I began to admire the perceptive art of many of the bullfight posters with their free forms and raw colors, done by Spanish artists to advertise who was going to participate on certain days. The artist would never be in exactly the same relationship to the fight that I had been, so the entire drawing would be different; but in many instances certain good sculpturesque ideas would be represented. Even from bad newspaper prints I could sometimes catch something, and I filled many notebooks with small drawings.

All these hints were centered upon a group of my own impressions that finally limited themselves to eight moments of the fight. I didn't try to make up anything from other sources, only to do these moments I had felt deeply myself. Nothing else, I knew, would have been convincing or meaningful.

In the meantime we continued our normal tourist activities. We used to spend afternoons in the Alcazar in the tropical gardens there, listening to birds and exploring terraces with topiary spirals and boxwood labyrinths. And driving through the Parc María Luisa, we visited the memorial to the Spanish poet Gustavo Adolf Bécquer, where I learned something else about the Spanish people. We found the memorial partly dismantled, the portrait shaft and its bust taken down, as well as the two seated figures of languishing ladies (because after many years sections of the base had been wedged apart by powerful tree roots), but still in recesses cut into the stone beside the seats there were copies of Bécquer's poems, and these books, we were told, if they were stolen, were always replaced by admirers of his. I thought of the poet's charming lines:

> Los suspiros son aire y van al aire.
> Las lágrimas son agua y van al mar.
> Dime, mujer: cuando el amor se olvida,
>   Sabes-tú adónde va?*

There is also that poet's "Volverán los oscuras golondrinas" (The dark swallows will return). These poems, romantic and tender, had endeared Spain to me long before I went there and had seemed to embody much of the evocative power of the Spanish language.

From Seville, we crossed the mountains and traveled by way of Jaén to the fabulous city of Granada. Seeing the crenelated red towers rising in the sky against the distant snow-capped Sierra Nevada Mountains glowing in shafts of sunlight, I found my breath catching, bewildered by beauty built into stone and brick, growing out of cliffs, piling up on the edge of precipices drenched with color.

---

* *Sighs are air, and turn to air.*
Tears are water, and go to the sea.
Tell me, woman: when love is forgotten
   Do you know where it goes?

The Alhambra remains the symbol of all the best and highest achievements of Moorish art and architecture, and this art has long haunted my imagination. I thought of the Moors in their white robes who once filled the halls here and wandered in the courtyards and gardens. Everywhere there was the sound of water. I heard that magical sound in archways of spray thrown across long narrow pools, in runnels that fell over rocky walls into and out of terraces, in the flow of water along channeled stone stair rails from one level to another.

Gregorio, who had been of invaluable service to us and whose face, marked with suffering, had been a sign to me of the strength and endurance and good humor of the Spaniard, now reported that he had another tour to attend to and that he must take leave of us. We felt a genuine regret. He had helped us with more than driving. He had steadily sensed our needs, had interpreted for us, and had generally bridged us over to the meaning of the life we had come to Spain to acquaint ourselves with.

Without a car now, Peggy and I took a night train to Madrid. As the sharp shafts of sunlight came through the edges of the window shades, I woke early and dressed and went to the dining car. There was only one unoccupied seat, which I promptly took, noticing a smartly dressed Spaniard across the table from me. In my best YWCA-student accent, I tried out *"Buenos días* on him and he replied hopefully in French, handing me the menu. I realized he suspected my limitations in Spanish; luckily my French was good and his more than good, so we talked together easily while the waiter brought my *café doble* and rolls. "Is this your first visit to Spain?" he asked, and from that we went to gypsies (I had seen much of gypsies) and from that to the composer Granados, and then for some reason we discussed Siamese cats. His interest in cats recommended him to me. Without too much connection, he told me he had been an architect, but was now making a collection of photographs, "Castles in Spain," pictures that he himself was taking of some of the finer Spanish "châteaux." He asked me if I'd care to see them one day while I was in Madrid.

The invitation appealed to me, and I phoned him: the name on his card was Loygorri Pimentel. A big collection of his photographs had just returned from an exhibition in Holland, he said on the phone, and it would be worth my while to come. When I arrived, he gave me a packet of slides which he told me to project on a screen in his study while he finished developing a strip of pictures. Never had I seen such magnificent views of castles and fortresses and dramatic Andalusian skies. When I had run through the slides, I felt as if I had never before realized the vastness of Spain and its architectural treasures.

Across the semidarkened room, I noticed a row of glittering blue eyes, three silent and secretive Siamese cats tucked into the pillows of a couch. Just then Mr. Loygorri returned from his laboratory in a long blue apron. From the large pocket I saw the furry head and bright blue eyes of a Siamese kitten peering out. He explained that this little creature was his mascot and constant companion. I felt an immediate affinity to this family setup, and it added greatly to my pleasure while my host unpacked the exhibit of his photographs just returned from Holland and set them around the room, ovewhelming me with still more pictorial wonders, each castle, fortress, or landscape (which he identified for me) having its dramatic backdrop of clouds.

This one visit was the end of our actual meeting in Spain, but the fragile little kitten enabled us to continue the friendship in letters, for when my own Siamese cat Kiki died, I sent Mr. Loygorri the fluffy blue sweater Kiki had worn for one of his own cats that was ailing, and he wrote that she lived in it from the day he received it.

It was following my visit to Mr. Loygorri that on a balmy spring morning Peggy and I drove to the Escorial. This vast edifice backed by a sky piled up with dark clouds made me think of Mr. Loygorri's photographs. But this particular scene also seemed to us strikingly evocative of an El Greco painting and, after lunch, with thunder and lightning added, we were impressed by the veracity of the great painter's powers of observation. I knew the intensity of effort it takes to memorize essentials, and then there is an element that goes beyond effort, and that is the instantaneous power of the scene. This renewed consciousness of the registering power of the immediate scene took me back to Seville and the bull-ring there, with all its troubling aftermath.

In this mood, imagine my surprise and delight when I noticed what seemed like an astoundingly familiar form beside the road—Gregorio. He was there, some ten days after we had left him, chauffeuring his new party. We had thought, when we said good-bye, that we might well never see him again in our lives. One may imagine how enthusiastic our greeting was.

Our stay in Spain was coming to an end. Peggy and I had one more major interest: the prehistoric drawings on the roof of the caves of Altamira in the northwestern corner of the country. These were near the ancient village of Santillana where we stayed. When I asked how far we were from the Altamira Caves: "Only a short walk, Señora. You follow the road signs and climb the hill until you reach the guardian's cottage." I started off at once, eager for what I would see. Peggy said she would join me later by taxi.

At the entrance cottage, a friendly guardian invited me to come in and rest in the cool shade of his hallway. My rudimentary knowledge of Spainsh struggled into action again. I explained as well as I could that I was an American artist, a sculptor, and friend of Abbé Breuil whose book on Altamira I had studied, and that he and Henry Field, formerly of the Field Museum of Chicago, had often spoken to me of these caves and their art. The face of the guardian lighted up with bright recognition of these names. "Oh, Señora, the Abbé spent four months here when he measured and copied these wonderful paintings so carefully and faithfully."

He put on his coat, picked up a flashlight, and led the way to the nearby iron gateway set into a stone entrance in the side of the hill. I confess that a feeling of eerie apprehension came over me at the thought that I was about to enter a place of such antiquity and that the gateway to the dwelling of the prehistoric warriors of this Cantabrian coast was now open for me, letting me freely explore the hidden mysteries of the ice age, as if glacial rivers and herds of huge woolly elephants might rush upon us.

Peggy had joined me, and we waited like enchanted children as the guide turned on an electric switch, lighting up the extraordinary paintings that covered the roughly formed ceiling, paintings still brilliant and fresh in color, having withstood the ravages of time in their dark gallery. After studying the designs of the life-size primitive animals, I began to detect the undulating surface of the ceiling itself. The prehistoric artist had obviously studied this before beginning his painting, for the actual protrusions and crevices were taken advantage of and used to emphasize and add modeling to the frescoes in a most discerning manner. His skill and draftsmanship, as well as his astounding knowledge of anatomy and of the motion of animals, were evident everywhere. I was reminded of the strong sure sense of line and motion in our American Indian paintings—a sort of blood-and-bone affinity between artist and animal. Obviously he could observe his prey in action while hunting, but afterward he was forced to draw from memory on the ceiling of a cave where only the flickering flare of a fire or torch helped him detect the rough forms and fill in large areas of the bodies with a mixture of animal grease and blood, red earth and ocher, using black burned wood for the outlines.

This was the end of our visit to Spain except for a short trip to the seaside resort of San Sebastián where, in 1929, I had modeled a rugged type of Basque peasant for the Hall of Man. Now my interest was the Prehistoric and Folklore Museum that adjoins the large chapel of San Telmo. My respect for the genus Man, to which I had given an important part of my life, had not been diminished by my recent view of his historic and prehistoric legacy. And the vigor of the Stone Age art I had just seen, with its direct confrontation of man and animal, was related in my mind to that other confrontation I had seen in Seville that, though ritualized and distanced into choreography, was still the same facing of death.

I took with me from Spain a several-volume history of Spanish bullfighting by Cossío. It was hard to read with my still relatively elementary knowledge of the language, but it trained me in Spanish, a useful by-product, and it had endless technical information—pictures of all the different types of bulls and their way of charging, for example. In the matter of charging, I learned how important a knowledge of the bull's vision is. In the first five minutes, the matador has to find out whether the bull has better vision in one eye than the other, and if so, he handles himself accordingly. Like a magician exerting a spell, if he wants to be sure the bull will respond, he uses the better sight. If he wants to put the bull at a disadvantage, he uses the poorer sight.

Only after this study could I do drawings that began effectively to embody my impressions. I learned the whole anatomy of the bull so well that I could draw a bull in any position I wanted, knowing how he was hooked together inside his skin. Only in that way, no longer needing to take time to refer back to authorities, could I draw spontaneously.

I did this studying after I returned to Paris. I went to my Paris home and stayed there through the summer and fall and then returned to New York. In New York, in the winter of 1952–1953, I began doing the actual sculpture, using my new knowledge, my sketches, and especially those searing moments during which the fight had fixed and focused itself in my memory. I worked on a stand I could easly revolve all the time, to get an all-the-way-around position of the man and the bull and their relationship to each other. The toreros were so built that they reminded me immediately of the Russian dancers, those strategists of space whose discipline demanded an equal, almost parallel, consecration.

Toreros practiced for hours on a tanbark floor, jumping backward on their toes so that they would not lose their balance if something was coming at them that they had to avoid in an emergency. The same kind of exercises were essential to dancers too, and they practiced them as endlessly. They had to develop ankle strength that would allow them to turn either foot to an impossible position without its shaking. They even spoke of their "emergency muscles." Pavlova exercised these muscles so that she could fall down unintentionally in such a way that she was never suspected of having fallen down, and she would ask me, if it happened during a rehearsal I was watching, if I'd noticed she had changed the pose. I would say, "Yes, I noticed," and she would say, "Well, I lost my balance and I had to cover." It was her training and control that gave her such skill as this that it could conceal a mistake with an improvisation. She'd all the time be telling students, "Strengthen your ankles. Balance, balance, balance." She'd always be using that word, and then she would wheel around to me and say, "I mean you too on ladders, going up and down ladders; I know, I've seen you in your studio. You stand on one foot and use your other foot as a balance. Yes, you couldn't prance around like that if you hadn't trained your feet to hold your whole body." And she would laugh. But that mastery of the feet and ankles is no laughing matter to a bullfighter or a dancer. It is basic, and the safety it represents is manufactured with infinite pains.

Beginner's scales—some students want to slough them off too, and start playing pieces. But the great players go over these scales so much you'd think they would become maddened, on and on and on, but they know the importance of shading from one finger to the other until they get just the effect they want.

In January I worked on "The Picador," a horse-and-bull group, struggling to get a convincing composition in three dimensions. I had been told in Spain that this would be impossible, and this challenge incited me. The daily hours of work continued into evening when I would again study anatomy and technique, to keep my knowledge of them instantaneously available and automatic. "The Picador" group resolved itself. The figure of the matador pointing his sword at the bull in "The Moment of Truth" I also managed to complete. Although I had begun "The Banderillero" some weeks earlier, this took me a long time to finish. The problem was to raise the man and the forward part of the bull up in the air with only the hind legs of the bull supporting this entire weight; but I had a feeling it would hold together satisfactorily when cast, and I was determined to reproduce this stroboscopic action fixed so firmly in my memory.

Work continued through the following winter, and then I finished the eight pieces I had planned. Now I decided to have a little exhibit to show why I was so concentrated all winter and had not gone out anywhere practically, just stayed home working. People don't understand that you have to work so hard and that there are no shortcuts. If there are, although I've lived rather long, I have never found any. I have to *work* my way through to knowledge, and there never seems any other way to get it.

I built a circular fence in my studio in the shape of an arena, and hung it with red and orange cloth, and inside this I put eight stands the same height as the fence, to hold the pieces. There were bullfight posters around, and I used hangings to cover any extraneous things so that the background was plain—just the arena and the bronze pieces. It was carefully planned to have an effect.

At about that time I heard of an exhibit of paintings by a Spanish painter named Francisco Coll. He was a lawyer by profession, but he had observed bullfights meticulously and was a very able and swift draftsman, as I found out when I visited his show. The gallery was filled with convincing and exciting work, and everything, so far as I could see, was marked "Sold." The woman in charge said, "Yes, there are only a half dozen drawings left." I was surprised. Who in New York knew the authenticity of this work or was interested? I had an impulse. I wrote a little note and left it for Mr. Coll, saying I didn't know know him, but I wanted to offer my congratulations. I had been to Spain and had done some bullfighting sculpture and would he like to come down to see my corrida? If he came, he might wish to bring with him whatever of his own was left unsold and set it around on my furniture—I was having some people in, and he might be able to sell the balance of his work. He came, set out his drawings from his portfolio as I had suggested, and after the people arrived

"Matador and Dying Bull"

"The Picador"

"The Banderillero"

and they had had enough champagne or punch and found him fun (he was very entertaining and spoke English well), they bought his work, all of it. And so he was sold out.

There were, meanwhile, purchases of my own work. John W. Davis, the lawyer who was formerly Ambassador to the Court of St. James's and who ran for President against Calvin Coolidge, was sitting on a high stool staring at the corrida and particularly at one of the bulls. He said: "You know, you call that a dying bull. He isn't dying."

I said: "No, that was a mistake. I'm glad you noticed it. He's just got his head down."

He said: "Yes, so have I. I've got my head down, but my horns are all right and I intend to keep on living and pushing. And I'd like to buy that bull."

He set the bull up in his apartment, and his sister, who inherited it from him, told me it was one of his dearest possessions.

The sale of this bull pleased me because it was so unexpected and spontaneous, and after that there were a number of sales. Mrs. Agnes Milliken bought another bull, and I sold "The Moment of Truth" and "The Banderillero." Later, Leo Cherne saw some of the bullfight pieces at the Tourist Office of the Spanish Travel Agency, and asked if there wasn't a "Picador"; and they told him that there was but that it was at my studio—they had been afraid of criticism by the SPCA if they put that one on display. So Mr. Cherne came to my studio and bought "The Picador" and another of the pieces for his office, where he already had a bull done by Rosa Bonheur's brother Isidor.

So my effort was well repaid and I was as happy as Mr. Coll. My friendly assist to him was to have an unforeseen result. He read my book *Heads and Tales*, and determined to translate it into Spanish. On a later trip abroad I went over a substantial part of his translation with him, but this was the last time I was to see Mr. Coll alive. Not too much later this agreeable, talented man passed away while writing me a letter to tell me about his progress with the book.

CHAPTER THIRTY-SIX

TRANSATLANTIC SEASONS

To RETURN to the late spring of 1952 when I came back to Paris from Spain. I had to go through a period of readjustment from the immediacy of that intense emotional experience. My little garden with the faithful white rosebushes in bloom helped me readjust.

We started cleaning and painting the villa. Brittany-blue paint began to shine on the window frames, and with effort some of the scars of former tenants were gradually removed. Édouard Schuré's grand piano was tuned and made ready for music.

Newspapers from New York announced the death on June 13, 1952, of Emma Eames. My memory went back to her standing beside this same piano, singing, so she told me, for the last time. It had started with our asking her to sing Baudelaire's *L'Invitation au voyage*. She said she couldn't; she didn't believe she had any voice left at all. Sam said, "You can't know unless you try." She said, "Let me whisper it," and so, without accompaniment, it came back little by little; she forgot her fears as the melody sustained her, and at the end she was singing with a beautiful clear tone, much to her own astonishment.

One day, Grace Frick and Marguerite Yourcenar phoned that they would come to see me, and this revived one of the memorable experiences of my recent trip, an evening in Granada that I spent on the hillside of the Albaicín. A series of cave dwellings cut in the rock there had been used to shelter Moorish refugees in the fifteenth century, but these refugees were burned out and massacred during the following century. Then the gypsies moved into the caves, fitting them up with odd collections of furniture, stiff unpainted chairs, brass bedsteads, and any trinket they cherished. Now they showed their dances and played typical music on certain evenings for the visiting tourists who were escorted by guides from their hotels, or driven in taxis up the steep winding roads to the entrances of the larger caves. The night I went, girls costumed in orange and white polka-dotted ruffled skirts smiled and showed their glittering white teeth. Some older women, keeping more aloof, took their seats around the edge of the low-ceilinged cave; a crowd of eager-eyed youngsters gathered at the entrance; and a few rather dark and beady-eyed young men in tight-fitting trousers and silk shirts paired off with the girl dancers. The party got off to a rather awkward, self-conscious start. Presently the tempo quickened and the gypsies clapped and started shouting; the serious guitar players forgot the tourists, and the dancers whirled and stamped their heels with ever-increasing fervor. One eight-year-old girl worked herself into an almost trancelike state of ecstasy dancing with a boy twelve years old, and they quite outdid all their older rivals.

I had in the meantime noticed two ladies sitting opposite me—one of these was Grace Frick, and we smiled at each other, for she had recognized me by my white felt tam-o'-shanter. Just then the eight-year-old gypsy finished her wild but excellent performance, and dashed over to her fat mother next to whom I was sitting. The child tried hard to sit on her mother's lap, but slipped off twice. I told her to try sitting on my lap, which she did with alacrity and I at once felt more at home, and a part of the show.

When we left, Miss Frick and her companion, whom she introduced to us as Mlle. Marguerite Yourcenar, taxied with me back to our hotel. The following day was an important one in Mlle. Yourcenar's life, as it happened. There at the hotel she received a telegram from her publishers in Paris that her novel, *Les mémoires d'Hadrien*, had just been awarded the Prix Fémina, one of the leading annual French literary prizes. I had since my return to Paris read the novel and enjoyed its extraordinary re-creation of the travels and accomplishments of the Emperor Hadrian, as if one became an integral part of that Roman emperor.

Miss Frick made the distinguished translation of the book into English, and perhaps was at work on it at the time they called on me in Paris. They had just come from a visit to Marie Laurencin, and brought with them two small oil paintings, portraits of themselves, that she had presented to them. We reminisced about our Spanish experiences, the marvels of Granada and of that Spain where Hadrian was born and to which he had returned; we recalled the gypsies and our evening of the caves and our perilous taxi trip up and down the mountain roads.

I had just been re-reading Flaubert's *La Légende de St. Julien l'Hospitalier*, and mentioned how its climax haunted my imagination and, since my visitors were sympathetic, I told them how I had gone, under its influence, to see the church of St. Julien le Pauvre, finding it a place of shadowy silence and meditation.

A certain look came over Mlle. Yourcenar's strongly framed face, as if she was aware of the influence of such moods.

Eugène Rudier's Funeral

Soon after this I received news of the death of Eugène Rudier. It seemed like the conclusion of a great period of art, and it caused consternation both among his workmen and among the many sculptors who would now hardly know how to get along without this *maître-fondeur*. His funeral was held at the foundry. In the courtyard we had gathered early in the morning. The bier was set on a platform, surrounded by tall white candles; in the background was Rodin's "Gate of Hell," and on the sides the huge lead figures and dragons of the Versailles fountains that were being rearmatured and strengthened. These silent witnesses added a dramatic effect. Monsieur Marcel Aubert of the Rodin Museum read a tribute. On either side of the entrance was a gigantic wreath, one from the foundry workmen, the other from the Musée Rodin. Madame Rudier, aged eighty-six, walked at the head of the cortège all the way to the church with many of us following her behind the bier. At the church, after the High Mass, Fauré's *Requiem* was sung.

One day, later in the summer, I drove again to Malakoff where Madame Rudier and the workmen were about to cast the last piece before the ovens were cooled off for the final dismantling of this famous foundry. It turned out to be my portrait of Eugène Rudier made in 1932, and it was impressive to watch the aged widow of Rodin's *fondeur* standing motionless beside the glowing ovens, overseeing every move made by the workmen as they poured the molten metal into the sand mold. She told me she was going to present the portrait of her husband to the Rodin Museum, and this she later did. It was placed in the hall of bronzes upstairs in the Hôtel Biron.

Since my return from Spain, I had picked up the threads of the Épinal project and consulted with the French architect who represented Mr. Delano in this undertaking. Various plans had developed for my visiting Épinal with some government officials, but constant postponements kept me rather on edge. I was naturally anxious to have the work started in time so that I could see the proportions pointed up on the wall before my departure.

At long last Colonel Falks of the A.B.M.C. picked me up at seven o'clock one morning for the drive to Épinal. The last sections of stone were being set into the "attic" of the memorial and I had an extended conference with Monsieur Juge, the chief carver. At the start of work, in my studio in New York, I had considered the condition under which visitors arriving would view the façade of the memorial. It would be generally a midday light from overhead and would require heavy undercutting. To simulate the condition, I had arranged overhead lights in the studio, but even so, it was hard to tell how it would come out in stone, on the final location. With the help of the enlarged photos of the panels that I had brought with me, I was able to explain to Monsieur Juge some of the effect I wanted.

VISIT TO LONDON

In the beginning of September, I left for London where I saw a comprehensive exhibit, at the Royal Academy, of Leonardo da Vinci's paintings, drawings, and inventions.

A few days later I lunched with Sir Osbert Sitwell in his beguiling home in Carlyle Gardens, the walls covered with pictures, many of them colorful clever ones, the furniture in the sun-drenched drawing room shining with its gold-and-white baroque carvings and decorations, all kinds of colored glass sparkling on the shelves and tables, and gay watercolors making even the walls join in with such bright sparkle as I had never seen in a room before. I followed Sir Osbert through the rather dark halls across the courtyard in the back where we lunched in a candlelit dining room. At coffee I read him a quotation from Byron that I had come across browsing in the King's Library at the British Museum, copying down verses from original manuscripts on display:

> How sweet it were in concert to adore
> With those who made our mortal labors light,
> To hear each voice we feared to hear no more,
> Behold each mighty shade revealed to sight,
> The Bactrian Samian Sage and all who taught the Right . . .

The last lines of this quote from *Childe Harold's Pilgrimage* intrigued me, for I could not fathom who this Samian Sage might be. I asked Sir Osbert if he knew. "I think there is a Bactrian wine," he said. "Now we must find the Samian Sage."

"Pythagoras, perhaps?" I ventured, but he was doubtful. "Let's write Marianne Moore. She will know, I'm sure!" so we did, and by return mail came her answer—Zoroaster.

I went with Stella Reading to her country home, Swanborough Manor at Lewes in Sussex, and the following morning I took a plane back to Paris, where I had an appointment to meet Henry de Monfreid, the adventurer and author. We had not met since 1937, and we caught up on the news about each other. He confessed dolefully that he was seventy-seven years old, but he still seemed active and resilient. He showed me his watercolors made in Africa, and also his latest book, *Tombeau des Éléphants*. His most successful book, he told me, was *Secrets de la Mer Rouge*. He asked me if I could model his portrait if he posed for two days; I agreed to try, and to our mutual surprise and pleasure it came off well! I gave him the original plaster after having it cast into bronze, planning to exhibit this at the annual show at the National Academy in New York.

Returning to New York, I felt very much under par, and consulted Dr. Simard, who managed to get me fixed up in time to attend an evening at the Alliance Française at the Plaza Hotel during which M. Jean de Lagarde, the French Consul, was to bestow upon me the Order of the Chevalier de la Légion d'Honneur. My mind was in a trance from the effects of drugs and apprehension, and I could not hear the words of the citation. At the close, however, I caught sight of my wonderful friend Père Teilhard sitting in the first row; this unexpected view of him startled me out of my state of semiconsciousness and revived me.

A few days later, I had the good fortune to meet the French actor Jean-Louis Barrault, who electrified us all by his flashing intelligence. A great pantomimist, he showed us in slow motion how, on the level floor of the stage, he created the optical illusion of seeming to be climbing stairs. In a spirit of fun, I suggested that he should dress as Pierrot and go to Wall Street at night when it was deserted, especially if there was a moon hanging over the spire of Trinity Church. He had been there, he said, by day, but would surely return with this new thought for a ballet that he might call *Pierrot in Wall Street*. When, on a return engagement to New York he carried out the idea, I found it exhilarating to view it from the audience as a finished number. The scenic effect was produced by a cleverly arranged moving picture thrown on the backdrop curtain. He called the sketch *Adieu to New York*, and gave it at his last performance.

PORTRAIT PROBLEMS AGAIN

The Rutgers University Board of Trustees commissioned me to do a portrait of Dr. Selman A. Waksman, who had just won the Nobel Prize for biochemistry with his discovery of streptomycin and aureomycin. From the first sitting I realized that it was going to be a difficult problem to persuade this overworked and tired scientist to remain in the studio long enough for the kind of intuitive observation I would need to interpret his "inner man." Seldom, indeed, did a sitting last two hours. This brought on the exhausting effort, between seances, of working from memory and photographs far into the night, and I was almost desperate when, at one of the sittings, he stated he could not pose again. I had to add his right arm and hand in one hour and achieve a result satisfactory to us both. His kindly good nature made it impossible for me to insist on his giving me more time. In spite of these difficulties, I felt that the final portrait had caught much of his essential character, of concentration and humanity. As to the quality of his humanity, I was well aware that he had generously given all the royalties from his discovery to Rutgers University; to date these had amounted to $2,400,000, to be used to build an Institute of Research.

Guldie and I sailed for France on May 6, 1953. Our first day in Paris began with a transport strike that paralyzed buses and subways; and a few days later electricity and gas companies shut off most of the power, and some of the trains were taken off, so it was not difficult to realize that France was without a government. Nothing dramatic ensued, however.

My back went lame again after working in the garden for a while, and made me remember that not so long ago I had been unable to move as a result of muscle spasms and phlebitis. How quickly one can forget pain!

I drove to the Gare de Lyons to welcome Agnes Milliken arriving from Rome. We had planned a trip the following day to the Vosges Mountains to see the carving on my Battle Monuments Building. After taking a train to Nancy, we drove in a taxi an hour and a half to Épinal and had our first impression of the full-size carving in stone. The design was legible and clear, and the south façade seemed nearing completion except for the inscription on each side of the eagle and all around the building under the cornice. Juge the carver and I examined the joints in the stones; I was shocked to see that they were uneven and filled with white cement, and I insisted that this must be corrected and that he also make changes in certain areas where the drawing was inaccurate. The panel representing War called for many corrections and more accurate pointing. As a whole, however, the effect was better than I had dared to hope.

CORONATION WEEK

After this excursion, I packed up to go to London for Coronation Week. I was guest of the Milliken clan in a fairy-tale adventure—my first trip on the deluxe British through train the "Golden Arrow." I stayed in a charming little flat in London. We visited the British Museum, and I was glad to see some of my old favorites again, especially the Kwannan Goddess from Japan. I had actually seen the workmen carving this same wooden figure out of a tree over one hundred years old when I was in Japan in 1931.

In the afternoon we went to my cousin Herbert Haseltine's distinguished show of bronzes of domestic animals and Indian maharajas set up in his usual perfect style, red damask hangings, shadow boxes, and special lighting.

One day I motored with Ruth Draper to see Sir Arthur Keith at Downe, Kent, taking along fruit and flowers. He was happy to welcome us with his Scotch bonnet on his head and his "Malvina"—the warm Shetland shawl I had given him—wrapped around his shoulders. He showed us all over the Darwin house, put on Darwin's top hat, and sat in the chair in which Darwin wrote his *Origin of Species*. Sir Arthur's mind was as alert and keen as ever, and his eyes still twinkled.

Coronation Day, June 2, 1953, was one of drenching rain and bitter wind, the coldest June 2nd on record since 1871. We rose at 6:30 A.M., had a good cup of tea, and drove to the Dorchester Hotel, where we arrived before the crash gates closed at 7:00 A.M. Here we saw the coronation on TV and later went to the outdoor stand that overlooked a long stretch bordering Hyde Park and commanding a splendid view of the procession. In spite of a pouring rain, they marched past in regal grandeur, the water streaming down the faces and bodies of riders and horses. The Queen and the Duke of Edinburgh drove in the golden coach drawn by eight white horses, the young sovereign waving her hand and smiling with gracious dignity to the thousands of her subjects, who greeted her with thunderous cheers.

Agnes Milliken and her sister motored me to the airport at Heathrow the following morning where, after seeing me off on the plane for Paris, they presented the small second-version bronze of my portrait of Thomas Paine to the village of Thetford, his birthplace.

In Paris the weather had changed, and it was bright and sunny. Gifts of flowers arrived at the villa, and we were kept busy trying to arrange them. The big room was so lovely with every vase filled that it made me want to paint it. So I bought canvas, oil colors, and brushes at the art store at Montparnasse and started in painting one of the flower arrangements in the big room with the casement windows thrown open. This new experiment in color values was such a change from sculpture that it acted as a fine recreation. But while advancing two steps I felt I slipped back three in my painting efforts, and could only console myself with the words of Paul Valéry in discussing the artist whose *"peine bien aimée le fortifie"*! (well-loved suffering strengthens him).

I also happened to read, at this time, Flaubert's notes on his writing of *Salammbô*, six years of constant corrections and revisions to produce this one book. By a curious power of suggestion, it put me suddenly in the mood to work again on my own long-delayed autobiography. If his courage and patience could only be contagious!

At the end of my Paris stay, I went again to Épinal to supervise the finishing of the carving of the angel.

THE ROAD MARKER

Back home, I was asked to design a granite road marker, ten feet high, for the Milliken Mills in South Carolina. Here was a chance to think in another direction, to do something contemporary in feeling, original and functional. All my life it has been my practice to take any kind of commission that was offered me, however unexpected it might be or unfamiliar to me. And just because I have been adventurous that way, expecting the unexpected, I have in a sense prepared for it by learning all I could as I went along.

Before attempting to do the Milliken Mills marker, I went down to South Carolina to see the site where it would be placed. It was to point down a small side road off a main highroad, and it would have to be conspicuous, even startling, because cars would go by on the highroad at high speeds. It had to stop them.

I also wanted to see the industrial plant the marker would point to, so that I could make a design that would fit it. The mill, I discovered, was a perfectly modern, flat-top, windowless, enormous plant totally unexpected in that area. An arrow-like shape began to take form in my mind, which would be in character with that plant, jutting out annexes and additions, but with no break in the roof line. The arrow would be held aloft by a stone strut lunging forward in the direction of the arrow, and up this strut would run a row of stone threads from stone bobbins. The name of the mill would be in raised letters on the arrow and on a circle the arrow would transpierce.

My client approved this design, and the model was given to the carvers. Finished, it was set up at the junction of highway and mill road, and I must say there have been no complaints that it failed to do its job.

CHAPTER THIRTY-SEVEN

ITALY AND RETURN

THE DOCTORS, after my muscle spasm and phlebitis attack, were still trying to build up my strength, but I certainly did not feel normal or even fit for work. Dogged persistence can drive one for a period and make survival possible, but the signals were set; I knew there were "dangerous curves ahead" if I did not plan a long and complete holiday. For some reason I had a sudden longing to see Italy again. I hadn't been there since 1910, my first trip abroad with Mother.

In keeping with this spirit of "remembrance of things past," a few days before leaving I attended our fiftieth class reunion of the Brearley School. Twelve of us gathered at the Cosmopolitan Club for luncheon before the ceremony at the school building. As one would expect, we scrutinized one another carefully. To our surprise and pleasure we recalled first names and found many who had worn their years with grace.

The Alumni Association had arranged in the adjoining hall a large showing of photographs of my work, and the Spring 1954 Bulletin had included an illustrated article showing portraits, racial types, dancers, and bullfighting groups, a sort of chronological survey of fifty years of hard work, adventure, and travel.

Travel! As I began the long boat trip to Naples on the *Independence*, I found it a welcome change after the final exhausting days of packing and closing the studios, and my companions—Agnes Milliken and her granddaughter Anne Stroud, aged ten—were diverting and gay fellow voyageurs.

Going to a country without knowing the fundamentals of the language has always seemed a mistake to me, so I had been taking Italian lessons again, and studied quite diligently, until now I could at least make myself understood and read well enough to find my way about in shops and restaurants.

350

THE BREARLEY SCHOOL, CLASS OF 1904—MH IN CENTER OF REAR ROW

We landed at Genoa, where we took a drive up to the hilltops back of the city and enjoyed feeling terra firma again. From there we sailed on to Naples, where the approach evoked memories of my trip with Mother long ago; but now, in contrast, all practical problems were taken care of; by some magic wand the customs were behind us and we had a hotel room with a balcony view over the bay to Vesuvius. From Naples we motored to Pompeii and Herculaneum, and crossed the verdant country to Grottaferrata to Villa Senni, the house of Agnes's sister Mary, who was married to Count Senni. Numerous members of the family welcomed us, and Mary's pleasure in seeing Agnes after a year's absence added to the gaiety of the family reunion. Mary, Countess Senni, had lived so long in Italy that it was difficult to realize she was an American and a true matriarch, iron-willed and goodhearted. She adored gardening and raised roses and irises of notable splendor.

We took many side trips from the Villa Senni, including a day's visit to Lauro, where an old friend of Count Senni's, Prince Lancelotti, lived with his daughter in a sixteenth century fortified castle perched on a precipitous cliff high above the little town.

Then I moved to the Minerva Hotel in the old quarter of Rome on the square designated by a white obelisk on the back of a chunky stone elephant. Here I was able to get a quiet little room where I was surrounded by roses given me when I left Villa Senni. I wanted to absorb all the impressions I had had to experience so quickly.

I ventured forth to walk about the quarter, and girded myself to face the miles of sculpture in the Vatican Museum. I visited the museum in the Baths of Diocletian where I found two of my first loves in marble—the Cyrene Aphrodite and the Kneeling Boy. Their everlasting beauty renewed my faith in the immortality of perfection.

One day, an unanticipated pleasure, the Sennis took me to visit the picturesque home of Princess Caetani. Hidden away—remote from any city or even town—she and her husband managed to cultivate a romantic garden beside a rushing mountain stream. The ruins of Ninfa, within which Prince Caetani rebuilt a house of stone, were originally part of a lost village of early Roman days. From this house, despite utter isolation, without a car of her own or even a telephone, the Princess kept in close touch with the literary activities of contemporary poets and writers, and published the famous quarterly review *Botteghe Oscure*. After tea in the enchanted garden, we motored up the sharp hill road to Cori, where Gianandrea Senni proved himself an ace in driving through winding streets just wide enough to permit his "Fiat 1400" to reach the topmost terrace of the temple site. The Greek Temple of Hercules commands a magnificent view of the country.

. A final visit at Villa Senni, and I moved on to Florence, where I was met by two Dominican Sisters in charge of the Art Institute of Pius XII. This is near Fiesole, in the former Villa Schifanoia of Mr. and Mrs. Myron C. Taylor, who gave it a few years ago to the Pope as a place for studying music and the arts. In New York, before I sailed, Mr. Taylor had invited me to visit the villa, and the visit was timed with his and his wife's arrival to hear the student musicians give a recital. There were about twenty students, some of them Sisters who came from America, Greece, Yugoslavia, and Italy.

One day we went to Mr. Bernard Berenson's villa, I Tatti, with its renowned library and gardens, perhaps the most romantic in all Italy. I confess to a pleasurable lift when the librarian pointed to my own two books on one of the library shelves.

A surprise was waiting as the train drew into the Milan station. I saw my good friends Marquis de Rosales, the sculptor, and his wife standing on the platform. Though we had not seen each other for twenty-seven years, we recognized each other, and it was a heartwarming reunion. Rosales had been my teacher in Paris before the First World War, when he was on the crest of his career as a sculptor. His many kindnesses to me and his invaluable guidance in my modeling were never forgotten, and through the years of separation we always kept informed of each other's activities.

That summer my Paris home was again a place of work after the relaxation of my Italian trip, and at the end of the summer I had a new experience of renting. Lydia Foote, the daughter of my good friend Anne Archbold in Washington, had seen some paintings that I had made of my garden and villa, and wanted to try her luck there. Happily, the venture turned out well. She enjoyed her stay and made friends with the neighbors.

Back in New York, I had periodic visits from Father Teilhard de Chardin that brought a new light into the routine of my working days—a new light on art. I have never been one to ask too many questions, but I had been thinking about modern art ever since the Armory Show at the beginning of the century. I'm not easily able to become passionate about new ideas and movements. As an example: Matisse and Picasso—some of Picasso's early paintings convinced me, but I was not at all receptive to his later work. Or Henry Moore. When he began, I was surprised, but interested, and when he did the drawings during the war, I admired his skill in handling crowds, how he could bring them down into a very simple kind of drawing—a tour de force. But his later work, like Picasso's later work and much of the art of my time, troubled me. Then Father Teilhard reminded me of the rule: *Reculer pour mieux sauter.* (One draws back the better to leap forward). Progress in art, as in everything, is not limited to periods of five or ten years—or even fifty or a hundred. These times of tension and controversy may be signaling a change for the better, because even a grappling battle is good—somebody gets close to somebody else. And in the process, it may even be stimulating for our inner beings to have to try so hard to understand.

What Father Teilhard told me about art was only part of his optimistic message that went beyond art and even beyond the narrow limits of theologic argument to present the rising line of human evolution in which he believed with such a burning brightness of faith.

Occasionally he would come to the studio or I would see him at the homes of friends. He told me he was preparing to give a series of lectures at the Wenner-Gren Foundation, and later I attended these lectures that enlarged his general theory. Since he was busy, I didn't see him often, but he was one who could make you feel close to him in spite of his preoccupations, and I was grateful to be one of the group of his friends.

Although he appeared frail and frequently referred to the need of preparing oneself to end well, we were none of us in any way alerted to the proximity of his death, which occurred on Easter Day, 1955. After attending Mass in the Cathedral, he took a walk in Central Park and went to a friend's house for tea in the afternoon. There he was stricken with a heart attack, and died immediately.

His funeral service was a simple Mass in the Church of St. Ignatius Loyola.

CHAPTER THIRTY-EIGHT

FINALE TO MORTALITY— ALMOST

IN EARLY JULY I moved to Kittery, Maine, to spend a month with Marianne Moore in the Louis Hydes' house. This was a little sea captain's house with a steep wooden staircase that led originally, I suppose, to the attic. The man who had owned the house previously, Professor F. O. Matthiessen of Harvard, had left his library there, a mine of readable and interesting books. Marianne took full advantage of it. When she wasn't so occupied, we would go off together to do watercolors. This was typical of our several summers together (one at Penobscot Bay): we would spend a sympathetic couple of hours in the afternoon that way, perfectly independent of each other. We would go to a granite quarry, for example, that to me was a very exciting place as a whole—all pinks and grays, beautiful colors of stone. I'd be trying to get all of it in at once, as usual, the three floors of ladders going down to the water below, the derricks, the men working. But Marianne would select just one thing, a piece of chain on a pulley, and paint that. And she painted it very well. She did excellent miniature watercolors, perfectly evocative and imaginative.

Toward the end of the month, the radio announced the approach of Hurricane Connie. I may say that this was not the first hurricane I had experienced with Marianne in this same house. Unconcerned, she had written through a previous one without interruption, by the light of six candles (since the electricity had gone off) and telling me to keep the fire going. I had thought that a curious request, with the wind tearing by at eighty miles an hour, dashing things against the house and pulling the whole netting off the veranda and throwing it in the road. So this time, when Hurricane Connie was announced, I decided to advance our scheduled departure for Northeast Harbor to reach it before Connie caught up with us.

355

It was exciting to be in a race with the elements. We packed and started early. It took us less time than usual to reach Camden, where we ate lunch while the clouds were threatening. After we left Camden, the heavens opened and poured. Our car radio announced that nobody should go on the road between Camden and Ellsworth because it was inundated and impassable, but since we were already in the middle of it, and progressing, we decided to keep on. At Northeast Harbor, our destination was my recent traveling companion Mrs. Agnes Milliken's place where she had offered us a house for the continuation of our holiday. We reached Ellsworth and telephoned Mrs. Milliken, and she said, "Why, I just heard on the radio you couldn't possibly come through from Camden, so I thought you were spending the night there." I said, "No, we had already started, and since we were unthinking, foolhardy people, we kept on."

We arrived at the guest house that Mrs. Milliken had put at our disposal to find it stacked with food and open fires burning in the rooms. After settling in and hearing that the hurricane had blown itself out to sea, we reverted to our usual undramatic tasks. In the morning we went painting in the pine woods. We continued painting and driving around each day, and by the time we were ready to leave for New York, Marianne looked rested and refreshed.

In November, Henry Shepley, the Boston architect, called to discuss a project for the façade of the new Joslin Clinic for Diabetes. I dared to suggest depicting the History of Medicine in a series of panels. Such an idea had been in my head for years. Now came the hoped-for chance to express it in plastic form. Luckily, Dr. Joslin approved of this plan and came to my studio to look me over and examine my other work.

Collecting data on the origin and evolution of medicine kept me busy after the daylight hours. We decided on the first panel—it was to tell the story of Imhotep who lived about 2980 to 2950 b.c. This renowned builder of the Step Pyramid at Saqqara near Cairo was a learned scholar who practiced medicine with such distinction that his fame for healing spread far and wide. He became the ruler of Egypt, and after his death the people and priests worshiped him as a god and many temples were built in his honor and served as centers of healing.

The panel after Imhotep was to celebrate the origin of medicine in India, dating to 2500 b.c. Nobody in this country seemed to know much about the subject. Sympathizing with my determination to use only absolutely unquestionable data, my friend Swami Nikhilananda helped me get in touch with heads of institutes of learning, libraries, and medical schools in India, and from them I received dependable information and early engravings and designs that were most useful to me. From these I formed an idea of the four-armed god of Indian medicine. In his four hands he held the lotus bowl, the shell, healing herbs, and Vedantic teachings. I placed him against a background of the sacred mountain, with the serpent power of Kundalini encircling the world, center of the struggle between health and sickness, good and evil. In an inscription I indicated that the earliest physician, Dhanvantari, had been made a god. It was

IMHOTEP PANEL OF THE FRIEZE ON THE FAÇADE OF THE JOSLIN CLINIC

HEAD OF A YOUNG GIRL IN GREEN BRONZE, 1958 (*Peter A. Juley & Son*)

hard for me to arrive at this simplified design. All the panels had to be equally simple and uniform in effect, since they would appear next to one another, in low relief with incised outlines. Every part of the panels called for the most careful drawing.

The next panel was China, 2000 B.C., and included the names of Shen Nung, Hwang Ti, and Kien Lung, who were great early leaders, and in the background I had the reversed circles inside an encompassing circle—the yin and yang—symbolizing negative and positive influences. The main figures showed a herbal therapist and a patient holding out his arm to have the doctor or sage make a diagnosis by means of little points marking the circulatory system.

For Greece I had Hippocrates and Aesculapius, and then I had the first Christian figure, St. Luke, patron saint of doctors. For the Renaissance, there were Vesalius and Sanctorius, and so the panels led to the later great figures of medical history, particularly, where possible, those who had had a part in the study and cure of diabetes: Bernard Naunyn, George R. Minot, and Frederick Banting and Charles Best who discovered insulin in 1922.

There was an interesting side story to the panel about Thomas Willis, founder of the British Royal Society and discoverer of the "circle of Willis," a hexagonal network of arteries at the base of the brain. The person who made the first drawing of that "circle" was Sir Christopher Wren, who illustrated Willis's book *Cerebri Anatome*. I obtained a reproduction of his original drawing from the London College of Physicians and Surgeons and put it in the panel.

My enthusiasm and admiration for the wonderful dedication of the men to be represented led me at first to prepare more subjects than could eventually be included in such a limited space, which was a band of marble stretching 126 feet across the front of the building. Besides the panels there were intervals of carved lettering that would explain the evolution of medicine in the periods between the portrait panels. It was very hard, then, to make a final selection, and there were some differences of opinion. I held out strongly for St. Luke, and had to remind the hospital judges that Christ had called St. Luke "the beloved physician." Pasteur was objected to because he wasn't an actual doctor, but I said: "Well, he cured people, thousands of them. He didn't have to be an MD to do that." I had put into the Pasteur panel his essential tools, which I got directly from the Pasteur Institute in Paris, and I liked this panel. I offered to give up the whole enterprise unless he was kept—to surrender all my notes and studies. I was finally allowed to keep him. After the excitement had calmed down, I said, "There are always some rogues in every gallery, and this is my pet rogue."

In all, I was occupied for the better part of two years in the research and preparation of these panels. They were modeled full size, four by five feet, and carefully finished in plaster, and when all were completed they were shipped to Boston and carved onto the marble panels that were already built into the wall of the rather austere modern façade of the Joslin Clinic.

NEW PROJECT

When the Joslin frieze was well launched and the 159 studio was filling up with the plaster panels stacked against the walls, an unexpected dinner party given by my friend Margo Plass introduced me to a most interesting personality, William Francis Gibbs, marine engineer and naval architect.

He had been urged to have his portrait made, but he was opposed to the suggestion, and told me quite frankly that he had come to the dinner under protest and that nothing could interest him less than sitting still and being stared at by a sculptor who would no doubt see all his faults but would not be able to discover his virtues. He left almost immediately after the dinner, but agreed to come to the studio and see "what all this damned business of sculpture is about!"

Our first encounter was rather turbulent, and he tried to hide behind a mask of granitic severity. His kind eyes, however, were not to be disguised by any mask; and when I asked to be admitted to his downtown workrooms, where I knew he studied the small-scale models of ships, his astonishment was genuine. "No, I can't show you any ships or plans, but I'll show you the perfect model of a fire engine—a complete and working replica of the last model of steam fire engine used in New York City—it's a honey!"

The mask had completely vanished, and the real personality was revealed —the enchantment of a piece of perfect craftsmanship with every part functioning as it should was not to be denied. This visit was a confirmation of what I had often found to be an infallible guide—to see a man in his own laboratory or workshop was the direct way to discover the man behind the mask.

Here was the man who had designed the swiftest line afloat—whose firm had designed two-thirds of all new boats for the United States Navy during the war—and whose pride was the performance of his "Fair Lady," the S.S. *United States.* I had to disagree with him violently when he insisted that he had a queer-shaped head. The finely chiseled features were covered with taut pale skin, and his thin white hair seemed to follow the contour of the sleek bow of his great ship.

Finally I finished the first version of the portrait, but I was not satisfied, and began another. This one was more spontaneous and sure, and was completed without bloodshed—much to the relief of both the sitter and the sculptor. We were both happy, indeed, that the bronze when shown to his wife was obviously a great surprise and delight to her.

One evening shortly after the new year 1959 I had gone to hear John Gielgud recite *The Seven Ages of Man*—a wonderful feat of memory—and after the performance went with some friends to tea at the Plaza, blissfully unaware that a fire starting from the oil burner raged in my cellar at 159. I learned only later that evening that firemen had saved the house while I was out. Doors and windows had been broken open; the cellar was a black shambles. The sooty oil smoke drifting through both 159 and 157 had covered everything with oily black spots. I began coughing, and realized that my lungs were having a tough time to extract enough oxygen to keep my heart going. I recovered from this, but I knew that my health was gradually going downhill from other, unknown, causes; I continued carving a wood panel until it became too much of a strain and I was forced to stop and take a long rest.

A long-hoped-for evening of music by an open fire in my big upstairs room! I had Pa's piano tuned to prepare for a visit by George Copeland on March 23. Mr. Horst Froelich came with him, and after dinner we started off with the music: Debussy, Ravel, Bach, and Chopin. I began to wonder if so much beauty could be safely condensed into a single evening. Later I went across the room toward the landing at the top of the stairs, turned, and said, "Music like this, played so sensitively here in my own house, seems too good to be true . . ." and without a warning I blacked out and fell to the floor with my head and shoulders down three steps.

When I returned to consciousness, I woke up on the big divan. My two friends, having seen me fall, had picked me up and carried me there, and after five or six minutes I had opened my eyes. Mr. Copeland appeared so pale and apprehensive that I immediately asked him what had happened to him. "To me?" he said. "Nothing . . . but to you, Malvina . . . You aren't hurt? You don't feel battered by your fall? We hardly dared lift you for fear of broken bones!"

"No, I felt nothing and knew nothing of my fall. I just blacked out and had a marvelous sense of spacelessness and overwhelming peace. It was like dying, I guess. I remember saying that this evening 'seems too good to be true,' and now I have a touch of regret—that I missed such a finale to mortality."

We called the doctor; he was away until the following morning at eight o'clock. I took some codeine I had on hand, and after persuading my friends to go home, much against their will, I fell asleep until the doctor telephoned the next morning. He came at once and called in a heart specialist. They decided to take me to the hospital. Never having been in one as a patient before, I made attempts at resistance, but finally gave in and they drove me in a taxi to Columbus Hospital, where I was quickly put to bed under an oxygen tent. Completely immobilized, I felt like a captive butterfly pinned to a board, but had no desire to move or speak. The cold clean oxygen gave relief to breathing, and drugs were easing the pain in my chest. I was totally detached from reality, and the white Sisters and figures moving about the room were phantoms in another world.

After six weeks of expert doctoring, and being nursed by the dedicated Sisters of the Mother Cabrini Order, I recovered from a coronary thrombosis, double pneumonia, and severe pleurisy. Quite enough to ferry anyone safely across the river Styx and land him on the other side.

PART V

CHAPTER THIRTY-NINE

MY "POSTHUMOUS" LIFE

MY STRENGTH was sapped out of my muscles, but somehow my spirit had been reinforced, and the silent hours had given me a sense of faith and security that I had never felt before. I was overcome with gratitude for the sensitive expert care of my French doctor Simard and Dr. Siragusa, the heart specialist on the staff of the hospital.

They gave orders, when I returned to my studio on the ground floor of 157, that I was to live there and not go upstairs until permitted. So I rigged up a sort of Arab tent, putting the silken curtains I had long ago brought from Tunis all around the bed on wires strung from the studio ceiling. This made a place of quiet shelter where I could rest. It was quite a challenge, this enforced horizontalism after the long life of a sculptor who had rarely sat down except to meals.

Guldie, my faithful and devoted secretary and factotem, spared me the duty and care of housekeeping and contributed endlessly to my recovery. I think she was as surprised as I was to witness my docile obedience to doctor's orders— "Be a good girl and surprise everybody" was a suitable motto.

I had made reservations long before this debacle to sail on the *Mauretania* on May 28, and I determined to keep to the original plan; off we went for the sea change and seven days of blissful anonymity, "we" being myself, Guldie, and my good friend and fellow sculptor Lucinda Duble. The ocean healed and gave us of its strength and we arrived refreshed in Paris and were diverted by the spectacular clouds and familiar streets. We crossed the long routes to the fifteenth arrondissement to my villa with its high, ivy-covered walled garden. Of course, the following days were again mostly horizontal, my powers being slow in returning.

As time slipped on, various friends would come in to see us, and a French doctor supervised my health. Lu Duble would go off on her own each morning, and at teatime would regale me with accounts of her adventurous discoveries. Gradually I gained enough energy to motor with her to Meudon, where I showed her the house, museum, and garden of my beloved Maître Rodin, and then we would sit at a tiny table at the Café de la Paix and watch the world go by.

Alas, the time came when I had to start to think about disposing of the more important pieces of furniture, for I had been urged in no uncertain terms by my doctors and lawyer in New York to liquidate my property in Paris and reduce my responsibilities.

The wrench of such a separation would naturally entail emotional regrets, but I had recently been made the initiate of an order that no longer clings to nonessentials, having been stripped and disciplined by powers beyond its control. With a sense of finality, I engaged packers to put my marble portrait of Pavlova and the Paderewski "Statesman" in bronze into double cases for shipment to New York.

A period of good luck now brought me unexpected encouragement. This was when the Rosenbach Foundation in Philadelphia purchased my alabaster portrait of Rita Lydig. Rita's sister, Mercedes de Acosta, had brought the director of the Foundation to my studio. He remembered seeing this alabaster many years ago at its only public showing, and appeared overjoyed to find that he might now include it in the Rosenbach collection.

Also at about this time, *Sculpture Inside and Out* and *Heads and Tales* were both reissued after being out of print for many years, and both sold well in a lower-priced edition. I was particularly pleased that the reduced price made them far more available to students.

In May of 1961, Guldie and I sailed for France and met "Gazelle" (Frances) Rich, who waved to us on arrival at the villa. Her pretty face smiling above the window boxes of bright red geraniums gave us a cheery welcome.

My first task was to select and pack books, which I sent to the home for old artists at Nogent. Many other books filled a row of cartons destined for the American Library in Paris.

Antique dealers began to arrive, and the furniture was sold room by room, leaving the house with only the absolute necessities and us living like gypsies. The odd types who would appear to bid on rugs, tables, and chairs were a curiously interesting lot. They ranged from titled, smartly dressed dealers to sad and wilted *petits commerçants* who ran sidewalk booths and supplied some of the shops or flea markets along the quais. The latter roamed about the garage and garden, picking up the last remnants of the sale, things so forgotten and hidden away that I did not even remember their existence.

Only the harpsichord Sam had worked on, but had never completed be-cause of his illness—which, alas, had continued untempered by time until his death—was left in the big top-floor living room, a ghost of our dream and a lonely symbol of unfinished music and beauty.

I could not go on—at this point I had exhausted all my determination not to let this experience get the better of my emotions. I quickly decided with Fran Rich to go with her in her car to Brittany. We wired my friend Mildred Capron, who was filming the Finistère coast, to meet us in Port Manech. We found a room in a *pavillon* in a pine forest near the edge of the shore where we stayed four days.

We visited my old Breton friends at Concarneau and Saint-Guénolé and witnessed a wild tempest that swept in cloudbursts along the whole coast, caus-ing many fatalities. In spite of the storm, the Charlot family gathered together for a reunion, and we sat around the table, drinking to everlasting friendship.

Mildred dauntlessly determined to continue filming the rocky coast in the grip of the howling wind, but the heavy rain finally stopped her and we moved on to Rennes. Simon Charlot then was kind enough to take me home to Paris, where I could complete the tasks I had interrupted.

Returning to New York in the fall, I faced the long-postponed necessity of clearing out all movable objects from my studio so that a gang of painters could set up a scaffolding and clean the dust of years from skylights and steam pipes too high for ordinary long ladders to reach. In this upheaval I decided to reduce my collection of supplies and tools, and I sold hundreds of pounds of plasteline and gave a truckload of other supplies to the Sculpture Center.

Once order was restored, the light clean walls and bright skylights gave me a sense of renewal, and with the encouraging permission of my doctor, after a halt of eighteen months, I began to work once more at sculpture on condition that I rest every two hours and accept no commissions limited by deadlines.

With a feeling of trepidation I began a life-size portrait of an old friend, Bayard Dodge, to be placed at the American University in Beirut, where he had been president for twenty-five years. I soon discovered that my Daemon had not deserted me and that even though I was beginning a kind of posthumous life, I could work with more security and assurance than I had felt before my illness. To have the soft material take shape, to be mentally liberated once more in the struggle of my craft was an invigorating experience. The work progressed faster than either of us had thought possible, and after four sittings I was able to tell him the portrait was completed.

THE PROBLEM OF POSING

Doing portraits again brought back in flood what now seemed an inex-haustible experience of posing subjects. What I knew now went back to my first experience with Father, and the lesson I learned then remained the same through the years: at the heart of posing is getting essential understanding, getting be-hind the surface model-sculptor relationship to the real person. At times, as with the William Francis Gibbs head, I had taken my subject to his natural workshop and habitat. But you can't do this with everyone. You may be limited to studio sittings, and then the key to understanding is to feel, to absorb the model sub-consciously through an immediate emotional rapport. What will block such a rapport is thinking you can simply look at him and make his shape. If the person senses that you are seeking a mere likeness, he will offer you a poker face. We all have a set of such poker faces we resort to for different occasions, but the sculptor's problem is to get behind the barrier.

Talking is one way to reproduce in the studio the natural reactions that re-veal the subject as he would be at home or at work. But this is not so simple as it sounds. You are not free to talk yourself, since you must be busy looking at the subject, making comparisons, making the infinite number of quick judgments that go into the work of modeling. But you can listen. You can be attentive to anything the subject wants to say. You don't force him with questions, since what is important is that he speak spontaneously; and you don't even listen too carefully to the content of what he's saying, since its usefulness to you is only that it changes the aspect of his face.

Sometimes incidents will occur during posing that help bring the model's character into view. While I was doing the portrait of Thomas J. Watson, head of IBM, he skipped a couple of appointments, and the next time he arrived at the studio, there was a large-lettered sign THINK hung on his chair on the model's stand. This luckily did much to promote good humor and *détente*.

Particularly important are the rest periods when the model is moving around, when he relaxes and leans over a table and begins to read something and you suddenly see him in a different light, with a new expression and atti-tude. Sometimes I put the person on a low fire bench where he is almost squat-ting on the floor, and that gives me a completely fresh point of view on him. It reminds me always of Rodin's instruction on how to do a head.

He kept saying to me: "Don't think that it's just straight on that you're sup-posed to look at a person. You must crouch down and look up and see whether you have the person right from below, and then you must go up on a pair of steps and look down and be sure that you have the person's form right as seen from above." You may find that what you see from above doesn't resemble a head at all, and similarly from any different point of view you take. As Rodin said, you have to go around and above and below and through before you can be sure you've observed the form of a head at all. After suffering from a few years of this kind of observation training, you can at least realize more quickly what you have to hunt for.

People are often surprised when I say I look at the model from above. "How do you manage that?" Then I show them how it's done, how you step up on the model's stand and are at the right height to examine the model in his chair. You look down on him and you look down at your bust, and you generally see a discrepancy from that point of view and you're able to correct it. By such cor-rective steps, you handle a great deal that is ordinarily neglected in modeling. From a three-dimensional approach you even move on to the fourth dimension when you make the psychological observations described above, when you watch what happens when a visitor comes in, for example, and joins you, what changes then, for inevitably there will be a change in the model's physiognomy. You may think you see just a momentarily different expression, but if you are modeling that person, this expression should create a significant variance in form. There isn't a static thing in our makeup, and the human face is a library of details. The sculptor's art is to fix these details rapidly in clay as he becomes aware of them, for unless he can register them, he's lost.

Something particularly significant may happen when one sculptor makes the portrait of another. I have in my studio an unfinished head that Mestrovic made of me, started and never finished, but as far as he went with it, I was aware that it was the expression of a direct, rather overpowering interest he had in portraying an artist's face. One artist working with another should be the reflection of something valuable. I was conscious of it with Pavlova, and when I posed for Mestrovic I felt like a sculptor giving back to him what I knew he wanted, and it was that interplay of professional understanding and sympathy that gave its quality even to the unfinished head.

Every head is a challenge, and no sculptor ever feels that in the head he finally does he has exhausted the vein of character. So he often tries again and again, not only preliminary stages of the same portrait, but successive portraits that begin to give him a sense of reward or relief.

THOREAU PORTRAIT

The New York University's Hall of Fame for Great Americans asked me to make a portrait of Henry David Thoreau. At the public library I found a postal-card photo of a painting made of him at twenty-four years of age by his sister. This moved me deeply, for it was obviously done with love and understanding. It also happened that at this time, in honor of the hundredth anniversary of Thoreau's death, an exhibit was held at the Morgan Library in Thirty-sixth Street where one could browse about and read the original pages of the thirty-eight volumes of his famous journals. These were written in ink, and every page was filled from margin to edge with disciplined regularity. Some of the volumes lay open in glass cases, and I could read the actual sentences as they were created in Thoreau's mind, sentences which, quoted many times since, have become famous for their homespun wisdom and philosophy. These pages and a collection of his letters were road marks along the way to guide me in the quest of the true character of the man. Articles and books written about him often gave conflicting opinions, but the passages by Van Wyck Brooks in *The Flowering of New England* and R. W. Emerson's memories of his youthful friendship with Thoreau were convincing and most helpful to me.

Writing to Concord, I obtained a few photographs of a contemporary portrait of Thoreau made in marble from life and memory, but lacking a sense of vitality.

Many published reproductions showed Thoreau wearing a beard, but he did this for a year or two only, and I considered it nontypical. The sister's painting

HEAD OF WILLIAM FRANCIS GIBBS

HENRY DAVID THOREAU, OVER-LIFE-SIZED BRONZE IN THE HALL OF FAME
(Peter A. Juley & Son)

was certainly the best help I had, and after working hard on the first version I built up the over-life-size one showing him as a mature man.

His character possessed me, and I worked with deep emotion as I joined him in his solitary walks in the woods and shared his love for every living thing that he found there. Under this influence, the work progressed steadily and with conviction.

It was submitted to the jury of sculptors. As always, I found waiting for the decision an ordeal. I remembered Thoreau's words, "The mass of men lead lives of quiet desperation," and for the moment I could witness to the truth of his statement. At last I learned that they had approved of my conception.

I had tried to express his rough-hewn exterior and sensitive sad awareness of his physical illness; I had tried to express what had allowed him to accept peacefully the inevitable and immutable law that carries us across the horizon of mortality. When his aunt asked him if he had made his peace with God, he answered, "I was never aware that we had quarreled."

It seems incredible that a man of Thoreau's stature and fame should have had to wait one hundred years after his death to be elected to the ranks of Great Americans and to be included in the Hall of Fame. I felt grateful and privileged indeed to have been chosen as the sculptor for this assignment, which luckily my return to health had enabled me to undertake.

After the placing of this bronze, I was asked to model a Thoreau medal, which was to have on one side a profile of Thoreau and on the other a design of my own choosing. For the reverse side I worked out a view of Walden Pond with a few pine trees framing the water and the rays of a rising sun leading to the lines, "Only that day dawns to which we are awake," one of Thoreau's evocative sayings. The fully designed medal was to be reduced to small size and distributed by the Medallic Art Company and New York University's Hall of Fame for Great Americans.

I often used to keep two or three projects going at the same time in the studio because I found the change for a day or two gave me a fresher approach to each portrait. Now I found myself doing the same thing. Before finishing the Thoreau bust, I started a study of Marguerite Yourcenar. There could not be a more contrasting problem in physiognomies. The many photos taken of this gifted French author whom I had first met in Spain were all around me, and by a process of acute concentration and flashes of memory I managed to model her portrait until I finally wrote her that I could go no further unless I could actually look at her for at least an hour.

The appointment was arranged for the day she was planning to sail from New York on a long cruise. The sitting was an intense one, and rather frightening as I saw at once the need of surgery, and Marguerite quite naturally gasped with apprehension. I told her I would painlessly remove her right ear and replace it slightly lower down. This was done so quickly that there was no time for argument. It solved a problem that had been troubling me and cured all my doubts about the correct construction of this head that was now finished after so many hours and weeks of "absent treatment."

NATIONAL ARTS EXHIBIT

Not long after this, a group of friends persuaded me to cooperate in their effort to arrange an exhibit of my work at the National Arts Club. There was an undeniable reticence on my part, especially when they announced that I would be guest of honor at the annual dinner. I realized that the doctor's caution to "avoid any emotional strain" was urgently directed to just what was threatening me now, and try as I might to control my conflicted feelings, Nature suddenly took charge and laid me low, and the doctor ordered me to give up any thought of being able to attend the big dinner. Instead I was taken to the hospital and forced to accept treatment for water in my lungs. I must leave to the reader to imagine my frustration and regret, further, my distress of mind at having disappointed so many good people by my ill-timed collapse. My friend Ray Kinstler, the painter, brought me a sound-track recording of the dinner where, it seemed, the speakers had bravely carried on without the guest of honor in a most moving display of loyalty and friendship, but it was two months before I could bring myself to the test of listening to this recording. Then I was greatly touched by the fine speeches of Paul Manship, Stuart Cloete, and C. D. Batchelor abetted by the Master of Ceremonies, Staats Cotsworth. Batchelor had made a charcoal drawing of the Brittany fishing boat *Malvina* that was circulated among the guests and signed around the border by over two hundred of them.

During this period I had also done a bust of lovely Katherine Cornell. Thoreau, Katherine Cornell—it sounds simple, but my head now felt tired, and with a sense of having used up my limited budget of strength I decided to fold my tent and take a trip to my old faithful New England coast. My friend Mildred Capron would join me with her Volkswagen bus. Recently I had had the nostalgic pleasure of seeing her film *The Spell of Brittany* at Town Hall, which had brought back my Finistère trip in startling clarity. With enthusiasm we started for our own rocky coast, motoring up to Rye Beach and on to Prouts Neck. Never having seen this section of the coast, I was enchanted by the sweep of rocky ledges, the counterpart of paintings by Winslow Homer, who lived on this rugged shore for many years. The jagged and colorful ledges slanted downward under the edge of the sea and some, shaped like large logs, looked like specters of a petrified forest flung by some prehistoric landslide helter-skelter down the steep slopes into the ocean. After a few watercolor attempts to reflect these dramatic new impressions of rocks, frustration forced me to give up and just absorb the sharp cool salty air as tonic to the soul as well as the body, and do nothing about it but breathe deeply and be thankful for such a chance of total relaxation.

Letters from my good friend Professor William Ernest Hocking had urged me to come to the White Mountains, where he had been living for many years hidden away in his isolated farm 1,250 feet above sea level at a place called Madison. His children and grandchildren were with him, and they hunted up a little inn for us at Tamworth, about six miles from his farm, nothing nearer being available. Mildred and I decided to move there in a leisurely westward drive from Prouts Neck.

We found the view from the Hocking farm overlooking the White Mountains an ever-changing glory of nature, reaching its climax when the sunsets spread the panorama of vivid sky colors over the receding ranges of blue and gray mountains. After this rewarding visit, Mildred Capron and I motored southward to Stockbridge, where I stayed with Peggy Cresson and enjoyed the familiar charm of the Berkshire hills and Peggy's warm hospitality.

My friends the Louis Hydes wrote to me that their "captain's cottage" at Kittery would be free for the end of the summer. This tempted me to spend the last weeks of August and the start of September in this alluring place. So ended this happy summer that seemed to bring me a long step back to my former health.

When I had returned home to 157, it went through my mind that Professor Hocking, with his great talents and spirit, with his lifetime of notable contributions to American thought, should obviously have his portrait done. Since he was now far off, I could do it only by memory, and it amazed me that I had been right there, sitting beside him, and had not, as I usually did, recorded him in my mind. Still, I was now determined to do a bust of him, and I believed that subconsciously I may have registered enough to go on. As one clue to his character, I had recently found out that he could quite casually sit down at the organ and play Bach and that he had painted well in oils, including portraits of his family and a particularly sensitive and successful one of his son. He was in his late eighties, but students in his philosophy classes of the twenties and thirties at Harvard still remembered him and spoke of his unquestioned influence. He was a figure of marked vitality apart from age.

Therefore, as I modeled, I refused to use age marks for crutches. I had a few photographs on dust jackets of his books, but no large-scale formal portrait photograph. I kept on working concentratedly for the better part of a week, and then I felt that I must verify certain dimensions by actual measurements, and the description of these I drew on paper and sent to him. Would he be so kind, I wrote him, as to take in hand the calipers that I would send him and render me the invaluable service of jotting down just a few dimensions?

A day or two after the notations were returned to me, I was able to write to him, "It's now finished as far as I can question it, and we will set it aside and compare it with the original when you come down to the meeting of the Institute [of Arts and Letters] in April or May." When he arrived and came to the studio, I said, "I'm going to put you in this light and look at you, and I'll put up a big mirror so that you can look at yourself, and we'll be honest with each other and see what more has to be done." Under this scrutiny, we found that the portrait was as close as I could expect to get. It was a good likeness; though, as I explained

MEDALLION IN STONE OF HENRY CLAY FRICK,
LATEST WORK OF MH

HEAD OF WILLIAM ERNEST HOCKING

HEAD OF KATHARINE CORNELL

in discussing posing, I know that if all you have achieved in sculpture is a good likeness, you are hardly making a start; but there was something else I had got behind the eyes, expressive of himself and apart from any measurement. He said, "Don't go on with it; don't do any more, because as far as I'm concerned, that's the man I shave every morning."

When his family saw it, they were happy, and it was cast into bronze. I gave him the first bronze, and his children bought several additional copies.

Early in 1964 I received a commission to make a bas-relief portrait of Henry C. Frick to be carved in stone for an Italian Renaissance building his daughter was erecting as a gift to the City of Pittsburgh, to house an Institute of Art. The portrait would be a limestone medallion sunk into the surface of the building front, over the main entrance. It was a very stimulating problem, and I was particularly pleased that I would be working again in stone after a somewhat long period away from that medium. I prepared a plaster original, and the actual carving was done by Bruno Mankowski, since union regulations prevent sculptors from doing their own work when it is part of a building. In the final stages, Helen Frick very kindly arranged to have a small stairway put up to the scaffolding so that I could go up myself and touch the stone and guide the completion of the work. Mr. Mankowski received me on the scaffolding with unusual sympathy, and I believe that both of us enjoyed those final hours together and of course I was reminded of many previous scaffolds I had mounted to carry out projects in stone.

A most happy event: on February 11, 1964, a mild winter day, I was taken to a dinner and meeting of the National Sculpture Society where a large number of my colleagues had gathered, among other things, to celebrate my receiving the Society's gold Medal of Honor, a medal I learned had been given only a few times in its long existence. The medal was a handsome one made by Laura Gardin Fraser, widow of the eminent sculptor James Fraser.

This honor surprised me. I was not at all prepared for it. I was not very active at the moment, and certainly I was not one to look back at what I had done in my life. When you do take that backward look, you wonder how you got such a rather large amount of work accomplished.

Out of the blue—another of life's surprises, totally unexpected, but so timed by the hand of fate that it came as another much-needed reinvigoration.

From Calgary, Canada, a visitor appeared in the studio one recent autumn day. Eric Harvie was introduced by Mr. Rudolph Wunderlich of the Kennedy Galleries, and to my surprise and gratification he not only looked over the contents of the two studios but also expressed his desire to purchase a collection of my bronzes. It seemed that he had already built a museum in Banff and had acquired a large group of sculptures and paintings and Indian artifacts that had been on public display for some time.

I had to confess never to have heard of this project nor indeed did I know anything about the place named Calgary except that it comes into our news each year as the home of the great cattle roundup and world-famous rodeo of rough-riding cowboys.

This visit and the ensuing ones seemed to me to be something of a fairy tale, but the result was real enough. To make the necessary arrangements, I communicated with the staff of the Field Museum (now called the Chicago Natural History Museum) with whom I had not too long before been in touch. In 1960 I had suddenly decided to go to Chicago, after twenty-five years, to see Stanley Field and wish him a happy eighty-fifth birthday. We revisited "our hall" and had a reunion lunch the following day with fellow staff members. Now, with letters back and forth, I obtained permission to send my set of original plasters of half-life-size heads and one-third-life-size figures to the foundries to be made into bronze replicas for Mr. Harvie. The statement "made into bronze replicas" sounds very simple, but these plasters all had to be checked and mended, since they had been boxed for about thirty years and some of the armatures had rusted and the deterioration had caused cracks on the surface.

The foundries today are so overcrowded with work, chiefly of the modern school, that it became a struggle for me to get a first group done, not to mention repacked and shipped to Canada, before starting another group on its way. The consolation during succeeding months was the understanding and consideration shown by Mr. Harvie, a man of unendingly cheerful patience.

As I write the story, it seems a hardly credible good fortune, coming so long after the original work. The Chicago Hall of Man is the permanent exhibition of the one hundred and four life-size subjects of my study of the races of man. Now it seems assured that there will be a collection in permanent material of the original series made on the road during the long treks to the habitats of faraway tribes.

We know "so little about so many," and yet we are all brothers in this family of man. Let us try to understand one another, and not be too quick to condemn. Another surprise to our judgment may be just beyond the next hill. We must keep on exploring:

> To follow knowledge like a sinking star,
> Beyond the utmost bound of human thought. . . .
>
> Made weak by time and fate, but strong in will
> To strive, to seek, to find, and not to yield.

The quality of greatness can live behind masks, and often seeks a hiding place; its fragile power shrinks from contact with reality. It shines out like a beacon in the night; a word, a gesture, or a flashing glance may give the clue; then actions follow thought, and the inner secrets reveal themselves. We become aware of something new, of unfolding beauty; the soul unsheathes itself and flowers into being, creating an adventure of renewal.

The humblest may have this quality; the poorest may be princes of the spirit. What marks them out from their fellowmen? Is it their consciousness of God? Are they so gifted, or so fortunate?

The quality of greatness triumphs in a moment of selfless heroism. It shines out through humility. It moves the heart to share another's pain. It builds itself a fortress of its Faith, a faith in things unseen. It is not by what we have, but by what we love that we are known—what motivates the gift, not what it is— what lies behind our acts, not what we say aloud. Some are remembered because they are brave, some because they inspire laughter, some because of an inward power that cannot be denied. These furnish their own momentum, never leaning on others or borrowing energy. They can be stripped of every advantage, yet they persist and turn defeat into victory. If you have been so blessed as to know them, they live in your memory. Even if you tried, you could not efface them. They have become part of life, a thread in the ever-growing, everlasting pattern.

THE PAST

The past is such a curious creature,
To look her in the face
A transport may reward us,
Or a disgrace.

Unarmed if any meet her,
I charge him, fly!
Her rusty ammunition
Might yet reply!

EMILY DICKINSON

LIST OF SCULPTURED WORKS
by Malvina Hoffman

1906   "The Way of a Serpent on the Rock," plaster
       "Despair," bronze

1910   "Richard Hoffman," marble
       "Samuel B. Grimson" (Honorable Mention, Paris Salon, 1910), bronze
       "William Astor Chanler," bronze
       "Robert Bacon," bronze
       "Russian Dancers" group (First Prize, Paris, 1911), bronze

1912   "Mrs. Irwin L. Laughlin," face in marble
       "Mrs. Irwin L. Laughlin," bust in marble
       "Bacchanale Russe" (original statuette, fourteen inches), bronze
       "L'Après-midi d'un Faun" (statuette), bronze
       "John Keats" (finished in 1926), marble

1913   "Frileuse" (fountain; three studies, 1910–1913), bronze
       "Mort Exquise" group, marble
       "Roger Kahn" (bas-relief), terra cotta

1914   "Les Orientales" group (Pavlova and Novikoff), bronze

1915   "Roger Kahn" (portrait bust), marble
       Pavlova, "La Gavotte" (statuette; Honorable Mention, San Francisco, 1915),
          bronze; (National Academy, Watrous Medal), wax
       "Boy and Panther Cub" (fountain, twenty inches), bronze
       "Boy and Panther Cub" (five feet, six inches), bronze

1917   "Richard Hoffman 3rd," marble, plaster
       "Bacchanale Russe" (over life-size, Luxembourg Gardens, Paris), bronze
       "Bacchanale Russe" (over life-size, Cleveland Art Museum), bronze
       "Frederick Pierce" (portrait), marble
       "Colonel Milan Pribicevic in Uniform" (bust), bronze
       "Column of Life" group (later version 1939; with "Oriental Pedestal" six
          centers of Kundalini in low bronze reliefs), marble and bronze

1918   "Fidelia M. Hoffman" (life-size high-relief face), marble
       "Fidelia M. Hoffman" (life-size portrait of head), marble
       "Modern Crusader" (Colonel Milan Pribicevic in helmet), bronze
       "James G. Croswell," bronze
       "Offrande" group (George Widener Medal, Pennsylvania Academy; Helen
          Foster Barnett Prize, National Academy), marble and bronze
       "General Sir David Henderson" (portrait), simili pierre
       "Colonel Philippe Bunau-Varilla" (portrait), bronze
       "John Muir" (portrait), bronze

1920   "Hindu Incense Burner" (seated figure), bronze
       "Henry C. Frick" (portrait), marble

1920–1922 "The Sacrifice" ("La Douleur est la Mère de la Beauté"), Caen stone

1921   "La Péri" (dancing group, Pavlova and Stowitz), bronze
       "Bill Working," bronze
       "The Misses Cromwell" (bas-relief in conjunction with Edward McCartan),
          bronze

1922   "Robert Bacon" (posthumous portrait), bronze
          "Paderewski the Statesman," bronze
          "Paderewski the Artist," bronze
          "Paderewski the Man," bronze

1923   "Paderewski the Friend," plaster

1923–1925 "Hand of Jean-Julien Lemordant," bronze

1924   Frieze, "Bacchanale Russe" (26 panels), plaster
          "Mrs. E. H. Harriman" (portrait), marble and bronze
          "Paul M. Warburg" (portrait; also reduced to seven inches, second version
            [posthumous], 1932), bronze
          "Samuel B. Grimson" (portrait in helmet), bronze
          "Anna Pavlova as Byzantine Madonna" (bas-relief), plaster
          "Anna Pavlova" (mask), wax
          "Anna Pavlova" (half life-size), bronze
          "Anna Pavlova" (hands folded over her breast; life-size), marble

1924–1925 Bush House, London "Anglo-American Friendship" group, stone

1925   "Boy Neptune" (fountain), bronze
          "Agnes Yarnall" (bust), stone
          "Jean-Julien Lemordant" (bust), simili pierre
          "Ivan Mestrovic" (over life-size portrait), bronze
          "Bill Resting," bronze
          "Frank Damrosch," bronze

1926   "Kneeling Girl," marble and bronze
          "Torso" (man of Breton Memorial), granite

1927   "Vita Nova" (hands over life-size), simili pierre
          "Vita Nova" (ten inches), bronze
          Memorial, "Four Horseman of the Apocalypse" (in the round), plaster
          "War" (one of the Four Horsemen, mosaic), colored cement
          Two "Pegasus" heads, two gateposts, stone
          "Dr. William H. Draper and Dr. William K. Draper" (bas-relief portraits),
            bronze
          "Senegale," black Belgian marble

1927–1932 104 portraits, heads, busts, and figures for the Hall of Man, Chicago, three in
            marble; bronze

1928   Equestrian group: "Death," "Pestilence," "Famine," "War" (bas-reliefs), plaster
          "Martinique Woman" (over life-size), black Belgian marble
          "Cockfighter and Cock," bronze
          "Arab Stallion" (eighteen inches), bronze
          "Mme. La Motte," simili pierre
          "Coal Man," coal
          "Brick Man," brick
          "Lady Next Door" (also known as "The Witch"), simili pierre
          "Mattressmaker," bronze
          "Mme. Emma Eames" (bas-relief, first version), marble
          "Giovanni Boldini," bronze
          "Java Woman" (mask), black Belgian marble

1929   "Martinique Woman," sandalwood
          Siamese cat "Kiki" (first version, sitting up), simili pierre and bronze
          Siamese cat "Kiki" (second version, asleep), marble, bronze
          "Rita de Acosta Lydig" (portrait bust), alabaster
          "Malvina Hoffman" (first version, relief), stone
          "Malvina Hoffman" (second version, with hand), stone
          "Dr. Albert Simard," bronze
          "Pulpit," Church of the Heavenly Rest (Memorial), stone

1930   "Percy Memorial," stone, background bronze
"Jewish Mausoleum," Jacob Epstein, Baltimore (architectural drawings, interior and exterior to scale)
"John G. Shedd" (portrait), bronze
"Stanley Field," bronze
"Cambodian Dancer" (rehearsal figure), bronze

1932   "Bali 'Fan Dancer' " (eighteen inches), bronze
"Cambodian Dancer in Costume," bronze
"Mongolian Archer," bronze

1933   "Egyptian Dancer, Nyota Inyoka," bronze
"Uday-Shankar" (seated figure), bronze
"John Thomson Hodgen" (bas-relief), bronze
"Marquis of Reading" (portrait), bronze

1935   "Marcel Griaule Pierrot" (life-size head), bronze
"Felix M. Warburg" (life-size portrait), bronze
"Kinnicutt Fountain," St. Mark's School, stone
"Mrs. George G. Frelinghuysen," marble
"Frances Rich" (life-size head), marble

1935–1937   "Memorial Panel for Groton School Chapel," stone

1936   "Elemental Man" (over life-size), plaster
"Adolph Ochs" (portrait), bronze
"Girl on the Beach," marble and bronze

1937   "Miss Anne Morgan" (portrait, three-quarter figure; bust), bronze
"Goddess of Safety" group (in the round), aluminum and bronze
"Bali Dancer" ("Bow and Arrow" figure), bronze
"Frank Roberts, Liberian Dancer," bronze
"Lila A. Stewart" plaque (bas-relief memorial), bronze

1938   "Orpheus and Eurydice" (seven inches), bronze; (twenty inches), stone

1939   "Pagan's Prayer" (one-third life-size figure and life-size figure), bronze
"Thomas L. Chadbourne," bronze
"St. Francis and His Animal Friends" (fifty-eight inches), bronze

1941   "Artur Bodansky" (portrait), bronze
"Ernest Peixotto" (portrait), bronze
"Paderewski—Last Phase" (head), bronze

1942   "Winnie" (nude figure of woman holding drapery back of her; Coty Award for Best Design and Style of Year), bronze
"Mrs. Garfield King" (posthumous portrait head), terra cotta
"Archie Gibbs" (portrait of merchant mariner twice torpedoed same night, four days on Nazi submarine), colored plaster
"Charles Armand de Rougé" (medallion three-quarter life-size), electroplate

1943   "Basque Sailor" (heroic head), plaster
"Adelaide Nutting Medal," bronze

1944   "Dr. Sanford Gifford" (posthumous portrait; head only; three versions), bronze and terra cotta
"William Adams Delano" (life-size portrait bust), bronze
"Wendell L. Willkie" (study and two versions; posthumous), bronze
"Unicorn" (book end, eight inches), bronze on marble
"Lion" (book end, eight inches), bronze on marble

1946   "Weddell Garden Memorial Plaque" (relief eighteen inches by twenty-four inches and thirty inches by forty inches), Tennessee marble
"Christ Walking on the Water" (set in carved frame), bronze
"Thomas J. Watson" (life-size portrait bust), bronze
"Randolph Winslow" (life-size portrait, posthumous), bronze

"Rosen Memorial Shaft" (for Katonah Churchyard), granite
"Edward S. Harkness" (life-size head and shoulders, posthumous), bronze

1947   "George B. Cutten" (life-size portrait bust), bronze

1948   "Jester" champion poodle, bronze on marble
"Dr. Leconte de Nouy" (life-size portrait, posthumous), bronze
"Henry James" (life-size portrait, posthumous), bronze
"Dr. Harvey Cushing" (life-size portrait bust, posthumous), bronze
"Armand de Rougé" (plaque reduced)
"Père Teilhard de Chardin" (two versions, life-size portrait bust), bronze
"Memorial Plaques" for IBM offices—"He telleth the number of the Stars,
He calleth them all by their names," bronze

1948–1949 Memorial Flagpoles for IBM, bronze on granite

1949   "Dean Virginia Gildersleeve" (life-size portrait bust), bronze
"Lucy Archbold" (life-size head), bronze

1948–1950 War Memorial sculpture for Épinal, Vosges, France, American Battle Monuments; "Panels" incised into wall surface; "Angel" (three feet, for over altar
in Chapel); "Two Roundels" (for over entrance to Museum and Chapel)

1950   "Royal Air Force Trophy" (figure), bronze
"Swami Vivekananda" (three-quarter figure, posthumous portrait), bronze

1951   "Henry E. Perry" (posthumous portrait), bronze
"Sri Ramakrishna" (posthumous portrait bust), alabaster and bronze

1952   "Citizen Thomas Paine" (over life-sized bust for Hall of Fame), bronze
"Walter Rosen" (posthumous portrait bust), bronze

1953·   Bullfight series: "Dying Bull," "Young Bull," "Picador" (man, horse, and
bull), "Banderillero," "Matador with Capa," "Matador with Sword," "Ve-
rónica" (matador with hat), "Momento de la Verdad" (man and bull),
bronze
"Dr. Selman Waksman (life-size portrait bust), bronze
"Holy Mother of India" (posthumous portrait bust), bronze
"Henry de Monfreid" (portrait head; Honorable Mention, National Arts
Club), bronze
"Milliken Road Marker," granite

1955   Kimber Awards: "Ruth Slenzcynska" Music Award (three-inch medal), bronze;
Genetics Award for National Academy of Sciences, bronze
"Brotherhood of Man" (Medallists Society, New York City; medal portrait
profiles of four races), bronze
"Portuguese Horseman" ("Rejoneador"), man in flat hat and horse, bronze
"Portuguese Horseman" ("Rejoneador"), man in court costume and horse,
bronze
"Quality of Mercy Is Not Strained" (plaque in memory of Helen F. Draper,
presented to American Red Cross, New York City Branch), bronze
"William Francis Gibbs" (life-size portrait bust), bronze
"Alice Laughlin" (posthumous portrait), terra cotta
"St. Andrew" (bronze relief on wooden background), bronze

1956   "Dr. Charles Malik" (portrait head), bronze
Joslin Hospital, Boston, project (thirteen bas-relief panels depicting the evolution of medicine for the façade of building), stone

1957   "John Keats" (mask from Malvina Hoffman head of Keats), terra cotta
"Dr. Elliott P. Joslin" (bas-relief portrait, round), terra cotta

1958   Tiny Figures: 1. Man lifted in arc over standing figure; 2. Upper man, handstand on figure below; 3. Upper man's head against side of standing man;
4. José Limon in dance pose; 5. "Russian Dancer," left knee bent, right ex-

tended; 6. "Torch Bearer," standing figure; 7. Three men, head and feet on ground, two above, handstand on man below, all in bronze cast directly from wax

"Unknown Lady" (life-size head), stone

"Marshall Field 3rd" (life-size posthumous portrait, bas-relief), bronze

1959   "Trinity School Plaques" (Cole Medal), bronze

1961–1962   "Katharine Cornell" (life-size portrait head), bronze
"Bayard Dodge" (life-size portrait head), bronze
"Walter Rothschild" (posthumous bas-relief portrait), bronze
"Henry David Thoreau" (over life-size bust, placed in Hall of Fame), bronze
"Henry David Thoreau—Young Thoreau" (life-size bust), plaster
"Marguerite Yourcenar" (life-size portrait head), terra cotta

1963   "Professor William Ernest Hocking" (life-size portrait), bronze
"Swami Nikhilananda (life-size portrait), bronze
"Frank Talbott" (life-size portrait head), bronze
"Henry Clay Frick" (bas-relief portrait), stone

NATIONAL SCULPTURE SOCIETY MEDAL OF HONOR PRESENTED TO MH IN 1964